"Simultaneously intimate and sweeping in scope, [...] in close to dictators and would-be dictators across decades and [...] nents. We are left with a disturbing look in the mirror. Throughout, Ruth Ben-Ghiat's clear prose rings with a rhythm and cadence that today's nonfiction too often lacks."

—Sarah Chayes, author of *On Corruption in America* and *Thieves of State*

"Ruth Ben-Ghiat . . . specializes in male menace."

—Jon Blitzer, *The New Yorker*

"For the reader inured by the drip-drip-drip of stories of brazen corruption over the course of years, it is bracing to see a half-decade's worth of reporting so carefully distilled. . . . Ben-Ghiat does not shy away from revealing America's role in enabling dictatorships around the world. . . . It's a chilling current through the book and one that pricks the conscience of a reader."

—Talia Lavin, *Washington Post*

"With a steady gaze and an eye for the telling detail, Ruth Ben-Ghiat delivers a timely analysis of how a certain kind of charisma delivers political disaster—and some valuable hints about how it can be resisted, and the virtues we will need to rebuild democracy."

—Timothy Snyder, author of *On Tyranny*

"Deep insight and a vigorous style . . . [A] brilliant contribution to the political psychology of democracy."

—Joy Connolly, president of the American Council of Learned Societies

"Ruth Ben-Ghiat delivers a superb examination of how close the US came to fascism—and how it has propped it up before."

—Charles Kaiser, *Guardian*

"Ben-Ghiat teaches us about the leaders. . . . [She] cogently states that the secret of the strongman is that he needs the crowds much more than they need him."   —Federico Finchelstein, *New Republic*

"[Ben-Ghiat], a historian who has written previously on Italian fascism, is at her best when describing the history of Mussolini's rise, and the way that insouciant Italians and foreign powers facilitated it."
     —Francis Fukuyama, *New York Times*

"Ben-Ghiat's portrayal of fascist-era tyrants, murderous Cold War dictators, and would-be tyrants in our own day gives us a gripping and illuminating picture of how strongmen have deployed violence, seduction, and corruption. History, she shows, offers clear lessons not only about how these regimes are built, but also how they must be opposed, and how they end."
     —Daniel Ziblatt, coauthor of *How Democracies Die*

"Ruth Ben-Ghiat is an indispensable resource on authoritarianism, past and present. Everyone who cares about American democracy should read this book."   —Sarah Kendzior, author of *Hiding in Plain Sight: The Invention of Donald Trump and the Erosion of America*

"What separates this book from the many others that examine tyrants and tyranny—is the analysis that puts this phenomenon in perspective."
     —David M. Shribman, *Boston Globe*

"Rich in anecdote. . . . Ms. Ben-Ghiat is at her most persuasive when she writes of the importance of the strongman's cult of personality."
     —Tunku Varadarajan, *Wall Street Journal*

"A surpassingly brilliant public intellectual."
     —Virginia Heffernan, *Trumpcast*

"This incisive study casts a wider geographic net than two recent books that have placed Trump on a continuum of authoritarian leaders: Géraldine Schwarz's *Those Who Forget*, which set him in the context of rising far-right movements in Europe, and Eric Posner's *The Demagogue's Playbook*, which compared him to American tyrants."   —*Kirkus Reviews*

"This is a thought-provoking look at how authoritarianism has shape-shifted from WWII to today."   —*Publishers Weekly*

STRONGMEN

OTHER WORKS BY RUTH BEN-GHIAT

Italian Fascism's Empire Cinema

Italian Mobilities (edited with Stephanie Malia Hom)

Fascist Modernities: Italy, 1922–1945

La Cultura Fascista

Italian Colonialism (edited with Mia Fuller)

Gli Imperi: Dall'antichità all'età Contemporanea (editor)

STRONGMEN

Mussolini to the Present

RUTH BEN-GHIAT

W. W. NORTON & COMPANY
Independent Publishers Since 1923

Copyright © 2021, 2020 by Ruth Ben-Ghiat

All rights reserved
Printed in the United States of America
First published as a Norton paperback 2021

For information about permission to reproduce selections from this book, write to
Permissions, W. W. Norton & Company, Inc., 500 Fifth Avenue, New York, NY 10110

For information about special discounts for bulk purchases, please contact
W. W. Norton Special Sales at specialsales@wwnorton.com or 800-233-4830

Manufacturing by LSC Communications, Harrisonburg
Production manager: Anna Oler

Library of Congress Cataloging-in-Publication Data

Names: Ben-Ghiat, Ruth, author.
Title: Strongmen : Mussolini to the present / Ruth Ben-Ghiat.
Description: First Edition. | New York : W. W. Norton & Company, 2020. |
Includes bibliographical references and index.
Identifiers: LCCN 2020034208 | ISBN 9781324001546 (Hardcover) |
ISBN 9781324001553 (ePub)
Subjects: LCSH: Dictators. | Dictatorships. | Authoritarianism. | Heads of state—Africa. |
Heads of state—Europe. | Heads of state—Latin America.
Classification: LCC JC495 .B48 2020 | DDC 321.9092/2—dc23
LC record available at https://lccn.loc.gov/2020034208

ISBN 978-0-393-86841-8 pbk.

W. W. Norton & Company, Inc., 500 Fifth Avenue, New York, N.Y. 10110
www.wwnorton.com

W. W. Norton & Company Ltd., 15 Carlisle Street, London W1D 3BS

4 5 6 7 8 9 0

CONTENTS

—

Part III: LOSING POWER

ACKNOWLEDGMENTS

STRONGMEN REFLECTS A LIFETIME of thinking about authoritarian rulers and their destructive impact on individuals and societies. My seaside hometown, Pacific Palisades, California, was an unlikely place to have birthed a teenager's meditations on regimes and their atrocities. Yet many exiles from Nazism resettled there or in adjacent towns, from the composer Arnold Schoenberg to the writer Thomas Mann. Even in the 1970s and 1980s, their traces were everywhere, inspiring me to learn more about their histories. A seminar on German exiles that I took during my undergraduate studies at the University of California, Los Angeles, taught by the historian Robert Wohl, gave me the historical context. The senior thesis I did on the conductor Otto Klemperer's transition from Berlin to Southern California introduced me to the pleasures of working in archives and interviewing people. They have not lost their pull decades later.

This book also draws on my firsthand experience of how the mainstreaming of far-right political forces damages democracy. I am grateful to the Fulbright Scholar Program for granting me a fellowship that put me in Rome in 1994 when Silvio Berlusconi's center-right coalition brought neo-Fascists into the government for the first time since 1945.

I knew Italy well, but felt the political ground shifting under my feet as Italians publicly expressed feelings of nostalgia and admiration for Fascism that they had previously kept private. More than once, I heard shouts of "Heil Hitler" and "Viva Il Duce" coming from the German beer hall across the street from my apartment.

Almost two decades later, when Donald Trump began his presidential campaign, I had a similar feeling. Watching Trump retweet neo-Nazi propaganda, call for the imprisonment of Democratic presidential candidate Hillary Clinton, and lead his followers in loyalty oaths at rallies seemed all too familiar—and filled me with dread. By then I had published extensively on Italian Fascism, documenting how the regime convinced Italians to see violence as a necessary agent of racial and political cleansing and imperial domination. Drawing on this expertise, in 2015 I began to write opinion pieces to warn the public about the dangers Trump posed to American democracy. By the time he was inaugurated in January 2017, I had mapped out the authoritarian playbook he would use to consolidate power. It is no consolation that my predictions proved accurate. I thank Stefano Albertini, Director of the Casa Italiana Zerilli-Marimò at New York University, my colleagues in NYU's history and Italian studies departments, and James Devitt, Managing Director of Public Affairs, NYU, for their support of these activities. I'm grateful to my first editors at CNN, Richard Galant and Pat Wiedenkeller, who helped my work reach a wide audience.

This book draws on datasets, archival documents, and scholarship in history, gender studies, political science, visual culture, and more. My most precious sources have been the accounts of people who experienced strongman rule, as told through memoirs, graphic novels, records of police and military interrogations, and interviews. I am also very grateful to the men and women who consented to be interviewed by me for this book. Some of their stories are told publicly for the first time here.

So many colleagues and friends around the world patiently answered my queries and assisted me in myriad ways. This book could not have been written without them. I'm grateful to Alan Angell, John Bawden, Mohamad Bazzi, Isak Bengiyat, Giorgio Bertellini, Eliot Bornstein, Nina Burleigh, Randall Bytwerk, Mauro Canali, George De Castro Day, Fred Cooper, Jessica Davidson, Emidio Diodato, Mansour El-Kikhia, Rebecca Falkoff, James Fernández, Antonio Feros, Federico Finchelstein, David Forgacs, Mimmo Franzinelli, Mark Galeotti, Alfredo González-Ruibal, Stephen Gundle, Benjamin Hett, John Hooper, Iván Jaksić, Geoffrey Jensen, David Kerzer, Adam Klasfeld, Marwan Kraidy, Jo Labanyi, Olga Lautman, Francesca Lessa, Michael Livingston, Sergio Luzzatto, Nicoletta Marini Maio, Hisham Matar, Christopher Mathias, Molly McKew, Jennifer Mercieca, Enrique Moradiellos, Lee Morganbesser, Sebastien Mort, Giovanni Orsina, Fraser Ottanelli, Juan Cristóbal Peña, Galadriel Ravelli, Gianni Riotta, Roberto Saviano, Laura, Alex, and Fabio Selvig, Richard Steigmann-Gall, Alexander Stille, Mary Helen Spooner, Dirk Vandewalle, Cristian Vaccari, and Stephen Wiley.

Jorge Dagnino invited me to lecture at the Universidad de los Andes and was a wonderful host. I am grateful to Alfo González Aguado for facilitating interviews during my stay in Santiago. I thank Barbie Zelizer for bringing me to the University of Pennsylvania's Annenberg School for Communication to teach a course on propaganda. I learned much from the discussions that followed my talks at Stanford University, Northeastern University, SUNY New Paltz, the University of Pennsylvania, the University of British Columbia, James Madison University, and Cambridge University. Diane Coyle, Anwar Fekini, Mia Fuller, Stephanie Malia Hom, Olga Lautman, and Lisa Tiersten generously read portions of the manuscript, and Andrea Chapin's careful edits made it much sharper.

I was lucky to have help from research assistants Andrés Fernández Carrasco, Charles Dunst, Ezel Sahinkaya, Giulio Salvati, and Maysam Taher. Nicola Lucchi did a wonderful job of sourcing images. Alexander Langstaff read the entire manuscript, improving it, and prepared the bibliography.

A big thank you to my agent, Wendy Strothman, who believed in this book from the start and gave me wise counsel throughout the writing and publishing process. Alane Mason, Vice President and Executive Editor at W. W. Norton & Company, read the manuscript several times, transforming it with her superb edits and keen sense of structure and flow. I am grateful for her time and dedication. Mo Crist, Janet Greenblatt, and Rebecca Homiski expertly guided the book through production, and Kyle Radler and Steve Colca handled publicity and marketing with professionalism and good cheer.

My friends inspired me with the example of their own lives and work. Thank you to Stefano Albertini, Giovanna Calvino, Diane Coyle, Daniela Del Boca, Troy Elander, Mia Fuller, Rhonda Garelick, Stephanie Malia Hom, Nita Juneja, Kate Loye, Giancarlo Lombardi, Jenny McPhee, Cinzia Mulé, Ellen Nerenberg, Franco Pirone, Jacqueline Reich, Dana Renga, Marina Sagona, Igiaba Scego, Ruti Teitel, David Tokofsky, and Lisa Tiersten for sustenance and conversation. My family, dispersed among many time zones and countries, encouraged me throughout. Thank you to Shlomit Almog, Gal Almog, Simonida Benghiat, Dusica Savić-Benghiat, Michael Benghiat, Stacy Benghiat, Victor and Viti Benghiat, Bezalel and Zehavah Tidhar, and my parents, Raphael Benghiat and Margaret Robison. Closer to home, the Canders family kept me in good spirits with their humor and hospitality.

This book is dedicated to my daughter Julia and my partner Bill Scott, who heard more about authoritarian leaders past and present than they ever wanted to and lived far too long with piles of books, organized by leader, invading the house. I feel blessed to have them in my life.

PROTAGONISTS

Idi Amin: President of Uganda, 1971–1979. He entered office through a military coup and was forced into exile by opposition forces.

Mohamed Siad Barre: President of the Somali Democratic Republic, 1969–1991. He entered office through a military coup and was forced into exile by opposition forces.

Silvio Berlusconi: Prime minister of Italy, May–December 1994, 2001–2006, 2008–2011. He came to power each time through elections. His 1994 government fell due to corruption charges. He was voted out in 2006 and resigned in 2011 during the eurozone crisis.

Jair Bolsonaro: Brazilian president, 2019 to the present. He came into office through elections.

Rodrigo Duterte: President of the Philippines, 2016 to the present. He came into office through elections.

Recep Tayyip Erdoğan: President of Turkey, 2014 to the present. Prime minister of Turkey, 2003–2014 and 2018 to the present. He came into office through elections.

Francisco Franco Bahamonde: El Caudillo (The Leader) of Spain, 1939–1975. He came to power through a military coup and led

Nationalist forces during the Spanish civil war (1936–1939). He died in office, of natural causes.

Muammar Gaddafi: Brotherly Leader and Guide of the Revolution of Libya, 1969–2011. He came to power through a military coup and was executed by opposition forces during the 2011 revolution.

Adolf Hitler: Chancellor of Germany, 1933–1945; Führer (Leader) of Germany, 1934–1945. President Paul von Hindenburg appointed him chancellor. Hitler committed suicide in April 1945.

Saddam Hussein: President of Iraq, 1979–2003. He came to power via military coup. Imprisoned in 2003 by American occupation forces, he was tried by the Iraqi Special Tribunal for crimes against humanity. In 2006 he was sentenced to death by hanging and executed that year.

Narendra Modi: Prime minister of India, 2014 to the present. He came into office through elections.

Benito Mussolini: Prime minister of Italy, 1922–1925; Head of State and Il Duce of Italy, 1925–1943; Head of State and Il Duce of the Republic of Salò, 1943–1945. King Victor Emmanuel III appointed him prime minister. The Fascist Grand Council removed him from power in July 1943 and imprisoned him. In September 1943, Adolf Hitler had him freed and placed him at the head of the Republic of Salò, a Nazi client state. Italian partisans executed him in April 1945.

Viktor Orbán: Hungarian prime minister, 2010 to the present. He came into office through elections. As of April 2020, he rules by decree.

Augusto Pinochet Ugarte: President of the Governing Junta of Chile, 1973–1990; president of Chile, 1974–1990. He came into office through a military coup and was voted out of office by a 1988 plebiscite.

Vladimir Putin: President of Russia, 2000–2008, 2012 to the present. Prime minister, 2008–2012. He came into office both times through elections.

Mobutu Sese Seko: President of Zaire, 1965–1997. He came into office through a military coup. Born Joseph-Désiré Mobutu, in 1972 he changed his name to Mobutu Sese Seko Kuku Ngbendu Wa Za Banga, which translates as "the all-powerful warrior who, because of his endurance and inflexible will to win, goes from conquest to conquest, leaving fire in his wake." He was forced into exile in 1997 by opposition forces.

Donald J. Trump: President of the United States of America, 2016 to the present. He came to power through elections. In 2019 he was impeached by the House for abuse of power and obstruction of Congress. The Senate acquitted him on both counts in 2020.

NOTE ON TERMS
AND LANGUAGE

I GIVE THE FULL NAME of individuals on first mention, then the
last name only. For individuals from the Spanish-speaking world,
I give both the paternal and maternal surnames on first mention, then
just the paternal. For example, Augusto Pinochet Ugarte is referred to as
Pinochet throughout the book.

There is no dominant spelling for some proper names. I use Gaddafi
to refer to the Libyan dictator throughout the book, but readers will see
Kadafi, Qaddafi, and other versions used in quotes and sources.

I use fascism for the general system of interwar government and Fascism for the Italian dictatorship. Following common usage, I use neo-
Fascism and neo-Fascist for movements and individuals that espouse
all varieties of fascism after 1945, and anti-Fascism and anti-Fascist for
movements and individuals that oppose all varieties of fascism throughout the twentieth and twenty-first centuries.

I use terms as they appear in sources and discussions of the time.
Mobutu Sese Seko renamed the Congo Zaire, so I use Zaire to refer to
that country during the years of his rule (1965–1997). When speaking
of the century-long repression of LGBTQ+ individuals, I use "homo-

sexual" for the twentieth century and "LGBTQ+" for the twenty-first century.

All translations from French, Italian, Spanish, German, and Portuguese sources are my own unless otherwise noted.

STRONGMEN

INTRODUCTION

O<small>N</small> N<small>OVEMBER</small> 4, 2008, when many world leaders waited to hear the results of the American presidential election, Italian prime minister Silvio Berlusconi was in his Roman residence preparing to have sex. "I'm going to take a shower," he told Patrizia D'Addario, his partner for the evening. "And if you finish before me, wait for me on the big bed."

> D'Addario: Which bed? Putin's?
> Berlusconi: Putin's.
> D'Addario: Oh, how cute. The one with the curtains.

Whether the bed was a gift from Vladimir Putin or the former Russian president and then-prime minister had merely slept there is unclear. Yet Berlusconi's "Putin bed" symbolized the intimacy of a friendship sustained by the leaders' common drive to exercise as much personal power as their political systems allowed and to appear to the world—and each other—as virile.[1] The men broke a record for bilateral visits among heads of state. In February 2003, they bonded at Putin's retreat in Zavidovo, near Moscow; in August they held a press conference in Sardinia, where Berlusconi had a villa. In the play by Dario Fo and Franca Rame, *The*

Silvio Berlusconi and Vladimir Putin in Zavidovo, Russia, February 2003.
VIKTOR KOROTAYEV / AFP / GETTY IMAGES

Berlusconi and Putin in Sardinia, Italy, August 2003.
STR / AFP / GETTY IMAGES

Two-Headed Anomaly, which premiered that year in Rome, Putin was killed and his brain transplanted into Berlusconi.[2]

The Berlusconi-Putin relationship brought two supremely transactional individuals together as they traced two paths for twenty-first century authoritarian rule. The former developed an autocratic style of governance within a nominal democracy. He exerted strict control over his party, Forza Italia, and his ownership of commercial television networks gave him more influence over the formation of public opinion than any Italian leader since Benito Mussolini. Putin suppressed democracy as he domesticated Parliament, the media, and the judiciary, assassinated and jailed critics, and plundered the economy.

The close relationship of the two premiers worried Ronald Spogli, the American ambassador to Rome. In January 2009, he warned Hillary Clinton, secretary of state of the new Barack Obama administration, that Berlusconi regularly voiced "opinions and declarations that have been passed to him directly by Putin." Berlusconi's private envoy, Valentino Valentini, traveled frequently to Russia on his behalf, and the two men handled Italy's Russia policy, leaving the Italian Foreign Ministry "in the dark." Spogli suspected that a "nefarious connection" accounted for the secrecy. The Italian leader was likely profiting from deals between the Italian and Russian energy companies ENI and Gazprom in exchange for supporting Russian efforts to "dilute American security interests in Europe."[3]

When a Wikileaks document dump later made Spogli's memos public, the Italian Parliament launched an investigation. It confirmed that Berlusconi was poised to make a percentage profit from an ENI-Gazprom South Stream pipeline to be built under the Black Sea. By the time construction on the pipeline began in 2012, sex and corruption scandals and the eurozone crisis had driven Berlusconi from office. That year, *Berlus-Putin*, the Russian adaptation of Fo and Rame's play, opened in Moscow. In the revised version, Berlusconi dies and his brain is transplanted into Putin, the political survivor between the two.[4]

—

OURS IS THE AGE OF THE STRONGMAN, of heads of state like Berlusconi and Putin who damage or destroy democracy and use masculinity as a tool of political legitimacy. In America, Turkey, Brazil, and other geopolitically important nations, such rulers have exploited their countries' resources to satisfy their greed and obstructed efforts to combat climate change. Their dependence on corruption and censorship and their neglect of the public good mean that they handle national crises badly and often bring ruin upon their people. How to combat this authoritarian ascendance is one of the most pressing matters of our time.[5]

The initial responses of illiberal heads of state to the 2020 COVID-19 pandemic are a case in point. All crises are leadership tests that clarify the core values, character, and governing style of rulers and their allies. Yet a public health emergency exposes with particular efficiency the costs of a perennial feature of autocratic rule: the repudiation of norms of transparency and accountability. The coronavirus outbreak started in Xi Jinping's China, a country of entrenched one-party rule. Wuhan doctor Li Wenliang warned his peers in December 2019 about the virus's destructive potential. The Chinese police silenced him, classifying his truth-telling as "illegal behavior," since it conflicted with government assertions that the disease was "preventable and controllable." In Hungary, Prime Minister Viktor Orbán used the pandemic to complete his process of autocratic capture. He declared a state of emergency and then instituted rule by decree to give himself dictatorial powers. In Brazil, where democracy is under assault, President Jair Bolsonaro claimed that COVID-19 was no worse than the flu and fired his health minister, Luiz Henrique Mandetta, for advising the public to practice social distancing. In each case, the leader's priority was not to save lives, but to maintain or expand his power. With climate change likely to cause increased levels of disease and scarcity, the spread of the strongman style of rule doesn't just endanger democracy, but also poses an existential threat.[6]

"NO HISTORIAN CAN GET INSIDE the heads of the dead . . . But with sufficient documentation, we can detect patterns of thought and action," writes Robert Darnton.[7] This book aims to do just that by looking at the evolution of authoritarianism, defined as a political system in which executive power is asserted at the expense of the legislative and judicial branches of government. I focus on Benito Mussolini, Adolf Hitler, Francisco Franco Bahamonde, Muammar Gaddafi, Augusto Pinochet Ugarte, Mobutu Sese Seko, Silvio Berlusconi, Recep Tayyip Erdoğan, Vladimir Putin, and Donald Trump, with Idi Amin, Mohamed Siad Barre, Jair Bolsonaro, Rodrigo Duterte, Narendra Modi, Viktor Orbán, and others making cameo appearances.

To illuminate the entire arc of authoritarian rule, starting with how democracies are degraded or destroyed, I do not include Communist leaders like Xi who take power in an already-closed system. I do acknowledge the ways Communist and other authoritarianisms developed through mutual influence. Zairean anti-Communist president Mobutu learned from the personality cults of Communist leaders like Nicolae Ceausescu of Romania and China's Mao Zedong. He took one of his titles, the Helmsman, from the latter.[8]

Some readers may wonder why I do not discuss strong female leaders in modern history, such as Britain's prime minister Margaret Thatcher or India's prime minister Indira Gandhi. While some of these women may have had certain strongman traits (Thatcher's nickname was "The Iron Lady") or engaged in repressive actions against minority populations, none of them sought to destroy democracy, and so they are not addressed here.

MANY STUDIES POINT TO recent historical events to explain today's turn away from democracy, like the 2008 recession and increases in global migration that heightened racist sentiments. Other works go back to the collapse of Communism in 1989–1990. Unleashing nationalist and tribalist sentiments in Eastern Europe, it encouraged the resurgence of the far right in Western Europe as well. Putin, the former Communist functionary who is now a leader of the global right, successfully rode that tide of political upheaval and ideological transformation.[9]

Populism is a common term for the parties and movements that carry forth this illiberal evolution of democratic politics. While populism is not inherently authoritarian, many strongmen past and present have used populist rhetoric that defines their nations as bound by faith, race, and ethnicity rather than legal rights. For authoritarians, only some people are "the people," regardless of their birthplace or citizenship status, and only the leader, above and beyond any institution, embodies that group. This is why, in strongman states, attacking the leader is seen as attacking the nation itself, and why critics are labeled "enemies of the people" or terrorists.[10]

Strongmen argues that today's leaders also have deeper roots. They recycle rhetoric and actions that go back to the dawn of authoritarianism in the 1920s and are invested in rehabilitating their autocratic predecessors. Putin has approved the erection of statues of Joseph Stalin in cities like Novosibirsk and Moscow, and Russian scholars who write about the mass graves of Stalin's victims have been imprisoned.[11] Berlusconi spread the lie that Mussolini "never killed anyone." Bolsonaro makes the false claim that Nazism was a left-wing phenomenon. Austrian chancellor Sebastian Kurz sent fascist-nostalgia signals in 2018 when he called for an "axis of the willing" among Hungary, Italy, and Austria (all fascist or collaborationist states during World War II) to combat illegal migration. To understand today's authoritarians and their allies, we need a historical perspective.[12]

FOR A POLITICAL SYSTEM THAT affects the lives of so many, authoritarianism remains a surprisingly fuzzy concept. We still lack a common language to speak about the governments of twenty-first century authoritarian rulers who repress civil liberties but use elections to keep themselves in power. Orbán celebrates his transformation of Hungary into an "illiberal democracy," using the term Fareed Zakaria coined in a landmark 1997 article in *Foreign Affairs*. More recently, labels like "hybrid regimes," "electoral autocracies," or "new authoritarianism" (the term used here) proliferate as scholars seek to classify this new wave of antidemocratic rule.[13] A long view of the authoritarian style of governance, which highlights baseline features that recur in different historical circumstances, as well as what changes over time, can help us to understand authoritarianism as it manifests today.

From Mussolini through Putin, all of the strongmen featured in this book establish forms of personalist rule, which concentrates enormous power in one individual whose own political and financial interests prevail over national ones in shaping domestic and foreign policy. Loyalty to him and his allies, rather than expertise, is the primary qualification for serving in the state bureaucracy, as is participation in his corruption schemes. Personalist rulers can be long-lasting rulers, because they control patronage networks that bind people to them in relationships of complicity and fear. Making all political activity bolster his own authority allowed Franco to stay in power in Spain for thirty-six years.[14]

The leaders discussed here have all put their mark on the authoritarian playbook—a set of interlinked tools and tactics that have evolved over a century. *Strongmen* focuses on propaganda, virility, corruption, and violence, as well as the tools people have used to resist authoritarianism and hasten its fall.[15] The practices and behaviors of today's rulers—and those of their opponents—have their own histories. When Putin poses shirtless, he recalls Mussolini's pioneering bodily display. Philippines president Duterte boasts of throwing enemies out of helicopters, evoking Chilean dictator Pinochet's practices. Resource extraction has inspired strongman partnerships from Mussolini and Hitler to Berlusconi and Putin. American president Trump's 2019 view of his country's interest in Syria is in this spirit: "We're keeping the oil. We have the oil. The oil is secure. We left the troops behind, only for the oil." I bring into focus histories of violence and plunder that are too rarely examined in a transnational and transhistorical frame.[16]

Strongmen adds to discussions of authoritarianism by highlighting the importance of virility and how it works together with other tools of rule. The leader's displays of machismo and his kinship with other male leaders are not just bluster, but a way of exercising power at home and conducting foreign policy. Virility enables his corruption, projecting the idea that he is above laws that weaker individuals must follow. It also translates into state policies that target women and LGBTQ+ populations, who are as much the strongman's enemies as prosecutors and the press. Anticolonial leaders like Mobutu and Ugandan president Amin were often as misogynist and anti-homosexual as their racist imperialist peers.

The authoritarian playbook provides continuity through the book's three periods of strongman rule: the fascist era, 1919–1945, the age of military coups, 1950–1990, and the new authoritarian age, 1990 to the present, the first two unfolding in dialogue with continuing Communist governance. Part I, Getting to Power, focuses on how such leaders get into office. Part II, Tools of Rule, first examines their projects of national greatness, revealing the logic of their policies. I then explore their use of propaganda, virility, corruption, and violence to stay in power. Part III, Losing Power, tracks resistance to the strongman, the decline of his authority, and his exit from office. Moving through Europe, the Americas, and Africa, *Strongmen* covers a century of tyranny under leaders that promise law and order and then enable lawless behavior by financial and sexual predators. It reveals how such leaders think and act, who they depend on, and how they can be opposed.

—

FOR ONE HUNDRED YEARS, charismatic leaders have found favor at moments of uncertainty and transition. Often coming from outside the political system, they create new movements, forge new alliances, and communicate with their followers in original ways. Authoritarians hold appeal when society is polarized, or divided into two opposing ideological camps, which is why they do all they can to exacerbate strife. Periods of progress in gender, labor, or racial emancipation have also been fertile terrain for openly racist and sexist aspirants to office, who soothe fears of the loss of male domination and class privilege and the end of White Christian "civilization." Cultural conservatives have repeatedly gravitated to antidemocratic politics at such junctures of history, enabling dangerous individuals to enter mainstream politics and gain control of government.[17]

From the start, authoritarians stand out from other kinds of politicians by appealing to negative experiences and emotions. They don the cloak of national victimhood, reliving the humiliations of their people by foreign powers as they proclaim themselves their nation's saviors. Picking up on powerful resentments, hopes, and fears, they present themselves as the vehicle for obtaining what is most wanted, whether it is territory, safety from racial others, securing male authority, or payback for exploitation by internal or external enemies. A wildly gesticulating Mussolini demanding justice for his country struck some as a histrionic "carnival-barker Caesar," but the politics of raw emotion he employed remains powerful today. So do the rhetoric of crisis and emergency and the comfort of knowing who to blame for the nation's troubles—and who to trust to solve those troubles once and for all. As the anthropologist Ernest Becker observes,

> It is [fear] that makes people so willing to follow brash, strong-looking demagogues . . . capable of cleansing the world of the vague, the weak, the uncertain, the evil. Ah, to give oneself over to their direction—what calm, what relief.[18]

As he gains a following, the aspiring leader tests out tools like propaganda and corruption that will later help him rule. The decay of truth and democratic dissolution proceed hand in hand, starting with the insurgent's assertion that the establishment media delivers false or biased information while he speaks the truth and risks everything to get the "real facts" out. Once his supporters bond to his person, they stop caring about his falsehoods. They believe him because they believe *in him*.[19] Many future autocrats pose as fresh alternatives to a morally bankrupt political system, even if they have a police record (Mussolini, Hitler) or were under investigation (Trump, Putin, Berlusconi). "All they have ever cared about are their own interests and those of their corrupt followers," a pro-Fascist lawyer wrote about the Italian political establishment in 1922, sounding like those who support populist parties and authoritarian leaders a century later.[20]

While not every ruler uses repression to get to power, all of them are skilled in the art of threat. Proclaiming a personal capacity for violence while running for office is a common twenty-first-century tactic, as when Trump declared he could shoot someone on Fifth Avenue and not lose any followers in January 2016. Some warn the nation that they intend to target certain categories of people. "I am telling the Filipino people not to vote for me, because it will be bloody," declared Duterte in 2015 of his vow to kill thousands of drug dealers and criminals if elected president.[21]

Shock events, or grave incidents that often prompt declarations of states of emergency, drive forward authoritarian history. They propel some individuals into office and give others who are already in power the excuse to do things they've wanted to do anyway, like securing their hold on government and silencing the opposition. In such situations, the temporary state of emergency may become normalized, "no longer the exception but the rule," as the anti-Nazi philosopher Walter Benjamin put it. For a century, knowing how to capitalize on calamity, whether you had something to do with it or not, has been an essential strongman skill.[22]

—

IN HIS 1931 BOOK *The Technique of the Coup d'Etat*, the Italian-Austrian journalist and writer Curzio Malaparte cautioned that Mussolini, in power for a decade, was "a modern man, cold, audacious, violent and calculating," and predicted that Hitler, then rising in popularity due to the Depression, would be even worse. The Austrian might look like a waiter and rant like a fool, but Germans had acclaimed him as "an ascetic, a mystic of the cult of action," just as many Italians had responded to Mussolini. If Hitler got into office, Malaparte warned, he would try to "corrupt, humble, and enslave the German people, in the name of German liberty, glory, and power."[23]

Journalists, aides, and others who have witnessed the strongman's dangerous character firsthand echo Malaparte's chillingly accurate forecast. Authoritarianism has had vastly divergent outcomes as it evolved over a century. The fascists committed genocide, while twenty-first-century leaders tend to favor targeted assassinations and mass detention. This makes the coherence of the collective portrait that emerges, the traits of one ruler eerily echoing those of others, more striking. Hitler resembled many later leaders in being an indecisive and insecure ruler behind his all-powerful Führer facade, his opinions sometimes reflecting the last person he had spoken to. Mobutu was hardly the only authoritarian to be "obsessively concerned with slights to his Presidency," as US ambassador to Zaire Brandon Grove asserted. Nor was Mussolini alone in spending hours each day reading the press "where every item dealing with him . . . has been marked by subordinates. He reads them with the air of a man seeking something," in the journalist George Seldes's 1935 observation. Putin continues the lineage of personalist rule in translating his private preoccupations with "loss of status, resentment, desire for respect, and vulnerability" into state policy.[24]

The strongman's impulsive and irascible nature (most have severe anger issues) and the "divide and rule" practices he follows to prevent anyone else from gaining too much power produce governments full of conflict and upheaval. Erdoğan's unpredictable decision-making, which is worsened by surrounding himself with family members and flatterers, is typical. So is the time the authoritarian leader's officials spend doing damage control when he has once again "insulted adversaries, undermined his aides, repeatedly changed course . . . and induced chaos." Gaddafi took chaos to an extreme, repealing entire legal frameworks from one day to the next. Being unpredictable energized him, as it did Amin and others who "have ideas of grandeur, think that they have the answer to complicated problems and in a sense lose touch with reality," in the words of Dr. David Barkham, Amin's personal physician. Amin's self-imposed title—His Excellency, President for Life, Field Marshal Al Hadji Doctor Idi Amin Dada, VC, DSO, MC, Lord of All the Beasts of the Earth and Fishes of the Seas, and Conqueror of the British Empire in Africa in General and Uganda in Particular—says it all.[25]

On one issue, the strongman has been consistent: his drive to control and exploit everyone and everything for personal gain. The men, women, and children he governs have value in his eyes only insofar as they produce babies, fight his enemies, and adulate him publicly. Each tool of his rule has its place within this scheme. Propaganda lets him monopolize the nation's attention, and virility comes into play as he poses as the ideal take-charge man. Repression creates confinement spaces full of captive bodies. Corruption lets him claim as his own the fruits of the nation's labor. The writer Jon Lee Anderson sums up a common authoritarian pathology of possession: "the technologies of paranoia, the stories of slaughter and fear, the vaults, the national economies employed as personal property, the crazy pets, the prostitutes, the golden fixtures"—anything that can chase away their fear of not having enough or losing what they already have. When they finally depart office, dead or alive, there is a sense that "their mania had left room in the country for nothing else."[26]

Personalist rulers can be the most destructive kinds of authoritarians because they do not distinguish between their individual agendas and needs and those of the nation. Their private obsessions set the tone for public discourse, skew institutional priorities, and force large-scale resource reallocations, as happened most famously in Hitler's war against the Jews. Authoritarian history is full of projects and causes championed by the ruler out of hubris and megalomania and implemented to disastrous effect. Mussolini's 1935 invasion of Ethiopia to give Italy an empire bankrupted the Italian state. Mobutu's massive projects for the Congo River—two Inga Falls dams and an Inga-Shaba power line—caused a debt crisis in Zaire. Trump's border wall with Mexico has claimed federal funds meant for defense and disaster prevention.

Authoritarianism has been reputed to be an efficient mode of governance, but my study of the dynamics and costs of personalist rule shows that the opposite is true. If the leader or his inner circle is under investigation, governance revolves around his defense, with time and resources focused on exonerating him and punishing those who might expose him, like prosecutors and journalists. Killing dissident elites and driving entire families into exile squanders generations of talent. Seizing or ruining profitable businesses, some built up over decades, hurts the economy. Far from being a productive force, illiberal rule has had devastating consequences for the earth and many millions of its inhabitants. [27]

"A DICTATOR IS IN GENERAL a man who comes from below and then throws himself in an even deeper hole . . . the world watches him . . . and jumps into the void after him," said Charlie Chaplin in 1939, capturing the authoritarian leader-follower dynamic.[28] *Strongmen* examines why people collaborate with these leaders, sometimes for decades, no matter the cost to them or the country. It also reflects on a truth that the autocrat goes to lengths to conceal: he is no one without his followers. They are not merely the faces that cheer him at rallies, his corrupt coconspirators, and the persecutors of his enemies, but the force that anoints him as the chosen one and maintains him in power.

In popular culture, the strongman's brand of charisma is often depicted as a spellbinding force that makes people do his bidding. Yet theorist Max Weber made it clear a century ago that charisma, which he defined as the attribution of "supernatural, superhuman, or at least especially exceptional powers or qualities" to an "individual personality," exists mostly in the eye of the beholder. Most strongmen have uncommon powers of persuasion. Their followers and collaborators are the ones to "make" their reputations, though, by acknowledging their abilities. This makes the leader's charismatic authority inherently unstable. His aura of specialness can dissipate if public opinion changes, leaving him without any legitimacy, unlike in dynastic and other forms of authority. That is why authoritarian states invest in leader cults and why they increase their use of censorship and repression if the leader's hold on his people starts to disintegrate.[29]

Elites are the authoritarian's most important promoters and collaborators. Afraid of losing their class, gender, or race privileges, influential individuals bring the insurgent into the political system, thinking that he can be controlled as he solves their problems (which often involves persecuting the left).[30] Once the ruler is in power, elites strike an "authoritarian bargain" that promises them power and security in return for loyalty to the ruler and toleration of his suspension of rights. Some are true believers, and others fear the consequences of subtracting their support, but those who sign on tend to stick with the leader through gross mismanagement, impeachment, or international humiliation.[31]

Foreign elites also prop up strongmen. This book highlights two categories of enablers. From Hitler to Pinochet to Erdoğan, mountains of foreign debt support the economic miracles authoritarians are said to perform. Deutsche Bank has funded authoritarian states from Hitler's Germany to Putin's Russia, as well as lending to businesses like the Trump Organization that are suspected of helping autocrats and their cronies to launder their money. Financial institutions in the United States and the United Kingdom, working with international law firms, allow strongmen to hide their illicit wealth in anonymous accounts and shell corporations abroad. So did the Swiss, whose vaults and banks, ruled by banking secrecy until 2018, store some of the money of Gaddafi, Mobutu, and other despots.[32] Public relations and lobbying firms have also played a prominent role, advertising strongman states as productive and stable. Charm offensives help to cover over the chaos and corruption. "The more trouble the client was in, the better the party," recalled an associate of Edward von Kloberg III, who represented Ceausescu, Iraqi president Saddam Hussein, and Mobutu.[33]

THE HISTORY OF THE STRONGMAN can make for difficult reading. These rulers promise a bright national future, but the emotions they elicit are bleak. The line between everyday life and horror in their states can be razor-thin. Amin entertained diplomats at Kampala's swanky Nile Hotel, enjoying the knowledge that his security forces were beating dissidents in the basement. Pinochet's military made some leftists watch the torture of people they knew on a blue-lit "stage." Gaddafi had a "Department of Protocol" to procure his sexual captives. As the philosopher Hannah Arendt argued, authoritarian states thrive on the synergy of bureaucracy and violence.[34]

Along with these histories, there are others of hope and inspiration. *Strongman* relates the quiet heroism of men and women who tried to keep social bonds and family ties strong "under the most adverse external conditions imaginable, across space and time," as Gabriele Herz wrote from the Moringen work camp in Germany in 1937. Herz, a Jew, felt fortunate to have gotten off relatively lightly, emigrating with her family after nine months in captivity. Her memoir pays tribute to the solidarity she found in Moringen and the resilience of her fellow prisoners. Victoria Hösl, a Communist worker, sent a picture of herself, sketched by a graphic artist inmate, to her son, whom the authorities had placed in a convent after the Gestapo took her away. "I recognized you right away, dearest Mommy, even though I haven't seen you for years," he wrote back touchingly.[35] Such stories of love that resists the state's attempts to destroy it call out to us today.

PART I

GETTING
TO POWER

ONE

FASCIST TAKEOVERS

F ROM AN EARLY AGE, the first man to transform a democracy into a dictatorship showed the qualities that have marked strongmen of the twentieth and twenty-first centuries: a violent temperament, opportunism, and a way with words. All of these set Mussolini apart from other children in his working-class village of Predappio, in the Romagna region of Italy. By the time he became a schoolteacher known for carrying brass knuckles and sexually assaulting women, he had already stabbed a classmate and a girlfriend. His student and future wife Rachele Guidi recalled how frightened she was at the ferocity of his calls for Socialist insurrection.[1]

Mussolini could transform himself into a gentleman, though, with anyone he felt could advance his career. His rise was linked to his ability to charm powerful male conservatives and influential women who taught him how to behave at crucial moments of his political life. The Russian-born Italian Socialist Party (PSI) official Angelica Balabanoff promoted him within Italy's vibrant left. By 1912, he headed the PSI's revolutionary wing and edited the Socialist newspaper *Avanti!* Two years later, Mussolini was expelled from the PSI for supporting Italy's intervention in World War I (Socialists felt the war weakened international worker solidarity). Many observers felt his political career was over, but soon he debuted the newspaper that served as a laboratory for his ideas about Fascism: *Il Popolo d'Italia*. It was funded in part by Italian and foreign industrialists and financiers who profited from Italian mobilization, which came in May 1915.[2]

Fascism and the modern strongman emerged from the vortex of World War I (1914–1918), a conflict so catastrophic that many combatants felt no words could express its horrors. The first total war, so named for its erosion of civilian and military boundaries, caused a systemic shock. The Ottoman, Habsburg, German, and Russian empires all fell. Out of those five turbulent years and the Russian Revolution (1917–1921) came fascism and Communism. Both political systems were founded on a rejection of liberal democracy and the worship of male leaders who promised to harness the energies of modernity to create superior societies.[3]

Mussolini understood that the world would never be the same after the war. Old parties and the "old men" who ruled them would be "swept aside," he asserted in 1917, the year his own war experience ended due to wounds sustained in a training exercise. The battlefields had created a "trenchocracy," an elite made by combat rather than aristocratic birth. These men knew that "he whom you cannot teach to fly you must push, that he may fall faster," as Mussolini had concluded from reading the German philosopher Friedrich Nietzsche, who influenced Hitler as well. Emerging from a matrix of violence, fascism gave political expression in Italy and Germany to such pitiless attitudes, attracting veterans who exchanged state-issued military uniforms for black and brown shirts. Bringing the mentality and tactics of the war home, these combatants regarded persecuting domestic enemies as a patriotic duty—as it would become for civilians, too, once Mussolini and Hitler got into office.[4]

Fascism disrupted the existing field of politics, confusing many by putting two things together that were supposed to be opposites: nationalism and Socialism. Leftists were the earliest and most consistently persecuted targets of fascist regimes. Any real progressive elements in the original 1919 Italian Fascist program, like the demand for 8-hour days for workers, soon vanished. Yet Mussolini, a former Socialist, knew the power of insurrectionary language to mobilize people. He pitched Fascism as "both subversive and conservative": it favored national unity instead of class conflict, imperialism and force instead of international solidarity, and promised modernization without loss of tradition.[5]

Both the National Fascist Party (PNF), founded in 1921 by Mussolini, and the National Socialist German Workers' Party (NSDAP), which Hitler led as of 1921, electrified followers with the idea that revolution could be used to suppress rather than enable the sweeping political and social emancipation wrought by the war. Reversing female empowerment at a time of mass male injury and declining birth rates was one target of fascism; neutralizing workers galvanized by the Russian and 1918 German and Hungarian revolutions to demand more rights, another. The spread of atheistic Communism also seemed to threaten White Christian civilization, as did the perceived loss of imperial controls over peoples of color. The 1919 Versailles Treaty deprived Germany of its colonies, and the Paris Peace Conference that produced the treaty recognized the world's first independent Arab state, the Tripolitanian Republic, inside Italian Libya.[6]

The disaffection with conventional politics and politicians after a ruinous war created yearnings for a new kind of leader. The cults that rose up around Mussolini and Hitler in the early 1920s answered anxieties about the decline of male status, the waning of traditional religious authority, and the loss of moral clarity. Those who saw these men speak in person, like Heinrich Class, chair of the Pan-German League, and the critic Ugo Ojetti, felt they were witnessing "something entirely new in the political life of our nation": the comfort of "the world reduced to black and white," presented by someone with "absolute faith in himself and in his own powers of persuasion."[7]

Out of the crucible of these years came the cults of victimhood that turned emotions like resentment and humiliation into positive elements of party platforms. The Versailles Treaty, which blamed all of the conflict's damages on Germany, fueled charges by the Führer and many others that foreign and domestic elites had "stabbed Germany in the back." Italy had allied with France and Great Britain and came out on the winning side, but Mussolini gained equal traction from his complaint that Italy's victory had been "mutilated" by more powerful nations, since the Versailles Treaty did not give the country the city of Fiume and other territory.[8]

Mussolini borrowed the "Duce" title (taken from the Latin *Dux*, for military leader), the black shirt, and the Roman salute from Gabriele D'Annunzio. The imperialist poet pioneered their use when he occupied Fiume in protest in 1919–1920. Mussolini went much further, though, applying the Socialist language of class conflict to argue that a revolution was needed to liberate "proletarian" Italy from discrimination by the "plutocratic" Great Powers. Mussolini prepared the script used by today's authoritarians that casts the leader as a victim of his domestic enemies and of an international system that has cheated his country.[9]

—

THE FASCIST COMBAT LEAGUES that Mussolini founded in 1919, in the midst of a severe postwar economic crisis, were a symptom of Italy's extreme polarization. Between 1919 and the founding of the Italian Communist Party (PCI) in 1921, close to 2 million industrial workers and peasants took part in strikes and farm and factory occupations. Fascist squads, heavy with veterans, started as private militias financed by industrial and agrarian bosses to end the labor unrest. Thousands of Socialists and left-leaning priests were murdered and their homes and offices trashed and burned. In border areas like Trieste, squadrism also expressed racialized, anti-Slav sentiments. "Even those who have seen proper action at the front have been amazed at how much violence there is," wrote a young Florentine squadrist in 1921.[10]

Mussolini's partnership with conservatives provided a template for later authoritarians. On their own, the Fascists would have gone nowhere—those who ran independently in the 1921 elections got 0.4 percent of the vote. In alliance with Prime Minister Giovanni Giolitti's National Bloc

Benito Mussolini, 1920s.
PHOTO 12 / ANN RONAN
PICTURE LIBRARY /
AGEFOTOSTOCK

coalition, though, they entered Parliament as the PNF. Neither Giolitti nor his peers worried much about Fascist violence. Taming the left was the competency the ruling class most desired in a leader, and they stuck with Mussolini until it was too late to save Italian democracy.

By then, word of Mussolini's mystique was spreading. Robust and 5 feet 7 inches tall, with a bald head and jutting jaw, he seemed to inflate in front of a crowd. He reminded many of Maciste, a popular Italian muscleman and film star. Mussolini's intense gaze attracted much attention, as it seemed to be powered by a mysterious energy source. One admirer felt overcome by Mussolini's "magnetic energy"; another felt "electrified." The young officer Carlo Ciseri hated politicians until he saw Mussolini speak in 1920. "I immediately felt hugely drawn to him. I liked his words, I liked his pride, his force, and the look in his eyes. . . . I have seen something exceptional in this man," he wrote in his diary [11]

"Does Fascism aim at restoring the State, or subverting it?" Mussolini teased his followers, playing on his movement's ideological ambiguity. He was the sole reference point and interpreter of Fascism for his motley crew of backers that included bankers, rural dwellers, and housewives. Imperialism also held Mussolini's Fascism together. Although Italy then occupied Eritrea, Libya, Somalia, and the Dodecanese Islands, Mussolini claimed that imperial France and Great Britain invoked a double standard by denying Italy the right to an empire. "It is our destiny that the Mediterranean return to being ours," he told Italians in 1921.[12]

After so much violence, Mussolini did not have to stage a coup to take power. King Victor Emmanuel III, commander of the Italian armed forces, could have easily disarmed the Fascists, who never counted more than 30,000 in a country of about 40 million people. Instead, this shy man chose the path of least conflict, appointing Mussolini to the post of prime minister in October 1922. The American ambassador to Rome, Richard Washburn Child, had already assured Mussolini that the United States would not object to a Fascist-led coalition government. While violence prepared the path, the March on Rome, celebrated by Fascists to this day on October 28 as a populist uprising, was an elite-approved transfer of power.[13]

Over the next two years, as blackshirt violence continued, Mussolini pioneered authoritarian strategies to weaken Italian democracy. He turned Parliament into a bully pulpit and denounced negative coverage of him and Fascism as "criminal." He created the Fascist Grand Council and the Voluntary Militia for National Security as parallel governance and defense structures, but elites did not heed these red flags. The art critic Margherita Sarfatti, the most important of the Italian leader's lovers of the 1920s, polished his image to help him win over financial and industrial elites. Privatizing the electric, telephone, and insurance sectors helped even more. Italian Parliament passed a Fascist-sponsored electoral reform that gave any party receiving over 25 percent of the vote two-thirds of seats. This measure, plus voter intimidation and fraud, gave the Fascists 64.9 percent of the vote in the April 1924 election.[14]

Mussolini, now known as Il Duce, was on top of the world—and then the Socialist leader Giacomo Matteotti threatened to ruin everything. Matteotti, trained as a lawyer, was all that Mussolini was not: tall, urbane, and known for his integrity. Fascist thugs had already physically assaulted him several times for denouncing Fascist electoral interference and destruction of the rule of law. Matteotti ignored the shouted death threats coming from Fascist deputies in May 1924 as he called out Italy's slide into "absolutism" in Parliament, joking to his allies, "now you may write the eulogy for my funeral."[15]

The fastest way to lose your life to a strongman is to publicly denounce his corruption. Matteotti wasn't just an outspoken anti-Fascist, but also a crusader for government ethics, who had spent nights and weekends compiling an exhaustive dossier of PNF crimes. It contained evidence of illegal financial transactions, such as bribes paid by the American oil company Sinclair (already tainted by the American Teapot Dome Scandal) to Fascist officials in return for a monopoly on oil exploration rights in Italy. Mussolini's brother Arnaldo, who served as his fixer, featured in the documents that Matteotti was set to read at the next parliamentary session.[16]

And so on the afternoon of June 10, witnesses saw two men attack Matteotti on Rome's busy Lungotevere and drag him into their car, which was subsequently discovered outside of Rome. The killers acted like amateurs. One of them, Amerigo Dumini, a former squadrist who often introduced himself as having eight murders on his resumé, was found with Matteotti's bloodstained trousers. The car was quickly traced to Cesare Rossi, head of Mussolini's personal secret police and his press office. It had been seen parked at the Ministry of the Interior the preceding night.[17]

Although Matteotti's body was not found until August, Rossi and Dumini were arrested, and special prosecutors launched a murder investigation that put Mussolini on the defensive. The opposition press accused Il Duce of complicity in the crime. As street-corner shrines to Matteotti proliferated all over Italy, Mussolini's conservative allies pressed him to step down. Veterans, long his core supporters, turned in their party cards. Rosa B., a tarot card reader from Turin, had warned the prime minister the year before of "a calamity soon to come your way. . . . Prepare yourself, Duce, for the Fall, for Ingratitude and Ignominy." Now her prophecy seemed accurate. Few people came to see him now about jobs or favors—a real measure of his decline in status. By December, rumors of his resignation prompted public celebrations. "Really, there are two dead men, Matteotti and Mussolini," Ojetti observed.[18]

As his biographer Laura Fermi, who grew up under his rule, notes, Il Duce was ill equipped for the rejection he faced during this period. "[U]sed to flattery and applause, he could not face the once-crowded waiting rooms of his office, now suddenly empty, gelid, immense." Losing sleep and plagued by an ulcer, the Italian leader extricated himself from an impossible situation by applying the strongman's golden rule: do whatever is necessary to stay in power. On January 3, 1925, a day after the Liberal leader Giorgio Amendola told the London *Times* that Mussolini "was finished," the Italian leader announced the first fascist dictatorship, challenging Parliament to impeach him and declaring himself and his party to be above the law.

> I, and I alone, assume political, moral, and historical responsibility for all that has happened. . . . If Fascism has been a criminal association, I am the head of that criminal association. . . . Gentlemen, Italy wants peace, quiet, work, and calm. . . . We will give it by love, if possible, or by force, if necessary.[19]

A series of assassination attempts against the new autocrat led to the Laws for the Defense of the State (1925–1926) that created a secret police (Organization for the Vigilance and Repression of Anti-Fascism, or OVRA) and banned strikes, political parties, and more. Anti-Fascists fled abroad or went into hiding, and many were killed. Former prime minister Francesco Saverio Nitti, in exile in Zurich, appealed to the king to "liberate our country from its humiliation" by "violent ignorant men." He received no reply.[20] To take care of unfinished business from the Matteotti killing, Mussolini pardoned all political criminals in July 1925 and fired the magistrates overseeing the ongoing Matteotti investigation. Their replacements delivered the judgment of involuntary manslaughter, clearing him of direct responsibility for the crime and setting him up to rule without limitations on his power. Mussolini lacked one last guarantee of his survival: international legitimation and economic aid. In 1926, J. P. Morgan partner Thomas Lamont, another Fascist proselytizer, brokered a $100 million loan from the American government to the regime. Implicitly sanctioning Mussolini's power grab, the act started a century of US support for right-wing authoritarian leaders.[21]

In less than three years, Mussolini had destroyed Italian democracy, bought off elites, and domesticated the press and labor. When former prime minister Giolitti, who had given Mussolini his start by putting his extremist party on the ballot, died in 1928, neither Mussolini nor the king attended the funeral. Among the new dictator's greatest admirers was Hitler, known as "the German Mussolini" before coming so fully into his own that he, and not Il Duce, is often seen as the epitome of fascism.[22]

—

THE THIRD REICH BEGAN the way it would end: in flames. The fiery landscapes of World War I forged many of the men who followed Hitler, torches in hand, as he promised them a new Germany. One fire, the Reichstag-gutting blaze of February 27, 1933, proved particularly fateful. While there is no consensus among historians about the fire's origins, when Dutch Communist Marinus van der Lubbe was found in the building that evening, Hitler had an excuse to proceed with mass arrests of leftists and strip all Germans of civil liberties. "You are now witnessing the beginning of a great new epoch in German history," he told the British journalist Sefton Delmer that night as they watched the flames consume Parliament. "The fire is the beginning."[23]

Hitler had been in his early twenties when he made an important discovery. He felt most alive when losing himself in something he found sublime, like a Richard Wagner opera or the sound of his own voice. He had moved to Vienna from Linz after his mother's death, and while his desired careers as a painter and architect went nowhere (he was rejected twice from the Academy of Fine Arts), he found he had a talent for captivating and cowing people with extended verbal tirades. Hitler shared Mussolini's violent temperament, but he favored verbal aggression, rather than physical assault, as a means of gaining obedience and attention. "Adolf's claims on me were boundless. . . . I had to be at his beck and call," recalled his friend August Kubizek, presaging Hitler's behavior as Nazi leader.[24]

Hitler's ambition led him to Germany, where he won two Iron Crosses for his service in World War I. The striking oratory that had helped him become the head of the NSDAP now attracted attention. From his Munich base, he harangued against Jews, the "black parasites of the nation" who might have to be placed in "concentration camps"; Marxists; war profiteers; and foreign powers, all of them out to rob Germany of its future. Hitler's vocal and emotional force brought to him collaborators like Joseph Goebbels, later his minister of propaganda. "What a voice. What gestures, what passion. My heart stands still. . . . I am ready to sacrifice everything for this man," Goebbels confided to his diary after hearing Hitler speak. Convinced of his providential mission, Hitler took to holding multiple rallies in a single evening, usually arriving late and with an entourage, like the *divo* he was becoming.[25]

Mussolini had squadrists, and Hitler had the SA (Stormtroopers), a paramilitary force cofounded by Ernest Röhm that drew its members from World War I elite shock troops. From providing Hitler with protection at rallies, the SA grew to become the NSDAP's own hit squad. German democracy was under attack by the political extremes, and clashes between the SA and left-wing paramilitaries were common. Runaway inflation and Germany's default on reparations payments, which led the French and the Belgians to occupy the Ruhr area in 1923, increased the sense among some Germans that extraordinary action was needed to save the country.[26]

Yet Hitler had little traction beyond his small base of fanatic followers. His failed November 1923 Bavarian Beer Hall Putsch had damaged his reputation and sparked a prohibition on the NSDAP holding office. No press but the NSDAP's own would publish Hitler's lengthy work *Mein Kampf* (*My Struggle*), which he wrote while in prison in 1924 for the putsch attempt. Hitler also had no live audience, since his hate speech had gotten him banned from public speaking in many German states. A 1926 NSDAP poster calling for a protest against the ban depicted him as a populist truth-teller muzzled by the "crooks and fat cats" who controlled Weimar democracy.[27]

Feeling stymied, Hitler redoubled his efforts to obtain Mussolini's counsel on how to bring a fascist takeover to Germany. Il Duce ignored the Austrian's requests for his photo, irritated that an evident loser asso-

NSDAP poster calling for a protest against Hitler's speaking ban, 1926. COURTESY OF THE BUNDES-ARCHIV, KOBLENZ

ciated himself with his Fascist brand, but Hitler was undeterred. He installed a bust of the Italian leader on his desk, dismissed remarks from NSDAP associates that he suffered from "Mussolini-intoxication," and pestered Mussolini's Berlin liaison, Army Major Giuseppe Renzetti, for a meeting.[28] Hitler had already learned from Mussolini the importance of making himself palatable to a larger public to gain entry into the political mainstream. In 1925 he promised to abide by the Weimar constitution to get the NSDAP ban lifted, and his speaking ban ended in 1927. Hitler also hired Heinrich Hoffmann, who later became his official photographer. This 1929 portrait, which highlights his intensity and masculine capability, became an iconic image after 1933. The businessman Ernst von Hanfstaengl introduced this cleaned-up Hitler to the moneyed social circles that mattered, just as Sarfatti had done for Mussolini.[29]

Adolf Hitler, 1929.
HEINRICH HOFFMANN / EVERETT COLLECTION / AGEFOTOSTOCK

Hitler was ready when the economic crisis hit Germany and the NSDAP became the second largest party in the 1932 elections, sandwiched between the Social Democrats and the Communists. At last Mussolini sent him an autographed picture (Hitler speedily replied "this is a great honor for me"). The NSDAP sold 287,000 copies of a slimmer edition of *Mein Kampf* between 1930 and 1933. Hitler's audiences multiplied as he exerted what observers saw as "an almost mystical power of attraction" at rallies, unleashing frenzies of raw emotion that expressed Germany's pain and anxiety. "We don't want to hear anything more about the government, we want only ADOLF HITLER as our leader, as the sole strong hand, as dictator," wrote the Silesian official P. F. Beck to Hitler in 1932.[30]

As in Italy, the action of a few conservative elites, rather than popular acclaim, got the strongman into power. Around 1930, the media magnate and German National People's Party head Alfred Hugenberg and the German president Paul von Hindenburg had begun to court Hitler, thinking he would support rearmament and help them subvert the left's growing electoral strength. In January 1933, on the strength of the NSDAP's electoral showing, Hindenburg made Hitler chancellor, allowing him to rule by decree, as had his immediate predecessors, rather than by parliamentary majority. German conservatives thought Hitler would be their tool. The industrialist and NSDAP funder Fritz Thyssen saw Hitler's rule as a transition to restoring the German monarchy. "I, too, misjudged the political situation at that time," Thyssen would write after fleeing Germany in 1939.[31]

Having waited a decade to get into office, Hitler had no interest in Renzetti's advice to follow Mussolini's example and "make your moves carefully, and don't rush." The February Reichstag fire ensured that he didn't have to. The building still smoked when Hindenburg issued an emergency decree ending freedoms of press, assembly, and more. Thousands of leftists were detained in prisons and warehouses while Dachau, the Reich's first concentration camp, was being converted from an arms factory. In March came the Enabling Act, which allowed the Führer to rule without consulting the Reichstag or the president. In less than two months, Hitler had secured the ability to govern without any checks on the exercise of his authority. His fascist takeover surpassed Mussolini's in its speed and intensity. As the Italian exile Giuseppe Borgese observed, a cat had birthed a tiger.[32]

—

WITH HIS HIGH-PITCHED VOICE, 5-foot 3-inch frame, and faint presence on camera, Franco might have seemed an unlikely candidate for leader longevity. Yet he proved to be a key transition figure from the age of fascist takeovers to the era of military coups. Franco possessed the crucial strongman talent of knowing how to change his rhetoric and alliances to suit the current political environment. He was a fascist in the 1930s and a pro-American client during the Cold War. Violence against leftists was the constant.[33]

By the mid-1930s, Spain had become the latest battleground between left and right. Between 1923 and 1930, Spain experienced authoritarian rule under General Miguel Primo de Rivera. His government prepared some Spaniards to accept dictatorship—and others to fight to the death against it. The leftist-led Second Republic that began in 1931 cast out the Bourbon monarchy, separated church and state, expanded worker rights, granted women voting rights and legal independence, and reduced the military's officer corps—measures conservatives and the right saw as the start of social anarchy. As in Germany, the Depression further fueled political extremes. In 1933, a center-right government took power, and the fascist Falange movement soon took shape.[34]

Franco had made his reputation as a military commander fighting insurgents in Spanish Morocco, where the idea originated that he possessed special powers. In 1916, as a twenty-four-year-old officer, he survived a stomach wound that would have killed most men—suggesting to his Moroccan troops that he had *baraka*, known in Islamic cultures as a divine blessing bestowed on someone marked for a special destiny.

The notion that a higher power intended him to save Spain from Marxism became an element of his charismatic authority. In 1934, Franco was given "emergency dictator" powers to put down a revolt and strike by miners in Asturia. "This is a frontier war against Socialism, Communism, and whatever attacks civilization in order to replace it with barbarism," he declared.[35]

The civil war that brought Franco to power started when the center-right refused to accept the results of the February 1936 election that brought a Popular Front government of left-wing parties to power, sparking cycles of violence and rumors of a coup. Prime Minister Manuel Azaña sent Franco off to the Canary Islands to ward off a conspiracy against his government, but the cautious Franco was the last man to join the July uprising planned by Generals José Sanjurjo and Emilio Mola.[36]

Francisco Franco, July 1936.
BETTMANN / GETTY IMAGES

Once the coup began, Franco surprised his peers by speedily securing personal agreements with both Mussolini and Hitler for weapons, supplies, and funding. And only Franco had at his service, from his years in Morocco, the equivalent of a fascist paramilitary in the violent and freewheeling Spanish Foreign Legion. Along with his Moroccan troops, known as *Regulares*, it formed the Army of Africa. Italian and German planes airlifted his units from Morocco to Spain, where Franco treated Spanish leftists like a colonial enemy to be exterminated. Hitler and Mussolini, who had sent troops of their own to Spain, applied his tactics to their own adversaries during World War II.[37]

Already Generalissimo of the Nationalist forces, in October 1936 Franco declared himself head of a military-run insurgent state. He was the only major participant in the coup left standing by the time the civil war ended with the Nationalists' victory in April 1939. Whether or not Franco possessed *baraka*, he did have the strongman brand of luck, which often involves competitors meeting a bad end. General Mola and General Sanjurjo both died in plane crashes, and other generals involved in the uprising were executed by Republicans or met with accidents.[38]

Franco's grip on power held long after Mussolini and Hitler died. His brutality and cunning were an inspiration to Pinochet, who attended his funeral in 1975. In Madrid, the Chilean leader also conducted some off-the-record business related to his intent to carry Franco's far-right torch. He hired the neo-Fascist terrorist and propagandist Stefano Delle Chiaie, who was a fugitive from Italy and had lived in Spain under Franco's protection, to work for his own secret police. The tools fascists used to rule found new life in the age of military coups.[39]

TWO

MILITARY COUPS

A LEOPARD NEVER CHANGES its spots, goes the saying about human nature, but Mobutu, nicknamed "the leopard of Zaire" for his leopard-skin hats, survived for thirty-two years in office by adapting to please his patrons, in the Franco manner. Two grand historical movements, decolonization and the Cold War, fueled the second strongman era. Mobutu embodied both. After an American-backed military coup brought him to power in 1965, Mobutu managed to be simultaneously anti-imperial, anti-Communist, and pro-capitalist. He nationalized economic resources and expelled European capitalists, but also served as a tool for Americans and Europeans to contain Communism in Central Africa and preserve their economic and strategic interests. During Mobutu's 1970 White House visit, President Richard Nixon hailed Zaire as a "strong, vigorous and stable country" and a "good investment." Conveniently, Nixon overlooked Mobutu's corruption and his public execution of cabinet officials four years earlier in front of a crowd of 50,000.[1]

World War I had created the conditions for the age of fascist takeovers, and World War II prepared the age of military coups. The destabilizing effects of the war on British and European imperial territories fostered what the civil rights activist Malcolm X called a "tidal wave of

Zaire's president Mobutu Sese Seko and US president Richard Nixon at the White House, 1970.
COURTESY OF THE RICHARD NIXON PRESIDENTIAL LIBRARY AND MUSEUM

color": anti-imperial insurrections that changed the face of power. Franco's loss of Spanish Morocco in 1956 was part of a vast transfer of authority to non-Europeans that took place in India, Vietnam, Algeria, the Congo, and elsewhere from the late 1940s to the 1970s. In 1969, the year Gaddafi seized power in Libya, successful military coups also occurred in Sudan and Somalia.[2] This new crop of leaders used their peoples' anger over the tyranny of Western colonizers to rally followers. Those who became authoritarians, like Gaddafi, Barre, and Mobutu, adapted traditions of colonial violence for their own purposes.

Military service had always been an avenue of advancement for ambitious men from occupied nations, and coups appealed as a way for such outsiders to get to power. Repurposing the combat and communications training given them by the imperialist enemy was sweet revenge. Amin served in the King's African Rifles forces in British Kenya, and Mobutu enlisted in the Belgian Congo's *Force Publique*. Barre was a member of the *Zaptié* military police corps in Italian Somalia, and Gaddafi and his fellow Libyan conspirators received military training in Great Britain and America. A transnational body of knowledge about armed conflict informed the military strongman's rise to power. The success of one coup inspired others. Just as Hitler watched Mussolini's actions carefully, so did Gaddafi learn from Lieutenant Colonel Gamal Abdel Nasser's 1952 overthrow of the monarchy in Egypt.[3]

Military coups may be less common today, but they have been the most common path to authoritarian rule, accounting for 75 percent of democratic failures globally since World War II. They are certainly the most dramatic instances of change. They often happen in the morning, meaning that you could leave for work or school living in a democracy and return home to a state of emergency—or never return home again.[4] When coups are bloody, the shock of soldiers using force normally deployed against external enemies on their own people prepares the public for a transformation of the military's role within the state. The strongman who triumphs via military coup may pose as a patriarch, but this father doesn't hesitate to butcher his own. The word *coup* translates as a "cut" or "hit" in many languages, and it often entails the removal of objectionable elements said to endanger the nation.

Wherever and whenever they happen, coups are almost always undertaken in the name of "the people," even though in a well-executed coup the people had no idea it was coming. Justifications for coups repeat over a century, such as preventing economic disaster, avoiding leftist apocalypse, or removing corrupt leaders. Many strongmen who come to power by coup leave it in the same fashion. Two-thirds of dictators were removed by coups between 1950 and 2000. Takeover by coup paid off for Gaddafi and Pinochet, who stayed in office for forty-two and seventeen years, respectively. Their countries are still marked by their rule and haunted by their memory.[5]

—

COUPS ARE BY NATURE surprise events, but Gaddafi's overthrow of King Idris I was shocking, not because of its violence (it was initially largely bloodless), but because no one in power had ever heard of him. On September 1, 1969, an unidentified voice addressed the nation:

> People of Libya! In response to your own free will, fulfilling your most heartfelt wishes . . . your armed forces have over-thrown the reactionary, backward, and corrupt regime . . . As of now Libya shall be free and sovereign . . . we shall build glory, revive heritage, and avenge a wounded dignity.

When the speaker was revealed to be a twenty-seven-year-old captain from a poor and illiterate Bedouin family, it caused more consternation. How had this outsider Gaddafi pulled off such an efficient operation?[6]

Unlike Franco, who joined his coup at the last minute, Gaddafi's was the fulfillment of a lifelong dream. Gaddafi's goal was to replicate Nasser's takeover, and as a student at Benghazi's Royal Military Academy in the 1960s, Gaddafi was already recruiting for his own Free Officers movement. Six feet tall and lean, with intense eyes and striking features, Gaddafi exerted a charismatic hold on fellow conspirators like Abdessalam Jalloud, his future right-hand man and prime minister. The nine months Gaddafi spent in England in 1966 studying military communications further hardened his hatred of Western imperialists and their secular and materialist cultures.[7]

Gaddafi's anti-colonialism also had a more personal origin. The Italian occupation of Libya (1911–1943) and the Fascist genocide of Gaddafi's Bedouin people fostered his sense of being victimized by colonial crimes. Significantly, Gaddafi's first major speech as a leader was delivered on the thirty-eighth anniversary of the Italians' 1931 execution of the spiritual teacher and guerrilla warfare master Omar al-Mukhtar. The events of the Mussolini era are key to understanding the politics of revenge that galvanized Gaddafi throughout his life.

Although Italy had occupied Libya since the Italo-Turkish War

Muammar Gaddafi, 1973.
MICHEL ARTAULT / GAMMA / GAMMA-RAPHO / GETTY IMAGES

(1911–1912), the military had been unable to expand into the interior. The 1918 declaration of the Tripolitanian Republic led the liberal government to change its tactics. General Rodolfo Graziani, nicknamed the Butcher, air-dropped letters and bombs on the house of resistance leader Mohamed Fekini to get him to submit to Italian rule. Denouncing this "correspondence by bomber" as "uncivilized," Fekini responded, "I have absolutely no fear of your airplanes and I take full responsibility for my actions. None of us will live forever." Only the addition of chemical weapons to the Italian arsenal once Fascism came to power quelled the Tripolitanian resistance. Fekini relocated to Fezzan and in 1930 went into exile, crossing the desert to safety as airplanes strafed him on Graziani's orders.[8]

In the eastern region of Cyrenaica, an assault of more than 10,000 soldiers and dozens of gas-equipped bomber planes failed against the guerrilla tactics of the Bedouin foot soldiers of the Senussi, the regional religious order and governing clan. To break the resistance, in 1930–1931

Graziani deported over 100,000 Bedouin and seminomads to concentration camps in the desert, where about 40,000 died of execution, starvation, and disease. The Italians captured resistance leader al-Mukhtar, photographing him in chains before hanging him in front of 20,000 Bedouin. Poems and songs honoring al-Mukhtar as a martyr circulated among Libyan families, including Gaddafi's.[9]

Thirty years of Italian occupation, which ended when Italy lost Libya in World War II, left Libyans with a 40 percent infant mortality rate and a 90 percent illiteracy rate. One-third of the population perished—Gaddafi's grandfather, an early resister, among them—and another 14,000 Libyans were driven into exile.[10] This devastation presented many challenges for the British- and American-backed King Idris, who took power in 1951. Presiding over a limited-rights monarchy, King Idris had little interest in guiding Libya to democracy. In 1963–1964, Paris-educated Mohieddin Fekini, Mohamed Fekini's son, served as prime minister and undertook reforms, including giving women the right to

Omar al-Mukhtar before his execution by Italian military, 1931.
HISTORICAL VIEWS / AGE FOTOSTOCK

vote. But resentment was reaching a boiling point. Libya had become the world's fourth largest oil producer by the late 1960s, but oil profits remained in the hands of King Idris's Libyan and foreign allies.[11]

When the king and queen departed for a trip around the Aegean that summer, their 400 suitcases implying a lengthy stay abroad, the time seemed right for action. British intelligence anticipated a coup by Abdul Aziz el Shalhi, a colonel from a powerful family who would unseat the king while ensuring elite continuity. El Shalhi's group began coup preparations the night of August 31, only to discover the next morning that they had been preempted by Gaddafi. The new leader sentenced King Idris to death in absentia and arrested anyone seen as close to the monarchy, el Shalhi and most army officers included. The young officer Jaballa Matar was in London when the coup happened. He flew home, enthusiastic about the prospect of change, and was escorted directly from the airport to prison for a five-month "reeducation."[12]

Gaddafi's personalist style of rule manifested quickly. Appointing himself commander in chief of the Libyan Armed Forces and head of the Revolutionary Command Council (RCC), he forced his associates to remain anonymous so that he alone was the face of the new government. Foreign diplomats and press obtained the names of some cabinet officials, but RCC members' names and photographs were not officially made public in Libya until four months after the coup. Acquiring such power made Gaddafi more volatile, and two RCC members resigned within a few years, tired of his his temper and being kept in the dark about major policy changes. Three more plotted a coup against him, previewing the turmoil of future decades.[13]

Abundant high quality oil, Arab unity, freedom through Socialism, and anti-imperialism were the pillars of the new government. The last element included anti-Zionism, although Gaddafi didn't follow Nasser in hiring former Nazi propagandists for their expertise in anti-Semitic messaging. The Libyan ruler wanted fewer Europeans in his country, and he would soon expel the Italian community, making an exception only for foreign oil technicians. Oil plays a starring role in many authoritarian bargains, and possession of it kept Gaddafi in power by funding the nota-ble benefits he gave his people: free education, cheap housing, and more.[14]

Yet oil money couldn't buy everything. Coming to power via military coup meant Gaddafi had no mass party or movement behind him. Four months after the coup, he created popular congresses to decide who sat in the General People's Congress, Libya's legislative body. He then added the Arab Socialist Union as a grassroots political organization. The RCC held all of the actual power, though, and Gaddafi claimed that Libyans wanted it that way. "They want the RCC to lead them," he told the activ-ist and scholar Ruth First in 1971. Fear of state repression soon replaced the initial revolutionary jubilation: as of 1972, all political activity outside the aegis of the Arab Socialist Union was punishable by death. Many Libyans sought refuge in traditional tribal loyalties, avoiding national politics altogether. "In a Bedouin society, with its lack of government, who can prevent a father from punishing one of his children? It is true that they love him but they fear him at the same time," Gaddafi wrote in his story "Escape to Hell," its title summing up how millions of Libyans experienced the outcome of his anti-imperial revolution.[15]

—

"UNCONDITIONAL SURRENDER! No negotiation! Unconditional sur-render!" Pinochet screamed into the phone to Vice Admiral Patricio Carvajal the morning of September 11, 1973. Socialist president Salva-dor Allende was barricaded in the La Moneda Presidential Palace, and resistance to their coup had been fierce in Santiago. Some on the left had prepared for such an event with paramilitary training, but the Chilean Army soon had the upper hand. "How do you face a tank with a hand gun?" said Ana Maria, a Communist Party operative, who tried it. "You kill a few, but there are thousands behind them. They multiply. What can you do?"[16]

Until that day, Chileans thought they had escaped the fates of their Latin American neighbors who lost their freedom through military coups.

Takeovers in Guatemala and Paraguay in 1954 put military juntas in office, with Brazil and Bolivia turning authoritarian in 1964, followed by Argentina in 1966. As in coups inspired by decolonization, one overthrow influenced another. All of them were justified by Cold War national security doctrines espoused by anti-Communist democracies like the United States. In the interest of containing the expansion of Soviet influence, they legitimized regime change in Latin America, along with torture and mass murder of leftists. The Operation Condor consortium of rightwing military juntas, which Pinochet headed, came out of this climate. It shared intelligence about counterinsurgency and repression, drawing on the expertise of former Nazi Protection Squadron (SS) officers Walter Rauff and Klaus Barbie and neo-Fascist terrorists like Delle Chiaie, who found safe harbor in Chile and other Latin American regimes.[17]

Allende, a man of great charisma, counted both Franco and Cuban Marxist leader Fidel Castro among his personal friends. His anti-imperialist economic and social program included nationalizing Chile's copper mines (the country produced 20 percent of the world's supply) and expropriating 50 percent of farmlands and businesses to redistribute wealth. Influenced by anti-imperialist thought, he saw the presence of multinational corporations like ITT in Chile as a strike against national sovereignty and targeted them with a 1971 law against "excess profit."[18]

Such anti-capitalist measures raised a red flag for American officials. They deployed economic and psychological warfare to create the conditions to "give Allende the hook," as Nixon phrased it to his National Security adviser Henry Kissinger, who was promoted to secretary of state weeks after the coup.[19] "Make the economy scream," was CIA director Richard Helms's takeaway from a September 1970 meeting with Kissinger and Nixon. That directive led to a credit freeze and an embargo on international loans to Chile (Franco came through for Allende with $40 million). In 1971, Kissinger, who had fled Nazi Germany as a youth, encouraged Nixon to ramp up the pressure, claiming that Allende, like Hitler, intended to establish a "one-party state." CIA assisted truck driver strikes in 1972 severely disrupted the food supply, causing unrest.[20]

"There is a graveyard smell to Chile, the fumes of democracy in decomposition," Edward Korry, US ambassador to Chile, wrote approvingly soon after Allende's 1970 election.[21] In truth, the Chilean Army's dedication to constitutionalism had initially made the coup recruiting process difficult. "Parameter of action is exceedingly narrow and available options are quite limited," the CIA Santiago station chief complained to his Washington, DC, bosses. Admiral José Toribio Merino, a main author of the coup, worked hard to connect the CIA, the Chilean military, Chilean conservatives, and the far-right group Patria y Libertad. All of these actors, together with other American government agencies and the Brazilian military, created a climate conducive to a coup. Polarization between the Christian Democrat Party and Allende's Popular Unity Party also eroded Chilean democracy. With no legislative majority and an opposition determined to block his programs, Allende made recourse to legal loopholes and executive decrees, bringing calls for his impeachment. In August 1973, the Chamber of Deputies declared his government unconstitutional.[22]

"My aunt has died" was the CIA code phrase for the coup, and auntie had often been near death in the summer of 1973. On June 29, Santiago District Commander Pinochet, serving under Commander in Chief General Carlos Prats, an Allende loyalist, had neutralized a putsch by army officials against Allende's government. In July and August the political and economic climate further deteriorated. Socialist senator María Elena Carrera had "coup bags" prepared for her family in case they had to flee. When a smear campaign in late August forced Prats to resign, Pinochet took his place, becoming the top-ranking figure of the Chilean military. Yet his service to Prats meant that he was told about the coup only three days before it happened. Pinochet soon surprised everyone with his thirst for power and his cruelty.[23]

Allende was shocked that September 11 morning to see Pinochet's name listed in the junta, along with Merino, Air Force head Gustavo Leigh, and *Carabineros* head Cesár Mendoza. The Socialist leader remained in La Moneda when Hawker Hunter jets bombed it, and committed suicide rather than surrender. By late afternoon, the junta had declared martial law, and by evening Allende's body was on an air force flight to his burial place in Viña del Mar, far from the capital. When air force mechanic Mario González, assigned to guard the body on its journey, lifted the cheap pine casket, part of the plastic handle came off in his hand. González took it home, gave it to his wife for safekeeping when he was arrested in one of Pinochet's purges of the military, and later brought it with him into exile. It was his reminder of a democratic Chile that would take seventeen years to restore.[24]

LIKE OTHER STRONGMEN, Pinochet believed he'd been guided by a higher power into the position of being able to save his country. Unlike Mussolini, Hitler, Franco, and Gaddafi, no one who met him before he got into office had found him exceptional. Although he looked good in a uniform, Pinochet came across as average, gaining admission to the Chilean Military Academy only on the third try. His wife, Lucia Hiriart, who grew up around influential men as the daughter of a senator, never expected him to go beyond the rank of colonel. The coup gave him an opportunity to satisfy his secret desire for power.[25]

As tens of thousands of Chileans went into exile (200,000 did so in all), the junta declared a state of emergency, suspending civil rights and carrying out mass arrests of leftists. Prisons and detention camps, like Pisagua in the north, filled to capacity. The Red Cross counted 7,000 people in Santiago's National Stadium, its locker rooms turned into torture spaces. The paramedic Patricio was at Santiago's Barros Luco Hospital when the military took it over, and saw troops steal its blood bank and rape female staff. Later he went to the Concha y Toro vineyard outside the city and found forty workers dead.[26]

The Brazilian worker Jurandir Antonio Xavier was a Cold War coup veteran, having fled his native country for Bolivia, and Bolivia for Chile, where he had hoped to find "a little tranquility, a little repose." While the soldiers beat him, he "simply remained quiet, accepting every outrage." He survived and went into exile for the third time. Outside of Santiago, General Manuel Contreras and other military officials traveled in helicopters to hunt down prominent figures in the Allende government, killing almost one hundred people and sometimes hiding victims' bodies in mine shafts or dumping them into the sea. The "Caravan of Death," as it became known, rehearsed the methods of the junta's Directorate of National Intelligence (DINA) secret police. It was responsible for some of the first "disappeared" in Latin America.[27]

Political polarization and fear of the left prevented Chilean elites and moderates from acting against the junta after Pinochet's coup. Influential figures in the Christian Democratic opposition, like former president Eduardo Frei Montalva, misread Pinochet, just as Italian and German conservatives had with Mussolini and Hitler decades earlier.

Augusto Pinochet,
September 1973.
CHAS GERRETSEN /
NEDERLANDS
FOTOMUSEUM

Frei assured Chileans that the junta would restore order and then "return power to democracy." When he later opposed the regime, Pinochet had him poisoned.[28]

As Gaddafi had in Libya, Pinochet quickly asserted his primacy over his peers. At a press conference on September 18, 1973, he posed in a throne-like chair, his arms folded, with an officer standing guard behind him. Asked by the Dutch photographer Chas Gerretsen to remove his sunglasses, the general refused, saying, "I am Pinochet." He insisted on serving as head of the junta, claiming that control of it would rotate. "I am not an ambitious man; I would not want to seem to be a usurper of power," he declared. By December 1974, he had appointed himself president. By 1976, he had a lock on executive power, and in 1978, he had Gustavo Leigh, the only junta member who stood up to him, removed for insubordination. Rather than the collective governance that marked most anti-Communist juntas, Chile experienced seventeen years of personalist rule. By the time Pinochet left office in 1990, after losing a plebiscite vote, the Cold War had ended.[29]

THREE

NEW AUTHORITARIAN ASCENTS

—

O N JANUARY 26, 1994, Italians watching the news saw something unexpected. Berlusconi, the flamboyant billionaire owner of a business and media empire and the AC Milan soccer team, sat somberly behind a desk, announcing that he was running for prime minister:

> Italy is the country I love. Here are my roots, my hopes, my
> horizons. . . . Here I gained my passion for freedom. . . . I
> decided to enter the field and dedicate myself to the public
> because I don't want to live in an unfree country. . . . I now ask
> you to enter the field too, all of you—now, immediately, before
> it's too late. . . .

The movement he unveiled, Forza Italia, named after a popular soccer chant, had a conservative platform. It was pro–free market, family, order, and efficiency. Although Communism had ended five years earlier, Berlusconi played up the threat of leftist tyranny. He broke precedent, however, by starting his campaign via videotape, rather than at a real-time event where he would face journalists' questions. His bold move let Italians know that he was entering the field to disrupt the rules of play entirely. The political force Berlusconi unveiled took Italy by storm, allowing him to win the election just two months later. The center-right coalition he created brought neo-Fascists into government for the first time in Europe since 1945, opening the door to a new set of threats to democracy.[1]

WITH MILITARY COUPS LESS COMMON by the time Pinochet left office in 1990, elections became the way a new generation of strongmen would come to power. Elections had long been a mark of an open society and their absence a criterion of autocracy, but new authoritarians use elections to keep themselves in office, deploying antidemocratic tactics like fraud or voter suppression to get the results they need. The resources they devote to rigging elections are often well spent. Leaders who come to power by elections rather than coups are more likely to avoid ejection from office and less likely to face punishment. Once a new authoritarian establishes control, he may stay in office as long as some old-school dictators. A 2020 amendment to the Russian constitution allows Putin, who has already been president for a total of sixteen years, to remain head of state until 2036.[2]

Still, new authoritarians who run for office risk that their sins and secrets will be revealed by investigative journalists and anti-corruption watchdogs. Convincing the public of their competency can be challenging if they have ongoing legal issues. Berlusconi faced tax fraud and bribery charges during his election campaign, and Trump started his political career amid a slew of accusations of sexual assault and ongoing legal actions for fraud related to Trump University. That's why such men employ armies of legal, propaganda, and security operatives to spin or suppress harmful information that may emerge. Once in power, they create an inner circle of family and loyalists from their youth and their professional worlds. Many of these individuals have one degree or less of proximity to criminals. So does the strongman, but he has far less chance of prosecution than his associates, who almost always take the fall for him. From Mussolini onward, making sure you have immunity while those who have done your dirty work go to jail has been an essential strongman skill.

Two momentous events made Berlusconi's political career possible. Across Europe, the collapse of Communism in 1989–1991 created the conditions for the rise of a new right and a new authoritarian era. In the East, hypernationalist and tribalist sentiments and ethnic conflicts, long managed by the Soviet system, proliferated. The loss of state-mandated enemies liberated some, who felt "free to hate," in Paul Hockenos's phrase, on their own terms. Immigrants proved convenient new targets from the start. In Western Europe, too, the eclipse of Communist parties weakened the left and created a space for the right to assert itself. The populist Northern League (now the League), which proclaimed the establishment of a Federal Republic of Padania, was founded in northern Italy in 1991.[3] Along with a new wave of extremists came far-right politicians like Austrian Jörg Haider and Italian Gianfranco Fini who wore business suits and were willing to make compromises to get to power. Haider's Freedom Party got over 20 percent of the vote in the 1995 Austrian elections. Fini's neo-Fascist Italian Social Movement (MSI) had spent decades on the margins of Italian politics, but when Fini ran for mayor of Rome in 1993, he received 46.9 percent of the vote.[4]

Some Europeans who sought new models for rightist politics also looked to America. There, a more radical form of conservatism had taken hold during the 1980s, thanks to the support given to anti–big government and pro–White Christian sentiments during Ronald Reagan's presidency. The 1994 "Contract with America," coauthored by Republican politicians Newt Gingrich and Dick Armey, promised trust-based politics and fiscal responsibility. It influenced Fini, who some called "the Italian Gingrich," the French National Front Party's 1995 "Contract for France with the French," and Berlusconi's 2001 "Contract with Italians."[5]

Berlusconi also benefited from the "Clean Hands" scandal of 1992–1993, which exposed bribery and the illegal financing of political parties. It ended the First Republic and the political order that came out of World

War II. Both the dominant Christian Democratic Party and the Socialist Party collapsed. The only major party left standing was the Democratic Party of the Left, the social democratic heirs to the defunct Italian Communist Party, which had been the largest such party in Western Europe. Berlusconi posed as an alternative to a bankrupt political class and as a patriot who put aside his business career to save the country from leftist rule. Italy "needs a strong cure and strong men," he had said a few months earlier, channeling Il Duce.[6]

Berlusconi also feared a more personal removal of liberty, since he was one step ahead of prosecutors' charges when he was elected in 1994. As he later recalled, the years of "Clean Hands" were a time of "terror." His holding company, Fininvest, was dangerously in debt, and one influential figure after another whom he knew ended up in prison. When Berlusconi's brother Paolo, a Fininvest executive, came under investigation, Berlusconi realized he might be next. In December 1993, when news of his candidacy began to circulate, prosecutor Francesco Borrelli issued an ominous statement:

> Those who want to become political candidates should look
> within themselves. If they are clean, then they should go ahead
> serenely. But if they have skeletons in their closets . . . they
> should open their closets now and stand aside from politics,
> before we get there.[7]

For the strongman, politics is always personal. Berlusconi's appeal to Italians one month later to mobilize "now, immediately, before it's too late" could well have had another meaning. Becoming prime minister might save Italians from Communist tyranny, but it would also save Berlusconi by giving him immunity from prosecution.

In business, as in politics, Berlusconi was unafraid to take risks and break with tradition, starting with his activities in the 1970s–1980s in the fields of construction and media. Some of his steadfast partnerships date from these years, like that with Marcello Dell'Utri, who ran his advertising firm Publitalia. Dell'Utri was Berlusconi's link to the powerful Opus Dei Catholic sect and to southern interests that included organized crime (Dell'Utri would be convicted of Mafia association in 2004).[8] Berlusconi's 1980s battle to privatize Italian television shaped his neoliberal concept of freedom as liberation from government controls. Italian television had been limited to three state-owned Rai national networks, but by the 1980s, Berlusconi's Mediaset conglomerate owned the three largest private channels (Canale 5, Rete 4, and Italia 1). When Berlusconi's close friend, Prime Minister Bettino Craxi, used executive decrees to lift the ban on national programming by commercial networks, it smacked of favoritism to many.[9]

Berlusconi's networks changed the content and style of Italian television. His channels were heavy on variety shows featuring barely-clothed women, American shows like *Dallas*, and advertisements. Their news coverage reflected Berlusconi's "unusual relationship with factual truth," as the journalist Alexander Stille puts it, refuting or ignoring any negative press about him. By the late 1980s, Berlusconi had an 85 percent audience share of broadcast media and 95 percent of television ad revenues, as well as ownership of the *Il Giornale* newspaper and the giant Mondadori publishing house. The 1990 Mammi law made future such media concentrations more difficult, but did not affect Berlusconi's situation, and it allowed all networks to broadcast live. When he entered into politics in 1994, no one since Mussolini had possessed such power to shape public opinion.[10]

Berlusconi's election campaign marked the first time a political party was created and launched by a corporation. Forza Italia "clubs" in every town, wired for satellite television so he could appear virtually, provided the base structure. Publitalia employees did screen tests on potential parliamentary candidates and took care of marketing research and messaging. Berlusconi media properties blanketed Italy with billboard and other ads promising a "new Italian miracle," and the ubiquity of Berlusconi's face reminded some Italians of Mussolini's personality cult.[11]

Italy, the birthplace of Fascism, once again became a crucible of

"For a New Italian Miracle." Berlusconi campaign billboard, 1994.
FOTOGRAMMA

rightist political innovation. Berlusconi provided the glue of the winning center-right coalition of Forza Italia, the Northern League party, and National Alliance (AN), which Fini founded out of the old MSI. While campaign promises like creating 1 million jobs captured the news, Berlusconi, like strongmen before him, played on anxieties about living through an era of loss and transition. His strident anti-Communism let Italians take comfort in retaining a familiar enemy. Berlusconi ended up with the kind of eclectic supporter mix that had powered past authoritarians into office: priests, gangsters, housewives (a big Berlusconi fan base), and elites who supported him to protect their own privileges. "If he wins then we all win. If he loses then he loses alone," said Gianni Agnelli, president of the FIAT automotive company, with timeless cynicism.[12]

Berlusconi's wager paid off. Just two months after its creation, Forza Italia became the country's largest political force, winning 21 percent of the popular vote in the March 1994 elections. Although the volatile coalition fell apart after six months, bringing neo-Fascists into the government cleared the way for Fascism's rehabilitation. AN leader Fini had set the tone during the election campaign, declaring Il Duce "the greatest statesman of the twentieth century." Not a few Italians were relieved they could finally express positive feelings for Mussolini. A Roman dry cleaner surprised a longtime client by saying that the dictator "did great things for Italy; he only harmed subversives and Jews."[13]

Berlusconi's May-December 1994 government set a precedent for personalist rule in the new authoritarian age, making the solution of his own financial and legal problems a governmental priority. In July, while Fininvest was under investigation for bribery, he passed a decree to remove bribery and corruption as offenses warranting detention, although public protests forced him to revoke the decree. Berlusconi and his Forza Italia allies also sought to turn public opinion against the judiciary. His allies labeled the prosecutors who charged him with bribery in November 1994 as criminals "who aim to subvert the democratic order" through "an institutional coup d'etat." Mounting judicial woes led the Northern League to withdraw from the government. As magistrates interrogated Berlusconi in December, his center-right experiment ended and with it, many thought, his political career.[14]

Just as Franco was a transition figure between the fascist and military coup eras, so did Berlusconi serve as a bridge to twenty-first century authoritarians who discredit democratic institutions for personal benefit while mainstreaming extremist political forces. His rise to power filled the void created by the end of the Cold War and the postwar Italian political order, and his brief first government laid the foundations for something new. "I know how to create, I know how to lead people, I know how to make people love me," he said in 1996, summing up key strongman talents.[15]

—

NO ONE WOULD HAVE ATTRIBUTED similar qualities to Putin in the years before he came to power. Possessing neither Vladimir Lenin's sparkling intellect nor Stalin's gravitas, Putin was an improbable political idol in a country that, with Fascist Italy, had pioneered authoritarian leader worship. His intelligence training led him to mirror his interlocutor to build trust, rather than impose his own presence, as a charismatic leader was supposed to do. "There's already a cult . . . but there's no personality" was a joke during Putin's first term.[16]

All strongmen construct systems of rule meant to minimize the possibility of an undoing of their personal power, but living through the collapse of Communism, first in East Germany and then in Russia, made Putin's survival instincts particularly sharp. A formative event for Putin occurred in Dresden, where he worked as a Committee for State Security (KGB) case officer from 1985 through 1989. In December 1989, after the fall of the Berlin Wall, a hostile crowd of protesters gathered outside the Stasi secret police headquarters, where Putin and his KGB colleagues also worked, demanding justice for the oppressions they had suffered. Putin was no stranger to unpleasant encounters. He had been involved in many fights as a youth until studying martial arts channeled his aggression. He went outside to speak to the protestors, while colleagues frantically burned the fruits of years of intelligence work. "[N]o one seemed to care enough to protect us," Putin recalled of Moscow's delay in sending backup.[17]

Returning to a disintegrating Soviet Union strengthened Putin's idea that democratization brought weak leadership and social unrest. First came the August 1991 coup of military hardliners against Soviet Union president Mikhail Gorbachev, which was short-circuited by Boris Yeltsin, then president of the Russian Federation. Yeltsin's appeals to support the government, made from the top of a tank as he was flanked by hundreds of deputies and thousands of supporters, led to his becoming the first freely elected president of Russia in December.[18]

Yeltsin's government undertook economic reforms and neoliberal austerity measures that removed the Soviet-era social safety net and brought extreme economic hardship. Millions of Russians, men aged twenty-five to thirty-five in particular, died in the early 1990s from alcohol-related diseases, heart attacks, suicides, and homicides. The behaviors of elites who plundered the economy also expressed the collapse of values. Privatizations brought struggles among oligarchs for control of assets, and KGB officials smuggled vast sums of state gold and money out of Russia to offshore accounts. The combination of staggering wealth created at the top and mass misery soured some on the idea of democratization. "The worst thing about Communism is Post-Communism" was the rueful saying.[19]

Putin's ascent to the presidency came against this backdrop, although his early performance in government was hardly a success. Appointed deputy mayor of Saint Petersburg in 1994, he was censured by the city legislature for collaborating with criminal organizations regarding the regulation of gambling. The Ministry of Internal Affairs would later investigate whether he had siphoned funds from Saint Petersburg's budget to a construction company called Twentieth Trust. The company never paid back the $28 million worth of loans it received from the city, and it regularly transferred funds abroad.[20]

Putin's performance in government may have been sorely lacking in terms of accountability, but it showed his potential to Boris Berezovsky and other powerful figures around Yeltsin who wanted to tame the oligarchs. So, although "he didn't seem like a rising star" to American ambassador to Russia Thomas Pickering or most others, Putin was placed in Yeltsin's inner circle in Moscow in 1996, and in 1998 he became the first civilian head of the Federal Security Service (FSB, heir to the KGB). In August 1999, when Yeltsin faced impeachment by Parliament for his handling of the democratic transition, he and his inner circle chose as prime minister and presidential heir someone they thought would stabilize things and continue Yeltsin's legacy: Putin.[21]

"Who did you say Putin was?" asked Zhenya Molchanova, a Moscow hot dog vendor, when told the news on August 9, 1999, a reaction shared by most Russians. "It's hard to explain madness," the politician Boris Nemtsov commented of Yeltsin's choice. Military hardliners, supportive of an authoritarian rather than a democratic solution to the transition, were scornful. "We always hope for a Pinochet, but Putin is no Pinochet," said one retired officer. "President Draws Criticism from All Political Camps" read the *Moscow Times* headline.[22]

Less than a month later, the bombings that changed everything for Putin began. Between August 31 and September 16, 1999, multiple explosions, four of them detonated in apartment buildings, rocked Moscow and other cities, sending panic-stricken families to sleep in the streets and ultimately killing 300 people and injuring well over 1,000. Putin was still an unfamiliar face when he appeared on television to blame the Chechens. The 1994–1996 war that Russia had waged to prevent Chechen secession had ended with a cease fire, leaving tensions unresolved. Skipping the usual expressions of sympathy for the victims' families, Putin spoke the strongman's language, vowing to "rub out" the assassins: "We will hunt them down. Wherever we find them, we will destroy them."[23]

In the midst of this crisis, Putin appeared as a competent and capable leader, his fit body contrasting with Yeltsin's ill and aged figure. By January 2000, Russia had resumed war with Chechnya, Yeltsin had resigned, and March elections had been scheduled, making Putin, now acting president, a wartime candidate. He suddenly demonstrated an imperious side, refusing to debate his opponents or engage in grassroots campaigning. Given that doubts swirled about the source of the bombings (the bombs contained a hard-to-obtain military explosive, raising the possibility of FSB involvement), taking unscripted questions seemed unwise. An unknown quantity to the public three months earlier, Putin now won the March 2000 elections with almost 53 percent of the vote, the accusations of voter intimidation, ballot box stuffing, and vote switching presaging his later methods.[24]

Now some commentators renewed calls for a "Pinochet formula" for Russia, leaving out memories of the junta's mass violence and avoiding the fact that Pinochet was under house arrest in London for crimes against humanity. Kissinger was careful to cite Portuguese leader António Salazar rather than Pinochet as a model when he predicted that Russia under Putin would become "basically authoritarian." Putin's own ideas were put forth in the December 1999 essay "Russia at the Turn of the Millennium," which was posted on the Kremlin's website and set the tone for his rule. "For Russians, the strong state is not an anomaly to fight against . . . [but] the source and guarantor of order, the initiator and the main driving force of any change." Strongmen don't differentiate between personal and national interests, and for Putin a strong state was also a means of self-protection. Under his leadership, instead of a failing democracy, Russia would become "an authoritarian project in the process of succeeding," in scholar Karen Dawisha's words.[25]

———

"THAT'S SOME WEIRD SHIT," former president George W. Bush said of the inaugural address Trump delivered on January 20, 2017. It cast America as a desolate place of "rusted-out factories scattered like tombstones across the landscape of our nation." Its people were ripped off by foreign nations, its "wealth, strength, and confidence" gone, until Trump, advocate for "America first," entered the scene. Some of the populist language in this speech, which was written by the far-right propagandist and Trump campaign director Steve Bannon, came from the Tea Party. Yet the crisis rhetoric and positioning of the male leader as savior also followed a formula used by every strongman from Mussolini onward. What Bush saw as strange in the context of American democracy was normal in the authoritarian tradition. So was the tactic of leaving your audience uneasy and uncertain of what you will do next. "The time for empty talk is over. Now arrives the hour of action," Trump intoned.[26]

As had authoritarians before him, Trump saw himself as a maverick who could dispense with laws that less powerful individuals had to follow. Until 2015, business was the arena for the expression of this attitude, which he learned from his father. Fred Trump used tax dodges and fraudulent transactions to deprive the US treasury of hundreds of millions of dollars as the family built up a $1 billion real estate empire. Like Berlusconi, Trump applied to politics the lessons of business practices that skirted the line between legality and illegality. By the time he ran for president, his entanglements with the Russian Mafia had been documented for years.[27]

"Criminals got to go somewhere," said one New York City real estate broker of Trump Tower, Trump's residence and Trump Organization headquarters. Drug traffickers like Joseph Wiechselbaum, arms dealers like Adnan Kashoggi, and dictators like Jean-Claude Duvalier of Haiti all lived there. So did the Russian Mafia–connected real estate developer Felix Sater, who was convicted of securities fraud in the 1990s. He took Trump's daughter and eldest son, Ivanka and Donald Jr., on a business-scouting trip to Moscow in 2006 (Ivanka briefly sat in Putin's chair at the Kremlin) and was involved in the 2015 negotiations to build a Trump Tower Moscow. Trump Tower and its residents like Sater featured in investigations into "credible allegations of money-laundering by the Trump Organization," in Congressman Adam Schiff's (D-CA) words. "Dictators? It's OK. Come on in. Whatever's good for America," said Trump in 2019, now able as president to make deals with the devil(s) on a national scale.[28]

Trump had thought about running for president for years, but the stars aligned for the 2016 election cycle, when the uptick in global migration and the affront of eight years of Obama's rule created the right degree of resentment against people of color. "I am your voice," he told Americans who felt economically vulnerable and ill at ease in an increasingly multiracial society, his "protector" persona echoing past rulers who vowed to shoulder the nation's burdens.[29] As in Germany, Italy, and Chile during the final years of democracy, polarization in American politics had also reached a new high, creating a ready market for Trump's divisive rhetoric. A 2012 asssessment of the GOP by the political scientists Norman J. Ornstein and Thomas E. Mann captures key elements of an authoritarian turn that primed Republicans to accept Trump's candidacy:

> The GOP has become an insurgent outlier in American politics.
> It is ideologically extreme; scornful of compromise; unmoved by

conventional understanding of facts, evidence, and science; and dismissive of the legitimacy of its political opposition.[30]

By the time Trump started his campaign in 2015, the Republican party had largely abandoned democratic notions of mutual tolerance, and its commitment to bipartisan governance had waned. A robust right-wing media universe, from talk radio to Fox News and beyond, supported this shift. Before the coup in Chile, conservatives and rightists had labeled Allende as "the devil incarnate." A similar fury, fueled by racism, was directed at Obama, whose legislative agenda was blocked whenever possible by lawmakers misusing filibusters and other tactics. Trump had played a large role in creating hostility to Obama. In 2011 he had tested the waters as an openly racist presidential candidate, spreading a conspiracy theory that claimed that the then-president was born in Kenya and thus ineligible to govern. Now he rode the wave of anti-Obama sentiment.[31]

GOP powerhouses like Senate Majority Leader Mitch McConnell, along with conservative and right-wing elites, saw Trump as a vehicle to accomplish their own goals, which had been blocked during the Obama years. That could mean defending White Christian hegemony or implementing neoliberal reforms of entitlements, like cutting Social Security, with Pinochet's economic policies a model for some. As had strongmen before him, Trump depended on these establishment figures for credibility. Longtime Republican Senator Jeff Sessions (R-AL), an anti-immigration zealot, was among the earliest to pledge his support. "I hate to say it, I'm becoming mainstream," said Trump as he stood with Sessions at a February 2016 event. By then, though, the GOP had become an extremist party in terms of its platforms. It was closer to far-right European parties like Alternative for Germany than to mainstream German Christian Democrats or British Tories. Trump's right-wing populist views were a good fit.[32]

Trump's own campaign and advisory circles included numerous individuals who had promoted or worked for right-wing strongman leaders.

Bannon has made his life's work the advancement of far-right politics around the globe. He sees Mussolini as "one of the most important figures of the twentieth century." As former CEO of the right-wing propaganda outlet Breitbart and former vice-president of the data company Cambridge Analytica, Bannon supported Brexit, Italian League leader Matteo Salvini, Duterte, and many other far-right candidates and causes.[33] Kissinger, a longtime Putin adviser and a protagonist of authoritarian history, also served as an unofficial *consigliere* to the campaign, providing introductions to Chinese premier Xi and other leaders Trump admires.[34]

Like Kissinger, Trump adviser Roger Stone and Trump campaign manager Paul Manafort had a history of supporting strongmen that went back to the age of military coups. As part of the lobbying firm Black, Stone, Manafort, and Kelly, they worked for Mobutu, Barre, and for Philippines president Ferdinand Marcos during a 1985 election campaign that earned Marcos accusations of fraud. Manafort had transitioned to the new authoritarian age by representing Putin in 2006–2009, and he worked for the pro-Russian Ukranian president, Viktor Yanukovych, for a decade before he became Trump's presidential campaign manager. When a federal investigation revealed in August 2016 that Manafort had received over $12 million from a pro-Russia Ukrainian party, he stepped down. He became the first person sentenced during Robert Mueller's special investigation on Russian interference on Trump's behalf during the election, with deputy campaign manager Rick Gates to follow.[35]

Everything is a transaction in Trump's universe, and any partner valid if they help him realize his aims, whether that means increasing his wealth or helping him become president. Unlike the financially independent Berlusconi, who Putin courted at the start, Trump had long sought Putin's money and favor, for example for the building of Trump Tower Moscow. Trump and his family had been open about their status as supplicants. In a 2013 tweet, Trump asked if Putin would attend the Trump-owned Miss Universe pageant in Moscow and become his "best friend." His sons Donald Trump Jr. and Eric Trump stated publicly in 2008 and in 2014 that the Trump Organization had ample Russian funding. This history made Trump receptive to receiving Russian assistance in the political arena as well. His campaign had more than one hundred contacts with Kremlin allies in 2015 and 2016.[36]

Trump's treatment of his Democratic opponent, former secretary of state Hillary Clinton, showed his fidelity to strongman tactics. His calls for her imprisonment and allusions to her being shot were behaviors more readily associated with fascist states or military juntas. By the time a July 2017 poll showed that 47 percent of Republicans believed that Trump had won the popular vote (which Clinton won by 3 million), the era of what his campaign manager Kellyanne Conway called "alternative facts"—falsehoods that support Trump's view of reality—had arrived. So had a new era of American-Russian relations, as marked by the appointment of Secretary of State Rex Tillerson, former CEO of ExxonMobil and a 2013 recipient of Putin's Order of Friendship.[37]

For a century, strongmen have believed that society must be disrupted to allow a new order to take hold. Bannon had long wanted to "give the system a shock" to jump-start a right-wing populist insurgency. Now he had the power to test his theory. He asked White House senior adviser Stephen Miller to draft a list of 200 executive orders to be implemented over the first one hundred days of the Trump administration— a blitzkrieg designed to create disorientation and fear. That ambitious plan remained unfulfilled, but the order to ban individuals from certain predominantly Muslim countries from entering the United States went through. As intended, it threw the country into a state of chaos that stranded travelers, stymied federal employees, and prompted mass protests at ports of entry. It gave the public a visceral introduction to the psychological warfare that authoritarian propagandists had used for years, letting Americans know that this was no ordinary political transition. As Conway tweeted a week after the election, "Get used to it. @POTUS is a man of action and impact. Promises made, promises kept. Shock to the system. And he's just getting started."[38]

PART II

TOOLS OF RULE

FOUR

A GREATER NATION

O NE NIGHT HERR S., a factory owner living in Hitler's Germany, had a terrifying dream. Goebbels had come to visit his workplace, and Herr S. lined up his employees to greet the Nazi propaganda minister—except that he could not raise his arm for the required Nazi salute. For half an hour he struggled, as Goebbels looked on impassively. When at last his arm was in place, Goebbels told him, "I do not want your salute," leaving him humiliated in front of his staff. The dream returned again and again to haunt Herr S., and one version ended with his spine breaking.[1]

The idea of the strongman who brings his nation to greatness is a foundation of authoritarian history. Rituals like the "Heil Hitler" salute are central to the effort of collective transformation. They help the leader to train the bodies and minds of his people. Hitler borrowed the straight-armed gesture from Mussolini and made it mandatory within the NSDAP in 1926, ignoring complaints that he was imitating Il Duce. All German civil servants had to use it after July 1933, and it soon became a social norm and civic duty. The addition of a verbal greeting that named Hitler specifically (*heil* meaning health or salvation as well as to hail) boosted his personality cult. It also turned everyday moments into tests of political fidelity, since the salute required a visible gesture of physical submission to the leader—something Herr S. evidently resisted in his dream.[2]

Substituting for the humanizing handshake, the Hitler salute also aimed at accelerating Nazism's emotional training of Germans. It modeled their bond with the leader and their distance from everyone else—estrangement being a useful emotional state for overlooking your Jewish colleague's persecution or the disappearance of your disabled neighbor. Even within families, the rigid-arm salute could interfere with intimacy. Ingeborg Schäfer recalled that it kept her from holding hands properly with her father, a senior SS official, who saluted colleagues throughout their walks. Policing the salute kept informers busy. The Gestapo questioned a woman who failed to do it when entering a bakery. Students reported teachers who avoided it by entering class with their arms full of books. Jehovah's Witnesses who said "Heil" without the Hitler, refusing the veneration, were slapped on the street by Hitler Youth and put in concentration camps. Vaudeville shows like Traubert Petter's, which featured his chimpanzee, Moritz, giving the salute, did not last long. The Hitler salute made clear who the enemies were, since by 1937 Jews were banned from performing it. Yet, as in Herr S.'s dream, its real aim was to sap everyone's dignity and damage the bonds of civil society—a crucial goal of every authoritarian regime.[3]

—

THE STRONGMAN'S PROJECT OF national greatness is the glue of his government. It justifies his claims of absolute power and his narratives of risking everything to save the nation from domestic crisis and humiliation by foreigners. His national project may be organized around counterrevolutionary crusades against leftist subversives, as with Franco and Pinochet. Or, in the hands of anti-imperialist leaders like Gaddafi and Mobutu, it might revolve around action against the remnants of foreign occupation.

Virility, in the form of the leader's dominance over women and other men, has pride of place in his plans for national transformation. Discrediting other national male icons whose status threatens his reputation is often a priority, as with Pinochet's attempts to erase Allende's legacy or Trump's crusade to undo Obama's. Control over female bodies in the name of population growth is another constant, as are persecutions of LGBTQ+ individuals, who are seen as bearers of deviant and nonproductive sexualities. Perceived demographic emergencies due to the decline of White births and the invasion of the country by non-Whites, which inspired fascist policies, spur new authoritarian measures in Europe, Brazil, and America today.

Strongman national projects generally leverage three time frames and states of mind: utopia, nostalgia, and crisis. Utopia, the desire for a pristine and perfect community, links to the leader's promise to obtain what his people feel the country lacks or has been deprived of. Whether this is modernity and international prestige or the right to expansion, it always involves a glowing future that redeems a bleak present. Mussolini was unusual in starting time over by declaring 1922, his first year in power, as Year One of the Fascist Era. But his promise to "transform Italy so it will be unrecognizable to itself and to foreigners within ten years" was not atypical.[4]

Nostalgia for better times is also part of the equation, since the ruler's vow is to make the country great *again*. This involves the fantasy of returning to an age when male authority was secure and women, people of color, and workers knew their places. These leaders might invoke a lost imperial grandeur: the Spanish and Roman Empires for Franco and Mussolini, Imperial Russia and the Soviet Empire for Putin, and the Ottoman Empire for Erdoğan. Strongmen may also cite law-and-order governments of the national past to justify degrading democracy, as Bolsonaro does with Brazil's military dictatorship. As in Hitler's "Aryan civilization," these imperial fantasies often have a racial dimension. Today, rightists in Italy, Hungary, and Brazil invoke allegiance to "Christendom," harkening back to the Middle Ages, to defend a White European heritage seen as besieged by migrants or indigenous peoples.[5]

A third temporal frame, that of crisis, is the most particular to author-itarian rule. Crisis time justifies states of emergency and the scapegoating of enemies who endanger the country from inside the nation or across the border. It may be invoked by democracies at urgent moments, as in America after the 9/11 terrorist attacks, but is ongoing within authoritar-ian states as a response to political, demographic, or international threats. It also links to a conception of the state as an organic entity with the right to defend itself from threats to its safety and the right to expand into foreign territory to secure the resources it needs. Versions of this mode of thought and strategy, generally known as geopolitics, run through strongman history, influenced by the Nazi jurist Carl Schmitt, theorist of states of exception in governance and war. Pinochet's textbook, *Geo-politica*, was mandatory reading in the German-influenced curriculum of the Chilean Military Academy, and today Aleksandr Dugin's ideas on geopolitics have traction far beyond Russia.[6]

The strongman's ideal nation often exceeds his country's current bor-ders, with its members defined less by their physical location than by bloodline. Following this logic, imperialist maneuvers are couched as restoring "nationals" to the fold, as when Hitler incorporated the Czech Sudetenland into the Reich in 1938 and Putin annexed the Ukrainian territory of Crimea in 2014. Emigrants are valuable resources for this greater nation. Mussolini called emigrants "Italians abroad" and made Little Italies from Brooklyn to Buenos Aires outposts of Fascist allegiance and activism. Erdoğan asks Turks living outside of Turkey to be "ambas-sadors" for the fatherland, especially at election time. Duterte mobilized millions of Filipino expatriates on social media to help him get into office. India's prime minister performs his "Modi magic," aimed at the diaspora, at mass rallies on several continents and everyday on Instagram.[7]

As the strongman pulls the faithful to him, a parallel nation takes shape abroad—those forced to leave the country in order to stay alive. "Guilt is exile's eternal companion," writes Hisham Matar, who as the son of Gaddafi opponent Jaballa Matar became one of millions of exiles who followed their countries' fates from abroad. Even as an exile, criticizing the ruler can have consequences. Turkish basketball star and Erdoğan critic Enes Kanter, who has played for American teams since 2011, became stateless when the Turkish leader revoked his passport in 2017, branding him a terrorist. Nor do exiles always find safety in their new countries, since the possessive strongman relentlessly pursues "his" bodies abroad, using his secret police to gun them down (Mussolini, Gaddafi, Pinochet), kidnap them (Erdoğan), or poison them (Putin).[8]

This nation of unwanted and enemy people can be a place of sadness. Hisham Matar reflects that in exile he had perfected the skill of "how to live away from the people and places I love." Iván Jaksić, who left Chile in 1976 for the United States, longed for

> a certain texture of air, and light, and tones of voice and fragrances of sea, mountains and food, from which you are, perhaps permanently, removed. There is also the longing for the life that could have been . . . the desire to have lived a life without catastrophic breaks, a life in the place it was meant to be.[9]

Exile is also a place of resiliency and healing. The pastor Luis Caro traveled throughout Europe to offer aid to Chilean exiles suffering from the effects of torture and loss of friends and family. Living outside the nation also makes it easier to plan resistance operations, like those based in Paris and Cairo against Mussolini and Gaddafi. Foreign cities with large exile and emigrant populations can become sites of proxy struggles between the leader's allies and enemies. In the fascist era, these places included Los Angeles, where a robust pro-Nazi German community faced off with anti-Nazi exiles.[10]

One final principle anchors the sweeping changes that come with authoritarian rule: the leader's claim that he does not just represent the nation, as do democratic heads of state, but embodies it and bears its sorrows and dreams. Mobutu and Gaddafi both gave themselves the title of Guide to declare themselves as the sole figures that recognized their nation's potential and could lead it to greatness. The leader's rule is sanc-

"With you, we embrace glory." Gaddafi propaganda billboard.
M. PENSCHOW / F1ONLINE / AGEFOTOSTOCK

tioned by a higher power as he carries out the will of the people. A propaganda billboard from the early 2000s in which Gaddafi gazes toward the heavens while his country praises him ("With you, we embrace glory") suggests this double mandate. The divine blessing bestowed upon the ruler's actions is a consistent theme of personality cults. Pinochet's inspiration was the Virgin Mary, although most leaders were linked to the Heavenly Creator. "God wanted Donald Trump to become President," said former White House press secretary Sarah Huckabee Sanders, in this tradition. [11]

—

"IF WE SHRINK, GENTLEMEN, we won't make the Empire, we'll become a colony!" Mussolini told Fascist parliamentarians in 1927, reminding them with a wink to do their demographic duty. Years before Hitler came to power, Il Duce warned of a racial emergency, contrasting fertile peoples of color in Africa and Asia with Europeans who risked extinction. "Cradles are empty and cemeteries are expanding. . . . The entire white race, the Western race, could be submerged by other races of color that multiply with a rhythm unknown to our own," he declared. His landmark 1927 Ascension Day speech placed Italy in the vanguard of White racial rescue, with him as a "clinician" who undertook "necessary hygienic actions" to defend Italians from mafiosi, alcoholics, Slavs, political dissidents, and other degenerates. "We remove these individuals from circulation just like a doctor does with an infected person," he concluded chillingly.[12]

Encouraging the healthy to grow and protecting the nation by confining the unhealthy or helping them to perish: this was the Fascist logic of reclamation (*bonifica*) that would inspire strongman states for a century. Locking up and killing state enemies took them out of the procreative pool, while a "Battle for Babies" and the National Agency for Maternity and Infancy encouraged the right kinds of Italians to multiply. The dictator held a 1933 mass wedding for thousands in Rome, imposed an additional tax on bachelors over twenty-five years old, honored prolific mothers, and banned abortion and contraception.[13]

Strongmen probe the sore spots of the nation, stimulating feelings of humiliation and anxiety and offering their own leadership as a salve. Mussolini promised to restore the glory of ancient Rome while also modernizing Italy, correcting stereotypes about the country's backwardness and lack of martial fervor. His idea of Fascism as a "third way" to modernity, between liberal anarchy and Communist repression, appealed far beyond Italy. Beginning in October 1935, Italy waged an industrial-scale invasion of Ethiopia, a League of Nations member, the intent being to showcase Fascism's remaking of Italy and Italians. In 1896, when Italy was a democracy, the Ethiopians had defeated the Italian military at Adwa, an event viewed as so humiliating that it forced the resignation of then prime minister Francesco Crispi. Mussolini framed the occupation of Ethiopia as payback and a demonstration of the superiority of strongman rule. His May 1936 announcement of victory and the establishment of the Italian East African Empire marked the peak of his popularity.[14]

Expansion abroad and increased repression at home was Mussolini's formula for bringing Italy to greatness. Allied with Hitler beginning in 1936, he propelled Italy from one conflict to another. He sent troops to support Franco in the Spanish Civil War, then occupied Albania in 1939 to extend Italy's control of the Adriatic Sea. Permanent mobilization justified new purification measures. Apartheid-style laws for the Italian colonies, issued between 1937 and 1941, defended "racial prestige." Within Italy, persecution increased against groups seen as obstructing the regeneration of the nation, like homosexuals and ethnic minorities.[15]

Mussolini's 1938 anti-Semitic legislation may be seen within this context. It may have drawn on the Nazi's 1935 Nuremberg Laws, but Il Duce was an anti-Semite of long standing. He had tolerated Italian Jews for pragmatic reasons and some of them, like his lover-promoter Margherita Sarfatti, had been valuable allies. But now Fascist propaganda justified action against this highly assimilated minority (who made up 1 percent of the population) as the removal of diseased elements from the body to defend its overall health, "as with any other surgical operation." Italian Jews were now prohibited from marrying non-Jews or owning businesses with more than one hundred employees, and they were expelled from educational and cultural institutions and civil service jobs. Up to 70 percent of their assets were expropriated. The laws prompted the largest exodus of Italians after the emigrations of anti-Fascists in the 1920s, with almost 6,000 of a total 45,000 Italian Jews leaving the country. Sarfatti emigrated, and so did Enrico Fermi and his Jewish wife Laura Capon Fermi. The physicist picked up the 1938 Nobel Prize on his way to a new life in America, where he worked on the development of nuclear weapons with the Manhattan Project during World War II.[16]

—

In Nazi Germany, the fascist linkage of national greatness and racial purity reached its fulfillment, as did the geopolitical imperative to expand to get the land and resources the country needed. Taking to an extreme the eugenics practices ongoing in America and Europe, the Nazis claimed the right to curtail life "as the welfare of the people and the state demand," in the anthropologist Hans Weinert's formulation. Some Germans fell into a different category: they were allowed to live but not to continue life. The Nazis forcibly sterilized more than 200,000 "enemies of the Volk," from "asocials" like alcoholics and the work-averse, to mentally and physically disabled people not targeted for euthanasia.[17]

Within this large group, the fates of the biracial children produced by the union of German women and soldiers of the foreign powers that occupied the Rhineland from 1918 to 1930 remain less known. The presence of tens of thousands of soldiers from Senegal and other French colonies had long preoccupied Hitler, who claimed in *Mein Kampf* that the French had achieved "such great progress in Negrification that we can actually speak of an African state arising on European soil." When he came to power, he took action against this perceived racial threat. Hundreds of Afro-Germans were taken by the Gestapo from their schools and homes, with coerced permissions from their parents and guardians, tried by a commission of medical professionals for the crime of having a Black parent, and condemned to be sterilized. Marianne Braun, from Frankfurt, was only twelve years old when the Gestapo came for her in 1937; Josef Feck, from Mainz, was seventeen. Hans Hauck's grandmother came with him in the Gestapo car that traveled to a clinic where a vasectomy was performed without anesthesia. On his way out, Hauck had to sign an agreement to avoid sex with White women and a statement that the procedure had been voluntary.[18]

Strongman states turn the ruler's obsessions into policy. Hitler's fixation on the Jewish threat to Germany, which tapped into diffused public feelings of anti-Semitism, made ridding the nation of Jews the focus of Nazi policy. By the end of 1935, the Nuremberg Laws and other legislation had ejected Jews (a category defined by ancestry rather than one's own faith) from the civil service, many professions, and educational institutions and had stripped them of German citizenship. By then, over

60,000 German Jews (out of a community of over 500,000) had left their homeland for destinations as close as Austria and as distant as Palestine and the United States. "I was not prepared for the fact that it would render me not only homeless, but speechless, languageless," wrote the composer Arnold Schoenberg of his relocation to Southern California, where 10,000 to 15,000 others joined him over the 1930s.[19]

"Men and women fell into the arms of the new Reich like ripe fruit from a tree," recalled the historian George Mosse, another exile. The economic incentives granted by Nazism, like tax relief and access to thousands of jobs freed up by those fired or arrested, helped Hitler's popularity. Nazis spread the fiction that they "cared for everyone," recalls Friedrich C. Tubach, who grew up under Hitler's rule, citing collection boxes for the less fortunate among the racially pure. Marginalizing those who threatened the people's purity and survival was also a form of care, since Nazi morality saw the persecution of enemies as a righteous and patriotic act. Melita Maschmann recalls in her memoir that she experienced "intense happiness" immersing herself in the "National Community" through the League of German Girls (Hitler Youth's female wing). Ilse McKee, instead, disliked politics and politicians, but made an exception for Hitler, who she saw as "the savior that Germany needed."[20]

By the late 1930s, Hitler did seem a miraculous leader to many. He had created a greater nation without military conflict. He reclaimed and remilitarized the Rhineland in 1936, obtained the Sudetenland from Czechoslovakia via the 1938 Munich Agreement, and annexed Austria via a plebiscite that followed the 1938 Anschluss occupation. "Austria is free! Tyranny is over/No sacrifice, no tears in vain," rejoiced the Viennese Dr. Erich Oberdorfer in a poem sent to his Führer, who "rose like a star" to make "an unattainable dream" come true. The good doctor could not know that plenty of tears and sacrifice awaited the Reich: Hitler was just getting started.[21]

—

"OUR AIM IS TO NORMALIZE and heal the country," Pinochet told journalists at the junta's first press conference, ten days after the September 11, 1973, coup, adding that he couldn't say when the state of emergency would end. "It's like when you amputate the arm of a sick person, it's hard to predict how long they will take to recover." Pinochet justified his counterrevolution as a moral as well as political necessity. Destroying the left meant that Chile would be "purified of the vices and bad habits that ended up destroying our institutions." Two months later, US Assistant Secretary of State Jack Kubisch noted the "puritanical, crusading spirit—a determination to cleanse and rejuvenate" in Chile.[22]

While the junta's national project had several ideological pillars—neoliberalism, social conservatism, and Pinochet's authority—violence fueled it and made it possible. The junta justified the repression that followed the coup as the state's defense against "foreign agitators." In October 1973, Foreign Affairs Minister Ismael Huerta told the UN General Assembly that in September "more than 13,000 known foreigners, most of them extremists, were known to be in the country illegally," leaving out the fact that the vast majority of those targeted were Chilean.[23]

Far from being self-defense, violence was a means of forcing a "profound change in the mentality of the country," as one government official put it. The junta's *operación limpieza* ("operation cleanup"), which sought to cancel Allende's legacy and remove the signs of leftist culture from the public sphere, showed the junta's messianic spirit. Soldiers and civilian volunteer brigades destroyed statues and painted over murals, including work by Chilean artist Roberto Matta, and fascist-style bonfires blazed with books taken from libraries and the shops and homes of those who had been imprisoned or killed.[24]

Pinochet targeted universities early on for cleansing. New military rectors, who were guarded by armed soldiers, closed many philosophy and social science departments (these subjects were seen as leftist incubators). Faculty "prosecutors" handled denunciations of "extremist" colleagues. By the end of 1975, the regime had expelled 24,000 faculty, staff, and students, with thousands sent to prison. Allende's American translator Marc Cooper, visiting that year with a false passport, found Chilean universities veiled by a "self-imposed and discreet silence," just as the dictatorship intended.[25]

Nationalist pedagogy, American-tinged consumer culture, and far-right politics filled the gaps. Streets and schools were renamed for Chilean patriotic heroes—renaming being a favored way for authoritarian regimes to imprint themselves on the landscape—and television programs on military history proliferated. The Women's Centers Foundation (CEMA), run by Pinochet's wife, Lucia Hiriart, exalted mothers as emblems of "authentic Chileanness." New rituals and holidays celebrated Pinochet's success in saving Chile from Marxism, like the "Oath of Honor to the Fatherland" that thousands took on the coup's anniversary.[26] Extremists like former SS officer Walter Rauff, who had settled in Chile in 1958, connected with Nazi sympathizers within the German Chilean community and with student groups, passing on wisdom about authoritarian propaganda and repression to a new generation of democracy's enemies.[27]

Along with violence, neoliberal economic policies were the best-known part of the Chilean junta's national project. Milton Friedman, of the University of Chicago, visited the dictator in 1975 to present his plan for austerity measures that were implemented by Chicago-trained economists, like Minister of the Economy Sergio de Castro. Chile achieved prosperity in the 1990s after Pinochet left office. But in the late 1970s and early 1980s, this "shock therapy" caused economic crises that exacted huge social costs. Without the repression of labor, made easier by the muzzling of the press, the eventual economic growth that did occur would have been difficult to obtain. Pinochet may have promised to give every worker the ability to own a house, a car, and a television, but those workers could never get back their most precious possessions: the family members imprisoned or disappeared by the regime. That didn't concern wealthier Chileans, who hailed the Generalissimo for having saved the country from Marxism and dismissed criticisms of his human rights abuses as leftist exaggerations. "Pinochet was grand. He brought order and depoliticized the country," said the daughter of a well-off business-man. "I never saw anyone killed."[28]

—

SEVEN THOUSAND MILES AWAY, Gaddafi's path to national greatness was turning out to have a twisted trajectory. Everyone who lived in Libya after the 1969 coup quickly learned what his Revolutionary Command Council colleagues already knew: he was brutal and unpredictable. You could turn on the radio or television and learn that all existing laws had been repealed (1973) or that you had two months to sell everything you owned and leave the country. This last was the fate of the 40,000 Italians who lived in Libya and in July 1970 heard Gaddafi announce, "The time has come [for Libya] to recoup the riches of its sons and their antecedents that were usurped during the despotic Italian government"—a govern-ment that had ended almost thirty years earlier.[29]

"Nations whose nationalism is destroyed are subject to ruin," wrote Gaddafi in the *Green Book* that became his political religion's bible. Gad-dafi's national project revolved around anti-imperialism and the promo-tion of his versions of Socialism and Islam. Most anti-colonial rulers promoted indigenous cultures and histories that former European occu-piers of their countries had sought to erase. Barre imposed a writing sys-tem for the Somali language to replace the use of Italian and English. Mobutu promoted Lingala, Swahili, and Tshiluba over French. His 1970s *authenticité* policies banned Western first names, relabeled cities (Léopoldville, the capital named for King Leopold II of Belgium, became Kinshasa), and changed Congo's name to Zaire. He also forbid Western dress, mandating that men wear the *abacost*. The name of this tunic-like garment, inspired by "Mao suits" in China, condenses the French phrase "down with the suit," or *à bas le costume*.[30]

For Gaddafi, ridding the country of foreign cultural and economic influences was part of correcting imperial injustices. Over time, languages other than Arabic disappeared from shop windows and restaurant menus, and bonfires blazed with books and Western musical instruments, recalling the practices of the right-wing leaders he so despised. A "Libya First" policy awarded all government contracts to Libyans and required that businesses be Libyan headed and 51 percent Libyan owned and staffed. In March and June 1970, the British and American air bases El Adem and Wheelus (the latter was then the largest American air base in the world, employing 6,000 people) closed. "Wheels up, Wheelus," the US embassy in Tripoli cabled when the last American plane took flight.[31]

In July 1970 came Gaddafi's reckoning with Italians who had stayed in Libya after Italian rule ended in 1943. Prominent in commerce, agriculture, and tourism, Italians felt they powered the Libyan economy. For Gaddafi, they were a reminder of the "tyrannical and Fascist" government that had stolen Libya's land and destroyed its people. His announcement that Italians had to leave Libya in sixty days, when the state would freeze bank accounts and expropriate assets, upended the community. Plinio Maggi had moved to Tripoli from Catania as a child in 1938, and a Libyan friend warned his family of the impending order. The Maggis got a good price for their printing business, but had no time to sell their properties. The thousands of homes and vehicles, hundreds of restaurants, and over 91,000 acres of land Italians left behind were purchased by Libyans at subsidized rates on interest-free credit. "The feeling of holy revenge runs through our veins," cried Gaddafi, jubilant at "the end of the hated Fascist Italian colonization."[32]

Gaddafi also expelled the Libyan Jewish community, promising them compensation for their expropriated goods in the form of government bonds—the same arrangement the Fascists had with Italian Jews decades earlier. One group was exempted from expulsion: the 2,000 Italian experts who worked in Libya's oil industry. Gaddafi was not about to jeopardize his profits for ideological purity. Thicker than blood, and far more precious to him than human life, oil was the real fuel of his national project.[33]

Gaddafi claimed that Allah sent him to cleanse Libya of evil. The *ulema* (Muslim religious scholars) applauded his ban of alcohol and his closing of churches and nightclubs—until he nationalized *waqf* religious, educational, and charitable-use properties and declared the Qur'an to be the only source of Sharia law. Religious figures who pushed back, like Sheikh Mohamed abd al-Salam al-Bishti, Imam of Tripoli, were imprisoned or killed. With the excuse of nationalization, Gaddafi also marginalized tribes linked to the foreign-allied monarchy. Ethnic minorities like the Berbers, whose Amazigh languages were banned, came in for discrimination, while state propaganda depicted Gaddafi's Bedouin people as the soul of the nation.[34]

A skilled provocateur, the Libyan leader did not hesitate to play on Western fears of dark and fertile forces endangering White Christian civilization, especially when Muslims came to symbolize the enemy after the 9/11 terrorist attacks in America. "We have 50 million Muslims in Europe. Allah will grant Islam victory in Europe—without swords, guns or conquest—and turn it into a Muslim continent within a few decades," he declared in 2006.[35] The demographic policies of new authoritarians in Europe and America, like those of the fascists, reflect concerns of being "outperformed" demographically by non-Whites and non-Christians. "Europe has become the continent of the empty crib," said Katalin Novák, Hungary's minister for family and youth affairs, in 2019, reprising Mussolini's words.[36]

—

"CATHOLIC FAITH, NATION, PATRIA, FAMILY, ORDER"—with these words, Berlusconi's right-hand man Dell'Utri summed up the core values of Forza Italia and Berlusconi's national project in 2002. In returning to power in 2001 as head of Forza Italia, once again allied with the far-right AN and the Northern League, Berlusconi presented himself as saving the country from the left and the business-crushing state bureaucracy. In *An Italian Story*, the magazine-format autobiography his campaign had mailed to over 21 million families, Berlusconi proclaimed "the defense of freedom" as Forza Italia's "secular credo." He also boasted of his success in "constructing an empire," the phrase evoking what Mussolini had claimed to have done for Italians seventy years before.[37]

This proved a winning message, not just with the conservatives who voted for him in 1994, but also with "the forgotten": previously apolitical voters who distrusted career politicians but bonded with Berlusconi. The "Contract with Italians" the new prime minister signed in 2001 echoed the free-market and fiscal responsibility ethos of conservatives in Reagan's America and Thatcher's Britain. He promised to roll back government regulations and boost the economy with privatizations (including a controversial, never-implemented plan to privatize two of the three Rai state television channels). His emphasis on the bonds of affection between the people and the caring leader was his own innovation. "We want an Italy that knows how to love," Berlusconi claimed.[38]

"I am the most democratic man ever to be Prime Minister of Italy," Berlusconi asserted as he bent the institutions of Italian democracy to his private needs. When he returned to office in 2001, he had ten trials underway, on charges of accounting fraud, bribery, and more. Over two terms in office (2001–2006, 2008–2011) he had dozens of *ad personam* laws passed to protect himself from prosecution. His claim that he was "the Jesus Christ of Italian politics" referred to his role as savior of the nation *and* his martyrdom by the leftist press and judiciary. Senate president Renato Schifani accused magistrates involved in a 2002 Berlusconi trial of instigating "a coup attempt."[39] Berlusconi and his party also beat the drum of Communist threat to stoke fear in voters, playing on nostalgia for Fascism's law and order while whitewashing its violence. "Mussolini never killed anyone, he sent people into confinement to have vacations," Berlusconi told Boris Johnson and Nicholas Farrell in 2003, referring to dank Fascist prisons on islands like Ponza where torture had been practiced.[40]

"Why does xenophobia have to have a negative meaning?" Berlusconi asked in 2002, as he portrayed migrants and non-White populations as threats to Italy's stability. The Bossi-Fini law his government passed that year allowed for automatic deportation of migrants traveling on boats found in international waters, forced migrants who arrived in Italy into detention centers for up to two months, and made asylum contingent on long-term work and housing contracts. Illegal immigrants became Berlusconi's main targets as he moved further to the right in 2008, campaigning to return to office for a third term. Days before the election, he declared the presence of this "army of evil" in Italy to be a "national emergency." That year, when undocumented immigrants made up an estimated 6.7 percent of the population, polls conducted by the government statistics bureau ISTAT found that over 40 percent of Italians saw immigrants as the main perpetrators of crime in Italy.[41]

Berlusconi's government also capitalized on fears of White replacement due to fertile migrants and low Italian birth rates. The center-left shared the sense of a national population emergency. Yet the apocalyptic speech that Forza Italia undersecretary for health Carlo Giovanardi delivered to Parliament in 2008 closely echoed Mussolini's 1920s rhetoric:

> This is a country that is dying from low birth rates, from the
> aging of the population, from a migratory flow so massive that
> it renders integration difficult since there is no longer an Italian
> society into which non-EU immigrants can integrate. . . . If this
> is the trend, in two or three generations Italians will disappear.

Racial fears and practices harking back to Fascist persecution of Bedouin in Libya also resounded in Berlusconi's 2008 "nomad emergency decree." It destroyed camps in Italy inhabited by thousands of Roma people, some of whom were Italian citizens, on the grounds that they threatened "public order and security."[42]

The 2009 Benghazi Treaty between Italy and Libya, fruit of Berlusconi's friendship with Gaddafi, came out of this climate. It allowed migrant boats destined for Italy to be intercepted and returned to Libya without regard for legitimate asylum candidates on board. This did little to curb migrant entries into Italy, since only 10 percent of these occurred by sea, but it guaranteed Italy's supplies of Libyan oil and natural gas. Berlusconi called it his "diplomatic masterpiece," and it scored him points with conservatives and the far right, despite the $5 billion in reparation payments Italy agreed to pay for colonial-era damages over the next twenty years. The Libyan leader wore the photograph of the captured guerrilla fighter al-Mukhtar pinned prominently to his chest when he entered the land of the enemy for the first time. Reminding the world of the evils of Italian occupation and the genocide of his Bedouin people, Gaddafi refreshed the victimhood cult so important to his rule and distracted attention from the dreadful fate of present-day migrants and Libyans in his own detention centers and prisons.[43]

Berlusconi was often called the Mussolini of the twenty-first century. Like Il Duce, he made his image dominant in the public sphere, and he reoriented Italian foreign policy around his personal relationships with the despots he so admired. Taking advantage of his control of national media, Berlusconi remade Italian political culture. He mainstreamed the

Berlusconi greets Gaddafi in Rome, 2009.
STEFANO CAROFEI / AGF EDITORIAL / AGEFOTOSTOCK

far right, merging AN and Forza Italia into a new People of Freedom party, which governed Italy from 2009 to 2011. He detained and demonized migrants, promoted the agendas of autocrats like Putin, and exercised authoritarian and personalist leadership in a nominal open society. This Berlusconi formula would soon be exported to America.

—

"RUSSIA IS NOT A PROJECT—IT IS A DESTINY," Putin told Russian and international elites at the 2013 meeting of the Valdai foreign policy forum. Under his lead, Russia would escape the ruin of "Euro-Atlantic" countries that were

> rejecting their roots, including the Christian values that constitute the basis of Western civilization. They are denying moral principles and all traditional identities: national, cultural, religious and even sexual. . . . I am convinced that this opens a direct path to degradation and primitivism, resulting in a profound demographic and moral crisis.

Putin felt that Russia had been down that path in the 1990s, when experiments with democratization left the country at risk of becoming "not just a second but even a third tier country," as he had worried in 1999, just before he became president.[44]

Instead, the path to Russian greatness required the "defense of traditional values" and a "turn inward to protect the Russian state." Putin's anti-Western sentiment and attacks on liberal democracy increased after his 2012 return to the presidency. He used authoritarian scare tactics in his 2013 annual address to the nation, telling Russians to follow his lead or meet the fate of "retrogression, barbarism, and much blood . . . movements backward and downward, to the chaotic darkness, a return to the primitive condition."[45]

The Russian Orthodox Church has been Putin's faithful partner in his project to reshape Russian culture and society in the nationalist image. It has benefited from his largesse: thousands of old churches have been restored and new ones built. The militant version of Orthodox Christianity favored under Putin supports his view of LGBTQ+ individuals as dangerous to the social body. Homosexuality was decriminalized after the fall of Communism, but Putin made same-sex adoptions illegal in 2014. Many same-sex couples have emigrated due to the hostile climate.[46]

Putin's government justifies pronatalism and state policing of what it calls "nontraditional sexual relations" as correcting the plunge of Russian birth rates after Communism ended. The economic growth of the early 2000s, together with laws restricting abortion rights (2003) and granting eighteen months of partly paid maternity leave (2007), helped births to exceed deaths by the year 2013. The year before, life expectancy surpassed seventy for the first time in Russian history. Yet the state has done nothing to curb the sex trafficking that has caused the disappearance of millions of women, a trend that, as Russia crime expert Louise Shelly argues, "threatens the very survival of the Russian nation."[47]

Greedy for riches and territory and haunted by the collapse of the former Soviet Union, Putin seeks national greatness by expanding beyond current borders. He's used conventional military operations to pursue Eurasian domination, as in Chechnya (war and counterinsurgency operations, 1999–2009) and the Ukrainian territory of Crimea (annexed in 2014). He also acts abroad through political warfare meant to undermine Western democracies. His government has promoted Californian and Catalan secessionist movements and uses disinformation campaigns to aid foreign candidates and causes that benefit Russia (Trump and Brexit are two examples). At home, too, manipulating belief is Putin's key to staying in power. In the strongman tradition, he needs his people to think that there is no alternative to his rule.[48]

—

"SEND HER BACK! SEND HER BACK!" The voices of the majority-White crowd echoed through the basketball stadium of East Carolina University in Greensville, North Carolina, in July 2019. The chants were directed at Representative Ilhan Omar (D-MN), a Muslim and a refugee. Trump stood silently as the chants washed over him, his chin jutting forth belligerently. "He says what we're thinking and what we want to say," a Trump supporter had enthused at a 2018 rally in Montana, echoing a century of enthusiasm for leaders who have the courage to "pronounce clearly what others only whisper," as Margherita Sarfatti said of Mussolini.[49]

Omar, his target, has experience with strongman rule that bridges several periods of authoritarian history. Born in Somalia, she spent her early years under Barre, who established a dictatorship when he took power via a 1969 military coup. To escape the onset of civil war after Barre was forced into exile in 1991, she and her family spent four years in a refugee camp in Kenya before arriving in America in 1995. Coming into office as part of the wave of progressive victories in 2018, Omar, a frequent Trump critic, became an easy target for those who wish to purify the nation by ejecting people of the wrong faith and color.

Racism had long been an axis of Trump's national project and a space where the president's own long-held racist beliefs mingled with those of his heterodox group of backers. These include Confederate flag–waving Southerners who never accepted the end of segregation and GOP politicians who fear immigration will cause "the browning of America." Some of the latter, like former representative Steve King (R-IA), also amplify European far-right views. "We can't restore our civilization with somebody else's babies," King wrote in 2017, retweeting the racist Dutch leader Geert Wilders while wishing for an America "that is just so homogeneous that we look a lot the same."[50]

Muslims, Latinos, African Americans, and other people of color have been the targets of the Trump administration's plan to remake American society in the image of White nationalism. The nation's 2045 census projections see multiracial and Asian populations growing faster than Hispanics (185 percent, 93 percent, and 86 percent, respectively), but Latinos have borne the brunt of the president's wrath. Trump's February 2019 declaration of a "national emergency" over the "invasion of our country with drugs, human traffickers, with all types of criminals and gangs" reprised the language of Pinochet, Berlusconi, Duterte, and others.[51]

The intensity of the Trump administration's efforts to undo decades of advances for women, people of color, and LGBTQ+ communities recalls earlier authoritarian counterrevolutions. Many conservatives may feel nostalgia for an America of unchallenged White male power, but Trump's crusade to nullify Obama's legacy has echoed the fixations of other personalist rulers. The administration has redefined civil rights, traditionally linked to the struggle of African Americans for legal equality, as the protection of Christian "freedoms of religion and expression." An antiabortion rights and anti-LGBTQ+ Catholic activist lawyer, Roger Severino, runs the Office for Civil Rights, created by the Trump administration inside the Department of Health and Human Services. As in the Franco and Pinochet governments, Opus Dei–linked Catholics have occupied positions of influence, like Attorney General William Barr and Larry Kudlow, director of the National Economic Council. So have Evangelical Christians, represented in the administration by Vice President Mike Pence. Stephen Miller, tasked with the crucial job of tailoring immigration policy to defend the nation's Whiteness, has been connected to far-right networks for years. His depiction of Trump as a defender of "the principles of Western civilization" is all too familiar.[52]

Barr has been an important node of this ambitious project to bring sweeping changes to the nation and enhance executive power. Some have compared the attorney general to the Nazi jurist Schmitt, and he has at times sounded like ideologues from the rightist past. In November 2019, he accused the "left" of a "systematic shredding of norms and undermining the rule of law." Months earlier, Barr evoked the permanent war ethos of fascist and military strongmen in telling a police organization that Trump's government was waging an "unrelenting, never-ending fight against criminal predators in our society . . . a final victory is never in sight." In 2020, as coronavirus ravaged America and the election drew closer, Barr sought to push his authoritarian agenda forward. In March, the attorney general requested that Congress grant the Department of Justice the ability to ask judges to detain people indefinitely without trial, using the excuse of a state of emergency. In June, he fired Geoffrey Berman, the US attorney of the Southern District of New York. Berman's office had prosecuted Trump's former personal lawyer, Michael Cohen, as well as others associated with the Trump Organization, and was then investigating the president's current personal lawyer, Rudolph Giuliani. Neutralizing those who might expose the leader's wrongdoing has been a priority of strongman governments from Mussolini onward.[53]

———

IN A WORLD OF STRONGMAN RULERS who regard Muslims as a threat to the purity of the nation, Erdoğan is an exception. Like Gaddafi, Erdoğan declares himself the natural leader of Muslims and threatens to "open the gates" and unleash millions of Muslim refugees into Europe. He has financed mosque construction and Muslim religious education internationally as part of a design to revive the Ottoman Empire—without its distinctive multi-faith character. His military involvements in Syria and Libya have a similar expansionist aim. New maps of Turkey that appeared during the post-2016 coup attempt crackdown also assert territorial claims in Greece and Iraq.[54]

"[T]his uprising is a gift from God to us," Erdoğan declared a few days after that tumultuous July 2016 night. He used the coup attempt as an opportunity to reset his troubled government and consolidate his power. The 2013 Gezi Park protests, which saw over 7 million Turks contest his erosion of democracy and ruination of public space, hung over him like a shadow. So did a corruption investigation that year that involved several ministers of his cabinet. By 2016 the booming Turkish economy had also slowed, in part due to escalating government corruption. In February the *Economist* cautioned that "Erdoğanomics" might soon be in trouble.[55]

The failed military coup brought focus to the Turkish leader's ambitions to remake the nation. It gave him a pretext to act against his perceived enemies, chief among them the man he blames for the coup, the exiled cleric Muhammed Fethullah Gülen.[56]

The officers who tried to remove Erdoğan from power on the night of July 15–16 accused him of turning Turkey into "a country ruled by autocracy." Lack of a unified anti-Erdoğan sentiment within the military doomed the coup, as did the use of an outdated playbook. The plotters seized television and radio stations and communicated via a WhatsApp group text. They did not shut down the Internet, though, and viral images of troops shooting civilians turned public opinion against them. "Do what it takes to stay alive," one of them had texted at dawn on July 16, realizing that their takeover had failed. "I'm closing the group. Delete the messages if you want." Luckily for historians, not all of them did.[57]

The repression that marked Erdoğan's post–coup attempt state of emergency is well known. A sweeping purge started with the Turkish army and continued with the Kurdish opposition, individuals associated with Gülen's Hizmet movement, and members of the judiciary, the press, and academics. The coup plotters who survived got life in prison. The Turkish leader also replenished state finances in the favored authoritarian manner, seizing over 600 businesses with a collective valuation of over $10 billion during the second half of 2016. By July 2020, over 170,000 people had been dismissed from state positions; over 94,000 had been jailed, many on charges of terrorism; 3,000 schools and universities had closed; and thousands of Turks, including entrepreneurs and journalists, had gone into exile.[58]

Erdoğan's use of the cult of victimhood and rituals around it to consolidate his power has received less attention. As so often with strongmen, direct communications with the people at a fateful moment proved decisive. On the night of the coup, as rumors circulated that Erdoğan was dead or in exile, the president suddenly appeared on CNN Turk. Pursued by the military and not trusting any available landline, he had used the FaceTime application of his iPhone to call the network, demanding to speak to the nation. CNN Turk anchor Hande Firat held her own iPhone and lapel microphone up to the camera. The sight of Firat's French-manicured fingers cradling his small image added to the sense of Erdoğan's vulnerability.

Like all authoritarian leaders, Erdoğan knew how to seize the moment. "We will overcome this," he told Turks on television, using the first person plural to bond Turks to him. "Go to the streets and give them their answer. . . . There is no power higher than the power of the people." His FaceTime call drew viewers into an unfolding saga that transcended party politics. Erdoğan later framed the public's robust response to his appeal for help as a referendum on his popularity. In fact, had most Turks ignored it, he would perhaps not be in power today. A month after the coup, his approval ratings had risen from 50 percent to 70 percent.[59]

The anniversary of the coup has become an occasion to celebrate Erdoğan's survival and his ability to vanquish state enemies. In 2017, Turks who tried to make calls from their mobile phones heard a voice message from the president. Erdoğan was congratulating them on the "July 15 National Day of Democracy and Unity," the new holiday created in honor of the coup's defeat. The real point of the gesture was to remind his people of his control of telecommunications. A new topography of allies and enemies also appeared. The Bosphorus Bridge was renamed the "Martyr's Bridge," in honor of those who lost their lives defending Erdoğan that night. A "traitor's cemetery," pointedly created on the premises of a dog shelter, holds the body of at least one of the coup plotters.[60]

The strongman brand of nationalism is founded on emotions of fear and victimhood. Stoking past and present grievances is as important as optimistic visions of what the nation could become. Accordingly, as the coup attempt recedes in time, the threat it commemorates must increase. In 2019, Erdoğan linked it to the West's attempt to "subject our nation to slavery." By then, he had been reelected with expanded powers: since 2018 he has served as president *and* prime minister. This has made his reshaping of the nation through mass detention and the transfer of power to his family and allies easier. "It is social and political engineering," says Bekir Agirdir, general manager of the Konda polling firm. Erdoğan sees it differently. His dream is a Turkey that revives Ottoman glory by extending "from Vienna to the shores of the Adriatic Sea, from East Turkistan to the Black Sea." To realize this greater nation, domestic repression is a small price to pay.[61]

FIVE

PROPAGANDA

IN 1979, GADDAFI AGREED to sit for an interview with the Italian journalist Oriana Fallaci, who had grown up under Mussolini's rule with an anti-Fascist father. Fallaci was renowned for her bluntness and for making wily and powerful individuals say things they later regretted. Kissinger boasted to her that as Nixon's secretary of state, he had always acted alone, like a "cowboy" who arrives on his horse to save the day. He later recalled his 1972 interview with Fallaci as "the single most disastrous conversation I ever had with any member of the press." Pinochet got cold feet and canceled on her at the last minute.[1]

When interviewing autocrats, Fallaci probed behind their facades of omnipotence. With the volatile Gaddafi, her strategy was to "give him enough rope to hang himself," exposing him as a hypocrite. Few foreign journalists interviewing authoritarians have been as confrontational or as effective:

> Gaddafi: [O]nly the people count in Libya today.
> Fallaci: Really? Then how come everywhere I go I see only your image, your picture? . . .

Gaddafi: What do I have to do with that? The people wanted it this way. What am I supposed to do to stop them? Can I prohibit it?

Fallaci: Oh yes, yes you can. You prohibit so many things, all you do is prohibit . . . As a child I saw the same thing with Mussolini.

Gaddafi: You said the same thing to [Ayatollah] Khomeini.

Fallaci: True. I always make that comparison when I interview someone who reminds me of Mussolini.

By then, Gaddafi had retreated into his victim persona, denying he supported terrorism and telling Fallaci, "[Y]ou have always been the ones who have massacred us," referring to the West in general and the Italians in particular. After a decade in power, Gaddafi was not used to being challenged, and Fallaci hit a sore spot in pointing out the fatuous nature of his claim that "the people rule" when only one person's image was visible in Libya: his.[2]

"IN PROPAGANDA AS IN LOVE, anything is permissible which is successful," said Nazi minister Goebbels, who oversaw, with Hitler, one of the most comprehensive campaigns of mass persuasion in history.[3] For one hundred years, authoritarian leaders have invested in propaganda to instill loyalty and fear, motivating people to carry out their agendas of nationalization, persecution, and thievery. Few strongmen had a Goebbels equivalent, but all of them shared the German's "ends justify the means" mentality. Many of them also came to politics with experience in the arts of mass communication and dissimulation. Mussolini and Mobutu were professional journalists and, like Hitler and Gaddafi, knew how to use their voices and bodies for maximum impact. Berlusconi and Trump had experience with marketing and television. Putin grew up with Soviet propaganda and honed his skills at deception doing intelligence work. Pinochet and Franco's military backgrounds schooled them in the optics of power and pageantry.

Early modern French and English monarchs encouraged the idea that they had special powers, or a "healing touch." Personality cults like Gaddafi's are different. They depend on modern technologies of mass communication and surveillance, so the leader can seem omnipresent as well as possessed of magical properties. Developed at the same time as the Hollywood star system, personality cults share an important quality of celebrity: the object of desire must seem accessible, but also be remote and untouchable. Central to the strongman's propaganda strategies, such cults also enable his other tools. They leverage his cult of virility by depicting him as the nation's protector. They also justify the use of force against "enemies of the state"—that is, anyone who dares to question his miracle-working powers.[4]

At its core, propaganda is a set of communication strategies designed to sow confusion and uncertainty, discourage critical thinking, and persuade people that reality is what the leader says it is. Time and again, strongmen have succeeded in this endeavor, using propaganda strategies that have often stayed the same even as information media have changed. From Mussolini's use of newsreels to Trump's use of Twitter, authoritarians have had direct communications channels with the public, allowing them to pose as authentic interpreters of the popular will. Rallies have long been a favored means of contact, but rulers also use radio, newsreels, television, and social media to help them maintain their charismatic authority. From the Nazi assemblies at Nuremberg, with Hitler's name spelled out in Klieg lights, the strongman has turned politics into an aesthetic experience, with him as the star. The communication codes and celebrity cultures of film, television, and now digital storytelling shape the leader's self-presentation and the images he releases of both followers and enemies. So do advertising and marketing strategies. For a century, strongman states have sought to rebrand their countries as modern and efficient to attract tourists and foreign capital.[5]

Propaganda is also a system of attention management that works through repetition. The state disseminates the same message through multiple channels and institutions to synchronize society around the leader's person and his ideological priorities. It mobilizes sound, visual, and print media, architecture, ritual, and more to drip-feed slogans and ways of thinking, leading individuals "in the same direction, but *differently*," as the sociologist Jacques Ellul wrote in 1965.[6]

Modi has invested considerable resources in marketing himself and telling his story through digital technology and social media, Instagram in particular. Whereas Berlusconi used satellite television to appear simultaneously at rallies throughout Italy in the 1990s, Modi uses holograms. His NaMo App, available in English and a dozen Indian languages, features "exclusive content," including a page for donations to his Bharatiya Janata party.[7] Whatever the medium, a paradoxical truth holds: the more skilled the leader is at this mediatized politics, the more his admirers see him as authentic and feel a personal connection with him.

Strongman states have always learned from and imitated one another, and the public nature of propaganda has facilitated cross-pollination. Fascist regimes developed through mutual influences. Goebbels visited Italy in May 1933 to study Mussolini's propaganda apparatus while he planned the Reich Chambers of Culture. Gaetano Polverelli, head of Mussolini's press office, warned Il Duce that the Nazis might be infringing on his Fascist brand. But the 1933 Nazi Ministry of Popular Enlightenment Goebbels headed then inspired the 1937 Italian Fascist Ministry of Popular Culture, which in turn influenced Franco's press policies and cultural bureaucracy.[8] Fascist and Communist propaganda also developed in tandem. Italians paid close attention to the personality cults of Lenin and Stalin, and students at Italy's national film school studied Soviet montage theory and viewed uncensored films by directors Dziga Vertov and Sergei Eisenstein.[9]

Radio has been a propaganda powerhouse for autocrats from Mussolini onward. More affordable for consumers than television, the cinema, and the Internet, radio is also accessible to the illiterate, and can be listened to while one is working or performing other tasks. Television then replaced it as the authoritarian's ideal medium for connecting with the people as it spread his ideas through children's shows, documentaries, and news. What Pamela Constable and Arturo Valenzuela observe about television's function in Pinochet's Chile—"It kept people home [and] created a direct link between the individual and the state"—has been true of all autocracies. Today's laptops and smartphones have helped digital content to surpass television and radio in most developed areas as a portable propaganda feed.[10]

As leaders stabilize their rule, they use propaganda to legitimate their authority. Discrediting the press is a kind of insurance policy. When journalists turn up evidence of the government's violence or corruption, the public will already be accustomed to seeing them as partisan. Even those who demonstrate their loyalty can never be certain of their standing with the leader. Any critique, no matter how veiled, can lead to arrest, meetings with security forces or censors, or public denunciations by the leader and his allies on television, radio, or Twitter. This encourages self-censorship, which makes the construction of an alternate reality easier.

Authoritarian states invest heavily in the manipulation, falsification, and concealment of information. The anti-Fascist exile Gaetano Salvemini's 1931 warning that Italian Fascist statistics were "systematically tampered with for the glorification of the dictatorship" rings true a century later.[11] The blatant lie can sometimes be effective, as the Nazis knew, but some of the most successful propaganda builds its falsehoods around a grain of truth. The perennial strongman message that foreigners are breaching the border to engage in criminal acts is one example. A fabric of lies is woven around the fact that large numbers of foreigners *do indeed* cross the border, omitting vital information such as when they arrived and with what motives. Information manipulation on this subject often includes attempts to link immigration to elevated crime rates and terrorism. In 2019, when Trump's Department of Justice was forced to admit that its data on the subject were false, it refused to change the official record—that paper trail of lies was needed to justify future repressive actions.[12]

Propaganda aimed abroad, often generated in partnership with public relations firms, plays an important role in legitimating strongmen. Leaders use "soft power" strategies to lure foreigners to the country for vacations, film productions, and international sports competitions, clearing the streets of vagrants and confining dissidents for the occasion. Mobutu's 1974 "Rumble in the Jungle" world championship heavyweight fight between Muhammad Ali and George Foreman, held in Kinshasa, earned the dictator lots of publicity. Such events can also backfire, as when African American runner Jesse Owens's 1936 Berlin Olympics win contradicted Hitler's claims of Aryan superiority. Yet turning foreigners and journalists into brand ambassadors counters the bad press from political exiles and brings the strongman prestige and access to foreign loans. Individuals who vacationed in Franco's Spain during the 1960s, their guidebooks listing the leader's Valley of the Fallen memorial but not the mass graves of his victims, fell into this trap.

Propaganda may seem to be all about noise, but silence and absence are equally important to its operation. Strongmen disappear people, and they also disappear knowledge that conflicts with their ideologies and goals. Pinochet closed down philosophy departments, and Orbán banned gender studies. All twenty-first-century authoritarians suppress climate change science, lest that discourage the plunder of national resources that generates profits for them and their allies.[13] The film director Federico Fellini, who started his career during Fascism, called censorship "a system of violence" against "subjects it wants to bury and prevent them, indefinitely, from becoming reality." In strongman states, where speaking out can bring professional ruin or physical harm to you and your family, self-censorship can be a survival strategy.[14]

The history of propaganda is also a history of its failure. The same mechanisms that make propaganda effective can lessen its impact. Repetition can cause people to tune messages out. Chilean graphic artist Guillo (pen name of Guillermo Bastías), who lived through the Pinochet regime, captured the echo chamber quality of propaganda operations. Years of indoctrination to one truth can also lead to the cynical conclusion that there is

Pinochet's propaganda machine.
GUILLO / COURTESY OF GUILLO

no truth and nothing means anything. Moreover, strongman states provide opportunities for their populations to gain knowledge of alternate political systems. Gaddafi paid for thousands of young Libyans to attend college in the United States and other democracies. While abroad, some of them connected with exiled dissidents and returned home as resisters. Revenue-hungry regimes have often imported American entertainment that can deliver alternative messages, even in censored form. In 1938, American productions made up over 73 percent of box office receipts for films in Fascist Italy, and American shows composed between 64 and 80 percent of television offerings in Pinochet's Chile.[15]

EVERY AGE HAS ITS NEW MEDIA, and Mussolini's deployment of nonfiction film and Hitler's use of radio mark the interwar era. Only about 30 percent of the population could read Italian when the Italian dictatorship started (most people were fluent in dialects), making visual propaganda crucial. The Istituto Luce, the state nonfiction image factory founded in 1924, narrated Fascism's history through newsreels and documentaries. Cinemas were required to show them before feature films; PNF meetings, parishes, and schools screened them; and mobile cinema trucks brought them to remote locations in Italy and the colonies.[16]

The launch of the star system in Hollywood and Europe influenced Mussolini's image and marketing, Film was silent until the very early 1930s, but Mussolini's skill at knowing how to use his body on camera, using exaggerated gestures, made him a *divo*. For the journalist Seldes, Mussolini resembled an actor who "is magnetic and dynamic . . . erupts like his own Vesuvius and uses his hands, eyes, shoulders, and breath for the purpose of hypnotizing the mob."[17]

The 1935 Istituto Luce newsreel "Il Duce Tries His Hand at Threshing Grain" made Mussolini's sturdy masculinity central to his personality cult. In it, Mussolini threshes wheat bare-chested, wearing futuristic pilot's goggles for a modern touch. This was not the first time he had gone shirtless for the cameras. Starting in 1933, he appeared in a bathing suit during his annual vacation at the Adriatic beach resort of Riccione. This was the first time a head of state had engaged in manual labor in a state of undress on camera, though, and Il Duce's performance created such a sensation that he reprised it in 1937 and 1938. Until Putin publicized his pectorals in the twenty-first century, Mussolini remained the lone example of a leader engaging in repeated body display of this nature. The prudish Hitler always remained fully clothed, even when shoveling soil to mark the start of Autobahn construction.[18]

Film also made Mussolini an anti-Communist icon in America. The first foreign leader to speak directly to Americans (in English) in a sound newsreel, he also starred in the 1933 biopic *Mussolini Speaks*, which called him "the answer to America's needs," as though he were running for office

A shirtless Mussolini threshes wheat, 1935.
MARKA / TOURING CLUB ITALIANO / AGEFOTOSTOCK

in the United States. Between 1927 and 1935, Mussolini appeared in over one hundred American newsreels and had his own nationally syndicated newspaper column, courtesy of his admirer William Randolph Hearst. "Outside of Italy he could not crack heads, he had to win minds," the exile Salvemini said of Mussolini, who had a squad of powerful Americans helping him do just that.[19]

Mussolini faced a challenge early on to the success of his personality cult: the presence of the pope, a rival infallible authority, on his home turf. He and Pius XI came to an understanding with the 1929 Lateran Accords, which recognized Catholicism as the state religion and created a sovereign papal state. The pope warned in his 1930 encyclical *Casti connubi* that the state should have no jurisdiction over the family. But the Vatican did not publicly object as the regime framed Fascism as a political religion founded on devotion to a dictator reputed to have special powers. He could make sterile wombs fertile or halt the flow of lava from Mount Etna in Sicily before it could destroy a village. When He appeared in public (the pronoun was now capitalized, as for a deity), people thronged to touch him. Thousands of Italians wrote to him each day, praising his miracles, although most asked for favors or money, and a few wanted to have his baby. Margherita V. of Florence told Mussolini in 1936 about her fantasy of taking Communion with him, in a literal sense, his body having merged in her imagination with Christ's in the holy wafer. Duce, she wrote, if only you could "enter into my tongue, glide down my chest, then have you come to rest on my poor heart!"[20]

By then the declaration of victory over Ethiopia had made Mussolini even more popular in Italy. He had accomplished what no democratic politician had dared to even attempt: taken on richer nations to get Italy the empire it deserved. "Who, but He, can help you?" the *Corriere della sera* asked its readers. "He is everywhere. . . . Have you not felt that he was listening to you?" Although those listening were likely informers, Mussolini did seem to be everywhere. His slogans circulated in books, films, posters, ads, and inscriptions on monuments. His name resounded from radios, in classrooms populated by small Benitos, and in the Sardinian town of Mussolinia. His face peered out from offices, tram stops, women's bathing suits, and Milan's Duomo. He was the humble son of a blacksmith and the Founder of the Empire, a man who was modern, rustic, and classical—a twentieth-century Caesar.[21]

Violence that destroyed the opposition press, together with censorship of the surviving media, made this facade of omnipotence and competency possible. The young liberal publisher and journalist Piero Gobetti was an early victim. "Make Gobetti's life difficult," Mussolini told his prefects, leading to multiple arrests and a savage beating on the street. A weakened Gobetti died in 1926, soon after he went into exile. Family members of journalists who left Italy were often beaten and their property seized by the state. Some nonloyalist publications were forced into financial ruin, a tactic Orbán and others use today. Senator Luigi

Albertini, editor of the *Corriere della sera* since 1900, had praised Mussolini when he was a new prime minister as the man who "had saved Italy from the danger of Socialism." Yet his paper, which had the largest circulation of any daily newspaper in Italy, always remained too independent for Fascist tastes. Once Mussolini became dictator, he forced Albertini's resignation.[22]

Mussolini never stopped being a journalist and served as editor-in-chief of Italy. He spent hours every day reading the newspapers, looking to punish critics and anyone who did not praise him enough, and he dictated front-page layouts, down to what fonts to use. By 1928, when he proclaimed the Italian press "the freest in the whole world," coverage of poverty, train wrecks, suicides, killings of anti-Fascists, bank failures, and corruption were all off-limits. As of 1931, daily directives told journalists what to say and what and whom to ignore. "Don't have headlines with question marks," read a 1939 order: the strongman state must never leave room for doubt. Foreign correspondents were "bribed and intimidated, flattered or censored," wrote the *Chicago Tribune*'s Seldes after he had been expelled from Italy for reporting on the regime's repression and misinformation.[23]

Propaganda needs propagandists, and the regime coopted the poor and talented by putting them on state payrolls. Academics, most of them state employees, could be pressured through bureaucratic measures. First came a 1931 loyalty oath to the king and Fascism, which served as a loose model for a similar Nazi oath. Then came a 1932 requirement to join the PNF to apply for jobs or promotions. Invitations arrived to wear black shirts at ceremonies and amplify the regime's messages. May we count on you, Professor, to speak in Bologna or Buenos Aires about Italian claims to French Tunisia? We thank you in advance for your collaboration! Many learned too late the rule about cooperating with authoritarian regimes: as with the related world of organized crime, the moment you agree to do one thing, the trap is set for you to do another.

—

HITLER HAD SOME ADVANTAGES over Mussolini in his quest to create "one public opinion," as Goebbels called it. Germany had no pope or reigning monarch with independent communications, and it had a high literacy rate and more newspapers in 1933 than Italy, Britain, and France combined. The Nazis took over, purged, or shuttered many of them (5,000 newspapers became 2,000 by 1938), firing and imprisoning thousands of journalists in 1933 alone, including for racial reasons. A law that year made editors and publishers liable for journalists' transgressions so that the media would police its own.[24]

Above all, Hitler had Goebbels, who drew on crowd psychology, advertising techniques such as repetition, and the use of triadic slogans ("One People, One Reich, One Führer"), to make subjects like "the Jewish question" urgent and compelling. Goebbels built Hitler's personality cult, presenting him as the embodiment of Germany's national destiny. Nazi art often depicted him as a superman or a figure touched by divine benediction, but the Führer was approachable enough to those who asked him to be their children's godfather and sent him herbal teas or honey if he sounded hoarse. Curt Rudolph Kempe, a hairdresser from Seiffen, a village near the Czech border, asked permission to make a pilgrimage on foot to Berlin to cut Hitler's hair.[25]

The Nazis used radio to build the Hitler cult, weaken class and regional identities, and acclimate Germans to ideas of persecuting state enemies. Over 6,000 radios were installed in factories, marketplaces, and other sites, ready for "National Moments," when sirens wailed and radio wardens made sure everyone listened to the latest tirades of Hitler and his proxies. Once the state subsidized an affordable "People's Receiver" (the Volkswagen of radios), the audience soared from 4.5 million in 1933 to 16 million in 1942, when over 70 percent of Germans owned one. By then, radio had made Hitler an intimate and regular presence in Germans' lives for almost a decade.[26]

Hitler's voice, so laden with emotion that it stilled thought, was his chief propaganda weapon. Those who heard him speak, like the Italian writer Italo Calvino and the American journalist Janet Flannery,

Hitler rehearses in front of a mirror, 1927.
HEINRICH HOFFMANN /
WORLD HISTORY ARCHIVE /
AGEFOTOSTOCK

remarked on how his speeches built from relative calm to a state of "fanatic-hysterical energy." As he spoke, he became "like a man hypnotized, repeating himself into a frenzy." Like all strongmen, Hitler had worked hard on his charisma. In 1927, Hoffmann photographed him rehearsing the gestures that drew on Weimar-era Expressionist cinema. The hypnotism lessons he took from Erik Jan Hanussen and the voice lessons from the actor Emil Jannings also paid off. Through body and verbal language, Hitler expressed Germans' pain at humiliation, fear of plague-carrying Jews, and desperate hope for a better future. Former NSDAP luminary Otto Strasser warned from exile:

> Hitler responds to the vibrations of the human heart with the sensitivity of a seismograph . . . proclaiming the most secret desires, the least admissible instincts. . . . His words go like an

arrow to their target, he touches every private wound in the raw, liberates the mass unconscious . . . telling it what it most wants to hear.[27]

Rallies were the fascist strongman's favorite form of political theater and Mussolini and Hitler used them as sites of emotional training to create "a violent, lordly, fearless, cruel youth," ready to do what was necessary for the nation. "Women and girls, Jews are your ruin," banners proclaimed at a 1935 Berlin gathering. The crowds seen cheering the Führer performed work no less important to the regime than building roads. Film director Leni Riefenstahl's 1934 documentary *Triumph of the Will* depicted the leader descending from the sky in an airplane to receive his fans, an image Mobutu adapted: Zairian television news opened with his face hovering in the clouds.[28]

Who would the strongman past and present be without those crowds that form the raw material of his propaganda? His secret is that he needs them far more than they need him. Once Goebbels discovered that Hitler was wooden in a studio and required the energy and adulation of crowds to inspire his oratory, his speeches were recorded at rallies and other public occasions. Mussolini seemed to find crowd worship an aphrodisiac: he would ask his mistress Clara Petacci to watch him from the balcony of Piazza Venezia before they had sex. "They seem mad, it is a delirium . . . an inexplicable feeling of joy, of love," Petacci wrote in her diary in October 1937 of one such occasion. By then, years of Fascist rule had given Italians expectations of being transported at such events. "The reason Mussolini's words had a magic effect on the crowds is that both he and the crowds expected them to have just such a magic effect," wrote his biographer Laura Fermi, who saw many performances of Il Duce in her youth.[29]

The images fascist states produced of their rallies show the genuine emotion and affection these leaders elicited. They don't show the carrots and sticks employed to fill those vast spaces: schools and workplaces closing; postcards that requested your presence; delegations bused in from the provinces, lured by a free trip to the capital. Nor do they zoom in on details that might suggest a different reception of the leader. The news-reel of the rally convened in Rome's Piazza Venezia on October 2, 1935, to announce the invasion of Ethiopia gives the idea that those present were jubilant. If the reel is paused, though, some of the young men and women who face the regime's cameras listen silently, their faces sober or neutral. I may be here, but I am not cheering your war, they say. You cannot claim me for your propaganda. These images rebuke the strongman in the middle of his spectacle without saying a word.[30]

The repetition and aggression of fascist propaganda weakened its effects over time. Political education ranked tenth on a list of interests among female members of the Nazi labor organization who were polled in 1937. Italian informers' reports of 1937–1938 lament a "notable damp-ening of Fascist faith" among students raised under Mussolini. Many

Italians listen to Mussolini's announcement of war on Ethiopia, Rome, 1935.
ISTITUTO LUCE

Italians and Germans listened to foreign radio for alternative information. Even so, enough people assisted these regimes in imprisoning and exterminating people to judge fascist propaganda as having been effective.[31]

In the decades following World War II, as the age of military coups began, the personality cults, fabrication of falsehoods, and other elements of fascist propaganda all found new application. A new wave of repressive regimes in the Middle East, Africa, and Latin America, some headed by charismatic personalist rulers, would show the truth of the philosopher Hannah Arendt's 1951 observation:

> The ideal subject of totalitarian rule is not the convinced Nazi or the convinced Communist, but people for whom the distinction between fact and fiction (i.e., the reality of experience) and the distinction between true and false (i.e., the standards of thought) no longer exist.[32]

—

THE POSTWAR STRONGMAN had a new and very powerful weapon in his propaganda arsenal: television. The Nazis had limited television programming starting in the mid-1930s, but not until the 1950s did the global spread of this communications vehicle fully open up new avenues of persuasion and intimidation. The philosopher Theodor Adorno's assertion that television could continue fascist tyranny by fostering "intellectual passivity, and gullibility" was good news to postwar autocrats, who knew that discouraging critical thinking was key to maintaining themselves in power. Each one used television to build his personality cult by making the leader a familiar and constant presence. Franco's face appeared in Spanish television broadcasting's nightly sign-off.[33]

With Mussolini and Hitler dead, it fell to Franco to bring authoritarian strategies into a new communications era. Yet the cautious and culturally conservative Spaniard was the least suited of the three for the task. "The media, the power of radio waves, cinema, and television, have opened the windows of our fortress . . . contaminating the purity of our environment," he intoned in a gloomy 1955 Christmas message.[34] Franco changed his tune when he saw that television revitalized Spanish propaganda. Ministry of Information "tele-clubs" for people in rural areas took off, with 800,000 clubs for communal viewing in existence by 1972. By 1976, the year after Franco's death, over 90 percent of the population viewed television daily. Although television news contained the same false information as government-controlled radio and newspapers, the modernity of the medium made it seem more objective and trustworthy. Some Spaniards had a point of comparison: the population of the French border town Perpignan doubled on weekends when Spaniards arrived to see films and read news censored at home.[35]

In the 1960s, with internal dissent increasing, Franco embarked on a campaign of image rehabilitation. He agreed to some economic liberalization, which his Opus Dei–linked technocrats implemented, and in 1969 he granted Spanish Protestants and Jews freedom of worship. He hired American lobbyists like Charles Patrick Clark and public relations firms like McCann Erickson to remove the stain of his fascist violence. Hollywood producers given good deals to shoot movies in Spain released flattering images of the country in anti-Axis movies like *Patton* even as Franco gave refuge to accused Nazi war criminals. Travel industry luminaries Conrad Hilton and Eugene Fodor sold tourists on the country while putting aside its repression. These rebranding efforts paid off. Foreign investment soared from $40 billion in 1960 to $697 billion in 1970, while Franco's propaganda machine banned mention of continuing poverty and repression.[36]

—

PINOCHET CONTINUED FRANCO's double-faced tradition, torturing and executing his people while drawing on a sophisticated communications operation to sell Chile to foreign capitalists as a stable law-and-order country. The Italian neo-Fascist DINA operative Delle Chiaie had no luck, though, when he advised Pinochet to stop wearing sunglasses to project a softer image abroad. "I do what I want to," responded the general. Pinochet could count on the misinformation turned out by the American-Chilean Council he partly funded. Headed by Marvin Leibman and William F. Buckley, the council's reports downplayed the junta's violence and emphasized its neoliberal economic policies and its stability.[37]

The destruction of press freedom was a top junta priority. The Catholic Church Vicariate of Solidarity's radio and press survived as sources of alternate information, as did the Christian Democrat–linked Radio Cooperativa. But eleven daily newspapers shrunk to four, and 50 percent of Chilean journalists lost their jobs in the months after the coup, with many killed or imprisoned and dozens more prosecuted in the 1980s. In 1975, as the neoliberal economic experiment began, Chilean television ended its state funding and invited in American television and advertising agencies. A flood of American television programming followed. During the 1980s, when 78 percent of Chilean households or more owned a television, light entertainment shows like *The Brady Bunch* and *Hawaii Five-0* had a 60 to 80 percent market share.[38]

Propaganda works through a play of presence and absence. What's there and what's been cut or is hidden are always related. Chilean exiles who returned on visits felt the aura of threat behind the shining new skyscrapers of Santiago's business district, nicknamed "Sanhattan," and the gaps left by the disappeared. There may have been less petty crime under Pinochet, but there was more crime that left you scarred forever and started with DINA agents breaking down your door. When the exiled director Miguel Littín entered Chile in 1985 disguised as a Uruguayan businessman to film an exposé, the spotless streets and "material splendor" merely reminded him of "the blood of tens of thousands killed or disappeared, and ten times that number driven into exile."[39]

—

GADDAFI FACED A SITUATION not unlike Mussolini's when he came to power in 1969: the Libyan population was more than 75 percent illiterate. From a propaganda point of view, this presented an opportunity to fuse education with indoctrination, and Libya's oil revenues funded free education for men and women. Gaddafi's 1975 *Green Book*, like Mao's 1964 *Red Book*, intended to create a political subject suited to his revolutionary aims, but mass illiteracy meant that radio and television dominated in state propaganda.[40]

The Fascists had broadcast Arabic-language radio programming in Libya, with speakers installed in the main squares of large cities. Yet Gaddafi had been influenced by Egyptian leader Nasser's Cairo-based *Voice of the Arabs* radio transmissions of the 1950s and 1960s. The Libyan dictator soon had his own Voice of the Great Homeland channel that presented him as the new guide of pan-Arab identity. Other channels, with 19 hours of programming per day by the 1990s, served Libyans at home. Spanning the television, video, satellite broadcast, and Internet media ages, Gaddafi's forty-two-year dictatorship became more repressive over time. The feared paramilitary Revolutionary Committees, charged with suppressing dissent, also had media oversight after 1980. "The regime wanted to win the battle at any price," said former journalist Abdallah Rached.[41]

Gaddafi's use of television to present violence as mass spectacle drew on colonial and regional example. The Italians had assembled 20,000 people to watch Libyan resistance leader al-Mukhtar's 1931 execution, and Mobutu, likewise, hanged cabinet members in front of 50,000 in 1966. Television magnified these effects, allowing people in Hussein's Iraq to watch trials and executions of accused traitors while in cafés, souks, and homes. In Libya, where broadcasts started in 1968, the 1971 televised trial and death sentence of King Idris in absentia had huge symbolic value. But such shows needed a live body—ideally one already half dead—to instill maximum fear.[42]

University of Tripoli students who protested the regime starred in some of the first televised hangings in Libya on April 7, 1976. The popularity of the broadcast prompted Gaddafi to dedicate that date every year to student executions, and classes were interrupted to force students to watch. Rebroadcast at peak viewing periods like Ramadan, trials and executions exposed alleged anti-Socialist behavior or corruption, retried people previously arrested (a sequel, in television terms), or settled accounts with resisters charged with CIA or Muslim Brotherhood collusion. "And now we will see the confessions of the stray dogs," the announcer would say, as though cutting to the weather report.[43]

The 1984 execution of Sadik Hamed Shwehdi made violence into mass spectacle. The crowd assembled at Benghazi's basketball stadium included schoolchildren on a class trip. They saw a bound and terrified Shwehdi, sitting alone on the floor as he confessed his ties with anti-Gaddafi activists abroad (he had recently returned from studying in America). The crowd cheered as judges read his death sentence. When he struggled on the gallows, a young woman who had been inciting the crowd from the stands ran up and pulled on his legs until he was still. Huda Ben Amer, soon nicknamed Huda the Executioner, became a political star whose jobs included minister of sports and youth. The age of the masses "inflames feelings and dazzles the eyes," the *Green Book* stated. Gaddafi used television to do both, fostering terror and conformity.[44]

Maintaining Gaddafi's personality cult was a propaganda priority. The longer Gaddafi was in power, the more dramatic he became in his dress and behavior. He would suddenly pause during a speech and gaze toward the heavens, as if waiting for divine inspiration. While Libya had no "Gaddafi salute," public invocations of his greatness took on a talismanic value—"may Allah and the Revolutionary Committees acknowledge my good faith." Images of him, some gigantic, saturated Libyan society to give the impression that he was everywhere and saw everything, just like his secret police.[45]

—

By the time Gaddafi's regime fell in 2011, new authoritarian rulers were putting their own mark on the history of propaganda. They mix rallies, censorship, and personality cults with social media to create the news they need to stay in office. Holding elections means that they are more dependent than ever on censorship and the manipulation of information. They still silence and slander critics, but also flood the media space with noise and confusion, drowning out messages that may threaten their power.

Making misogynist and racist comments to shift media attention away from their corruption and incompetence is a common tactic. In 2019, Trump called the late representative Elijah Cummings's (D-MD) majority-Black congressional district "a disgusting, rat and rodent-infested mess" to turn attention away from Cummings's investigation (as chair of the House Oversight Committee) of daughter Ivanka Trump and son-in-law Jared Kushner's use of private email accounts for state business. That same year, when a *Globo* journalist asked Bolsonaro about his son Flávio's possible corruption, the Brazilian president told the reporter that he had a "terribly homosexual face," knowing the comment, and not his family's corruption, would dominate the news. Today's strongmen are well aware that every minute the public and the press spend on the outrage du jour is time they're not mobilizing for political action or investigating abuses of power.[46]

Rather than ban all opposition media, new authoritarians deny licenses to media outlets, bribe, sue, or threaten their owners, call for advertising boycotts to cause financial ruin, and stage hostile takeovers. In a spectacular 2018 mass genuflection, media luminaries in Orbán's Hungary "donated" almost 500 media properties to a government-allied foundation. In parliamentary elections later that year, "opposition views could not even reach significant portions of the electorate," in analyst Gábor Polyak's words, just as the Hungarian prime minister intended.[47] New authoritarians use platforms like Facebook and Twitter to target critics and spread hate speech, conspiracy theories, and lies. What today's strongmen give up in old-style top-down synchronization, they gain in amplification and penetration. This includes messages intended to raise hatred for the press. The Committee to Protect Journalists found "an unprecedented level of hostility towards media personnel" around the world in 2018, with record-breaking numbers of journalists killed, jailed, and held hostage.[48]

—

"IN RUSSIA WE ONLY HAD TWO TV CHANNELS," quipped the comedian Yakov Smirnoff, remembering the days of Soviet rule. "Channel One was propaganda. Channel Two consisted of a KGB officer telling you: turn back at once to Channel One." Putin came to power a decade after the demise of Communism, and his media policy bridges old-school and twenty-first-century methods. Hostile takeovers of oligarch-owned television networks NRT and ORT early in his presidency gained him control of news and political broadcasting. His post-2012 crackdown has made Russian media into a messaging machine for pro-Putin and anti-Western sentiments. Dozens of journalists who reported on corruption and other taboo subjects have been arrested or murdered in Russia and abroad.[49]

Communist-legacy sabotage and manipulation techniques and new-generation political warfare all figure in the Kremlin's propaganda arsenal. As time passes, Putin needs more misinformation to sustain illusions of his competency. Cybersecurity is the official rationale for his planned national Internet, which will have a domestically confined routing and domain name system to control the information flow into "Fortress Russia." As younger Russians have shifted news consumption to online platforms and to the independent channel NTV from state television, the Kremlin has put resources into the RT network (formerly Russia Today), which reaches more than one hundred countries. The most popular global news source on YouTube, RT is viewed by many living in Russia as well. RT's global television audience grew by one-third between

2015 and 2017, although in 2020 it still trailed far behind CNN and the BBC. To expand viewership to the United States, exposing Americans to Kremlin propaganda, RT America has hired Fox News talents like Rick Sanchez and Scottie Neil Hughes. In 2017, DirectTV added RT to its roster of satellite dish network channels.[50]

The expansion of RT is just one facet of the Kremlin's focus on political warfare that favors informational, diplomatic, and economic measures over physical confrontation. It has had success, especially against Putin's main adversary, American democracy. Cyberattacks like disruptions of electrical utility grids and the 2016 infiltration of American Democratic National Committee servers aim to show dominance. Whether directed at Russians or foreigners, Putin's propaganda does not just seek to create alternate truths; it also seeks to create confusion through disinformation and undermine the ability to distinguish truth from fiction. Mussolini's censors banned question marks in press headlines, locking down meaning. Putin's operatives create question marks around everything.[51]

Putin's personality cult, anchored in his display of virility, melds Soviet-style sternness and patriotism with homages to post-Communist capitalist accumulation. His face can be found on myriad consumer items, with a price point for everyone, from special-edition gold Apple Watches, to bedding, T-shirts, and pottery. Like other strongmen, Putin has been "a mirror in which everyone . . . sees what he wants to see and what he hopes for," as pollster Yuri Levada says. Everyone can find "their" Putin in the annual calendars the Kremlin approves for release, whether he's straddling horses and heavy machinery, smelling a flower, or lighting a candle in church.[52]

"I cannot actively stop this," says Putin of the proliferation of his image, with the same falsity as Gaddafi, since he's been quick enough to shut down caricatures of his person. As of April 2017, cartoons or other satires of Putin can be labeled "extremist material." In 2019, a broader measure made those who "disrespect" the state and its symbols, "society," or government authorities on the Internet liable for fifteen days in jail. "Soon we'll be telling jokes about authorities in whispers in the kitchen," wrote a Moscow lawyer on Facebook, describing a situation familiar to those who lived under Communist or other authoritarian regimes.[53]

—

"IF SOMETHING DOESN'T APPEAR ON TELEVISION, it doesn't exist," Berlusconi liked to say, and by that measure he had the fullest existence of anyone in Italy in the early twenty-first century. Berlusconi's media conglomerate, Mediaset, owned commercial television networks that commanded a majority of broadcast audiences in a country where 87 percent of inhabitants got their information from television by 2007. A landmark 2019 study found that heavy viewing of Mediaset's entertainment channels translated into a decline in civic engagement and a preference for simplistic populist rhetoric. This translated into an almost 10 percent bump at the polls for Berlusconi and his party over five elections from 1994 to 2008.[54]

During Berlusconi's governments of the 2000s, he retained control over his television, publishing, and advertising interests by putting family and loyalists in charge. His daughter Marina Berlusconi ran his holding company Fininvest, which had a controlling interest in Mediaset, in the publisher Mondadori, and in the advertising giant Pubitalia. Over time, his control of entertainment television gave him the ability to influence Italian society well beyond the sphere of politics. For example, many new authoritarians make sexist comments and pass pronatalist legislation, but Berlusconi also objectified women day after day for years in ads and shows on his television networks. He also developed new patronage networks that revolved around his control of entertainment programming. Some women who starred on his shows ended up in Parliament. A few were also involved as procurers or participants in Berlusconi's private quests for sexual pleasure—another example of how the tools of virility, propaganda, and corruption work together.[55]

Exploiting a degree of media control unheard of outside of dictatorship, Berlusconi brought the personality cult into the new authoritarian age. The omnipresence of his face in the public sphere encouraged Italians to see him as larger than life. He evoked Il Duce with slogans like "thank goodness we have Silvio" ("thank goodness for Mussolini" was the earlier version), while presenting himself as emblematic of the average man. "Italians see themselves in me, I'm one of them, one who . . . loves life, loves to have fun . . . and loves above all beautiful women, like any Italian worthy of respect," he told a Forza Italia youth group. So saturated was Italy with his image that a woman interviewed in the early 2000s by Italian psychologists studying dementia could no longer recognize her family's faces but knew Berlusconi's—along with those of Jesus Christ and the pope.[56]

Berlusconi also updated the strongman victimhood script for the twenty-first century. Posing as the target of liberal and left-wing press harassment, he had his media empire disgorge streams of stories that aimed to smear and intimidate members of the press and the judiciary. His use of legal harassment to drain the finances of opposition media outlets and encourage them to fire or silence critics earned him the nickname "Al Tappone" (*tappare* meaning to plug or gag) after the American gangster Al Capone. In the early 2000s, he targeted the journalists Enzo Biagi and Michele Santoro and the comedians Daniele Luttazzi and Sabina Guzzanti. Accusing them of making "a criminal use of public television, which is paid for by all," he had them fired from the state broadcaster Rai. That none of these individuals worked for companies under Berlusconi's direct control shows how twenty-first-century strongmen count on corporate conflict aversion to do their work for them. Media companies have strong incentives to sacrifice a few individuals rather than lose access or enter into expensive legal proceedings.[57]

"DON'T BELIEVE THE CRAP YOU SEE from these people, the fake news. . . . Just remember: what you're seeing and what you're reading is not what's happening." So declared Trump to a group of American veterans in 2018, continuing a century of strongman attempts to discredit and deny unflattering realities. Press freedom in America during peacetime has been fairly consistent compared with other countries, despite presidential untruths and cover-ups, from Nixon's Watergate to Bush's claim that Hussein had weapons of mass destruction.[58]

Trump departs from all previous heads of American democracy, though, in devoting so much effort to the destruction of the meaning of truth *in the absolute*. Without the degree of media control enjoyed by Berlusconi or Putin, Trump and his allies have worked hard to influence public opinion. Trump does not lie about one or two things. Rather, facts on any subject that conflict with his goals of power and profit are degraded through rumor and innuendo or simply altered or denied. The number of documented falsehoods he uttered as president increased from 5.9 a day in 2017 to an average of 22 a day in 2019, for a total of 16,241 in his first three years in office. This constitutes a disinformation barrage without precedent in America. As McKay Coppins has written, Americans have been subjected for years now to "the same tactics of information warfare that have kept the world's demagogues and strongmen in power."[59]

Like Berlusconi, Trump broke the mold of political communications in his country. While Berlusconi's team used his existing corporate and mass communications infrastructure to reach voters, Brad Parscale, Trump's digital media director, relied on the e-commerce model. In the lead-up to the 2020 election, the Trump campaign further expanded a gargantuan operation that during the 2016 campaign ran 5.9 million separate Facebook ads (versus the Clinton campaign's 66,000). "He was selling Trump, but he could have been selling sneakers," a rival strategist said of Parscale, summing up how civic and values-based politics are corroded as the perpetuation of the leader's power becomes an end in itself.[60]

As with Berlusconi, governing for the scandal-ridden Trump has been about self-defense. He has claimed that a mainstream press dominated by liberals and the left conspires to silence him, but has tried to shut out journalists he sees as critics, as when he temporarily revoked access to

White House press briefings for CNN's Jim Acosta in 2018. He asked former FBI director James Comey about imprisoning reporters in 2017. "The fake news is creating violence," he told reporters in 2018, preparing public opinion for future repressive measures against the press. By 2019, he was declaring in meetings attended by former national security adviser John Bolton and former defense secretary James Mattis that journalists should not just be jailed if they refused to divulge their sources, but physically eliminated. "These people should be executed. They are scumbags," he said, sounding like strongmen from Mussolini to Putin.[61]

Trump's vilification of the media has partly backfired. American investigative journalism has been revitalized, and "enemy" media like the "failing" *New York Times* and the *Washington Post* report increased digital subscriptions. Yet fringe and right-wing outlets have gained credibility. The 2019 White House Social Media Summit featured not just conservatives from the Heritage Foundation but also individuals tied to Praeger University, the far-right media outlet Breitbart, and the QAnon conspiracy theory. Along with engaging in twenty-first-century disinformation, Trump has kept the flame of past right-wing strongmen burning. He started his campaign by retweeting an anti–African American meme that previously appeared in the neo-Nazi outlet *Daily Stormer*. An image (now-deleted) that he tweeted in July 2016 of his opponent Clinton with a Star of David that read "Most Corrupt Candidate Ever!" had appeared a week earlier on a neo-Nazi Internet message board. Once in power, he brought individuals with deep connections to the far right into the White House, like Bannon and Miller. From 2015 onward, he has regularly retweeted and praised British extremist Katie Hopkins, who called for a "final solution" after the Manchester Arena Bombing in 2017.[62]

Twitter has been for Trump what newsreels were for the fascists: a direct channel to the people that keeps him constantly in the news. Dissected by pundits with the diligence of Communist-era Kremlinologists, Trump's tweets feature simple vocabulary and misspelled words, offering a curated sense of authenticity. Tweets have been his preferred propaganda delivery vehicles for falsehoods, and they have enabled him to distract attention from his corruption and policy failures. Designed for instant impact and encouraging feelings of omnipotence, Twitter is the perfect tool for an impulsive, attention-addicted strongman. "Boom. I press it, and within two seconds, 'We have breaking news'," said Trump of the effect of his tweets, like the March 2019 one that recognized Israel's claim of sovereignty over the Golan Heights and took US officials by surprise.[63]

Trump has differed from strongmen who came before him in one respect: his almost exclusive reliance on television for information about the world. His daily thoughts and moods have been determined by what has just been said on shows he watches. He has fired off tweets full of anger and agitation after viewing networks critical of him, like CNN or MSNBC. In contrast, many of his tweets on policy issues echo ideas aired on Fox News moments earlier. "Welcome to the studio!" Trump once said in welcoming journalists to the White House. With Fox host Sean Hannity recognized by White House aides as "the unofficial chief of staff," Fox has merited an executive producer credit.[64]

SIX

VIRILITY

—

"**D**UCE, I SAW YOU YESTERDAY during your tumultuous visit to our city," wrote Michela C. of Siena in December 1925.

> Our eyes met. I told you of my admiration, devotion, revealed
> my feelings to you. . . . Before your visit I was the unhappi-
> est woman in the world. Stuck in a bad marriage, with a cold
> man. . . . I feared I would never know love in my life. Now
> I know that I love you . . . I understood that I had touched
> your heart from the heated way you looked at me just before
> I fainted.[1]

History does not record whether Michela C. was one of thousands of women who, during two decades of Mussolini's rule, became part of his state-assisted machine of libidinal gratification. Young and less young, rich and poor, they came to his attention at rallies, events, or through letters they wrote to him. We don't know if Michela was among the five to twenty different women per week who received an invitation to meet Il Duce and climbed the stairs to his private quarters in Palazzo Venezia. When they emerged, 15 minutes later—the time it took for the "brief and violent" encounters he favored—they were persons of interest to Mussolini's security apparatus. His fixers and secret police stood ready to force an abortion, pay for silence, or make life difficult for the womens' boyfriends and husbands. One thing was certain: once Mussolini entered your life and your vagina, you were never free of him again.[2]

THE STRONGMAN WOULD BE NOTHING without bodies to control. He needs crowds to acclaim his projects of national greatness on camera, taxpayers to fund his follies and his private bank accounts, soldiers to fight his wars, and mothers to birth all of the above. The systems Mussolini and other leaders created to procure bodies for their sexual satisfaction may be seen in this context. Far from being a private affair, the sex life of the strongman reveals how corruption, propaganda, violence, and virility work together and how personalist rulers use state resources to fulfill their desires. Gaddafi was unusual in establishing a bureaucracy dedicated to this project, but whenever the ruler has a sex addiction, as he and Mussolini did, it subtracts time and energy from governance—up to several hours a day in their cases.

Many strongmen boast of their virile powers. Bare-chested photographs advertise the fitness and potency of Mussolini and Putin. Gaddafi, Berlusconi, and Trump vaunt control of desirable women, the former by surrounding himself with attractive female bodyguards and nurses, the latter two with former models and beauty pageant queens. Some broadcast their sexual stamina. "I can love four women at the same time," says Duterte; "If I sleep for three hours, I have the energy to make love for three hours after that," claims Berlusconi. "As a masculine egotist he sees women solely as beauties made for pleasure," reflected Mussolini's much-betrayed mistress Margherita Sarfatti at the end of her biography *Dux*. Most of the leaders featured in this book would fit that description and be proud of it.[3]

Presented by their personality cults as the ideal blend of everyman and superman, authoritarians make ordinary men feel better about their own transgressions. These were probably not as lavishly bad as what the leader was engaging in: hosting sex parties with underage women in attendance (Berlusconi), being spanked by porn stars (Trump), or keeping the twin sister of your wife as your mistress (Mobutu). The appeal of these leaders for many rests on their having the power to get away with things that ordinary men cannot, whether in the bedroom or in politics.[4]

Gaining favor after periods of economic and political gain for women, the strongman seeks to reverse shifts in social norms that threaten patriarchy and the satisfaction of "natural" male desires. Nazi ideologue Alfred Rosenberg's 1930 call for "the emancipation of women from the women's emancipation movement" was typical. So was Berlusconi's 2009 warning to Italian women that the state could not protect them from sexual assault, hinting that their own attractiveness made them fair game: "We can't deploy a big military force to avoid rapes. We'd have to have as many soldiers in the street as there are beautiful Italian women."[5] For a century, women have been the strongman's adversaries, along with prosecutors, journalists, and the political opposition. His machismo is not just empty posturing, but a strategy of political legitimation and an important component of authoritarian rule.

Putin is a case in point. His body display is an integral part of his identity as defender of Russia's pride and its right to expand in the world. The Kremlin releases images of him in macho poses, like the ones taken of him fishing during a 2007 vacation in southern Siberia. The government also deploys images of him as a hypermasculine thug to send a message when his power is threatened, as when he posed with bikers in a black leather jacket in August 2019 as tens of thousands of Russians protested him in the streets.[6]

Strongman rulers also display their virility to and for each other. Public events, like meetings and summits, where millions will be watching, are ideal occasions. Machismo figures heavily in their mediatized brand of politics. Hitler, preparing for his first in-person meeting with Mussolini in 1934, stoked the fires by telling an American journalist that he preferred "man to man diplomacy." Putin's virile friendship with Berlusconi was genuine, but the Russian is trained in the science of attraction

Putin fishing in the Khemchik River, 2007.
SOVFOTO / UIG / AGEFOTOSTOCK

and knows how to simulate male fellowship, as when he walked hand in hand with Modi for the cameras in Saint Petersburg in June 2017. Trump bonded with Orbán as they sat together at the White House in 2019, their craggy faces and heavy bodies projecting a kindred brutalist power. "It's like we're twins," Trump exclaimed.[7]

The leader sets the tone as his government propagates models of masculinity that suit his demographic and ideological goals. In most states, these compete with visions of gender roles advanced by advertising or American or other foreign cinema and television. Yet those who have grown up in authoritarian regimes testify that the leader's model of masculinity can easily be internalized. The Italian writer Italo Calvino, who came of age under the dictator's rule, recalled how his generation began to "carry around the portrait of Mussolini inside themselves even before they knew enough to identify it on the wall."[8]

Mobutu shows how the leader's misogynist predilections can translate into social practices that facilitate the exploitation and impoverishment of women. His 1987 Family Code contained provisions protecting women—for example, giving them the right to inherit their husband's property. In practice, men were able to claim their wife's property, even if they had abandoned their families. "We lost our dignity. We lost our status in society," said Mafiki Yav Marie, whose husband left her with ten children and tried to seize the home she had purchased.[9]

Mobutu himself fathered about twenty children and an unknown number of unrecognized offspring, including, perhaps, some with the wives of his officials. "He uses sex as a tool to dominate the men around him," said a former minister in his government. "You get money or a Mercedes-Benz, and he takes your wife, and you work for him." In the strongman world, this is a bargain struck like any other. It can be dangerous to be related to a woman claimed by the dictator. Hussein jailed the husband of Parisoula Lampsos, his lover for decades, and one of his sons reportedly raped her daughter. Many men who support these leaders' agendas of female subordination realize, too late, that the ultimate aim is to humiliate them as well.[10]

Just as the strongman finds ways to generate cash from national resources for his personal gain, so does he ensure that he has a pipeline of bodies for sex. Traditional means of encounter satisfied Pinochet. He spent time with female journalists "who came to interview him, but never published anything," as one of his former ministers recalled, and maintained a relationship with the Ecuadorean pianist Piedad Noé for decades. This caused his wife, Lucia Hiriart, to launch a morals crusade with her friend, DINA secret police chief Manuel Contreras, to punish any *other* military officer who had affairs. Only the Generalissimo and Contreras, with his own fifteen-year affair, were untouchable.[11] The ego and libidinal needs of Mussolini and Gaddafi required larger operations that involved secret police and other state employees. Berlusconi used his business network of beauty pageants and television shows to have a supply of women who could be leveraged for gratification and paid off or threatened when necessary, as did Trump before he took office.

IF STRONGMEN ARE such misogynist monsters, why do some women love them? Some appreciate the social welfare benefits they offer and feel elevated by inclusion in the national community. After all, those of the proper skin color, ethnicity, and religion have status above female *and* male enemies. Twenty-first-century leaders boost their popularity with female voters by appointing women to positions of authority. Putin's ex-wife, Lyudmila Putina, felt that the Russian president "doesn't take women seriously. He treats them with a certain contempt" (they divorced in 2013), but Putin has empowered female conservatives. The percentage of women in the Duma rose from 9.8 percent in 2003 to 14.6 percent in 2016. Valentina Matviyenko has been chair of the Federation Council since 2011, and Elvira Nabiullina has been chair of the Bank of Russia since 2013. The modern strongman can tolerate women in power as long as they work for him.[12]

Faced with women of equal authority, it's a different story, as Angela Merkel knows. Berlusconi's attempts to humiliate the German chancellor have included taking a long phone call in front of her while she stood waiting and reportedly saying that she was an "unfuckable lardass." Trump refused to shake her hand, and Putin made her wait for hours to see him and unleashed his dog near her to trigger her fear of canines. "I understand why he has to do this, to prove he's a man," said Merkel of this last episode. "He's afraid of his own weakness. Russia has nothing, no successful politics or economy. All they have is this."[13]

The strongman's shows of vulnerability as he risks everything for the nation can endear him to women and men. So can his theatrical displays of emotion as he bears the weight of his peoples' hopes and sorrows. Gaddafi wore his heart on his sleeve, or rather on his torso, since his lavish robes sometimes featured images of men he was honoring. Others make themselves accessible through the public sharing of moments of physical weakness, especially if these relate to their persecution by their enemies. In February 2019, Bolsonaro had pneumonia, one of several aftereffects of an assassination attempt by stabbing during his 2018 presidential campaign. He recorded a video message from his hospital bed wearing a gown and hooked up to monitors; thus, a man known for rape jokes and praising torturers showed a relatable side. Trump, the former reality television star, is skilled at simulating crowd-pleasing emotions. Rather than just salute the flag, like other presidents, he has hugged and kissed it with abandon, as at the Conservative Political Action Conference in February 2020. Trump's talk of wanting to be loved and of loving others, from his followers to North Korean dictator Kim Jong-un, has touched a chord. "He's an emotional guy. Passionate," said an admiring male attendee at the July 2019 Greenville, North Carolina, rally marked by racist chants.[14]

Observers over a century have seen both masculine and feminine

Donald Trump hugs the flag, February 2020.
RON SACHS / CONSOLIDATED NEWS PHOTO / AGEFOTOSTOCK

sides in strongman rulers. For every behavior that conforms to codes of machismo, there's another that hardly fits classical notions of the virile man who blends courage with self-control. Between their victim personas, vanity, endless demands for attention, and impulsivity, these men are *high-maintenance* (a term usually reserved for demanding women). Hell hath no fury like a strongman in a bad mood—which is any time he feels slighted or criticized or, if democracy still functions, doesn't get his own way.

The complex masculinity of the strongman is part of his charisma and his ability to stimulate libidinal energies of all kinds. Men and women both have longed for proximity to his special body. As the young Fascist Indro Montanelli fantasized in 1936, "When Mussolini looks at you, you cannot but be naked in front of him. But he is naked in front of us as well. . . . We rip off the clothing to go after the inimitable essence of this Man, who vibrates and pulsates with a formidable humanity."[15]

—

HAD MONTANELLI BEEN FEMALE, he may well have experienced Mussolini's pulsations, although it's doubtful he would have seen evidence of his leader's humanity. Il Duce took his pleasure with the women brought to his private quarters and then dismissed them immediately. Humiliating and violating women, and feeling powerful because *he and he alone* could have as many women as he wanted, was as much the point of these encounters as sexual satisfaction. His compulsive conquests acted out his beliefs about the submissive roles women should have under Fascism. Interviewed by the German journalist Emil Ludwig in 1932, he declared himself an enemy of feminism. "Of course I do not want women to be slaves, but if I proposed to give our women the vote, I would be laughed at. She must not count in political life."[16]

Mussolini had always had a busy sex life. Before World War I, for example, he was living (as of 1910) with his future second wife, Rachele Guidi, and seeing his future first wife, Ida Dalser. He was also spending time with and Margherita Sarfatti and courting the anarchist Leda Rafanelli while having quickies with countless others. Coming to power made managing his women easier for him and more dangerous for them, as Bianca Ceccato and Dalser found out. Ceccato served as his secretary at his newspaper *Il Popolo d'Italia* in 1918. Their relationship included many occasions of forced sex and a coerced abortion before she had a son in 1920. After Mussolini became prime minister in 1922, he had his secret police follow her and trash her apartment to remove any trace of their involvement, paid her to keep silent, and then threatened to take her child away when she wanted to marry her boyfriend. Dalser would not keep quiet about the son Benito Albino she had in 1915 with Mussolini. She ended up a prisoner in a psychiatric hospital. Benito Albino was also confined, and the dictator had him murdered by lethal injection in 1942.[17]

During his early years in power, with his wife Rachele still living in the Romagna region, Mussolini made his apartment on Via Rasella in Rome his bachelor pad. His housekeeper Cesira Carocci prepared his partners for intercourse and sometimes serviced him too. His brother Arnaldo disbursed funds for abortions, maintenance of illegitimate children, and silence. In 1929, when Mussolini made peace with the Vatican and Rachele and their children moved into Rome's Villa Torlonia, the dictator debuted a new personality cult theme of "family man" and transferred his sex life to his Palazzo Venezia office. Police chief and OVRA secret police head Arturo Bocchini became his chief enabler after Arnaldo died in 1931. Bocchini's operatives worked with Il Duce's personal secretariat staff to vet and track prospects and arrange for postcoital punishments or payments.[18]

Police files, diaries, and testimonies from Mussolini's inner circle and his last major lover, Clara Petacci, suggest that he had extramarital sex with up to four different women daily during his twenty-three years in power. His sex life is best visualized as a pyramid. Rachele, his wife, was on top, then his major lovers Sarfatti and Petacci, and then a dozen or so regular partners whom he saw once or twice a month. If he had children with the women, the relationships could go on for decades. Alice de Fonseca Pallottelli met Mussolini in 1922 and had two children with him in the 1930s. Il Duce gave her a monthly stipend, arranged for raises for her businessman husband, and bought her a car for her fiftieth birthday. The pyramid continued with a dozen semi-regular partners and ended with the thousands of women he summoned, screwed, and had surveilled. Many unrecognized mini-Mussolinis likely came out of all this activity, and an unknown number of husbands may have unwittingly raised the dictator's babies as their own.[19]

Authoritarian rule erodes trust and authenticity between people. So it's fitting that Mussolini and Petacci spied on each other throughout their nine-year relationship (1936–1945). Mussolini devoted hours each day to the aspiring actress almost thirty years his junior, checking in with her by phone a dozen times a day. He read her mail, transcripts of her phone calls, and police reports on her whereabouts. As for the well-connected Petacci, whose father was Pope Pius XI's doctor, she kept a record of her conversations with the Italian leader, spied on him, and cultivated relationships with his staff to neutralize rivals. She had the French journalist Magda Fontanges paid off and extradited from Italy. Yet Petacci brought to life the despot's fantasy: a woman who would "sacrifice her own existence and be totally dedicated to him, giving him the same gratifying sensation of dominating another's life that he had in politics," in the words of historian Mimmo Franzinelli.[20]

Fascism's misogynist cult of virility had come out of a cultural matrix that included the Italian Futurists, an avant-garde cultural collective whose 1909 manifesto made "disrespect for women" a modern commandment. The independence women gained during World War I fueled a desire to restore male authority.[21] The blackshirts' rape of women and public humiliation of homosexuals set the tone for the regime's use of the cult of virility to police sexuality. The institutionalized lawlessness of Fascism, layered onto the sexism of a traditional culture, made the dictatorship a haven for misogynists. The Neapolitan anti-Fascist Giorgio Amendola confessed that he had no notion of "sexual emancipation in a relationship of reciprocal respect" with a woman until he went into exile in Paris.[22]

Mussolini's hypermasculine persona on newsreels, posters, photographs, and more modeled the belligerent manhood encouraged by Fascist society. The Fascist film industry translated it into mass-market drama. Playing a pugnacious commander in Augusto Genina's 1936 colonial movie *The White Squadron*, the popular actor Fosco Giachetti imitated Mussolini's body language and speech patterns. Off-screen, Mussolini had myriad proxies, starting with his son-in-law Galeazzo Ciano, whose nickname was "the Jaw" because "when Mussolini thrust out his chin, Ciano thrust his own half an inch farther," in Laura Fermi's words. The bulging muscles of the statues of the Foro Mussolini sports complex remain as testaments to the exuberant manhood glorified by the state. So does Renato Bertelli's 1933 sculpture of Mussolini's profile, which resembles the tip of a penis. It was so popular that the artist sold miniature versions for coffee-table display.[23] Given the space that women occupied in Il Duce's life as a means of tension relief, career promotion, and ego gratification, depicting him as a phallus was an appropriate homage.

—

HITLER SHARED MUSSOLINI'S VOLATILE temperament and his need to dominate men and women around him. The Führer's frightening emotional intensity and verbal bludgeoning of his interlocutors were his main weapons of interpersonal aggression, rather than the Italian's physical and sexual assault. "An eighteen-year-old girl is as malleable as wax. A man must be able to leave his mark on every girl. That is all women want," said Hitler, his preference for young females reflecting a deep desire to shape those around him in his own image.[24]

The women Hitler spent time with before and after his ascent to power knew that the intensity displayed in his speeches was no act. Actresses and chorus girls, sourced for him by Goebbels and directors like Alfred

Zeisler, were subjected to monologues in his private quarters. His step-niece Geli Raubal was a near-prisoner during the two years she lived in a room in his Munich apartment before she killed herself with his gun at age twenty-three in 1931. His companion Eva Braun also shot herself in 1932 and made a second suicide attempt with sleeping pills in 1935 before her successful double-suicide with him by cyanide in the Führerbunker ten years later.[25]

Since the 1930s, discussions about Hitler's sexuality have centered on how it departed from the "masculine norm," with his relative physical restraint with women often taken as evidence of his lack of virility. The German left used the prominence of homosexuals like SA leader Ernst Röhm in early Nazism to smear it, and Hitler, as deviant. *The Authoritarian Personality*, published in 1950 by Theodor Adorno and a team of psychologists, retained this line of argument. Nazism's early tolerance for non-normative sexuality among its members is not surprising given that Weimar Berlin had been a homosexual haven, with an estimated 80 to 100 gay and lesbian clubs and bars. As Robert Beachy writes, many gay Nazis, "blinded by the homoeroticism of masculinist ideologies" prominent within the movement, did not believe that its machine of biological racism would turn against them.[26]

Those who contend that Hitler was secretly gay marshal the evidence. Until the eve of his suicide, he never married; as a young man he avoided brothels and casual hookups, in part due to his fear of germs and disease; and he kept a picture of his dead mother above his bed in several of his residences. Hitler's way of being a man led some observers to conclude that he was "both man and woman," either bisexual or, according to the postwar tabloid press, a hermaphrodite. "Outwardly so hard, he is touchingly soft within," wrote future deputy Führer Rudolph Hess, capturing the contradictory qualities that helped the Nazi leader gain the devotion of men and women. Although he kept his body clothed in public, Hitler's speeches left him bathed in sweat and gave onlookers the sense they had just made an intimate connection. "At times it seems as if [his words] are torn from the very heart of the man, causing him indescribable anguish," marveled the writer Michael Fry.[27]

In Hitler's long relationship with Eva Braun (1932–1945), lack of desire seems to have been less a problem than his insistence that the public see him as devoted only to Germany. Two months before her 1935 suicide attempt, Braun complained to her diary that "he only needs me for certain purposes." She had social power among the circle of intimates who gathered at Hitler's Berghof retreat, but was kept away from public events. At receptions, Goebbels's wife Magda played the role of First Lady, while Braun and her couture wardrobe remained unseen. Just as Hitler was fully and sublimely the audience's during his speeches, so did his leader cult depend on the fiction of him being completely available to the people whose will he embodied.[28]

Undoubtedly, Hitler's ability to bond deeply with other men shaped his career. His emotional intensity, as well as his racist proselytizing, reeled in Goebbels and many other top collaborators early on and kept them close for decades. "I know why Hitler loves me. . . . I so appeal to Hitler's vanity. But there is a further reason. It is my secret, and it is Hitler's too. I cannot describe the ecstasy I feel, the rapture, the high peak of my emotions," wrote the Nazi official and Hitler's personal lawyer Hans Frank, in Hitler's service from the late 1920s to 1945.[29] Ultimately, as in Italy, both men and women had to be subjected to the will of the leader, whose greatest pleasure was dominating and possessing everyone around him—a dynamic that continued into the age of military coups and beyond.

—

"TODAY . . . IS THE BEGINNING OF THE END of the era of harems and slaves," Gaddafi announced proudly in September 1981, presenting the first graduating class of Libya's new military academy for women. The female liberation movement that he was supporting would be "a bomb to shake up the entire Arab region, inciting female prisoners, whether in palaces or marketplaces, to rebel against their jailers, their exploiters, and their oppressors." Later, at home in his palace-like Bab al-Azizia compound, he would decide which of his own prisoners he would rape and abuse.[30]

Gaddafi's September 1969 coup gave Libyan women far more independence. It granted women and men equal legal status, opened new horizons for women through education, and promoted a degree of female autonomy. Feminist groups were prominent in the Women's Federation of his Socialist *Jamahiriya*, or "state of the masses." As Gaddafi publicly gained fame for these revolutionary measures, he privately constructed a system to procure and confine women for his personal satisfaction. In Gaddafi's case, the contradictions present in many authoritarian states between mobilizing women and restricting their rights were magnified, the compulsion to subjugate women taken to its extreme.[31]

"[W]as there ever a single woman whom he didn't want to possess at least once?" asked Soraya, only partly rhetorically. Kidnapped by his security forces in 2004, when she was fifteen, Soraya spent years in confinement. By the time she was taken to his Bab al-Azizia compound, Gaddafi's Department of Protocol had been operating for decades. A "services group" managed male partners, who were usually his guards, male guests, or army officials. The rapes normally took place in the basement of Bab al-Azizia. It was equipped with medical facilities, and Ukrainian nurses did blood tests and gynecological checks on new arrivals, since Gaddafi, like Hitler, was terrified of disease. There was also a bathroom with a Jacuzzi for golden showers, Gaddafi's sex den, and quarters for captives with lighting on day and night to make them lose all sense of the outside world. During the brutal sessions, which could last for hours, Gaddafi consumed Viagra like candy, and he was usually drunk and high on hashish or cocaine.[32]

Gaddafi extracted maximum value from his victims, forcing them to also serve as guards, housemaids, and servers when he entertained at home or when his wife Safia Farkash visited from her own villa within the compound. They also worked as bodyguards when he traveled abroad, mixed in with actual female soldiers. The foreign journalists who commented on those beauties in uniform, playing into Gaddafi's cult of virility, were doubtless unaware of what happened in private. The rapes continued in whatever lodgings they had abroad and in his camper on trips to the desert.

When US Secretary of State Condoleezza Rice visited Gaddafi in 2008, he insisted she dine in his private kitchen. He showed her a videotape he had made of her—a montage of photos of her with Putin and other male leaders, set to a song, "Black Flower in the White House," he had commissioned in her honor. Rice had no idea that the female servers and male guards she saw had another job downstairs. But L.S., who participated in a dinner for foreign guests as Gaddafi's wife's translator, sensed something about the women who cleared the plates that "made the blood run cold."[33]

As in Mussolini's Italy, secret police and bureaucrats worked to deliver bodies to a voracious leader. Yet Gaddafi went far beyond Il Duce, keeping his women captive. General Nuri al-Mismari, nicknamed General of the Whores, served as head of protocol. Some women he brought in were as young as thirteen. Others might be wives of visiting foreign businessmen or politicians or wives of his ministers and generals. As Gaddafi's fixer, al-Mismari also arranged for payments (sometimes billed as "investment agreements") to victims who might expose the regime abroad, and for punishment of female recruiters and guards who no longer wanted to participate in the sex abuse. The prominence of female enablers in Gaddafi's system offers another example of the strongman's paradoxical view of gender emancipation. Women advance in their careers by making it easier for the leader and his inner circle to harm other women.[34]

Gaddafi's system of kidnapping and sexual violence relied on scouts (often Revolutionary Guards) who looked for attractive girls in markets, schools, and on the street and photographed prospects for vetting. Some parents kept their daughters hidden, but scouts could see your child in the family car or shop and the next day come to take her away. Women and girls who were rejected by the leader and returned home might adopt a headscarf (a practice then relatively rare in Libya), as a relative of L.S. did after a two-week absence, but still be shunned by neighbors and devout relatives.[35]

Gaddafi preferred to choose his victims directly. Events at schools and universities and political assemblies did double duty as predatory opportunities. The University of Tripoli was a favorite hunting ground, and Gaddafi had a replica of his home sex dungeon constructed on campus for instant gratification. April 7, the terrifying "holiday" dedicated to the execution of male students, was Gaddafi's time to choose a new group of captives. A pat on the head by the leader was the signal to his security services to intervene. Selected by her school on such an occasion to give Gaddafi a bouquet of flowers, Soraya felt that touch: "And there my life ended." Eight years later, after countless beatings and violations, "I was now no more than an object, a hole." Reducing people to mere instruments of his desires for money, sex, and more is part of the strongman way of life and rule. In Gaddafi's case, unlimited wealth and unchecked power created a "monster who thought he was God . . . and thought about nothing but fucking," a description that might apply to some new authoritarian leaders as well.[36]

—

"WHAT HAPPENS WHEN YOU ELECT a sexist to run your country? Ask Italian women," the journalist Annalisa Merelli wrote in October 2016, warning Americans what the election of an outspoken misogynist might bring. During his two terms in office in the first decade of the 2000s, Berlusconi used his control of Italy's television and advertising markets to saturate the country with images of women in submissive roles. His sexism appealed to many in a socially conservative society where divorce was not legalized until 1970.[37]

Berlusconi's 1980s entertainment program *Drive In*, with its scantily clad females probed by a lascivious cinematography, blazed the trail. A

1986 phone call between Berlusconi and his close collaborator Marcello Dell'Utri about the former's New Year's plans with Prime Minister Craxi revealed that those women also had off-screen responsibilities:

> Berlusconi: The New Year is off to a bad start!
> Dell'Utri: Why?
> Berlusconi: Because two girls from *Drive In* were supposed to come and they stood us up!
> Dell'Utri: What do you care about *Drive In*?
> Berlusconi: What do I care? It means we're not going to fuck! If the year starts like this, it means we won't fuck anymore!"[38]

We don't know if these particular women paid a professional price for their bold move. But over the next decades Berlusconi's procurer-propagandist Emilio Fede, news director for the TG4 channel from 1992 to 2012, organized hundreds of beauty pageants around Italy to find women to star on Berlusconi's programs and be available, in theory, to service the Berlusconi circle. Some of these events, classified as "cultural initiatives," were publicly funded, and some were judged directly by Fede. Participating in them could jump-start a woman's career as a model or television star, including the prize of becoming a TG4 Little Weather Girl, or *meteorine*.

In 2008, Helen Scopel, a finalist for Miss Italia 2002, a Miss Padania, and a veteran of Berlusconi's prime-time shows, found out the real terms of employment. She lost her *meteorine* position for refusing Fede's requests for "favors." By the time she went public with her story on television in 2011, the connections between Fede's beauty contests and the sexual exploits of the Berlusconi world were clear. "Is Emilio Fede coming here to select the next participants for sex parties at taxpayers' expense?" asked a politician whose administration was supposed to pay 12,000 euros for hosting the Miss Pescara contest. That year, the United Nations (UN) Convention on the Elimination of All Forms of Discrimination against Women expressed concern "about the portrayal of women as sex objects" in Italy and "public statements made by politicians [that] undermine womens' social status."[39]

The UN report doubtless referred to the misogynist comments and actions Berlusconi made almost daily as part of his virile personal brand and management of media attention. There was the time he exited a meeting and grabbed a female police officer from behind, smiling for the cameras as he simulated copulation. Or the time he asked a female manager of a green energy company how she achieved sexual pleasure or told female winners of an academic award they were so talented he was tempted to invite them to a sex party. The goal, in these and many other cases, was to demean professional women and make viewers laugh with him, and at them.[40]

As Berlusconi's supporters liked to observe, he promoted women to cabinet-level positions, albeit in traditionally "female" areas, like the Ministry of Education. Mara Carfagna, minister for equal opportunities from 2008 to 2011, was a Berlusconi-world creation: she had been a Miss Italy contestant and a showgirl on Berlusconi's entertainment programs. As minister, she worked to reduce violence against women, sponsoring an act that made stalking a crime, while espousing anti–sex worker rights platforms and reportedly attending Berlusconi's sex parties. Carfagna's career trajectory suggests how Berlusconi changed Italian political culture, substituting traditional party patronage networks with others rooted in his private enterprises and needs.[41]

Berlusconi's female fans didn't care about his misogyny. His popularity with women remained unaffected even when news of his sex procurement scandal first broke. The Italian leader's charisma, his talk of kisses and hugs, and his comments about undertaking face-lifts and hair transplants to look good for women touched a chord. "I too was kind of a housewife," Berlusconi told housewives at the start of his political career, citing the chores he did as a boy as giving him knowledge of "how tiring" their jobs are.[42] Veronica Lario, the mother of Berlusconi's children, had a different perpsective. Berlusconi courted other women in public during their marriage, and after an episode in which he told Carfagna "if I weren't already married I would marry you immediately," Lario demanded an apology via an open letter in the newspaper *La Repubblica*. Lario started divorce proceedings in 2009 after Berlusconi attended the birthday party of an eighteen-year-old underwear model, Noemi Letizia, who mused aloud about becoming a showgirl or possibly a parliamentarian: "Daddy Silvio will take care of it," Letizia said confidently.[43]

The 2010 "Rubygate" scandal broke the spell for some of Berlusconi's longtime supporters. An unknown seventeen-year-old Moroccan dancer, Karima El Mahroug, known as Ruby, was released from police custody after she had been accused of theft. The release, it turned out, was at Berlusconi's personal request; El Mahroug was a Berlusconi favorite who attended his sex parties. But "Rubygate" wasn't just about the Italian prime minister's complicated private life. While Mussolini's prominent lovers, like Princess Giulia Alliata de Montereale, had sometimes influenced political appointments, this twenty-first-century scandal revealed that being intimate with the leader or procuring him women could land *you* in office. Nicole Minetti was one example. The dental hygienist first met Berlusconi when she worked as a hostess at Publitalia events and from 2007 to 2009 had roles on entertainment programs on Berlusconi's and state television networks. In 2010, with no political experience, she was put up for election as a regional deputy in Lombardy, taking office that year. The scandal revealed the logic behind her sudden promotion: Minetti had also worked as a recruiter, scouting girls for Berlusconi's sex parties and arranging their lodging and travel. As other such stories emerged, some charged that Italy had become a "whore-ocracy" (*mignottocrazia*), in which servicing Berlusconi opened doors to a political career. In Minetti's case, that career was short-lived. Charged with procurement, she was sentenced in 2019 to almost three years in prison.[44]

Berlusconi credited his friend Gaddafi with suggesting the euphemism "bunga-bunga" for his sex parties, which took place at his residences in Sardinia, Rome, or at Arcore, outside Milan. They involved local beauty queens and women brought in from all over the world. Along with Minetti, Berlusconi's news director Emilio Fede and Dario

Lele Mora, a talent scout for Berlusconi's Mediaset, handled lodging, payoffs, and gifts.[45] According to court testimony from El Mahroug and other women who attended the parties, several powerful men might be in attendance, or just one (Berlusconi) along with fifteen to twenty women, who might sing the Berlusconi hymn, "Thank goodness for Silvio." Pole and lap dancing followed dinner, with a few females invited to the after-party in Berlusconi's bedroom. Regular lovers got cash to help them start a business, a chance at a spot on a Berlusconi show, or a boost into politics. In El Mahroug's case, this amounted to $300,000 worth of goods and, according to prosecutors, payments of up to 4.5 million euros to keep her silent about her relations with Berlusconi, given that she was underage.[46]

The titillating aspects of "Rubygate" captured the media's attention, but the observations of female witnesses who saw the Italian prime minister up close are just as revealing. "Berlusconi? I feel sorry for him . . . forced to organize parties so he's not alone," said Chiara Danese, a former Miss Italy, who moved to America because she feared for her safety after testifying against Berlusconi. "He might seem happy, with all that money . . . but I think he's lonely," reflected El Mahroug of Berlusconi in 2011. Her statement applies to all strongmen, who are plagued by an inner emptiness, no matter how much money and power they accumulate and how many bodies they consume.[47]

———

"WHEN YOU'RE A STAR, THEY LET YOU DO IT," Trump said in 2005 about groping and kissing women, unaware he was being recorded by Billy Bush, producer of the *Access Hollywood* television program Trump was appearing on. When the tapes leaked shortly before the 2016 election, many thought his political career would be over. Instead, the revelation merely strengthened the misogynist brand of male glamour Trump had built over decades, including as owner of Trump Model Management (1999–2017) and the Miss Universe pageant (1996–2015). For decades the Miss Universe contest provided Trump with proximity to a large pool of women, and he often entered their dressing rooms when he knew they would be unclothed. Trump models were pressured to serve the boss, including as escorts for his powerful friends, as former model Jazz Egger charged in 2017.[48]

"During the Trump Era, will men finally start acting like men again?" asked the right-wing Infowars site days after the inauguration. Trump's followers see him as the dominant male leader America needs. They make posters of the president as John Wayne, Superman, and other male savior figures, which they bring to rallies and post on social media. In Trump's own mind, he is a buff fighter. In 2019, he tweeted an image from his personal Twitter account of his head photoshopped onto the body of Sylvester Stallone's character from the 1976 film *Rocky*. As a man in his seventies, Trump borrows other men's bodies to show his virility rather than display his own in the tradition of Mussolini and Putin.[49]

Reclaiming male authority after the Obama era also means creating an environment in which men can act on their desires with impunity. In 2019, the Department of Justice's Office of Violence against Women changed the definition of domestic violence on its website, limiting it to physical acts of harm. The DOJ no longer considers "sexual, emotional, economic, or psychological actions or threats of actions that influence another person" as "felony or misdemeanor crimes."[50]

Trump considers the #MeToo movement as "very dangerous" to men in power. His education secretary Betsy DeVos drove forward a revision to Title IX regulations that gives accused sexual harassers and assault-ers the right to cross-examine their victims (through a lawyer or other representative, with them present) during Title IX hearings. Trump has consistently come to the defense of prominent men like Fox News jour-nalist Bill O'Reilly (accused of sexual harassment) and Alabama politi-cian Roy Moore (accused of child molestation and sexual assault) and has sought to isolate and defame their accusers. In 2018, the psychologist Christine Blasey Ford testified to the Senate Judiciary Committee that Supreme Court nominee Brett Kavanaugh assaulted her in high school. Trump's mocking remarks about Ford's testimony, meant to call into doubt its veracity, set the tone for a wave of public hostility against her. Ford received death threats and had to relocate her family. Kavanaugh is now a Supreme Court justice.[51]

The president's prominent appointees have included men who have been accused of sexual harassment or domestic abuse. A partial list (all of them have now departed) includes Bannon and Trump's first labor secretary, Andy Puzder. His second labor secretary, Alex Acosta, gave pedophile and sex trafficker Jeffrey Epstein a deal that spared him jail time. Five male cadets at the Citadel accused Steven Munoz, who organized visits of foreign heads of state to the White House, of groping them. Sean Lawler, Trump's chief of protocol, carried a horsewhip around in the office to intimidate coworkers. The photographs of crowds of White male officials and staffers regularly released by the government show the reversal of gender and racial gains made during the Obama years.[52]

For Trump, as with Berlusconi, government became a tool of self-defense as his past was put under scrutiny. Dozens of women from every era of his life have accused him of sexual harassment or assault, from Miss Universe pageant and *Apprentice* contestants and Mar-a-Lago guests to Trump business and campaign senior staff. "Maybe he gets hit by a truck," Trump said to his lawyer Michael Cohen on a phone call in 2018 about David Pecker, then publisher of the *National Enquirer*, who was considering ending his longtime arrangement with Trump to keep accusations of the president's sex crimes out of the press. In keeping with strongman history, in the end it was Cohen who took the fall—for paying off porn star Stormy Daniels to remain quiet about her involvement with Trump. Cohen's three-year prison sentence started in 2019.[53]

SEVEN

CORRUPTION

THE ROASTED QUAIL, served on Limoges china, was cooked to perfection and accompanied by exquisite wines from one of the world's finest cellars. At Gbadolite, the site of Mobutu's palaces in the Congolese jungle, swans sailed across pristine lakes, servants glided through rooms sheathed in Gobelins tapestries and Carrera marble, and funds flowed in from the CIA, the International Monetary Fund (IMF), private banks, and the nation's cobalt, copper, and diamond mines. Pope John Paul II, preacher Pat Robertson, and CIA director William Casey all visited Gbadolite in the 1980s and 1990s, mingling with Mobutu and his ruling elite. Charming and cruel, Mobutu was always ready with some choice strongman wisdom: "If you want to steal, steal a little cleverly, in a nice way. If you steal so much as to become rich overnight, you will be caught." He followed his own advice, avoiding jail as he made Zaire into "a kleptocracy to end all kleptocracies, [setting] a standard by which all future international thieves will have to be measured," as US congressman Stephen Solarz (D-NY) stated in 1991.[1]

The Zairean ministers and officials in attendance at such official occasions, stuffed into the obligatory *abacost* tunic, knew that any of these lavish meals could be their own Last Supper. Frequent purges of ruling elites created a climate of insecurity and dependency on the leader, encouraging their complicity in his corruption. Participation in the system made them wealthy, but also, paradoxically, more vulnerable. At any moment they could be accused of corruption or nepotism and punished. In the first decade of Mobutu's rule, 29 of 212 elites went directly from high office to prison, another 26 were removed on charges of disloyalty or dishonesty, and 4 ministers accused of treason were hung in 1966 in front of 50,000 people. Over time, Mobutu conditioned political elites to avoid punishment, although some of them manipulated him as well.[2]

The career of Jean Nguza Karl-i-Bond encapsulates the risks and rewards of collaborating with strongmen. During his second term as foreign minister (1976–1977), he was accused of high treason, likely because the foreign press had cited him as a possible Mobutu successor. He endured torture in prison, but Mobutu overturned his death sentence in 1977, pardoned him in 1978, and named him foreign minister again in 1979. Karl-i-Bond went into exile, testified to the US Congress about Mobutu's corruption in 1981, and wrote a book a year later entitled *Mobutu, Or the Incarnation of Zairian Evil*. To stem the flow of bad press, Mobutu made him ambassador to Washington in 1986. Karl-i-Bond's skill in that post at legitimating the same crimes he had previously denounced won him a 1991 appointment as prime minister. Only eighty people mattered in Zaire, observed journalist Blaine Harden, with men like Karl-i-Bond in mind. "At any one time, twenty of them are ministers, twenty of them are exiles, twenty are in jail and twenty are ambassadors. Every three months, the music stops and Mobutu forces everyone to change."[3]

The Cold War made Mobutu's long rule and luxurious lifestyle possible. The age of decolonization marked a shift in the economic order, with the end of European empires bringing the removal of European state capital and the influx of new private and institutional investors. Mobutu's pro-Western anti-Communism set him up to be a primary recipient of funds from Europeans and Americans who sought to contain the left and continue their influence in a postcolonial age. Over the years his champions and investors included his lobbyists Paul Manafort and Roger Stone, US ambassador to Zaire Sheldon B. Vance, and the family of French president Giscard d'Estaing. In the 1980s, the d'Estaings controlled construction-related businesses that accounted for almost a third of Zaire's foreign debt. The IMF and the United States Export-Import Bank also lent Mobutu money, even after IMF banker Erwin Blumenthal warned in 1982 that they would likely never recoup their funds. By the time Mobutu was forced into exile in 1997, he had amassed a $5 billion fortune. Zaire lost $12 billion in capital flight and gained $14 billion in debt, with a 699.8 percent average annual rate of inflation and more than 70 percent of the population living in poverty on an average daily wage of $1.[4]

OFTEN DEFINED AS THE ABUSE OF public power for private gain, corruption involves practices that encompass bribery, conflict of interest, plunder of state resources, the use of tax and licensing regulations to extort or force bankruptcy, illegal raids on businesses, and profiting from privatization or nationalization. Dereliction of duty offenses may include sham audits or investigations and laws that facilitate or decriminalize wrongdoing. Mobutu's financial empire relied on kickbacks from private businesses, family ownership of national companies, siphoning international aid money and revenue from Zaire's diamonds and other natural resources, "loans" from state banks, and bribes.[5]

Co-optation is the term political scientists use for the way authoritarians bind individuals and groups to them. Here it is considered a form of corruption, given the ethical compromises and changes in personal and professional practices that cooperating with amoral and violent individuals entail. Strongmen use corruption in tandem with other tools. Purges of the judiciary result in a justice system that exonerates crooks or doesn't prosecute them at all. Journalists and activists who might expose thievery are imprisoned or smeared through propaganda. Virility makes taking what you want and getting away with it the measure of manhood. Authoritarians also create new patronage systems that offer jobs and opportunities for wealth, which help to overcome any moral hesitations some might have about collaborating. The core of the contract between the ruler and his enablers is the offer of power and economic gain in exchange for supporting his violent actions and his suppression of civil rights.[6]

Corruption is a *process* as well as a set of practices, and the word's Latin and Old French origins imply a change of state due to decay. As implied by popular sayings like "one bad apple spoils the whole bunch," corruption has always been associated with contamination and degradation, whether of physical objects (like fruit and computer files) or the soul. This notion of corruption captures the operation of strongman regimes. They turn the economy into an instrument of leader wealth creation, but also encourage changes in ethical and behavioral norms to make things that were illegal or immoral appear acceptable, whether election fraud, torture, or sexual assault. "What Putin and Erdogan could get away with at the beginning of their terms in office is nothing compared to what they can get away with now," noted the economist Daron Acemoglu in 2020.[7]

Rulers who come into office with a criminal record, like Mussolini and Hitler, or under investigation, as was the case with Putin, Trump, and Berlusconi, have a head start. They know that making the government a refuge for criminals who don't have to learn to be lawless hastens the "contagion effect." So does granting amnesties and pardons, which indebt individuals to the leader and make blackmailers, war criminals, and murderers available for service.[8]

Thirsty for profit and holding a proprietary view of office, personalist rulers exploit their nation's natural and human resources for economic gain. Bolsonaro warned indigenous communities that they must adapt to his capitalist exploitation of the Amazon rain forest or "simply vanish." Government fines for violating environmental regulations decreased by 34 percent his first year in office. Trump's authoritarian bargain with elites—profits for them, political support for him—motivates his administration's enthusiastic embrace of climate change denial. As of May 2020, one hundred environmental regulations had been rolled back, with dozens more in progress. All of these changes have made it easier for Trump's backers in the auto, agribusiness, chemical, and fossil fuel industries to pollute the earth and plunder natural resources with impunity. Oil and gas companies no longer have to report methane emissions. Mines no longer have to prove they can pay to clean up future pollution. Drilling is now permitted in the Arctic National Wildlife Refuge.[9]

This last action links to US secretary of state Mike Pompeo's claim that the melting of Arctic glaciers is a situation full of "opportunity and abundance," despite the mass displacement and ecological ruin it will cause. Pompeo sees global warming there as liberating 13 percent of the world's undiscovered oil, 30 percent of its undiscovered natural gas, and buried gold, diamonds, and uranium. This greed lay behind Trump's talk in 2019 of buying Greenland (which was never for sale) and the decision in 2020 to prioritize US investment in Greenland. The dictator in Gabriel García Márquez's 1975 novel *Autumn of the Patriarch*, who has the Caribbean Sea drained and sold to his US supporters, no longer seems so fantastical.[10]

Corrupting others works for the ruler only if he remains so powerful that the coercive tactics he uses on underlings cannot be used on him. To protect himself he relies on a "divide and rule" strategy that involves frequent upheavals of his cabinet to keep elites in competition with one another and loyal only to him. Officials may learn they've been fired by reading about it in the newspaper, like Fascist Party secretary Giovanni Giurati in 1931; while taking part in a rally, a favorite Mobutu tactic; by hearing about it on radio or television; or by seeing a tweet, while on the toilet, as happened to Secretary of State Rex Tillerson in 2018.[11]

Over time this constant upheaval creates a political class too weakened by rivalries to conspire against the leader and too cowed to tell him unwelcome truths. "For God's sake, don't upset the Führer—which means do not tell him bad news—do not mention things which are not as he conceives them to be," wrote the journalist Karl H. von Wiegand, summarizing a situation familiar to those who have worked for Gaddafi, Erdoğan, and others. The traits former CIA head Michael Morell listed in an

August 2016 *New York Times* op-ed, warning voters of Trump's unfitness for the presidency, sum up every personalist leader's style of governing:

> his tendency to make decisions based on intuition, his refusal to change his views based on new information, his routine carelessness with the facts, his unwillingness to listen to others and his lack of respect for the rule of law.[12]

Strongmen are family men, in their own fashion. To block criticism and engage in corrupt practices while minimizing the chance of exposure, they establish inner sanctums composed of family members and trusted cronies. The leader's children may run the official family business, as with Berlusconi and Trump, or the unofficial family business of money-laundering, which was the case with Mobutu's son Kongulu and many other offspring of autocrats.[13]

Sons-in-law also have a prominent role in strongman governance. Mussolini made his son-in-law Galeazzo Ciano foreign minister in 1936, used him as "a tool of his personal politics," and then had Ciano executed for voting in 1943 to remove him from power. Orbán's son-in-law István Tiborcz, a businessman, has amassed a net worth of over 100 million euros, but the Hungarian government dropped corruption probes initiated by the European Union (EU) against him. Berat Albayrak, accused by multiple foreign governments of illegal activities while serving as Turkish energy minister, is now Erdoğan's treasury and finance minister. Jared Kushner, a presidential adviser, pursues private Kushner and Trump family financial interests along with his government assignments.[14]

———

MUSSOLINI SET THE TEMPLATE FOR strongman corruption activities. He presented Fascism as cleansing Italy of war profiteers, then shut down investigations into war profiteering once he became prime minister to please the conservative elites and industrialists who backed him. Once he established dictatorship, he vowed to "drain the swamps" of Italy. He meant this literally: he transformed the Pontine Marshes south of Rome into cities like Sabaudia and Littoria. But he also vowed to cleanse Italy of all "delinquents" who spread contagion and gave Italy a bad name abroad.[15]

That entailed eliminating anti-Fascists, but also cracking down on organized crime. Mussolini viewed the Sicilian Mafia and other such organizations as a threat because they substituted for state power in areas and siphoned off state revenues. In 1925, he appointed a tough new prefect of Palermo, Cesare Mori, who arrested thousands of mafiosi, winning international fame—until his investigations went too far, uncovering collaborations between the Mafia and the Fascist Party. In 1928, Mussolini's brother Arnaldo Mussolini declared that Fascism had vanquished the Mafia. A year later, Mori was fired and given a job in Istria—as far away from Sicily as possible. The Fascist militia, now tasked with controlling the Mafia, instead adopted its methods, often in conjunction with party bosses. In 1934–1935, 40 million lire was embezzled from Palermo's municipal budget, leading the city's British consul, James Dodds, to remark that Fascist promises to "purify the administration" had been a sham. Fascism did not defeat the Mafia, but added a new one that operated under state authority.[16]

Race-based persecution also provided fascists opportunities for individual and state enrichment. Fascism's 1938 anti-Semitic legislation aimed to generate state revenue as well as impoverish Italian Jews. Armando Leoni gave the state a good deal on his profitable chain of thirty cinemas for special consideration of his claim that he was not Jewish because his mother was the illegitimate daughter of an Aryan Catholic maid. Giacomo Beraha, a banker and industrialist from Salonika who lost his Italian citizenship, paid 100,000 lire to stay in Italy. Fascist bureaucrats trafficked in false baptismal and Aryan status certificates, and Antonio Le Pera, director of the government agency for race and demography, figured in many OVRA secret police reports as a "speculator" who performed the miracle of transforming Jews into Aryans, especially if the Jews in question were wealthy.[17]

Fascist Italy was a laboratory for the divide-and-rule strategy that became a staple of authoritarian rule. Every three or four years, Il Duce fired more than half of his cabinet and undersecretaries to make sure no official felt too secure in his position. Becoming too competent or well known could derail your career, as the pilot and air force minister Italo Balbo found out. In 1933, his transatlantic flight to America put him on the cover of *TIME* magazine, and the city of Chicago gave him a parade and named a street after him. In 1934, Mussolini transferred him to Tripoli as governor of Libya. "This mistrust of his truly faithful followers is the greatest of [Mussolini's] defects," the general and minister of colonies Emilio De Bono confided in his diary in 1934, a year before the dictator dismissed him and took over his job. Mussolini hoarded job titles like he hoarded women, always occupying at least five cabinet positions.[18]

Franco, too, excelled at micromanaging. He directly or indirectly oversaw the hiring and firing of Spanish ministers, provincial governors, mayors of large cities, military commanders, and heads of major workers' unions. Pinochet appointed all Chilean mayors. Yet only Mussolini occupied so many jobs while also spending hours each day on his sex life, reading the press for news about himself, and interfering in small details of government, like when the trees along the road from Lodi to Piacenza should be pruned.[19]

Allied bombs and the prudent destruction of documents by the Mussolini family and PNF officials erased many details of Fascist financial malfeasance. Nor do we have a full picture of Il Duce's own income from royalties from his many publications or his earnings from his newspaper *Il Popolo d'Italia*. Yet reconstructions of his real estate holdings, many in his wife's name, suggest that he was a rapacious man who used any means, including deporting Jews who had desirable property, to get what he wanted. Meanwhile, he projected an image of a selfless and ascetic soul, unaware of his underlings' swindling, that convinced many Fascist sympathizers. "I read in the newspapers that you levitate rather than live: you give everything to Italy and so you don't eat drink or sleep," Michela C. from Tuscany wrote to Mussolini in 1925. The idea that the strongman remains "above it all" due to his special mission, while his cronies are the corrupt ones who lead his government astray, reappeared with each new authoritarian takeover, starting in Germany.[20]

—

"YES, IF HITLER COULD DO EVERYTHING HIMSELF, some things would be different. But he can't keep watch over everything." A 1935 police report from Bavaria summed up popular sentiment as accounts of embezzlement, fraud, and other crimes by NSDAP bosses circulated. The Führer had long crafted his image as a virtuous man, comparing himself in *Mein Kampf* to Jesus cleansing the temple of money changers. His abstemious habits as a leader (he was a vegetarian, didn't drink or smoke, and kept his girlfriend Eva Braun in the shadows) bolstered his purist credentials. "I am probably the only statesman in the world who does not have a bank account," he told Krupp factory workers in Essen in 1936. "I have no stocks or shares in any company." To keep up this anti-materialist profile, he declined to draw a salary, even as he earned millions of reichsmarks in *Mein Kampf* royalties, speaking fees, and gifts from admirers. His presidential funds were exempt from any accounting procedures, and he ordered the Gestapo to destroy his tax records to hide evidence that he never paid any taxes.[21]

The administrative structure of the Nazi state favored the distancing of Hitler from corrupt activities but made for inefficient governance. Frowning on Mussolini's micromanaging, the Führer delegated (some felt to the point of negligence, since he usually slept until lunchtime). He gave his ministers authority to build their own fiefdoms and encouraged them to compete for the title of most accurate interpreter of his everchanging desires. Bureaucracies and agencies proliferated, often with overlapping competencies, producing "the biggest confusion in government that has ever existed in a civilized state," as former Nazi press chief Otto Dietrich later charged.[22]

Material rewards compensated for any frustrations. Hitler kept his favorites close with secret stipends and bonuses that doubled their tax-free salaries, and his lax oversight permitted abuses. Although the courts prosecuted low- and mid-level functionaries for misappropriating NSDAP funds, the Nazi Labor Front paid for the maintenance of its drunkard chieftain Robert Ley's luxury villa and cruise ship. Taxpayers supported Nazi leader Hermann Göring's collecting and remodeling of multiple residences, including a castle. All these "little Hitlers" built their own chains of corruption, often hiring those with handy criminal skills. Anton Karl, convicted for theft and embezzlement during the Weimar Republic, became head of the Labor Front's construction department, known for his skillful use of bribery to gain contracts. "What sort of jacket do you need?" asked a tailor in a skit Werner Finck staged in 1934 at Berlin's Die Katakombe cabaret. "One with pockets wide open, in the current fashion," answered Finck, playing the tailor's customer. The Gestapo agents in the audience got the joke—they closed the show.[23]

To co-opt Germans, the regime linked benefits for the included to punishments for the excluded. A 1933 law that cost thousands of leftist and Jewish civil servants their jobs twinned with another law that erased debt for everyone else. A second debt eradication law in 1938, the year of full employment and the Kristallnacht pogrom, helped Germans to accept the "Aryanization" of the economy through boycotts, forced sales, and expropriations of Jewish businesses. Industrialists like Fritz Thyssen benefited most from the ongoing capital concentration in banking and other sectors, but regional economic offices got a 10 percent commission from the sale of Jewish firms, and "unofficial commissions" to bureaucrats were not uncommon. Benevolence for Aryans, brutality for the rest: this was Hitler's authoritarian pact. When violence escalated into mass murder, he would remain, for many, a "Führer without sin."[24]

—

MILITARY COUPS ARE OPERATIONS of high risk and, if all goes well, high reward for all involved—or so thought the officers who came to power in Chile and Libya. All of them soon found themselves in a position of subservience as Pinochet and Gaddafi quickly asserted their personal authority. In doing so, these leaders likely increased their time in office. Retaining sole control of patronage and punishment systems, personalist military rulers are less likely to be overthrown than those who share power with their juntas.[25]

In Chile, a military known for its rectitude quickly became subordinated to Pinochet's agendas of transforming the law into an ally of state repression and the armed forces into persecutors. The duty to serve the head of the country, no matter who it was or what he did, played a role in gaining compliance. So did the fear of being purged. A group of air force officers was accused of treason in 1974, and some of them were brought to court in chains as an example.[26]

Many military and civilian judges and lawyers welcomed the coup as means of staving off Socialism and accepted the state of juridical exception. This included using military tribunals to judge political crimes by civilians, 6,000 of whom were tried from 1973 to 1976 for treason (the omnibus charge). Years later, a former military prosecutor tried to make sense of this collective complicity:

> We believed in the letter of the law, and we tried to do our jobs
> well, but the whole system seemed to have gone insane. People
> were tried for war crimes even though we weren't at war. . . .
> We all went along with it, because we were afraid of losing our
> jobs . . . we all became part of it. Nobody escaped.[27]

American and Chilean propaganda about the regime's efficiency has obscured the chaos created by Pinochet's divide-and-rule practices. The

Chilean leader reshuffled his cabinet forty-nine times (ministers lasted an average of ten months), ordering ministers to resign en masse and announcing on television which ones would remain. He had overly competent or popular ministers monitored and sometimes sabotaged their work, and was known to reverse orders he had just given. General Nicanor Díaz Estrada was hired in 1973 as labor minister and fired eighteen months later without ever meeting alone with Pinochet, which spared him exposure to his boss's outbursts of anger. Pinochet also used material incentives to co-opt elites. Important judges and members of the Supreme Court had cars and drivers at their disposal; armed forces officers got education and housing loans.[28]

The junta's economic policies won Pinochet support from the sectors he cared about. Big capital benefited from neoliberal reforms that created what the Christian Democrat politician Genaro Arriagada called "one of the most accelerated processes of concentration of economic power" Latin America had ever seen. The Chilean leader's own family and inner circle also profited through control of businesses privatized by the regime. Pinochet's son-in-law Julio Ponce Lerou, who ran the government agency in charge of privatizations, obtained a chemical company with a $67 million annual profit, and Jorge Aravena, another son-in-law, got a large insurance agency.[29]

As in Franco's Spain, many of the technocrats who managed economic policy were linked to Opus Dei. Jaime Guzmán, a neoliberal lawyer and top Pinochet adviser, acted as a liaison with Catholic business elites who viewed wealth creation as a path to salvation. For the poor, the regime's austerity measures led to immense hardship, with 12.5 percent unemployment and another 5.1 percent only minimally employed by 1979. Chileans were trained over time to look the other way and not care about what happened to enemies of the state, including professionals who became street vendors after being fired or denied bank loans for political reasons.[30]

Every strongman needs international partners, and Pinochet's included the British and American financial establishments as well as the

American government and Operation Condor juntas. Pinochet hid his money in British offshore tax havens from Hong Kong to Gibraltar and in secret accounts, many in his family's names, with Riggs Bank in America. A fortune eventually estimated at more than $50 million, much of it coming from kickbacks on foreign arms deals, bought him an extensive library. The family used his wife Lucia Hiriart's women's centers foundation, CEMA, as a cover for lucrative real estate operations—a prime example of the kind of "moral cleansing" Pinochet's coup achieved.[31]

—

GADDAFI WAS A SELF-MADE STRONGMAN, enjoying none of the American largesse of Pinochet and Mobutu. He did have plenty of oil, which prolongs authoritarians' time in power and gives them little incentive to democratize. Scholars call this the "resource curse"; Gaddafi called it a blessing from heaven. Oil revenues funded Libya's generous social welfare provisions while freeing Gaddafi from compromises poorer rulers made to lessen their chances of being overthrown, like tolerating traditional elites.[32] The rapid rise in per capita income (from $2,216 in 1969 to $10,000 in 1979) boosted his popularity as he took away rights and built his patronage networks. He transferred wealth and power from tribes favored under the monarchy to previously marginalized tribes like his Qadhadhfa and their allies the Warfalla. Both tribes became prominent in the army and security forces, while the military as an institution was stripped of much of its power. Gaddafi "knows what he wants. He knows how to get it. . . . Barring some accident or assassination, he's going to last," said Harold G. Josif, who lived through the early post-coup years as deputy chief of mission at the American embassy in Tripoli, speaking in 1999.[33]

Like other strongmen, Gaddafi governed through chaos. His ministers and other leaders learned about major policy decisions on the radio, were often fired or posted abroad for being too talented, and endured the drama when Gaddafi felt insulted and threatened to resign or disappeared in a huff into the desert. Yet the Libyan dictator went further than others, reconfiguring entire bureaucratic structures on a whim. Large agencies, mass organizations, or entire legal frameworks could suddenly be abolished. The philosopher Hannah Arendt wrote of Hitler that his will was "so unstable that compared with it the whims of Oriental despots are a shining example of steadfastness." This applies doubly to Gaddafi, who used psychological uncertainty and upheaval to gain compliance and limit opposition.[34]

In 1979, Gaddafi gave his people a strongman surprise, declaring that he was resigning from all formal government positions. In theory, he turned over power to the people, in accordance with his theory of the "stateless state." In practice, he now exercised control informally, giving him even more opportunity to steal with impunity. The Revolutionary Committees now entered the picture as paramilitary enforcers charged with rooting out corruption. People who supposedly possessed forbidden assets endured televised trials, with informers calling in to denounce them. "It appears that falling out of favor politically can trigger the discovery of improprieties in business dealings that might not otherwise come to public attention," wrote US State Department official Elizabeth Fritschle in 2006.[35]

"We should have been another Dubai," Libyans lamented, citing the oil wealth of their homeland. Instead, many struggled to make ends meet in a dysfunctional state. With productivity low and individual initiative absent (Gaddafi banned the practice of law and other private professions in 1980), bribery and nepotism proliferated within public administration. A handful of politically connected families had control over food distribution, leading to chronic shortages. Gaddafi's own family and favorites built up fortunes through bribery, extortion, and siphoning off profits from oil and oil subsidiaries. Stealing oil was a fast route to riches: 5 million barrels, worth $500 million, disappeared in 2008. Threats kept potential whistleblowers at the National Oil Company silent. The regime's last head of the Ministry for Inspection and Popular Control, tasked with investigating oil industry malpractice, was Huda "the Executioner" Ben Amer, one of Libya's richest and most corrupt women.[36]

None of this stopped the gold rush for Gaddafi's money that ensued during the "reconciliation" years with the West that propped up his regime for an extra decade. After 9/11, Gaddafi vowed he would avoid the fate of Iraq's Hussein, whose country was invaded in 2003 by American-led multinational forces. The Libyan leader renounced extraterritorial violence, dismantled weapons of mass destruction, and shared intelligence on jihadist networks with the CIA and other foreign government agencies. As sanctions and travel bans lifted, Western arms manufacturers and dealers vied to sell their wares to Gaddafi. American companies won eleven of fifteen bids opened in 2005, facilitated by the lobbying and public relations work done by the Livingston Group, the Monitor Group, and Brown Lloyd James. In 2007, British Petroleum returned to Libya after three decades' banishment with a $900 million exploration deal.[37]

In return, Gaddafi got precious legitimation by the democratic world. While being crowned "King of Kings" of Africa in 2008 was thrilling, hosting important supplicants like French president Nicolas Sarkozy and British prime minister Tony Blair was even better. So was using influential foreigners like Francis Fukuyama and Anthony Giddens as megaphones for the "reformed" Libya. Best of all was getting "his" bodies back by collaborating with foreign intelligence agencies. Multiple governments agreed to have anti-Gaddafi Islamist dissidents extradited to Libya, where they were imprisoned and tortured for years.[38]

Through it all, Gaddafi's hatred of the West never dimmed. When Blair visited Libya in 2004, the Libyan leader showed him the sole of his shoe (a big insult in the Arab world) while he took British money. When the Arab Spring came to Libya in 2011, his new friends would turn on him, agreeing to NATO strikes on his military. By then the man born to illiterate and poor parents was the wealthiest man in the world, the estimated $200 billion he accumulated besting the worth of the other three richest men on the planet combined (Bill Gates, Warren

Buffett, and Carlos Slim). And a new generation of corrupt leaders was in office, starting with Putin, whose own wealth reportedly already surpasses Gaddafi's.[39]

—

NEW AUTHORITARIANS SHARE their twentieth-century peers' drive for personal enrichment at the public's expense. One-party rule and mass killing are now less common, making twenty-first-century leaders more dependent on propaganda and censorship to cover up their thievery and incompetence. Populating government with the very rich, as Trump and Putin do, means that buying the silence of coconspirators is not as effective. *Kompromat*, the Russian word for gaining cooperation through the threat of loss (from exposure of real or fabricated wrongdoing) rather than the promise of material gain, now rules.[40] When the ruler himself is under investigation, governance becomes secondary to his attempt to escape prosecution. He domesticates the press and the judiciary and increases loyalty demands on his party to avoid leaks. He might have laws changed to accommodate his malfeasance or amend the Constitution to prolong his stay in office and retain his immunity.

The end of the Cold War brought greater international efforts to prevent corruption (previously excused for geopolitical reasons, as with Mobutu). Accountability organizations appeared, like Transparency International (founded in 1993). In 1997, the Organisation for Economic Co-operation and Development issued an Anti-Bribery Convention, followed by the 2003 United Nations Convention against Corruption. That didn't mean that corruption declined in the new authoritarian age. Two trends mark strongman kleptocracy in the twenty-first century. First is the illegal takeover by authoritarians of profitable businesses, often with the excuse of cleansing the state of enemy influences. The scale of this predation is staggering. Between July 2016 and January 2020, for example, Erdoğan seized $32.24 billion worth of assets, including thousands of hospitals, foundations, banks, and large companies.[41]

Second, leaders and their elite allies launder money through real estate investments and joint ventures abroad with legitimate partners. The release of the Panama Papers in 2016 shed light on vast networks of offshore finance that trace back to the inner circles of Gaddafi, Putin, and other leaders. Along with Great Britain, America enables money-laundering by allowing anonymously owned companies to be registered in tax havens like Delaware and Nevada. The landmark 2019 Maloney Bill forbids this practice in America going forward, but does not affect existing companies. It's likely that Russian money is part of the estimated $300 billion laundered in the United States every year.[42]

—

PUTIN LIKES TO REFER TO HIMSELF as a "specialist in human relations" who is skilled at "working with people," but his past working *on* people as a KGB case officer is more evident in his governing style. His system of managed conflict places oligarchs in competition for state resources and his favor, while reminding them that *kompromat* or prosecution can ruin them at any moment—which is why most keep capital, family, and properties abroad. "In the special world, everyone's wealth is deliberately tainted," as Fiona Hill and Clifford Gaddy observe. Putin's inner circle, composed largely of trusted associates from his Saint Petersburg days, heads Russia's biggest state-owned companies, populates the boards of private enterprise, takes Mobutu-style "loans" from state banks, and has license to plunder state companies through no-bid procurement, asset stripping, stock manipulation, and extortion. By 2019, 3 percent of the population held 89 percent of the country's financial assets.[43]

Not only do legal and illegal economies intertwine in Putin's Russia, but criminal methods have also been normalized as a means of getting business done. Corporate raids by elite predators are one example. The case of William Browder, an activist Gazprom director and British citizen, is well known. In 2007, Putin's allies raided Browder's investment company, Hermitage Capital, and arrested his employees on fabricated charges of tax evasion (Browder had been banned from Russia two years earlier). Browder's lawyer, Sergei Magnitsky, subsequently died in detention, but Putin's government still tried him and Browder and sentenced both in absentia to prison. From 2000 to 2010, the state targeted a shocking one-third of Russian businesses for raids. Many thousands of business owners went into exile, avoiding the fates of over 70,000 others who were jailed between 2002 and 2012 on technicalities or made-up charges of tax evasion and other crimes. By 2018, one in six Russian business owners faced prosecution—a handy way to "put away the competition," in Russia expert Karen Dawisha's words.[44]

The energy conglomerate Gazprom, which produces up to 80 percent of Russia's oil, was judged in 2014 by *Barron's* to be "The Worst Managed Company on the Planet." Anders Aslund and other analysts see Gazprom as "an organized crime syndicate." After raiding a number of companies owned by Putin's enemies (like Vladimir Gusinsky), it was itself stripped of many major assets by Putin-allied Bank Rossiya, which by 2010 controlled Gazprombank, Gazprom-Media, and more. An incredible $60 billion worth of assets were exfiltrated between 2004 and 2007. Predation, as well as the 2008 recession, contributed to Gazprom's market value decline from $369 billion in 2008 to $60 billion in 2019. A 2018 report coauthored by Sberbank CIB analysts Alex Fak and Anna Kotelnikova suggested that Gazprom was not inept but rather "performing as designed" in enriching Putin-connected contractors. The Kremlin did not appreciate such honesty, and Fak was fired.[45]

Expropriating Russia's wealth and imprisoning business owners to grab their assets, Putin treats the country he governs much like Mobutu treated Zaire, as an entity to be exploited for private gain. Putin poses as a nationalist defender against "globalists," but uses global finance to launder and hide his money. He and his associates have removed an estimated $325 billion from Russia since 2006. Some of that illicit wealth was likely cleaned with the help of the Trump Organization, given that Russian investors were its central revenue source at the time Trump decided to run for president. "We don't rely on American banks. We have all the funding we need from Russia," declared Eric Trump in 2014.[46]

———

IN 2003, FACING THE CHARGE that his holding company Fininvest paid a 500 million euro bribe to a Roman judge in 1991, Prime Minister Berlusconi went on one of his television networks to proclaim himself a victim of a "witch hunt." No other liberal democracy allowed heads of state to be judged by the courts, he falsely stated. In fact, Berlusconi had returned to office two years earlier with ten court cases proceeding against him, and Parliament had obligingly passed a law that gave a degree of immunity to the individuals holding the five highest positions in government. Throughout his time in office, dozens of *ad personam* measures made it easier for him to disobey the law without consequences. Berlusconi repeatedly escaped conviction for past actions and used delaying tactics to run out the clock on new ones.[47]

The vastness of Berlusconi's media and other holdings made it hard to police his mixing of personal and business interests. "No one has the right to ask me to entrust my patrimony to unknown persons," he told the center-left when they asked him to put his assets into a blind trust. He turned them over instead to his children and longtime loyalists. Berlusconi's right-hand man, Marcello Dell'Utri, who was a Forza Italia senator throughout his time in politics, was convicted in 2004 of the crime of "Mafia association," a judgment validated by the Italian Supreme Court in 2014. Unsurprisingly, the Anti-Corruption and Transparency Service, which Berlusconi partly controlled, had few resources and less power.[48]

Berlusconi's ability to saturate the media with claims of his innocence kept his base faithful to him personally, even as his legal troubles eroded the authority of his center-right coalition. His ministers were reduced to lackeys, and as accusations against him mounted, showing loyalty to Berlusconi by launching smear campaigns against his enemies in the judiciary and the press became a Forza Italia ritual. More than a third of Italians who voted for him in 2006 said they were motivated by loyalty to him as a leader rather than to his party—a testament to how the strongman's personalist rule ultimately harms his political enablers.[49]

Berlusconi had a devastating effect on civil society by normalizing corruption. In 1996, when Clean Hands and anti-Mafia sentiment still resonated, over 30 percent of Italian voters ranked corruption as among the very top issues they cared about. By 2008, only 0.2 percent ranked it that highly. In the Lombardy region, prosecution of corruption fell from 545 cases in 1996 to 43 in 2006. By 2008, corruption was back to 1980s levels, only now the legal and reputational consequences were far lighter.[50]

Berlusconi's alliances with autocrats also corroded Italian democracy. His relationship with Gaddafi reflected the tangled history of Italy and Libya that had continued in the postcolonial age. Italy was one of Libya's biggest arms vendors; Libya was Italy's largest oil supplier; and Gaddafi had a 7.2 percent ownership stake in Unicredit, Italy's largest bank. In 2004, the two leaders announced the longest underwater pipeline in the Mediterranean, reaching from the Libyan to the Sicilian coasts. The oil provisions in the 2009 Benghazi Treaty continued these arrangments. The Italian leader lost no occasion to pay Gaddafi homage, even kissing the dictator's hand at the 2010 Arab League meeting held in Libya. When contrasted with his insults of democratic leaders like Merkel and Obama, such actions spoke loudly to his loyalties.[51]

Berlusconi's sycophantic and secretive relationship with Putin also damaged his reputation, highlighting his lack of accountability as a leader. Putin had started the courtship, using his experience as a KGB case officer charged with grooming collaborators. In 2001, when *Newsweek* Moscow bureau chief Christian Caryl asked the new president what intelligence skills he found useful as a politician, Putin mentioned the art of creating "a dialogue, a contact; you have to activate everything that is the best in your partner." In the early 2000s, when Russia aspired to full membership in the North Atlantic Treaty Organization (NATO) and wanted foreign lenders to write off crippling loans, German chancellor Gerhard Schroeder and President George W. Bush had been his targets.[52]

Berlusconi wanted to raise Italy's profile within Euro-Atlantic foreign policy and be personally recognized as an international power broker. He was happy to help Putin cultivate Bush and to champion Russia's entry into the international system.[53] In May 2002, Berlusconi arranged a summit between Bush and Putin at the Italian military base Pratica di Mare to sign a document that symbolically ended the Cold War. The NATO-Russia Council that came out of the summit proved Berlusconi's worth to Putin, and a mutually beneficial friendship unfolded.[54]

By 2008–2009, when Ronald Spogli, the American ambassador to Rome, sounded the alarm about the Berlusconi-Putin relationship, the dynamic had changed. Putin's heightened imperialism abroad and repression at home required Berlusconi to take more extreme positions to defend him. In 2008, Russia bombed military and civilian targets in Georgia in support of the separatists in South Ossetia. Berlusconi blamed the United States, not Russia, for inflaming regional conflict. A few months earlier, during a joint press conference, the Russian journalist Natalia Melikova brought up a taboo subject: Putin's relationship with the former Olympic gymnast Alina Kabaeva. As an angry Putin stayed silent and cameras rolled, Berlusconi mimicked shooting Melikova, knowing that the acclaimed investigative journalist Anna Politkovskaya had been shot to death less than two years earlier. As Spogli concluded, Berlusconi's "overwhelming desire to stay in Putin's good graces" was "leading him to go where others dare not."[55] Partnering with authoritarians and elevating himself above the law with the full cooperation of his party, Berlusconi bent the institutions of Italian democracy to accommodate his personal circumstances. A decade later, Trump would follow suit.

—

"AS TIME WENT ON, IT BECAME CLEAR that the sickness was a feature, that everyone who entered the building became a little sick themselves" wrote the journalist Olivia Nuzzi in March 2018 of the Trump White House and those who serve it.[56] Coming into politics with decades of improper business practices behind him, Trump was highly skilled at corrupting others. He set the tone for his associates with his blatant use of the presidency to further Trump Organization businesses. Through the end of 2019, Trump had visited Trump properties on 331 out of 1,075 days in office, meaning that one-third of his time was devoted to self-enrichment rather than governing. Using Trump properties for fundraising events and meetings with foreign groups and heads of state earned his private businesses $1.6 million in the first six months of his presidency alone. The Trump International Hotel in Washington, DC, and his Palm Beach Mar-a-Lago compound, both popular choices for GOP and lobbyist gatherings, "reshaped the spending habits of the federal government, turning the President into a vendor" of his own brand, as the *Washington Post* concluded in 2019.[57]

As in other countries, the rise of authoritarianism in America has meant the end of accountability and ethical standards in government. Overall 100,000 civil servants left, retired, or were fired as Trump rid himself of experts and critics. Retired ambassador Nancy McEldowney compared the sweeping changes to a "hostile takeover and occupation." A new Trump-era civil service employment application eliminated questions about real estate holdings, finances, and professional references. This made it harder to discover conflicts of interest and easier to hire those who can corrupt others or won't object to administration practices. Only press vigilance halted the nomination of Sid Bowdidge for assistant secretary of energy. His background managing a Meineke Car Care establishment seemed fine to the White House until it leaked that he had called Muslims "maggots."[58] Scorn for the Hatch Act, which forbids government employees from engaging in certain forms of political activity, has been another sign of the new lawlessness. At least ten Trump administration officials, including his adviser Kellyanne Conway, violated it. "Let me know when the jail sentence starts" was Conway's sarcastic response to a reporter's question about the impropriety.[59]

In the strongman tradition, Trump has used divide-and-rule and bullying tactics to weed out government officials who won't conspire in his corruption and subversion of the rule of law. He fired acting attorney general Sally Yates, FBI director James Comey, acting FBI director Andrew McCabe, and many others for a perceived lack of "loyalty" (Trump's term for doing his bidding). His administration has had a record 68 percent turnover of high-level positions. What an anonymous official in his service called his "impetuous, adversarial, petty, and ineffective" leadership approach, full of reversals of policy decisions, obligations to sing his praises at meetings, and rage at anyone who opposes his will, is normal behavior for personalist rulers. Ritual humiliation of male subordinates trains underlings to adopt a survivalist mentality, pitting them against each other. "A culture of fealty compounds itself, conformists thrive and dissenters depart or refuse to join," the journalist Evan Osnos concluded.[60]

Trump's attorney general, William Barr, has been an ideal partner. Barr has covered up Trump's illegalities and enabled schemes meant to help the president's autocratic allies and harm his enemies. He mischaracterized the results of the Mueller investigation to the public and helped Turkish bank Halkbank avoid indictment for participation in a multibillion-dollar effort to evade Iranian sanctions after Erdoğan pressured Trump—typical work for the head of "justice" in a personalist state. Trump lawyer and spokesman Rudolph Giuliani, another loyalist, has traveled abroad as the president's private envoy to take care of business relating to the Trump-Putin relationship, just as Berlusconi's "bagman," Valentino Valentini, did earlier.[61]

The Trump cabinet appointees who have kept their jobs the longest have understood that furthering Putin's geopolitical aims is an administration priority. During his confirmation process, Commerce Secretary Wilbur Ross lied to government ethics officials about conflict of interest investments, not wanting to divest his share in Navigator Holdings, a shipping company co-owned by Putin's son-in-law.[62] In January 2019, Treasury Secretary Stephen Mnuchin lifted sanctions on Putin ally Oleg Deripaska. In April, Deripaska's company Rusal made a $200 million investment in the home state of Labor Secretary Elaine Chao's husband, Senate Majority Leader McConnell, another Putin supporter. In August 2019 and in June 2020, continuing Berlusconi's work, Trump called for Russia's readmission to the Group of Seven organization, even as Russian television has mocked Trump as a Putin supplicant.[63]

"Amoral leaders have a way of revealing the character of those around them," wrote former FBI head Comey of his experience working for Trump. By choosing to reveal Hillary Clinton's use of a private email server just before the 2016 election, Comey had an indirect role in Trump's ascent to power. Serving Trump, he saw firsthand the allure and danger of charismatic rulers. Comey stepped back and was fired for refusing to engage in improper actions on Trump's behalf. In a 2019 *New York Times* op-ed, Comey described corruption as a process. It starts with the act of staying silent in a meeting while his lies "wash over you, unchallenged," making you and others present into "co-conspirators." It continues with requests for public tributes and escalates to attacks on institutions, including the one you serve. With each compromise, you hope he will be satisfied, but he returns to ask for more. What he wants—what all strongmen want—is to make you his: "You use his language, praise his leadership, tout his commitment to values. And then you are lost. He has eaten your soul."[64]

EIGHT

VIOLENCE

—

"THE TORTURE TOOK PLACE DAILY," recalled Cristina Godoy-Navarrete, who was arrested by Pinochet's forces in 1974 as a student and opposition activist.

> We would be blindfolded, strapped to beds and then it would begin. There were electric shocks administered to all over our bodies, and then there would be a rape. . . . Instead of toilet paper we were given pages from books by writers and philosophers to use. The secret police wanted to show their contempt for ideas.

Godoy-Navarrete was one of tens of thousands subjected to excruciating treatment in those years as the junta unleashed its cleansing of Chilean society from leftists, suspect foreigners, and anyone associated with them.[1] "Torture in Chile is not isolated sadism but state policy," wrote Rose Styron in a 1975 report for Amnesty International. What Godoy-Navarrete endured when her interrogators took control of her physical body distills the strongman's need for total possession and his efforts to break the will of his people. Forty years earlier, the Belgian resister and Nazi captive Jean Améry had known this syndrome intimately. The torturer, he writes, acts as an "absolute sovereign," claiming "dominion over spirit and flesh." Torture was "not an accidental quality of this Third Reich, but its essence."[2]

The history of strongman states sits uneasily with Hannah Arendt's claim that "violence can destroy power; [but] it is utterly incapable of creating it." Communist and fascist regimes, which came out of World War I's routinized slaughter, made violence the central means and often the end of political struggle. Institutionalized violence creates new hierarchies and power structures, new heroes and martyrs, and new norms and expectations. It changes both those administering it and those on its receiving end. However they use it, strongmen give violence an instrumental as well as absolute value. They believe that not everyone is born equal, and most also feel that not everyone has the right to life. Some people must be sacrificed for the good of the nation, and others simply get in the way.[3]

The authoritarian ruler uses all of his tools to persuade his people to spy on, lock up, and slaughter their compatriots. Propaganda encourages everyone in the country to see violence differently: as a national and civic duty and the price of making the country great. Friedrich Tubach recalled the "emotional charge" young men felt at being encouraged to "give one's instincts free rein" in the service of constructing a "utopia based on ethnic solidarity." For maximum efficiency, violence and propaganda should work symbiotically, as in Gaddafi's televised executions. The cult of male force, which is communicated by state media and the leader's example, sets expectations for perpetrators' behavior. "This is a dictatorship! There are no human rights! . . . There is only Pinochet and us!" screamed a Chilean torturer at his victim.[4]

Corruption assists in recruiting enablers and accomplices of state persecution, whether police and military who operate on the streets or elites who confer in boardrooms and private clubs. In the middle are bureaucrats, scientists, and propagandists who take care of the ideology, logistics, and finances of persecution. Authoritarian states have always promoted individuals who are willing to experiment with repression as a way of reshaping the nation, like SS official Adolf Eichmann for fascist-era mass killing, DINA head Manuel Contreras for Cold War–era torture, and Erdoğan's justice minister Abdulhamit Gül and Trump immigration adviser Stephen Miller for new authoritarian mass detentions.

While many collaborators are zealots, the strongman games the decision to work with the state by promising material and other rewards for persecution. Amin made sure that the officers who oversaw his murders of over 300,000 people lived rent-free and received regular gifts of whisky and luxury goods flown in from London. Violence is at the heart of the authoritarian bargain between the leader and followers who relinquish rights in exchange for economic gain and power.[5]

The strongman's violence reveals his avariciousness for bodies and minds to control—the more the better. The psychological damage wrought by a culture of surveillance and threat lies at one end of the spectrum of harm, fostering subjection and self-policing. With informers everywhere, one offhand remark or joke can lead to imprisonment. An Italian man ordered around a pet rabbit named Mussolini in a restaurant in the late 1930s and in consequence served a year of confinement. From Franco's Spain, the philosopher José Ortega y Gasset reflected on how "the threat in my mind of an eventual violence, coercion, or sanction that other people are going to exercise against me" bred conformity. The historian George Mosse never forgot the low-level "terror" and hypervigilance he felt as a Jewish youth in Nazi Germany. And the German leftist Eugen Nerdinger wrote a poignant poem: "You sit in bed, listen to the night/ . . . Will they come today to get me?" Millions living in authoritarian states around the world, gripped by similar fears, have lain awake, fearing a knock on the door.[6]

Public acts of persecution help strongmen to normalize the punishment of targeted groups and maintain the buzz of anxiety. Some penalize the disobedient, as when Hitler Youth chased "racial defilers" (Aryans in relationships with Jews) through the streets. Others justify continued repression by showing that the enemy is still numerous and active, like Pinochet's military sweeps of poor areas. [7] The public humiliation of prominent male enemies reinforces cults of virility. Jewish doctors and lawyers were the guests of honor and the entertainment at SA-organized "scrubbing parties" in post-Anschluss Austria as they cleaned the streets on their hands and knees, surrounded by jeering crowds. In Kastoria, during the Fascist occupation of Greece (1941–1943), Italian soldiers forced a priest to masturbate in front of Greek civilians and pumped air into Greek soldiers' rectums. [8]

Authoritarian violence is readily identified with the confinement of enemies in penal colonies, prisons, and camps. As Mobutu reminded Westerners who criticized his human rights abuses, European imperial powers provided a template for such practices. The Belgian Congo, German Southwest Africa, and Italian Libya all had concentration camps for insurgents—the Nazis learned from all of these experiences. The global history of camps shows that most internees die from disease, overwork, or starvation rather than from execution. Extermination sites like the Nazis' Treblinka, which were designed to kill people rather than house them, are atypical. [9]

The torture practices used by strongman states have a similarly complex history. The Soviets contributed "the conveyer" technique involving prolonged sleep deprivation. But the French played a bigger role in torture's development, from their use of electric shock in 1930s French Vietnam to the brutalities of the Algerian War. Torturers from democratic France and Nazi Germany shared expertise with Latin American military juntas. French Gestapo torturer Christian Masuy claimed paternity of the common technique of the "bathtub," known as the *submarino* in Spain and Chile, where the head is repeatedly submerged in water. Captives have reported its use in Putin's prisons, together with its "dry" variant (*submarine seco*), which quasi-asphyxiates the victim with plastic bags over the head. The United States already used torture for domestic policing (the "electric chair" being a holdover). The US Army's School of the Americas, founded in the US Panama Canal zone in 1946, taught torture techniques to right-wing militants from around the world. [10]

"One is not born a torturer," remarked a former torturer. For one hundred years, the strongman has guided the societies he rules through a transformation of culture and morals that legitimates harming others. While the satisfaction of following orders is part of the appeal for collaborators, authoritarian states also attract individuals who thrive in situations where inhibitions can be freed. "Is it order or disorder?" Mussolini asked of Fascism in 1922. For a century of authoritarians and their supporters, the answer has been: both. Only too late do some realize that the destructive energies the leader unleashes can be turned against them. In the strongman's world, everyone, torturers included, can be discarded when his or her usefulness has ended.[11]

—

"THE FASCIST STATE IS WIDE AWAKE and has a will of its own," warned Mussolini in 1932, his statement likely resonating with millions of Italians for whom physical aggression and intimidation had become commonplace.[12] While the rest of his cabinet was a revolving door, Il Duce kept Arturo Bocchini on as head of the political police and the OVRA secret police and as manager of his sex procurement operation. From 1926 to Bocchini's death in 1940, Mussolini met with him daily. After slaughtering thousands of Italians during the years of squadrism, Mussolini sought to minimize mass killing at home to market Fascism as a more humane alternative to Nazism and Communism. Fascist propaganda emphasized that the regime's Special Tribunal, established in 1926 to try "enemies of the state," executed "only" a few dozen Italians, most of them of Slavic origin. This left out the killings in other circumstances of many thousands of other Italians and the more than 700,000 Libyans, Eritreans, Somalis, and Ethiopians murdered before World War II started. By targeting mainly non-Whites outside of Italy and not persecuting Jews until 1938, Mussolini cultivated an image that he was a benevolent Fascist—an impression Berlusconi and his center-right government perpetuated.[13]

Some of Mussolini's most violent actions remain little known, like the genocide of Bedouin and seminomadic peoples in the eastern Libya region of Cyrenaica in 1930–1931. Marshal Pietro Badoglio and General Rodolfo Graziani vowed to cut off civilian support to resisters of Italian occupation, "even if the entire population of Cyrenaica has to perish," in Badoglio's words. They deported 100,000 Bedouin and seminomads to sixteen concentration camps in the desert. Almost a third of them died, as did 80 to 90 percent of their livestock. "We lived surrounded by constant terror and death from hunger and thirst, sickness and hanging," recalled Jamila Sa'īd Sulaymān. The Danish journalist Knud Holmboe reported from Cyrenaica that the "land swam in blood." He asked a Bedouin internee what the Fascists aimed to achieve. "Allah alone knows. I believe they want us to die," the man responded.[14]

The industrial-scale violence that marked the Fascist occupation of Ethiopia (1935–1941) also remains unfamiliar to many. "I'd rather be criticized for excesses than for deficiencies," Mussolini told General Emilio De Bono, with the 1896 Italian defeat by Ethiopians at Adwa on his mind. He ordered the biggest military operation since World War I on the League of Nations member: ten divisions, 300,000 men, and aerial drops of hundreds of tons of illegal chemical weapons, all of which caused an estimated 250,000 Ethiopian deaths during and after the war.[15] The scope and tenacity of the Ethiopian resistance inspired the African diaspora, and exiled Ethiopian emperor Haile Selassie I made front-page news when he denounced "the deadly rain that fell from the aircraft" to the League of Nations. Yet Ethiopia's plight did not retain the interest of White Europeans focused on Hitler's rise. In 1935, exiled German writer Thomas Mann judged Nazi anti-Semitism as "far more horrible than Mussolini's campaign, which was perhaps forced on him by necessity."[16]

Inside Italy, a network of hundreds of penal colonies, prisons, and camps from Lampedusa to Trieste incarcerated 100,000 of Fascism's enemies, some of whom spent fifteen years or more behind bars. In 1926, the Communist leader Antonio Gramsci and hundreds of other anti-Fascists, shackled in the fetid hull of a ship, made the crossing from

Palermo to the island camp of Ustica. Gramsci stayed there less than six weeks before he was transferred to mainland jails, where he died of neglect and ill health in 1937. Those who remained on Ustica sometimes faced torture as well as deprivation. Inmates there also included Italians caught up in Fascism's social hygiene dragnet, like alcoholics, as well as dissident Libyan notables—including the brother and nephew of the future King Idris.[17]

The number of Italian political prisoners quadrupled starting in 1935 as expansion abroad brought a crackdown at home. With camps and penal colonies overcrowded, the regime sent more anti-Fascists into confinement in remote southern towns. Fascist officials visited Nazi camps like Dachau and Sachsenhausen to explore ways to scale up state repression.[18] Italian homosexuals felt the difference. Even under democracy, socially conservative Italy had none of Weimar Berlin's tolerance for gay life. When the Fascists took over, they were unwilling to admit that homosexuality existed and made no mention of it in their 1930 penal code. Before, the state had imprisoned gays for brief periods on charges like pederasty. Now they interned them to isolate them from the rest of society. A Florentine man named Guglielmo, who had been arrested thirteen times in as many years, was sent to a Sardinian labor colony in 1939. Many homosexuals were confined on San Domino, on the Tremiti islands, between 1938 and 1940. They had no running water, electricity, or toilet facilities, but some found a paradoxical freedom there: they could be openly gay at a time when "you couldn't even go out of the house, especially if you were *femmenella*," as a former internee recalled, referring to effeminate or female-identifying men.[19]

Mussolini's drive to mold collective behavior to facilitate state persecution of his enemies was embodied in his 1938 anti-Semitic legislation. As Foreign Minister Galeazzo Ciano noted in his diary, Il Duce wanted Italians to become "less '*simpatici*' so they can be tougher, implacable, odious." Italy had a tradition of Catholic anti-Judaic sentiment, but no Eastern European–style pogroms in its history. Mussolini launched an intensive propaganda campaign to prepare his people to see Jews as a threat to their well-being. "Shame on you!" Dina M. of Trieste wrote to the Italian leader in December 1938, denouncing his "mimicking" of the Nazis. Propagandists celebrated the expulsion of Jews from schools, publishing, and the civil service as cleansing Italy of a culture "led by Jews or by Jewish sympathizers . . . without countries, ideals, or traditions," as one official publication explained it. Italians besieged the Ministry of National Education with requests for Jews' former jobs.[20]

Making Jews into state enemies liberated Mussolini, who had tolerated Jews while he needed their support and to distinguish himself from Hitler. The Axis alliance made that moot. "Jewish pigs, I will kill them all," or at least imprison them, he confided to his lover Clara Petacci in October 1938. "I have penned up 70,000 Arabs, I can easily confine 50,000 Jews. I will build a little island and put them all there." That island never materialized, and neither did a Nazi plan to deport Jews to Madagascar. But once the war started, Mussolini sent Italian Jews to concentration camps in Italy and beyond.[21]

—

IN THE AREA OF REPRESSION, the speed and intensity of Hitler's efforts set him apart from Mussolini. After a 1934 purge of the SA that left hundreds dead, including SA leader Röhm, and over 1,000 imprisoned, Mussolini's Berlin intermediary, Major Giuseppe Renzetti, expressed disapproval of the Nazis' indiscriminate use of camps for its enemies. Dachau, which had opened in March 1933 and held thousands of prisoners, was less than 20 miles from Munich. It was a pity that Germany didn't have islands like the Italians, Renzetti told Mussolini, referring to Ustica and other penal colonies that allowed "dangerous elements" to be "removed from the community."[22]

Those who passed through the gates of Nazi concentration camps certainly felt cut off from society. They entered a world where humanitarian values, like solidarity with others, were liabilities. Arendt contended that murderers were among the most likely to survive in the camps, not least because the Nazis promoted criminals to be kapos in charge of disciplining their fellow prisoners. Criminals proved to be some of the Nazis' best torturers, since they were "highly imaginative when it came to pain," in the political scientist Darius Rejali's words. Extermination camps like Chelmno and Belzec accounted for just six of more than 40,000 camps and other captivity sites through which 15 to 20 million people passed between 1933 and 1945.[23]

Dachau, the Reich's first concentration camp, became its model non-extermination site. It first held political enemies, then expanded to include Jehovah's Witnesses, Jews, and "asocial" and "work-averse" people, like vagrants, prostitutes, alcoholics, homosexuals, and criminals. Dachau pioneered the use of of psychological humiliation, labor, and physical brutality to disintegrate the prisoner's sense of self. Adolf Eichmann, an architect of the Holocaust, started his career there. When the Communist Hans Beimler entered Dachau in April 1933, the sign he was forced to wear ("A hearty welcome!") foreshadowed the perversity. His SS captors beat him so severely that he saw strips of his skin hanging from his tormentor's whip. He received multiple invitations to hang himself, with nooses conveniently placed in his cell. Beimler escaped and sent his torturers a postcard from Moscow, but many others took his place over the next twelve years.[24]

Many German Jews tried in vain to leave Germany as the dictatorship subjected them to public humiliation and violence. Some, like the linguist Victor Klemperer, had no viable job offers abroad. Klemperer's famous cousin Otto Klemperer, who became the conductor of the Los Angeles Philharmonic, had better luck. Other Jews thought that each persecutory measure would be the last. The strict immigration quotas of many countries meant that 300,000 Jews were still in Germany when the November 1938 Kristallnacht pogrom began.[25]

"For once the Jews should feel the rage of the people," wrote Goebbels in his diary during those days. News of the shooting of Ernst vom Rath, an official at the German embassy in Paris, had sparked popular violence that the Nazi leadership encouraged; 1,000 synagogues and prayer spaces and 7,500 shops and private homes were ransacked, burned, and looted. For non-Jews, life went on as usual. Students at one school watched as a nearby synagogue burned and the SA formed a human chain around it so fire brigades could not intervene. "And now back to our lesson," said the teacher after a few minutes, resuming her lecture on ancient history.[26]

—

BY 1938, A THIRD RULER, FRANCO, was making his own contribution to the history of fascist violence. During the Spanish Civil War, Franco deployed colonial warfare measures for the first time against a European adversary. Both Hitler and Mussolini sent troops to Spain to support Franco's Nationalists. Il Duce refused Franco's requests for chemical weapons so the Spaniard could kill large numbers of Republican fighters quickly, as the Italians had done with Ethiopians. So Franco brought his Army of Africa from Morocco to Spain to help execute a "radical cleansing" that entailed purging each foot of Republican-held territory before moving on. By 1940, 250,000 Spaniards were dead, 300,000 in exile, and 600,000 prisoners held in concentration camps. The Nationalists also previewed practices used by the Nazis on the Eastern Front during World War II, like throwing those they executed into giant pits that held up to 1,000 bodies.[27]

Spain stayed out of World War II, largely because Hitler found Franco's territorial demands in Morocco unreasonable. Franco sent a volunteer "Blue Division" to fight in Russia, but concentrated on consolidating his power at home. Between 1940 and 1945, he executed another 50,000 Spanish leftists and kept hundreds of thousands of them in prison. Another 200,000 Spaniards also starved in the countryside: Franco's scorched earth policies during the Spanish Civil War had caused agricultural and environmental disaster.[28]

Elsewhere in Europe, Franco's fellow fascists pursued policies of mass murder. Yugoslavia, which was partitioned by Italy and Germany in 1941, was decimated. In the Italian zone, twenty years of anti-Slavic propaganda and persecution culminated in executions and confinements that killed an estimated 250,000 people between 1941 and 1943. Echoes of the mass deportation and genocide of Libyans accompanied the Italian military's relocations of entire populations of Slovenians, Croats, and Serbs to concentration camps. In one, on the island of Rab, thousands of Slovene prisoners starved to death. Those taken to camps inside Italy often fared no better. "I found them lying in desperation on the bare ground . . . with the mark of death on their faces," said a visitor of the prisoners he saw in Monigo concentration camp on the outskirts of Treviso.[29]

In Eastern Europe, Hitler tested out his own application of imperial methods of repression. Since the 1920s he had believed that expanding eastward on the continent was Germany's destiny. In 1941, the year the Nazis invaded the Soviet Union, the jurist Carl Schmitt justified Germany's colonization of a space "without masters, uncivilized or only semi-civilized" as a means for the nation to get the food and resources it needed. For the Nazis, this was no ordinary conflict, but rather a fight for the survival of White European civilization. The annihilation of tens of millions of Jews and Slavs, both combatants and civilians, was built into this plan.[30]

It started with the Nazi occupation of Poland in September 1939. Years of propaganda helped German troops there to follow Hitler's orders to "close your hearts to pity." "Most of them could have been taken straight out of *Der Stürmer*," wrote the soldier Friedrich M. to his wife about the Jews he saw, referring to a popular anti-Semitic publication. Civilians sometimes did the German military's jobs for them. On July 10, 1941, the Christian inhabitants of the town of Jedwabne, bearing iron bars and axes, killed the Jewish half of the population, toddlers included. Many non-Jewish Poles survived by working for the Germans. Karol Wojtyla, the future Pope John Paul II, labored in a chemical factory and a quarry.[31]

The June 1941 Nazi invasion of Russia, which violated the Molotov-Ribbentrop nonaggression pact signed two years earlier, brought a showdown between the most violent regimes of the era. "Do not count days. . . . Count only the number of Germans killed by you," read a booklet the Red Army gave to Soviet troops. "Fight energetically" and show no mercy, German High Command told its soldiers as they killed and deported Soviet fighters and Jews. By November 1941, SS *Einsatzgruppen* special forces had murdered 500,000 Jewish civilians. The scale of destruction led one German official to wonder who would be left alive to serve as a labor force when peace arrived—not the 3 million Soviet POWs who starved in Nazi camps by 1945.[32]

Nazism had always held out the prospect of material gain as an incentive for participating in the state's persecutions of its enemies. This mattered even more when the goal was annihilation. In Poland and other Reich territories, the expropriation of assets brought opportunities for profiteering. By June 1941, the Nazis had seized half of Poland's businesses and a third of its large estates and had stripped churches and museums of valuables. Hitler's lawyer Hans Frank, now appointed Gauleiter of Poland, modeled the rewards of complicity. He seized Count Alfred Potocki's summer estate in Krzeszowice, decorating it and other properties he claimed with looted artwork by Leonardo da Vinci and Canaletto.[33]

Corpses, not art, enticed the anatomist Hermann Voss, dean of the Department of Medicine at Reich University of Posen. In July 1941, the Gestapo agreed to supply him with the bodies of Polish resistance fighters. "So many people are executed that there are enough for all three institutes," he wrote in his diary. Voss's side business selling skulls and skeletons also prospered, and his mood was excellent as he sat one day in April 1942 "right under the roof on our 'bone whitener,' soaking up the sun. To my right and left, Polish bones lay bleaching, occasionally giving off a slight snapping sound."[34]

Hitler's secretary in Ukraine, Christa Schroeder, also saw the East as a space with "enormous opportunity for development." She was one of many German women who found jobs in the Nazi empire as military support staff, nurses, and teachers. And another 3,500 women, some with criminal records, served as guards in camps like Auschwitz-Birkenau, drawn by the good pay and the appeal of having power. Others evaluated kidnapped Aryan-looking Polish or Ukrainian children for adoption by German families. German women and men benefited from participation in the Nazi racial hygiene and war machine.[35]

The mechanization of violence that distinguished the death factories of the Holocaust reflected years of experimentation with a strongman problem: how to kill and dispose of vast numbers of people quickly. The specially constructed facility in Buchenwald that allowed 8,500 prisoners to die each from a single shot to the neck was one result of an "authorization to invent," in the historian Raul Hilberg's words, that drove the "final solution" forward.[36] While far more Nazi victims died of shooting and starvation than gassing, gas chambers and crematoria were Hitler's contributions to a menu of authoritarian mass violence that included camps, executions, and aerial launches of chemical weapons. In 1941, 850 Soviet POWs and Poles served as testers for the effects of Zyklon B gas. While the crematoria were being built, vans based at Chelmno camp gassed Jews while en route to the body disposal site, for extra efficiency. SS official Walter Rauff, in charge of the vans, noted that 97,000 people had been "processed" in between January and June 1942. The four gas chambers that operated at Auschwitz-Birkenau as of 1942 could kill 2,000 at a time and 1.6 million a year.[37]

Whatever methods they used, the Nazis justified their violence as defensive in nature. "We must exterminate them or they will exterminate us," wrote Voss of the Poles whose bones he needed. To prevent unworthy lives from being born, sterilizations of mixed-race Germans continued during the war. Doris Reiprich, born to a Prussian mother and a Cameroonian father, cried so much on the way to her appointment at the clinic in 1943 that a guard let her go, and she later had two children. The Nazis showed no such mercy to the mentally and physically disabled and the terminally ill that they targeted for euthanasia. During the war, about 250,000 people, most of them German Christians, were killed by lethal injection, starvation, or gassing. Euthanasia, also known as Operation

T4, tested killing methods and trained personnel for the Holocaust: SS officer Franz Suchomel worked at the Berlin T4 center before transferring to Treblinka.[38]

Whether on Rab or in Mauthausen, fascist camps were designed to remove hope and solidarity among captives and obliterate their humanity. "Here there is no why," the Italian Jewish chemist Primo Levi discovered while in Auschwitz-Birkenau. "Here the struggle to survive is without respite, because everyone is desperately and ferociously alone." While the gas chambers ceased operation in 1945, fascist violence lived on, its marks remaining on survivors' minds and bodies. Italian and German perpetrators retained its techniques, plying their trade in Franco's Spain, in the Middle East, and in Latin America in the age of military coups.[39]

—

THE NATIONAL STADIUM, 38 Calle Londres, Tejas Verdes, Tres Álamos: these places map Nieves Ayress Moreno's imprisonment at the hands of the Chilean dictatorship. A twenty-three-year-old university student from a leftist family, Ayress joined thousands who were arrested in the wake of the September 1973 coup and held in the Santiago stadium. The beatings and electric shocks she endured during those two weeks were the prelude to a forty-month captivity that began in January 1974. Her experiences reveal how the junta's methods of violence related to its larger social and political goals: cleansing Chilean society of leftist influence and making Chile a center of the international struggle against Marxism—a fascist battle given new life by the Cold War.

"This is so you feel the Empire," Ayress's torturers shouted, referring to the force of the state and feeling omnipotent as they violated her with sticks and Coca-Cola bottles. At 38 Calle Londres in Santiago, solitary confinement alternated with beatings, electric shocks in her vagina and eyes, and rapes. Other experiences were designed to destroy her psychologically, such as watching her father and brother be tortured. In February 1974, Ayress was moved to Teja Verdes detention center on the coast, which future DINA secret police head Manuel Contreras had set up as a torture-training site. Sometimes she could hear Brazilians, Argentinians, or other foreigners in the room as the Chileans put rats and spiders in her vagina. Once, when her blindfold was loose, she saw a "German woman" who ordered a dog to violate her. When she became pregnant from being raped by her soldier captors, a gynecologist told her she should be proud of carrying a "son of the Patria." Her battered uterus soon spontaneously aborted. "One is no longer more than a body, a sack of flesh, a side of meat," Ayress later wrote.[40]

Several vectors converged to create the climate of terror that marked Pinochet's regime. The culture of violence in Cold War Latin America shaped events in Chile. Cold War national security doctrines saw fighting Communism as a transnational endeavor. Operation Condor, the intelligence, policing, and terror consortium set up by Pinochet in Paraguay, Uruguay, Brazil, Argentina, Bolivia, and Chile in the mid-1970s, put this credo into practice. The foreigners present at Ayress's torture sessions came out of the Condor matrix. So did the Brazilians who trained Chilean officials at the National Stadium. An international group of soldier-students from right-wing juntas, including Contreras, also learned torture and psychological warfare at the School of the Americas.[41]

One of the trainees at the School of the Americas was Miguel Krassnoff Martchenko, a Chilean military official and DINA agent who became an interrogator at the Villa Grimaldi detention site. In 1973, he arrested and tortured S., a twenty-three-year old leftist student. Krassnoff's blend of formality and ferocity stayed with S. years after. The elaborate politeness Krassnoff showed to S.'s mother in taking him away; the punctilious attention to bureaucratic procedure; and then, in the torture space, the unleashing of an assault on the mind and body meant to create a sense of total abjection. Krassnoff showed S. how "states of exception can be normalized in people," creating individuals who see the violence they inflict as righteous and purifying.[42]

The culture of DINA, created in June 1974 as a secret police agency, encouraged such personal transformations. As Mussolini had done with

Bocchini, Pinochet met daily with DINA head Contreras, who hired military, police, and civilians who took orders well but also thrived on transgression. Neo-Nazis who lived in Chile's large German community understood this mix of law and order and lawlessness, and the long-standing relationship of the Chilean and German militaries helped with recruiting. Former SS official and gassing expert Walter Rauff became a DINA adviser. Paul Schäfer's German settlement Colonia Dignidad became a DINA torture center and an important gathering place for neo-Nazis.[43]

Ingrid Olderock, Ayress's "German" torturer, came from this milieu. Born in Chile to German immigrants, the *carabinera* was Latin America's first female parachutist and a proud Nazi who admired Auschwitz-Birkenau guard Irma Grese. She drew on her talents as a prizewinning dog trainer when she headed DINA's female agent division. "I am an adventurer," she told a Chilean magazine, and in the mid-1970s she experimented with her dog in the junta's torture rooms. "Nothing prepared me for what happened," said Alejandra Holzapfel, a member of the Revolutionary Movement of the Left (MIR) who was tortured by Olderock in Venda Sexy, a detention center that specialized in sexual violence, where loud music played to hide the victims' screams.[44]

Foreign terrorists also worked for DINA, from Italian neo-Fascists like Stefano Delle Chiaie to the American Michael Townley, who grew up in Santiago as the son of the head of Ford Motor Company's Chilean operation. Townley and his wife, the Chilean Mariana Callejas, also a DINA agent, raised their children in a Santiago villa. The guests that attended their literary salon had no idea that Townley and a chemist made sarin gas, for use against the regime's enemies, in a DINA laboratory on the premises.[45] In September 1974, Pinochet tapped Townley for the DINA's first extraterritorial operation. Townley traveled to Argentina to plant a bomb under the car of Pinochet's former superior, General Carlos Prats, who was criticizing Pinochet from his Buenos Aires exile. The blast killed Prats and his wife, Sofia Cuthbert, instantly.[46]

By 1976, with his power absolute at home, his American backing secure, and Operation Condor in full swing, Pinochet felt invincible. Now he and Contreras wanted to assassinate the exiled Socialist economist and politician Orlando Letelier. A former minister of Allende's government, Letelier was mobilizing international opinion against the junta from Washington, DC. Pinochet had complained about Letelier to Kissinger when the latter came to Santiago in June 1976. Two weeks later, DINA received the order to come up with a plan. Townley wanted to use a sarin gas spray, but when he tested it on his usual guinea pigs—two Peruvian prisoners—he almost died along with them. The car bomb that detonated on September 21, 1976, in the American capital killed Letelier and a colleague, Ronni Karpen Moffitt, and injured Moffitt's husband.[47]

Pinochet's strike on his American patrons' center of power backfired. President Jimmy Carter cut off military and other aid, and a 1978 CIA report confirmed, "President Pinochet personally ordered his intelligence chief to carry out the murders." To save himself, Pinochet forced Contreras to resign and chose Contreras's rival, Odlanier Mena, to head the National Center for Information that replaced DINA. Ingrid Olderock was reassigned to a desk job, and Miguel Krassnoff took up a position in intelligence. By 1978, Villa Grimaldi and other torture sites were shuttered or transformed.[48]

Such changes were mostly cosmetic. President Reagan restored aid to Chile when he took office, and the growth of nonviolent protest and leftist armed attacks increased the junta's violence. Olderock did torture jobs privately for the government in these years. Her canine specialization fit with the preference for torture methods that gave human rights investigators less evidence. The junta had always tried to erase memories of its abuses. In 1975, it hired a hypnotist to try to make the British doctor Sheila Cassidy forget her torture for giving medical aid to leftists. A 1978 amnesty pardoned "concealers" as well as "authors" and "accomplices" of crimes committed since the coup. This sanctioned the removal of human rights abuses from military and police service records. The dead had a way of haunting the living, though. "The disappeared are driving me crazy. I don't believe they exist," said Supreme Court president Israel

Bórquez, who denied American requests to extradite Contreras for the Letelier killing.[49]

Survivors of the junta's violence became bearers of memories it wanted buried. This was the case with Nieves Ayress, who was released in 1976 after her mother, Virginia Moreno, brought her case to international attention. Expelled from Chile, Ayress told Amnesty International and other organizations her story and went to Cuba, where doctors reconstructed her uterus and gave her psychological therapy. The scars and pain remained after she settled in New York City in the mid 1980s, but she had a daughter, Rosita, with her Chilean husband Victor Toro, also a torture victim. Ayress's testimonies proclaimed the power of individual memory over the junta's politics of oblivion. Rosita's birth celebrated something more intimate: the state's failure to destroy her body and prevent her from giving life to another. "Here I am and here is my daughter" was her message to her persecutors from America as Pinochet's regime continued.[50]

———

THE AGE OF MILITARY COUPS was an age of extremism, and Gaddafi, like Pinochet, adopted terrorist methods in the early 1980s to eliminate exiled Libyan dissenters. The lawyer Mahmoud Nafa and the BBC journalist Mohammed Mustafa Ramadan were murdered in London; businessman Mohamed Salem Rtemi was shot dead in Rome; and Faisal Zagallai, a Colorado State University graduate student, was shot in his home (he survived). Hisham Matar, son of the opposition leader Jaballa Matar, attended his English boarding school under an assumed name, and his brother Ziad had to flee his school in Switzerland to escape Gaddafi's killers.[51]

The Libyan revolution was "a moving train. Whoever stands in its way will be crushed," said Gaddafi. The Revolutionary Committees were its engines. Over the 1980s, the committees grew into a paramilitary of 3,000 to 5,000. They infiltrated state institutions and business, controlled the media, and had their own courts to enforce revolutionary law. They took people to prison or to Gaddafi's sex dungeons and interrogated them on television. They hanged students on the gates of universities or in front of the Fascist-built Benghazi Cathedral, reminding some Libyans of Mussolini's methods. They staffed Libyan embassies, renamed "People's Bureaus," for access to assassination targets abroad. In 1984, one of them shot from the Libyan embassy in London into a crowd of Libyan protesters, killing a British police officer, Yvonne Fletcher.[52]

Just as Pinochet saw Operation Condor as a transnational effort to save civilization by exterminating the left, so did Gaddafi view terrorism as a means of creating an anti-imperialist, anti-Zionist world. He bankrolled a dizzying array of movements, including the Japanese and Italian Red Brigades, the Nicaraguan Sandinistas, the Abu Nidal Organization, and revolutionaries who aimed to topple Mobutu and Pinochet. In 1985–1986, his hand was seen in terrorist attacks at the Rome and Vienna airports, in a nightclub in West Berlin, and in the hijacking of the *Achille Lauro* cruise ship. He also sponsored camps in Libya that trained thousands of fighters for such actions. His World Revolutionary Center was his version of the School of the Americas.[53]

Like Pinochet, Gaddafi came to feel invincible. Unlike Pinochet, his country was on America's list of terrorist nations. In 1986, the United States surprised him by bombing his Bab al-Azizia compound and other sites. The trade bans, sanctions, and Libyan asset freezes that followed fueled his politics of victimhood, which further increased when Libya was held responsible for the 1988 explosion of a Pan American flight over Lockerbie, Scotland. Worried about rising internal dissent, Gaddafi turned on the Revolutionary Committees, attacking them for their violent excesses and diminishing their power. They now focused on repressing Islamists, a category that could include anyone who wore a beard and practiced Islam openly. "Going to the mosque was the route to prison," said Abu Farsan, a member of an Islamist resistance movement who went into exile in 1990.[54]

For most Libyan dissenters, prison meant Abu Salim, the forbidding fortress in Tripoli. Many Libyans had a friend or family member locked up there. Hisham Matar's cousin Ali spent twenty-one years in Abu Salim. The speakers in his cell blared propaganda songs and speeches from 6 a.m. to midnight so loudly "you could feel your muscles vibrate." Anwar Haraga had just returned from years in England studying computer engineering when the security services came for him in 1989. His beard and traditional clothing, tolerated abroad, were heresy in Libya. Haraga was still in Abu Salim in 1996 when a prisoner revolt over the awful conditions led to the massacre of 1,200 of the 1,600 to 1,700 inmates there. He survived because the keys the insurgents took from the guard would not unlock his cellblock, but he heard the others executed. The regime refused to release information about the prisoners it killed, and the disappeared of Abu Salim caused yet more popular hostility to Gaddafi as his rule dragged into the twenty-first century.[55]

—

"I SAW ALL MY LOVED ONES BEFORE MY EYES—I thought they were going to kill me," said Tolga (speaking under an assumed name) of the Turkish secret police that kidnapped him in Ankara in 2017 and subjected him to torture and threats of rape. Tolga worked for an institution in Turkey affiliated with Gülen, the cleric in exile in Pennsylvania accused by Erdoğan of planning the 2016 coup. Upon his release, Tolga left the country, but living abroad is no guarantee of safety. Erdoğan recalls Gaddafi's single-mindedness in pursuing his enemies. Those dissident Turks are *his* bodies to reclaim. "No matter where they run or how much they run, we will go after them," Erdoğan said of Gülen's supporters in 2018. At least eighty Turkish citizens have been abducted from more than eighteen countries over the last few years.[56]

Gaddafi's agents killed the "stray dogs" they found, whereas Erdoğan's agents jail many and assassinate relatively few. In the social media age, mass killing can easily generate bad press. New authoritarians like the Turkish president tend to warehouse enemies outside of public scrutiny.

They use targeted violence, information manipulation, and legal harassment to neutralize dissenters. They also attempt to impoverish them by expropriating any businesses they or their relatives might own. Each ruler finds his own formula, gauging the tolerance of elites and the public for violence. National traditions of detention and histories of repression also factor in.[57]

—

"THERE ARE THREE WAYS OF INFLUENCING A PERSON: blackmail, vodka, or the threat of murder," said Putin in 2000, reminding Russians of his days as a KGB case officer and former FSB head. All three methods have featured in his style of rule, although his government has often passed from threat to action, using Soviet-style political murder and torture, imprisonment, and poisoning against those who expose his crimes. The journalist Anna Politkovskaya was among these. She made fifty trips to Chechnya, covering human rights abuses during Putin's "dirty war" there. After a failed FSB attempt to poison her on an airplane, in 2006 she was shot in the elevator of her apartment building, becoming one of dozens of reporters killed for uncovering information Putin wanted buried.[58]

From the 1924 murder of anti-Fascist Giacomo Matteotti onward, exposing a strongman's corruption has been an exceedingly dangerous enterprise. In 2011, Boris Nemtsov of the People's Freedom Party, Olga Shorina of Russian Solidarnost, and others published the report "Putin. Corruption," which detailed how Putin and Medvedev stole from Russia. In 2013, Nemtsov testified before the US Senate Foreign Relations Committee. In 2014, he denounced the fraud and embezzlement of up to $50 billion in funds approved for that year's Sochi Olympics. In 2015, he was assassinated on the Bolshoy Moskvoretsky Bridge near the Kremlin, its cameras and patrols conveniently deactivated as he crossed.[59]

The ghosts of Communist repression haunt Putin's carceral system. Its more than 869 penal colonies, 8 prisons and 315 remand centers bring the "Gulag Archipelago" mapped by writer and historian Aleksandr Solzhenitsyn into the twenty-first century. In 2012, Nadezhda Tolokonnikova, a member of the feminist performance collective Pussy Riot, was sentenced to two years' imprisonment for "hooliganism." Sent to a Soviet-era camp in Mordovia, she was made to work 16 to 17 hours a day. After she exposed this forced labor through a smuggled-out letter, in 2013 she was transferred to a Siberian penal colony. Another prisoner, Ildar Dadin, in jail since 2015 for repeatedly standing alone holding a protest sign, has been a victim of torture. The number of political prisoners, who include Jehovah's Witnesses, in the Nazi tradition, is growing. There were 246 in 2019, up from 46 in 2015, although these numbers are likely much higher. Being a state enemy in Putin's Russia means cycling in and out of imprisonment, enduring journeys of up to a month in cattle-car-like conditions to reach remote captivity sites, and knowing that any sip of tea could be your last.[60]

Poisoning is Putin's signature mode of violence. The Russian leader has relied on this bloodless method that often kills on a time delay. Poisonings abroad are for Putin what shootings were for Gaddafi: advertisements of the state's ability to reach enemies anywhere. Alexander Litvinenko, a former FSB agent turned whistleblower, died after ingesting polonium-210-laced tea in London in 2006. In 2018, former Russian-UK double agent Sergei Skripal and his daughter Yulia survived poisoning with a nerve agent in Salisbury. Putin also poisons his adversaries in Russia, especially those who damage his reputation abroad. Vladimir Kara-Murza testified to the US Congress in 2012 and 2015 and to the Senate in 2017 about Putin's human rights abuses and corruption. He survived two lethal poisonings in 2015 and 2017. Anti-corruption crusader and politician Alexei Navalny received a "warning" dose of poison while in prison during the 2019 anti-government protests. He had already spent over three months total in prisons and penal colonies in 2017–2018 on fabricated charges of financial crime. "Putin is a serial killer. Western leaders should know that when they shake hands with Putin, they shake hands with a murderer" is Russian activist Leonid Martynyuk's take.[61]

Trump is not among those who see that as a problem. Two weeks into his presidency and days after Kara-Murza's second poisoning, Trump expressed his respect for Putin on Fox News. When host Bill O'Reilly reminded him that Putin was "a killer," Trump replied: "We've got a lot of killers. What, you think our country's so innocent?" The relativizing reasoning previewed Trump's own application of the authoritarian play-book, which presents the leader's measures against his enemies as necessary and justified.[62]

—

"I'D LIKE TO PUNCH HIM IN THE FACE," said Trump of a heckler at a February 2016 campaign rally in Las Vegas. "In the old days," protesters would be "carried out on stretchers," Trump continued, but "we're not allowed to push back anymore." In the tradition of the fascists, Trump uses his rallies to train his followers to see violence in a positive light. His speech in Las Vegas modeled an America where the press is penned up and anyone who criticizes the leader deserves a beating. Hate crimes have increased annually since Trump's arrival on the political scene, starting with a 17 percent jump between 2016 and 2017. A study by political scientists showed a 226 percent increase in hate crimes in counties that hosted a Trump rally in 2016.[63]

Like past strongmen, Trump used propaganda, corruption, and the cult of male force to create a climate favorable to persecution. Latino migrants, a main enemy, have been branded as a demographic and racial threat to American purity. His policies of mass incarceration have been in line with American traditions—the United States is the world's biggest jailer—and have drawn on practices inherited from previous administrations. Yet Trump's anti-immigrant crusade has gone much further. Of the approximately 400,000 people who spent time in Immigration and Customs Enforcement (ICE) custody in 2018, 70 percent had no criminal record (a change from previous administrations' policies). Racism, rather than crime prevention, has driven his policies. "Trump is building a deportation machine," charged Congress's Hispanic Caucus in August 2019.[64]

Trump used repetition and other propaganda techniques to guide the public to see his treatment of immigrants as necessary for the nation's safety. At sixty-four rallies held between February 2017 and August 2019, he mentioned immigrants more than 500 times, labeling them as criminals (189 mentions), killers (32), and predators (31). A blitz of 2,199 Facebook ads appeared between January and August 2019 warning of the consequences of an immigrant "invasion." This message apparently resonated with White nationalist Patrick Crusius, whose Facebook page featured Trump anti-immigrant slogans. On August 2, 2019, Crusius opened fire on a Latino-frequented El Paso Walmart, murdering twenty-one people and injuring dozens. "This is a response to the Hispanic invasion," his manifesto stated.[65]

The Department of Homeland Security, which oversees immigration policy, has become a haven for ideologues that take their cues from Trump adviser Stephen Miller. He is a quiet extremist—the most dangerous kind—who works behind the scenes. Miller promoted the "zero tolerance" policy in force for six months in 2018 and continuing unofficially, which made family separations at the border state policy. He has tried to remove immigrant children from schools, repeating fascist treatment of Jews. Customs and Border Protection (CBP) agents have echoed Nazi camp procedures in telling parents that their children are being taken away to have a "bath," then imprisoning or deporting the parents.[66] The unwashed children may be placed in detention centers. Or they might be assigned to Evangelical Christian adoption agencies like Bethany Child Services, a company long supported by Trump education secretary Betsy DeVos's family. Some adoption agencies make an effort to reunite the children with their families. Yet the scale of these forced separations—almost 70,000 in 2019—brings Trump's practices in line with states like Hitler's Germany and Pinochet's Chile, where children were taken from Jewish, leftist, and indigenous parents to be raised by more "appropriate" individuals.[67]

The ICE agents that round up migrants increasingly appear in neighborhoods in SWAT team formations, in full tactical gear. CBP agents, who operate within a 100-mile radius of the border, also see themselves as soldiers, and some refer to migrants as their "prisoners of war." Many treat their facilities as spaces of exception from professional and ethical norms. While drug smuggling among CBP agents was not uncommon during the Bush and Obama administrations, the demonization of migrants by Trump and his government has encouraged new levels of cruelty, such as the denial of visas to victims of sex trafficking. "Border Patrol is designed and made for someone like Donald Trump," says Jenn Budd, a former CBP officer who watched her peers embrace extremist ideas that since 2016 have received White House benediction. In America, too, many people have lain awake at night, fearing that state agents will bang on the door.[68]

It may seem overblown to compare Trump's detention spaces to those of other strongman regimes, but the similarities and differences are revealing. Prisoners in Nazi work camps like Moringen had mattresses or barracks and access to washrooms. Those in Trump's detention spaces often have been unable to wash and have slept on the ground, as in the Homestead, Florida, facility operated for the Department of Homeland Security by the private for-profit company Caliburn. Citing freezing temperatures, 24-hour lights, and lack of hygiene and medical care, Dr. Dolly Lucio Sevier compared conditions in camps in Clint and McAllen, Texas, to those of "torture facilities." The combined effects of disease (internees are denied flu vaccines), lack of food, water, and physical and sexual abuse led to at least seven child deaths in the first five months of 2019.[69] Extreme crowding, another staple of concentration camp abuse, featured in the reports of the inspector generals of Rio Grande and El Paso del Norte, both in Texas. In immigration processing centers there, adults were held in "standing-room only conditions for a week," and cells were so crowded that "adults had to stand on the toilets to breathe." Unsurprisingly, the government banned visitors soon after the reports went public.[70]

American public relations and lobbying firms stand ready to present repression in a softer light, as they have for so many foreign strongmen states. Qorvis, which represents Saudi Arabia, pitched a film to Caliburn depicting the "clean, warm, and safe" conditions inmates enjoy. As time goes on, such spin may be less necessary. "How do you stop these people [from crossing the border]"? Trump asked the crowd at a 2019 Florida rally. "Shoot them!" someone yelled. If intensive government propaganda campaigns continue, bolstered by the GOP and right-wing media, more Americans may agree that harming migrants is necessary to protect the country.[71]

PART III

LOSING POWER

NINE

RESISTANCE

———

IN 1938, GEORG ELSER, a thirty-five-year-old German from a small town in the Swabia region, decided he would kill Hitler. As a Communist, he was against international wars of the type the Führer seemed bent on starting. As a carpenter and joiner who also had access to explosives (he worked at an armaments factory and a quarry), he had the skills and the means to carry out his plan. Each year on November 8 at 9 p.m., Hitler gave a speech at the Munich beer hall where his failed 1923 putsch had originated. Elser decided to design and plant a bomb that would explode while Hitler pontificated. A time delay of 144 hours would minimize the chances anyone would connect him to the act. After testing explosive devices in the fields around his house, he took lodgings in Munich in August 1939. Every night, he went to the beer hall for a late dinner, hid while it closed, and spent hours hollowing out a pillar near the stage that would house the bomb. When the beer hall opened for business on November 3, the bomb lay inside the pillar, its timer activated, a cork casing muffling its tick.

On November 8, Hitler took his place on the stage and launched his invective. At 9:20, as planned, the bomb went off, causing the ceiling to collapse over the podium, killing five people and injuring sixty-seven.

The Führer was not among them, nor even on the premises. He had moved up the time of his speech and left the beer hall at 9:07, missing his appointment with death by 13 minutes. German guards detained Elser as he tried to cross the border to Switzerland, carrying fuses, sketches of the bomb design, a postcard of the beer hall, and his Communist Party badge. The Gestapo grilled him back in Munich, unable to believe that a single individual had engineered such a daring and sophisticated plan. Hitler examined his file with fascination. No one knew quite what to do with him, and he spent five years in isolation at Sachsenhausen concentration camp, with "special prisoner" status and his own workshop. Transferred to Dachau in February 1945, he was shot by the SS in April as the Reich collapsed. "I wanted through my act to prevent even greater bloodshed," Elser had told his interrogators upon his arrest.[1]

The history of strongmen is also the history of their opponents' efforts to remove them from power. Assassination is an occupational hazard of all political leaders, but the authoritarian's organization of state power around his person makes him an appealing target for those who want to try and sink a regime with maximum efficiency. Hundreds of assassination attempts have been directed at strongmen. Many people have rented hotel rooms and apartments that put the leader in the crosshairs of their weapons, whether a rifle pointed at Mussolini in 1925, a bazooka directed at Pinochet in 1985, or a sniper rifle and Kalashnikov aimed at Putin in 2008. "The bullets pass, Mussolini remains," the Italian leader wrote of the four attempts on his life in 1925–1926.[2]

The word *resistance* may conjure the armed insurrections of World War II against the Fascists and Nazis. Violence certainly features in its history. Around the world, resisters from outlawed movements or parties that oppose the regime with weapons have lived underground, cut off from family and friends. Maria Castro, a member of the far-left Chilean MIR, spent fourteen years in "internal exile." "What kept us going during those years was a very deep conviction that dictatorship was an evil too great for our people . . . that we had to resist, that each one had his or her work to do," she recalled.[3]

Most resistance in strongman states is non-violent, though, and unarmed protest has been among the most effective. It may start with solo or small group acts of protest, like the "Down with Hitler" graffiti the White Rose group left on the walls of government buildings in 1943 Munich. Public art and messaging proclaim the existence of individuals who are "refusing to accept the disinformation and lies . . . refusing to accept the abnormal as normal," in the words of the Chilean graphic artist Guillo. His 1987 caricature of Pinochet as Louis XIV on the cover of *Apsi* sent the magazine's editors to jail for "extremism"; being laughed at is something strongmen dread.[4]

Individual actions designed to be seen by the public break through the screen of official media and offer models of resistance that can be transformative. They seed the terrain for the mass nonviolent protests that can grow in response to state repression or when the leader's authority erodes due to a war going badly, an election that seems fraudulent, or economic hardship. A critical mass of visible protestors can remind international funders and the strongman's domestic allies that enabling him can have consequences.[5]

Strongmen use the public sphere to display their power to regiment bodies and minds. Resistance activities reclaim that space from the state and speak back to the government's violence, corruption, and exploitation. Such protests can be joyful collective occasions, as in the anti-Putin rallies in the winter of 2011–2012. They became spaces of warmth and solidarity despite the cold. Protests can also be stark refutations of the leader's claim on the body and soul, as in cases of self-immolation, which draw attention to injustice and call to others to do something about it. The Chilean Sebastián Acevedo set himself on fire in 1983 in front of Concepción's cathedral to protest his children's arrests by the junta. The street vendor Mohamed Bouazizi's 2010 self-immolation in front of a government building was a trigger for the Arab Spring.[6]

"Dictatorships put people to sleep, and the only ones brave enough to fight it are youth," said taxi driver Renato Gomez, a witness to years of Chilean protests in Santiago. Knowing little of other political realities, younger people may easily imbibe propaganda and adapt to authoritarian rule. Yet they also have the most to lose from living with leaders who use them as baby-making machines or cannon fodder and are often among the first groups to organize for action. Every strongman targets universities with informers who report on students, faculty, and staff.[7]

The history of resistance is also the history of what people of all ages don't do. In societies predicated on compliance, refusing to act sends a powerful message. Not listening to the radio when the leader speaks, not performing the Hitler salute (Elser observed both of these habits), or not sending your children to state youth activities all had repercussions. In Fascist Italy, Arturo Gunetti was the lone boy in his class not enrolled in his local Balilla youth group, as per the wish of his leftist father, and the only child with excellent grades failed by the teacher. Soon Arturo became a Balilla and his teacher changed his grades, but his father made Arturo take off his uniform the second he came home—at least his domestic space would be an anti-Fascist zone. From Il Duce onward, women have refused to become the tools of state demographic agendas. They have declined to procreate for the state, instead risking prison to obtain birth control and have abortions.[8]

Some of the most moving acts of resistance remain private. Individuals have secretly recorded deaths they witness as a way of opposing the state's erasure of its crimes. Hussein al-Shafa'i, a cook in Libya's Abu Salim prison, washed the blood off the watches of the men massacred in the 1996 revolt. He kept a mental note of the number of victims for fifteen years until Gaddafi died and he could speak out. A Spanish farmer in Teruel Province wrote down the number of executions he heard in the fields around him every night during the civil war. He hid his notebook with its record of over 1,000 deaths for four decades, showing it to investigators only eight years after Franco died. The devotion people show to the strongman's murdered rivals resists the state's politics of oblivion. The Italian writer Leonardo Sciascia's aunt kept a picture of anti-Fascist Giacomo Matteotti buried in her sewing basket during Mussolini's dictatorship. Carlos, a Chilean carpenter, sealed a photograph of President Allende inside the walls of his house after Pinochet's coup.[9]

Exile is the fate of many politically active individuals targeted by the state. While most resettle in democracies, immigration and employment circumstances can mean that resisters temporarily exchange one regime for another. Fleeing Hitler, the anti-Nazi theologian Dietrich von Hildebrand initially relocated to a family home in Fascist Italy. As many as 25,000 Chilean exiles lived under Brazil's military dictatorship, and a few joined a resistance group based in the southern city of Porto Alegre. Wherever they settle, those who speak out against authoritarian states from abroad may be targeted for assassination, especially if they are well known and can mobilize dissent; this was the fate of the Chilean Orlando Letelier. The 2018 murder of the Saudi Arabian journalist Jamal Khashoggi in the Saudi consulate in Istanbul is in this tradition.[10]

"But how to free ourselves of all the darkness and the veils behind which we have hidden for so many years? How to find ourselves again?" asked the Italian writer Natalia Ginzburg in 1944, while Italian partisans fought against the Fascists and Nazis. For millions, acts of resistance have been a path to the recovery of the self and the reaffirmation of dignity, empathy, and solidarity—all qualities the strongman seeks to destroy in his people.[11]

—

"CONFINEMENT IS A CELL WITHOUT WALLS, all is sky and sea; the patrols of militiamen serve as the walls. . . . The desire to climb over them becomes an obsession." So wrote the Italian Socialist Carlo Rosselli in June 1928, six months into his captivity on the island of Lipari, its 900 prisoners guarded by 500 men. A year later, Rosselli and fellow dissidents Emilio Lussu and Francesco Fausto Nitti took their fate in their hands and swam out to a motorboat that took them to Tunisia. We have "exchanged a prison in Italy for freedom in exile," Rosselli stated jubilantly before continuing on to Paris. Fascist police chief Bocchini sent Rosselli's brother Nello to Ustica and placed Rosselli's English wife, Marion Cave Rosselli, under house arrest. She had helped to procure the boat and smuggled out maps of the island in their child's diaper. Bocchini also fired the head of the Lipari prison colony, Francesco Cannata, who had recently cabled Rome that Rosselli was a "model *confinato.* Wish they were all like him."[12]

The Italian Communist Party, formed in 1921, was the only anti-Fascist force with the resources to sustain early underground networks. Their publications circulated widely: 150,000 leaflets and 12,000 copies of newspapers were distributed on May 1, 1930, alone. Directions given to the PCI by the Stalin-era Comintern often proved counterproductive, though, like banning collaborations with the non-Communist left. Some anti-Fascists air-dropped protest messages. Giovanni Bassanesi released 150,000 flyers on Milan in 1930, and Lauro De Bosis scattered thousands of anti-Fascist leaflets around Rome in 1931, including over Mussolini's stronghold, Piazza Venezia. Such initiatives were risky: De Bosis died when his plane crashed into the sea. By the mid-1930s, organized anti-Fascism inside Italy had been largely defeated.[13]

This made exiles' organizing crucial. In 1929, Rosselli founded the Justice and Liberty movement with Lussu and Nitti in Paris. His Liberal Socialism doctrine emphasized the autonomy of individual will within collective action and advocated collaboration with other opposition forces abroad—a winning unity in diversity formula. Part of a well-off Jewish family, Rosselli had money to finance anti-Fascist operations and was a skilled communicator in several languages. By the early 1930s, Justice and Liberty had more activists in Italy than the PCI. Seeing Rosselli as "the most dangerous of the anti-Fascists in exile" and his wife, Cave Rosselli, as an equal threat, the OVRA secret police ordered the spy Dino Segre to infiltrate the Rossellis' political circle. Segre was successful: 200 Justice and Liberty operatives were arrested in Italy in 1934.[14]

The Spanish Civil War galvanized anti-Fascists, and Rosselli joined thousands of Italian exiles who fought on the Republican side against

Franco's Nationalists and Axis troops. The English writer George Orwell, another Republican volunteer, felt like "a pawn in an enormous struggle being fought out between two political theories," but the fight was personal for Italians. They had to face the 70,000 Italians who served in the regular and volunteer armed forces Mussolini sent in 1937 to help Franco. Rosselli organized a Matteotti Brigade, named after the murdered Socialist leader, but most Italians fought in the Garibaldi Brigade, one of the Communist-organized international brigades that involved over 50,000 combatants from more than fifty countries. Spain prepared Italians for the fight of their lives at home against the Fascists of the Nazi-controlled Republic of Salò from 1943 to 1945.[15]

Some anti-Fascists in Spain saw proximity to so many Italian soldiers as an ideal counterpropaganda opportunity. They used radio to communicate across enemy lines. "Italians, sons of our land! You have been sent here, swindled by false and deceitful propaganda, or driven by hunger and unemployment," declared one Garibaldi Brigade message. In November 1936, Rosselli addressed his compatriots on Radio Barcelona. Appealing to "Italian brothers who live in the Fascist prison," he asked them to renounce the regime and join "a new world that is being born . . . today in Spain, tomorrow in Italy." Rosselli did not live to see that world come into being. The Fascist secret police had long recommended that he be "suppressed," and in 1937 French rightists murdered him and his brother Nello in Normandy, likely at the Italian regime's request. "History will decide the reason for their fate," said Mussolini obliquely of the killings. "Power is not always able to control the apparatus that represents it."[16]

From the late 1930s on, the Italian dictator saw his statement deployed against him at home. The threat of war and grinding poverty affected his popularity. When he visited Turin in 1939, the prefect had to conscript rural housewives to cheer him to ensure newsreel-worthy levels of excitement. Younger Italians trained by the regime to be its next elite began to communicate their malaise publicly. Informers noted university students' "hostility to the Rome-Berlin Axis," and the critic Giulia Veronesi noted the "deepening discomfort" among her peers as "the compromise in which we live" became harder to sustain.[17] Even official propaganda hinted at the growing disaffection. Roberto Rossellini's 1942 feature *A Pilot Returns*, which was supervised by Il Duce's son Vittorio Mussolini, is not an anti-Fascist film. Yet its story of an aviator who becomes a prisoner of war in Greece suggests an undoing of authoritarian ideals of emotional hardness. Highlighting acts of looking at and aiding those in distress, the film depicts something out of bounds for the Fascist era: sympathy for a suffering humanity beyond the boundaries of ally and enemy. Rossellini's 1945 resistance movie *Rome Open City* shows where this new vision led.[18]

—

IN JUNE 1942, TWO MONTHS AFTER *A Pilot Returns* premiered, one hundred people in Munich received a mysterious letter in the mail. Signed by "the White Rose Society," it presented Germans with a shocking demand:

> Adopt passive resistance—*resistance*—wherever you are, and
> block the functioning of this atheistic war machine before it
> is too late . . . and the last youth of our nation bleeds to death
> because of the *hubris* of a subhuman. Don't forget that every
> people gets the government it deserves!

Some brought the letter to the Gestapo, terrified to possess such blasphemy. Over the next six weeks, three more missives appeared, reaching thousands throughout southwest Germany and up to Hamburg. A fifth (written with Munich University professor Kurt Huber) appeared in early 1943.[19]

A thing of fragile beauty in any time and place, a white rose might seem an idealistic symbol of the fight against a corrupt and murderous regime. Yet the Munich University students who chose it as the name for their resistance group were eminently practical. They had absorbed lessons in mass communications from the regime they so despised. As the brother-sister conspirators Hans and Sophie Scholl stated, their goal was to create "compelling propaganda" that would "impact a large part of the population." While the Scholls grew up with an anti-Nazi father, they knew how the military and other Nazi institutions operated. A former Hitler Youth squad leader, Hans Scholl and fellow members Alexander Schmorell and Willi Graf alternated their university studies with service as medics on the Eastern Front, and Christoph Probst had also served in the military.[20]

Organized and fearless, the White Rose built a chain of collaborators that reached to Vienna. They expanded from letters to graffiti actions, like painting "Hitler mass murderer" on a Munich bookshop, and they distributed leaflets at train stations and phone booths. While they selected some recipients of their letters at random, most were chosen because their jobs put them in contact with many people, as with educators, doctors, and owners of restaurants, pubs, and bookshops. The letters asked the recipients to copy the messages and spread them "from person to person." Working in an analog era and in a police state, they tried to construct an anti-Fascist social network.[21]

The White Rose eluded the authorities throughout eight months of frenetic activity, even when the Gestapo hired a philologist to examine the letters for clues to the writers' identities. On February 18, 1943, the Bavarian president and Gauleiter Paul Giesler visited Munich University. When Giesler told women to put aside their studies and have babies, the White Rose collective led students in heckling him to his face. Perhaps euphoric at the response, Sophie Scholl threw copies of their sixth letter from a high floor. A janitor saw her and she and Hans were arrested. The siblings and Probst were executed by guillotine on February 22, with Schmorell, Graf, and Huber killed later that year. In death, the White Rose gained the mass audience they had dreamed of; Allied aircraft dropped tens of thousands of their letters over the country. "I had to act out of my inner conviction and I believed this inner obligation was more binding than the oath of loyalty I had given as a soldier," Hans Scholl told Gestapo interrogators, explaining his actions.[22]

Although Scholl didn't know it, a number of high-ranking military officers and operatives shared his sentiments. Hitler's reckless push to war and his 1938 takeover and purges of armed forces leadership spurred resistance in the defense world. The *Abwehr* (military intelligence) became a center of opposition under deputy head Major General Hans Oster. For maximum effectiveness, they worked with carefully selected civilians, like the anti-Nazi pastor Dietrich Bonhoeffer. During the war, German officers hatched myriad plots to kill Hitler, all of which failed due to malfunctioning explosives or other quirks of fate. The repositioning of an explosive-filled briefcase by an unwitting Hitler aide foiled the attempt by Claus von Stauffenberg, Oster, and others on July 20, 1944. The bombing of Hitler's headquarters in East Prussia left its target with minor injuries but killed and maimed multiple Nazi officers. It ended with the conspirators executed, their families imprisoned, and 7,000 military and civilian officials arrested and almost 4,000 executed. "I am invulnerable. I am immortal," a dazed Führer repeated to the doctor who treated him right after the explosion. For believers, Hitler's survival proved that he enjoyed divine protection. A conspirator concluded ruefully that Hitler had a "guardian devil" keeping him alive.[23]

Resisting the Nazis inside Germany was an isolating as well as highly dangerous enterprise. Myriad "solitary witnesses," from Elser to Josef Höfler, who smuggled Jews over the Swiss border, risked everything for their cause. Opposition took many forms, from the Socialists of the Bund to the meetings of Helmut and Freya von Moltke's Kreisau Circle, where aristocrats and other elites discussed how to end Nazism and transition to democracy.[24] Many Germans accepted Hitler's rule but took issue with certain policies, such as eugenics measures or the encroachment of Nazi ideology on religious liberties. When the regime tried to substitute religious instruction with a class on political education in some Württemberg religious schools in 1939, parents mobilized in protest. In one parish, forty-seven parents sent the local government officials a letter that demanded the protection of "full freedom of conscience." That they ended it with "Heil Hitler" also shows the parameters of pushback in a personalist state. Individual policies might be contested, but the Führer cult remained untouchable almost to the end.[25]

—

IN THE AGE OF MILITARY COUPS, leftists who wanted to train for armed struggle against far-right regimes had far more options than in the fascist era. New anti-imperialist networks joined Communist ones in catering to globe-trotting insurgents. Gaddafi's World Revolutionary Center trained men and women from dozens of countries, including Chile, although Castro's Cuba prepared more of Pinochet's enemies, including the MIR and the Communist Party's Manuel Rodríguez Patriotic Front (FPMR).[26]

On September 7, 1986, FPMR guerrillas were waiting for Pinochet as he returned from a weekend at his country house in El Melocotón, outside of Santiago. As Pinochet's convoy proceeded through the Maipo Canyon, a station wagon with a camper suddenly blocked the road, signaling the start of "Operation Twentieth Century." Light anti-tank rockets, grenades, M16 rifles, and more assaulted the convoy, which included Pinochet's brand-new armored Mercedes with bulletproof tires. The Generalissimo sat frozen as his driver, Army Corporal Oscar Carvajal, reversed at top speed. It was Pinochet's eleven-year-old grandson, along for the ride, who opened the back window curtains so Carvajal could see (the side mirror was covered in blood). Under continuous fire, the Mercedes took off for El Melocotón, leaving behind several wounded or dead members of Pinochet's security detail.[27]

When Pinochet appeared on television with a bandaged hand that evening, standing next to his damaged Mercedes, the reprisals against the FPMR and MIR had already begun. "I am no saint or Moham-med. If they give me a slap in the face, I strike back with two," Pinochet told journalists the next day. He did have the Virgin Mary watching over him: he had seen her outline in the shattered glass of his Mercedes. When his vehicle was exhibited to the public, many agreed that she had intervened to save him. Equally miraculous, for the dozen or so FPMR fighters, was the absence of fatalities among their ranks, given that few of them had combat experience. Commander Ernesto (José Valenzuela Levi) had been an officer in the Bulgarian People's Army, but some of his comrades had never used their weapons prior to the attack.[28]

As corpses of leftists bearing signs of government torture appeared around Santiago, many Chileans prayed for peace. By 1986, violence had exhausted the population. The junta's brutality had lost it supporters, and the Communists' armed response to regime violence seemed misguided to some. Many Christian Democrats and conservatives agreed with the Socialists' denunciation of a Communist strategy that "only means more pain and death for the people of Chile." Social mobilization and negotiation, not insurrection, was how the junta would end.[29]

Two events sparked broad-based nonviolent resistance. Pinochet had agreed to allow Chileans to vote in 1980 on a new constitution. It guaranteed him eight more years in office in return for holding presidential elections in 1988. But the government tried to influence the outcome of the plebiscite, declaring a state of emergency for the month prior to it to block countermessaging and using mayors personally appointed by Pinochet to count the results. The constitution was approved, with 67 percent in favor, but the experience jolted many Chileans and spurred a civil society movement to reverse government voter suppression measures before the 1988 election.[30]

The economic crisis of the early 1980s also sent people into the streets, protesting the resulting mass hunger and misery. By 1983, unemployment was at 50 percent in poor areas and 30 percent overall in a country where neoliberal policies had removed the social safety net. It also affected the middle and upper-middle classes. Massive foreign debt assumed by private Chilean enterprises had made the "economic miracle" possible. Now the government had to purchase the defaulted loans of the banks and financial institutions business depended on. By 1983, seven of nineteen commercial banks and eight of twenty-two investment banks were state-owned—a fact left out in accounts of the benefits Pinochet's neoliberal privatizations supposedly brought to Chile.[31]

Middle- and upper-middle-class people took part in the mass demonstrations that started in 1983. In May, the new Democratic Alliance of opposition parties held a National Day of Protest. Brutal state repression of that event did not deter the demonstrations and calls for national strikes that continued all summer. "We have taken a very important step . . . that of losing fear," said labor leader Rodolfo Seguel. In September, the crowd at a soccer match chanted "The military dictatorship is going to fall!" turning the National Stadium from a site of memories of terror into a place of dissent. A "different" country was emerging, noted CIA analysts in 1984. "Political activity—from party organizing to coffee shop debate—has returned to Chile."[32]

The Vicariate of Solidarity, founded in 1976 by Pope Paul VI at the request of the cardinal and archbishop of Santiago Raúl Silva Henríquez, made the Chilean Catholic Church a node of resistance activities. It assisted opposition politicians and labor activists, ran Radio Chilena, and undertook legal actions for families of the disappeared. Henriquez's successor, Juan Francisco Fresno, kept dialogue open between the government and the opposition.[33] Student activism also prepared the way. The hymns protesters sang at the Pontifical Catholic University evolved into broader demonstrations. Campus hunger strikes, prayer vigils, sit-ins, and marches flowed into the larger actions of 1983. That year, 67 percent of Chileans eighteen to twenty-four years old indicated a preference for civilian government—a remarkable majority given the climate of repression.[34]

Culture also became a vehicle of protest. In 1979, the Art Actions Collective (CADA) staged interventions that mixed resistance traditions dating to the Italian Fascist era with postwar performance art. In a 1981 project, six light planes dropped 400,000 pamphlets over Santiago. "We are artists but every man who works toward expansion of the spaces of his life, even just in how he thinks, is an artist," they read, reminding Chileans of the power of human agency. CADA's "NO+" slogan (for *No mas/no more*) had a huge influence. In 1983, during the mass protests, CADA invited artists to complete it on walls and other surfaces in Santiago. Soon "NO+ dictatorship," "NO+ torture," and other versions by the Chilean public appeared. NO+ became a visual symbol of protest for the duration of the dictatorship. CADA member Fernando Balcells later characterized the actions as encouraging "a radical opening to emotions, to memory, to pain, and the uncontrollable risk of the new," all of which countered the numbness and oblivion caused by years of authoritarian rule.[35]

Chile may have been changing by the mid-1980s, but Pinochet, nearly seventy years old, had no desire to do the same. He could not tolerate the exposure that came with even limited political liberalization. In 1984, the new magazine *Cauce* published evidence that Pinochet had built his weekend retreat in El Melocotón with public funds. The Christian Democrats accused him of fraud and misuse of public office. A furious Pinochet declared a state of emergency and temporarily shut down the publica-

NO+ art action, CADA, Santiago, 1983.
JORGE BRANTMEYER / CADA / COURTESY OF LOTTY ROSENFELD

tion. He reacted to the growing protests in the same repressive manner. In 1982, 1,213 people were arrested; in 1984, 5,314; and in 1986, 7,019. Pinochet's inflexibility and corruption increasingly concerned the junta, and his American government backers started to question their invest- ment. Elliott Abrams, who had served as President Reagan's assistant secretary of state for Latin America, recalled the moment bluntly. Pino- chet had "outlived any usefulness he had ever had. Even if you thought he was terrific in 1973, by 1983, it was time for him to go."[36]

—

The Libyans who met in February 1993 at the Hotel Ambassa- dor in Zurich to plan Gaddafi's overthrow could relate to that sentiment. Some of them were army officers from the Warfalla tribe, which had strong relations with Gaddafi's tribe and a privileged position in the mili- tary and security apparatus. Their coconspirators came from the National Front for the Salvation of Libya (NFSL), an exile opposition group founded in 1981 with a paramilitary presence in Libya. Once the offi- cers returned to Libya to recruit for the coup in Bani Walid, their tribe's stronghold, Gaddafi's security services let the group reach maximum size before arresting them all in October. As the televised interrogations and confessions started, the population of Bani Walid had to sign a petition demanding that their kin be executed.[37]

In some ways, Gaddafi had it easier than Pinochet. Libya had lit- tle culture of contestation when he took power. Oil riches also let him offer social welfare benefits to his people, which encouraged conformity. Yet the Libyan leader also created more categories of malcontents, as the military-tribal-exile nexus of the 1993 plot shows. He stripped the armed forces of power and then forced them into an ill-advised war on Chad (1978–1987), which ended in Libyan defeat. He also angered Isla- mists with his dismissals of traditional religious authority. This trans- lated into dozens of coup attempts by exiles and the military in the early 1980s alone.[38]

Like Pinochet, Gaddafi responded to heightened dissent with heightened repression. This turned young people, who were being groomed as the regime's next elite, against him. Thousands of Libyans with technological skills had spent years studying in Western democracies, funded by the Libyan government. The CIA counted 3,000 Libyans enrolled in universities and colleges in 1987 alone. Sadik Hamed Shwehdi, who was hanged on live television in the Benghazi basketball stadium, had joined an opposition group while he studied aerospace engineering in America. For students who stayed in Libya, being forced to watch your peers executed created fear and loathing.[39]

"An irritant but not a threat" was the CIA's summary 1987 judgment of the opposition in exile, which was composed of about twenty groups that involved about 10 percent of the 50,000 Libyans who lived abroad. While none of these groups gained army support sufficient for a mass mutiny, resistance also involved a long game of preparing Libyans to conceive of a different world—and a different leader. Gaddafi's opponents waged a countermessaging campaign from around the world. The NFSL, based in Khartoum until 1985 and then in London, printed 20,000 copies of its *Salvation* magazine each month. Egyptian radio broadcast the anti-Gaddafi program *Voice of the Libyan People*. The Libyan Constitutional Union, founded in Manchester in 1981, published "How to Undo a Military Coup."[40]

As the former army officer and NFSL leader Jaballa Matar found out, no adversary of Gaddafi was entirely safe. By 1979, Matar had moved to Cairo, putting his children in schools abroad. His articles on the need for democracy in Libya made him a prime target, as did his financing of a training camp in Chad, where the Chadian government retooled captured Libyan soldiers into anti-Gaddafi guerillas. In 1990, Egyptian State Security agents kidnapped Matar and returned him to Libya. He was imprisoned in Abu Salim along with his brother Mahmoud and his nephew Ali, all NFSL members. A sense of loss infuses his son Hisham Matar's memoir about his family's fate under Gaddafi. Seeing his cousin Maher Bushrayda, released from eleven years of prison after Gaddafi's death, Hisham Matar recognized "[t]hat slightly stifled gait all political prisoners have. As though oppression were a toxic sentiment that lingered in the muscles . . . and the grievance seemed not to be with fate of ideology but with humanity itself."[41]

—

By the time Gaddafi's rule ended in 2011, new media and other technologies had changed the practice of resistance and how authoritarian rulers sought to stop it. Putin blocked Zello in 2017, and Erdoğan banned Twitter and Facebook around the time of the 2013 Gezi Park protests. Governments also flood the social media platforms they do permit with trolls and misinformation and use digital infiltration to track dissidents at home and in exile. Today's resistance collectives include coders and encryption specialists who find workarounds for government censorship. They access virtual private networks and adapt apps like Tinder (which Hong Kong protesters used to organize protests in 2019).[42]

New media helps resisters organize and communicate with each other and the world, building horizontal networks of information exchange and solidarity. Today's protestors use digital storytelling practices to confront and expose state repression. Such narratives gave momentum to the 2010–2012 Arab Spring uprisings and brought attention to the plight of Russian activists during the government raids of August–September 2019. Now the dreaded knock on the door is streamed on Twitter, and we are in the room with the dissident as the police break in, as happened with Lyubov Sobol in Moscow. Now we watch the resister protect his contacts and documents in real time, as when Sergey Boyko, a Novosibirsk activist and former mayoral candidate, tweeted an image of a drone flying his hard drive out the window of his apartment as police banged on the door.[43]

By creating nodes of empathy and anger, social media helps to overcome the cynicism and paralyzing fear that authoritarian states foster. It also boosts the humanizing power of laughter born of caricature. Few

Chileans may have seen the 1984 mural of Pinochet as a Nazi pig in the La Victoria neighborhood of Santiago, but 2011 and 2017 images of Gaddafi as a clown and Putin wearing makeup went viral.[44]

At its core, though, resistance remains anchored in physical presence: people reclaiming public space and making a different nation visible and audible. In-person protest has created the images and tactics that still inspire protestors today. The Baltic Way human chain formed by 2 million people who joined hands across Latvia, Estonia, and Lithuania in 1989 to protest Soviet rule was echoed in Italy's 2002–2004 anti-Berlusconi *girotondi*, or ring-around-the-rosy human chains. In 2019, Hong Kong protesters paid the Baltic Way action homage. Around the world, one resistance action inspires others.[45]

—

IN 2010, PRIME MINISTER PUTIN RECEIVED a special birthday present: a calendar featuring lingerie-clad University of Moscow journalism students praising his virility. "You only get better with the years," "How about a third go?," the latter also an allusion to another Putin presidency (Dmitry Medvedev was then the nominal head of state). The calendar sparked a counter-calendar featuring other University of Moscow journalism students, these ones fully clothed, who sent Putin less welcome messages. "Who killed Anna Politkovskaya?" one asked, referring to the journalist murdered on Putin's birthday four years earlier; "Freedom of assembly always and everywhere," said another.[46]

The women who denounced state repression foreshadowed the mass protests over fraud in the 2012 parliamentary elections that returned Putin to the presidency. Putin's corruption and violence had been denounced and mocked during his preceding term. In 2006, an online journalist was sent to a penal colony for depicting him as a skinhead. In 2008, the Voina ("War") art collective performed group sex acts in Moscow's Timiryazev Museum of Biology to call attention to the ways that "those in power are fucking the people."[47]

The mass protests calling for "honest elections," held in the winter of 2011–2012, expressed a desire for systemic change and democratization. They mobilized up to 100,000 people in Moscow and tens of thousands in smaller centers. Publicized on social media sites like VKontakte, the protests drew people from all social classes, including previously apolitical individuals. Kira Sokolova, a teacher from Chelyabinsk, near the Ural Mountains, was one of these. Sokolova watched the December events on television and read online about election fraud and the work of anti-corruption activist Alexei Navalny. She joined Navalny's movement and became an election monitor. In May 2012, she traveled 34 hours to Moscow to attend the "March of Millions" held just before Putin's inauguration. For Sokolova, as for many others, the larger goal was changing Russian political culture so that "all of these lies, this filth, this vileness will diminish, and that some normal human values will triumph."[48]

Putin's body is central to his display of masculine threat, and those resisting him have made their own bodies arms of resistance against him and his state. Acts of self-immolations and mouths sewn shut by impoverished pensioners, dissident artists, and political prisoners became more frequent after 2011. The Pussy Riot collective's performances in subway stations and churches brought attention to misogyny as an integral part of Putin's Orthodox Church–backed rule. "Russia lacks political and gender emancipation, audacity, a feminist horsewhip, and a female president," the group declared.[49]

Putin has answered the waves of protest with more censorship and repression. Changes in the legal code now make it easier to put demonstrators in prison or ship them off to penal colonies. As happened with Pinochet in Chile, Putin's strategy may be backfiring. Pro-democracy protests are a continual presence in public life. "Wanting to intimidate society, the authorities only make it more angry," wrote the jailed twenty-one-year-old political activist Yegor Zhukov to the newspaper *Novaya Gazeta* in 2019.[50]

Opposition figures like Navalny now focus less on rallies and more on electoral strategies, starting at the municipal level. The government has sought to keep Navalny off of ballots and barred Sobol from running for Moscow city council in 2019. Putin's need to game the field of political competition is telling. Now sixty-seven, Putin is an aging strongman whose charisma no longer works its magic on the population. In 2019, his trust ratings declined to 33 percent, the lowest in thirteen years, down from 70 percent in 2015. If he had allowed free and fair elections in 2024, when his present term was supposed to end, he might well have lost his political hegemony. Putin's solution—amending the Russian constitution to stay in office until 2036—is a sign of weakness rather than strength.[51]

—

"SEE YOU NEXT SUNDAY, MAYBE," said the comedian Sabina Guzzanti, signing off from her new Rai 3 channel show *Raiot: Weapons of Mass Destruction* in November 2003, letting her audience know that this first episode might also be the last. One skit took on a proposed television reform law that would benefit the Italian prime minister's media empire. "It is up to comedians to inform about what's going on in Italy," Guzzanti proclaimed. In Berlusconi's state, this counted as a subversive action. The Italian premier sued Guzzanti and Rai 3 director Paolo Ruffini for defamation. Rather than defend Guzzanti, Rai canceled her show and banned her from all its channels. This left her without a national television audience, since Berlusconi owned all the major private networks. The remaining five episodes of *Raiot* that she taped have never aired.[52]

Resistance in degraded democracies run by personalist leaders, like those of Berlusconi and Trump, carries less risk of imprisonment or death than in the states of Erdoğan and Putin. Yet the private vendettas carried out by these heads of state can result in professional hardship and are often accompanied by the threat or actuality of physical harm. Prosecutor Francesco Saverio Borrelli's call to resist Berlusconi's corruption led to one-day strikes by magistrates in June 2002 and November 2003. Berlusconi responded by taking away the magistrates' security escorts, leaving them vulnerable to Mafia or other hits.[53]

The wave of civil society protests that spread in the early 2000s responded to these fraught situations. In March 2002, a Berlusconi proposal to make it easier to fire workers prompted trade unions to organize the largest march in postwar history, with millions gathering at Rome's Circus Maximus. Two months earlier, the *girotondi* movement had started, as Italians joined hands in concentric circles to symbolically protect endangered institutions like the Ministry of Justice and RAI. The hard left condemned the *girotondi* as "petit-bourgeois," but a September 2002 rally drew 1 million participants.[54]

Berlusconi may have succeeded in banishing critics and satirists from traditional media, but new media, whose power he underrated, proved a different story. On the Internet, his savior-of-Italy image and rhetoric were turned against him. His campaign for safer cities, meant to further his law-and-order governance, inspired pictures of *him* behind bars. The blog the comic Beppe Grillo started in 2005, which soon became one of the top-ranked worldwide, directed a stream of caustic critique at the "psycho-dwarf." A blog post that year was entitled "L'état c'est moi!" It included an image of Berlusconi's face superimposed on a portrait of Louis XIV, which updated Chilean graphic artist Guillo's print Pinochet caricature.[55]

In 2006, Berlusconi was voted out of office. His egotistical "miracle worker" message had raised unrealistic expectations of growth for a sluggish economy. Together with disaffection with his corruption, it contributed to his party's loss. But the center-left did not meet citizen expectations for anti-corruption reform during its own 2006–2008 government. Grillo channeled rising populist anger into a 2007 "Go Fuck Yourself" Day with protests in Bologna and 225 other Italian cities. The filmmaker Nanni Moretti, whose 2006 fiction film *The Caiman* ended with the prime minister leaving office to start a prison sentence, reflected on how Berlusconi's values and persona had colonized Italy. He diagnosed a Berlusconi "addiction" and a collapse of "public ethics . . . we consider normal, things that are not."[56]

Protests intensified when Berlusconi returned to office in 2008. With one trial proceeding against him and three more in preparation, the Italian leader was in full-throttle self-protection mode. When the new government soon passed a measure that gave him immunity from standing trial, it was the tipping point for some. Two days later a blogger-run Facebook page called on Italians to demand the resignation of a leader whose "proprietary conception of the state" made him "a very serious anomaly within Western democracies." By October 2009, when the Italian Constitutional Court repealed the measure that gave him immunity, Berlusconi's sex-party scandal had started to emerge.[57]

A December 2009 "No Berlusconi" Day saw demonstrations in more than one hundred Italian cities (300,000 mobilized in Rome), with protests continuing in 2010. The wave of public protest reinvigorated the Rai. Its union protested the suppression of news coverage of Berlusconi's legal and sex scandals. The popular Rai 1 anchor Maria Luisa Busi resigned in protest of the "unbearable climate." The 2009 manifesto "Against the Machismo of Berlusconi" by scholars and activists Nadia Urbinati, Michela Marzano, and Barbara Spinetti, published in *La Repubblica*, quickly got 100,000 signatures. "This man offends women and offends democracy," the authors asserted. "Let's stop him."[58] Two years later, when the eurozone crisis spread to Italy, the stage was set to do just that.

—

"[O]UR CONSTITUTION DOES NOT BEGIN WITH 'I, the President.' It begins with 'We, the People,'" said the writer and activist Gloria Steinem on January 21, 2017, speaking at the Women's March held the day after Trump's inauguration. The Washington, DC, event channeled America's tradition of feminist activism and the nonviolent ideology of the civil rights movement, including the 1963 March on Washington for Jobs and Freedom.[59] Then, a coalition of labor, civil rights, and religious organizations provided momentum. Now, social media played a determinant role.

The march originated in Facebook pages created by individuals across America after Trump's election. They asked people to demonstrate in defense of reproductive and other rights that the Trump administration would likely imperil. Over 400 organizations eventually partnered with the march, and its symbol—handcrafted pink pussy hats—turned Trump's misogyny and history of sexual assault against him. With 400,000 to 500,000 people joining in Washington, DC, and 3 to 5 million participating in over 400 marches across the country, it was the largest mobilization in American history.[60] It also changed the face of American politics. Many of the 3,000 women on the ballot in the fall 2018 midterm elections had been inspired by the Women's March to enter politics. Over ninety women were voted into office, including a record number of women of color.[61]

Protests continued a week later when Trump's ban on individuals from selected predominantly Muslim states from entering the country went into effect. Americans flooded airports and other border transit hubs. Immigration lawyers volunteered their expertise, and people walked off their jobs, as thousands of Comcast employees did nationwide. The demonstrations continued daily throughout the next months. The April 2017 March for Science drew attention to the government's assault on climate change science.[62] The United Resistance movement, created in January 2017, reflects the broad base of American protest against the Trump administration. It coordinates actions by organizations fighting for environmental, racial, reproductive, immigration, and labor rights. Its slogan, "when they come for one of us, they come for us all," based on a poem by the German pastor Martin Niemöller, who spent years in Nazi concentration camps, reflects the need for solidarity in resisting authoritarians.[63]

Individuals from within the political system have also played prominent roles in responding to the Trump administration's assaults on American democracy. Some pursue grassroots activism, as with the Indivisible movement created by former congressional staffers in December 2016. Others engage in legal pushback, like Protect Democracy, founded by former Department of Justice lawyers.[64] Civil servants have waged bureaucratic resistance by delaying implementation of executive orders they find unconscionable. Some have documented unethical behavior.

In September 2018, Inspector General Michael Atkinson told Congress of a whistleblower complaint about Trump's improper communications with Ukrainian president Volodymyr Zalensky. Atkinson's action opened investigations and hearings that led to Trump's 2019 impeachment by Congress—and to his own firing by the president in April 2020.[65]

A month later, a new wave of protests began in America, sparked by the May 25 murder of the Black truck driver and security guard George Floyd. "I can't breathe," Floyd gasped while White Minneapolis police office Derek Chauvin held his knee on Floyd's neck for 8 minutes. A terrified teenager, Darnella Frazier, recorded the scene on her smartphone and posted the video on her Facebook page. "Say their names! Black Lives Matter!" chanted the crowds who poured into the streets all over the country. They demanded justice for Floyd, Breonna Taylor (shot in her home, 2020), Philando Castile (shot in his car, 2016), and the many other African Americans killed by the police. A leading force of the 2020 protests, Black Lives Matter took shape in 2013 after a White man who killed an unarmed Black high school student named Trayvon Martin in 2012 was acquitted. It works at the local and national levels against the institutional racism and everyday violence and discrimination that Blacks face throughout America.[66]

Sustained mass protest requires opportunity, organization, and motivation born of outrage and the transcendence of fear. The conjunction of circumstances created by the coronavirus pandemic—mass unemployment and, for those with jobs, work-from-home flexibility—drove people into the streets. The raised stakes of having a White supremacist in the White House outweighed the risks of infection. Day after day, into the night, mixed-race crowds marched across bridges and filled streets and squares. By the end of June, millions had attended over 4,000 events held in over 2,000 towns and cities. Although property damage occurred during the first nights (the trucks backed up to take away stolen goods from stores belonged to professional looters), the demonstrations were mostly peaceful gatherings. The National Association for the Advancement of Colored People's #WeAreDoneDying campaign and Black Lives

Matter's goal of "centering Black joy" express the ethos of many 2020 protesters. They carry forth the righteous anger and optimistic belief in solidarity and the power of collective action that have characterized effective resistance movements for over a century.[67]

The protests also highlighted the rising dangers of resisting power in Trump's America. Many states had already elevated misdemeanor crimes related to protests to felonies and reclassified protests as riots, meaning participants can be criminalized as "economic terrorists and saboteurs." In 2018, West Virginia eliminated police liability for deaths occurring during police actions to disperse riots and "unlawful assemblies."[68] Moreover, many police officers came to the protests imbued with far-right ideologies. In 2015, an FBI counterterrorism report found "active links" between law enforcement and White supremacist and other antidemocratic groups. By 2019, studies of posts by former and retired police officers active in Facebook groups found that 1 in 5 current officers and 2 in 5 retired ones have made racist and dehumanizing comments about Blacks, Muslims, and other groups targeted by the Trump administration.[69]

During the May–June 2020 protests, police outfitted with combat-grade protection and tactical gear dispensed rubber bullets, tear gas, and blows. In Buffalo, on June 4, police officers pushed seventy-five-year-old Martin Gugino to the ground and stepped around him as he lay bleeding from the head from what was later diagnosed as a skull fracture. Trump not only defended police conduct, but also speculated on Twitter that Gugino was an "ANTIFA provocateur." Days earlier, Trump had declared his intent to designate Antifa a terrorist organization. The threat had no legal standing, since Antifa is a movement with no central coordination, but it gave security forces the message that they would be supported in treating protesters as though they were terrorists. Soon Barr formed a Task Force on Anti-Government Extremists. Echoing right-wing propaganda from Pinochet to Putin, U.S. Attorney General Barr claimed that the protests had been "hijacked by violent radical elements" and were "fortified by foreign entities seeking to sow chaos and disorder in our society." The over 400 incidents of police physically assaulting or arresting journalists who covered the protests suggests that Trump's anti-press propaganda had been effective.[70]

As in the past, artists have responded to the threats against civil rights and democratic freedoms. The 200 works featured in a 2019 School of Visual Arts "Art as Witness" exhibition included Nancy Burson's July 2018 *TIME* cover that superimposed Trump's face on Putin's. From 2017 onward, NBC's *Saturday Night Live* won large audiences with its satires of the president's administration and his relationship with Putin. The comedian Sarah Cooper's TikTok lip syncs of excerpts from Trump's interviews and speeches took the Internet by storm in 2020.[71] Robin Bell's projections on the facade of Trump International Hotel, from his May 2017 "Pay Trump Bribes Here" action onward, reach the public in a different manner. Bell's projections last 2 to 40 minutes, "depending on how fast [Trump] security reacts," and take on new life online. They offer "a visual reminder that what we are experiencing is not normal" and a message of solidarity, "letting people know that we listen and we care."[72]

Projection on Trump International Hotel by Robin Bell, May 2017.
PHOTO BY LIZ GORMAN / BELL VISUALS / COURTESY OF ROBIN BELL

—

THAT MESSAGE WAS POLITICALLY SUCCESSFUL in Istanbul in 2019, when Ekram Imamoğlu, the opposition candidate, won the race for mayor of Istanbul while demonstrating the power of positive emotions in politics. "We had two simple rules: ignore Erdoğan and love those who love Erdoğan," said his campaign manager Ates Ilyas Bassoy. Imamoğlu, then mayor of an Istanbul district, combines liberal views with an observant Muslim lifestyle. He had been chosen after much vetting as a strong prospect to beat Erdoğan's candidate, Binali Yildirim. Still, no one could have predicted the success of his platform of "radical love."[73]

Imamoğlu turned the strongman's politics of aggression and arrogance on its head. Instead of the mass rallies that stage authoritarian leader-follower dynamics, he walked the streets to "engage people directly, no matter what their ideology," greeting voters in cafes, mosques, and parks. Instead of menacing repression, he gave hugs. He countered Erdoğan's Justice and Development Party's (AKP) belligerent tone and predictions of apocalypse if they lost with a calming and optimistic campaign slogan: "Everything will be fine."[74]

When Imamoğlu pulled off an upset in the March elections (48.77 percent to Yildirim's 44.61 percent), the Erdoğan-allied electoral board cited irregularities and announced that the election would have to be redone. "They want conflict from us," Imamoğlu told his angry followers, but "we will insist upon embracing each other." Seeing the mayoral contest as a proxy vote about his popularity, Erdoğan (a former Istanbul mayor) made house visits to voters in each of Istanbul's thirty-nine districts during the new round of campaigning. His authoritarian tactics, like threatening to jail Imamoğlu for insulting a politician, did not go over well. When new elections were held in June, Imamoğlu increased his lead to 54.2 percent (versus 45 percent for Yildirim, who lost another eleven districts). "Maybe we should have given another message instead of 'survival,'" a source from AKP reflected.[75]

For one hundred years, the strongman has made political capital out

"Where there is Imamoğlu . . . there is hope." Campaign slogan, 2019.
MURAD SEZER / REUTERS

of such dire thinking, exploiting what Imamoğlu calls the "barriers of distrust and hostility that are created by the politics of fear." Those are the barriers that the new Turkish mayor explicitly campaigned to remove, in the spirit of resisters past and present. "Polarization is a universal problem," he says. "All around the world, populism is used to divide and rule. But I believe we can turn this trend upside down." Imamoğlu's victory holds out the possibility of a different future for Turkey and sends a message to strongmen everywhere.[76]

TEN

ENDINGS

—

O N OCTOBER 20, 2011, Gaddafi hid inside a drainpipe, hoping that his enemies would not find him. The Libyan Revolution had started eight months earlier, buoyed by the Arab Spring that had deposed Hosni Mubarak in Egypt and Zine El Abidine Ben Ali in Tunisia. Gaddafi had always dismissed the idea that he was next. *His* people loved him: he had given them the highest per capita GDP and life expectancy in Africa, and he was a different kind of man. "I am a fighter, a revolutionary from tents," Gaddafi said at the uprising's outset, warning that he would never surrender.[1] For his pursuers from the National Liberation Army, the military arm of the National Transition Council (NTC) interim government, the toll of forty-two years of terror outweighed any material benefits he had bestowed. Libyans lacked what mattered most: freedom. For the rebels who now closed in on his hiding place, Gaddafi's end was long overdue.

Every strongman's fall is different, but Gaddafi's involved dynamics common to others in the past. A disaffected population found momentum from events in other countries to take to the streets. Elites who had supported the leader for decades now subtracted their support. A central opposition force gained international recognition and the assistance of foreign military. Several generations of exiles returned to fight. Each group waged resistance against Gaddafi in its own manner, but enough of them came together at a fateful moment to make his end possible.

THE AUTHORITARIAN PLAYBOOK has no chapter on failure. It does not foresee the leader's own people turning against him, from military men he trained to young people he indoctrinated to women he rewarded for having babies. It has no pages on how to deal with becoming a national disgrace, someone who is pelted with tomatoes and eggs when he appears in public after leaving office, like Pinochet, or forced into exile, like Amin. Its discussions of how to control minds and exploit bodies do not extend to the deterioration of the leader's own. Aging and the ebbing of virile powers is difficult for leaders whose "entire sense of self is bound up in being revered," in psychological profiler Jerrold Post's words. Disappearing from the scene due to illness, as Mobutu did in 1996, can be dangerous for men already on the decline.[2] Nothing prepares the ruler to see his propaganda ignored and his charismatic hold weaken until he loses control of the nation and is hunted by his own people, as happened to Mussolini and Gaddafi.

For the strongman, such outcomes are unthinkable and yet ever-present. They fuel behaviors that make him feel safer and brush away thoughts of mortality. That might mean persecuting more enemies, firing more truth-tellers, hoarding more women and riches, or consulting astrologers (many are superstitious) about his fate and his legacy. Such rulers also brood about what happens to their peers. Hitler made sure he did not end up like Mussolini, and Gaddafi cooperated with Americans and Europeans to avoid ending up like Hussein. Analyst Stanislav Belkovsky notes that the Arab Spring revolts made a big impression on Putin, who knew that "the destiny of Gadhafi could be waiting for him." Trump's desire to stay in office indefinitely reflected the same fear of meeting a bad end, losing immunity from prosecution, or becoming a nobody. "You've got to put your name on stuff or no one remembers you," said the president, who showed familiarity with the anxieties about irrelevance that spur authoritarians' demands for loyalty and attention, especially in the end stage of rule.[3]

It's not surprising that most authoritarians leave office involuntarily. They are supremely ill equipped to handle the downward arc of leadership and life. They have trouble abandoning personal traits like hubris, aggression, and greed that served them to stay in power, even when these become self-defeating. Their theft of national revenue and resources may leave them unable to continue to fund the spoils system that kept elites loyal to them, leading to their loss of legitimacy. Believing propaganda about their infallibility can also be lethal. "I follow my instincts, and I am never wrong," said Mussolini, becoming the first of many who ignored experts and relied on the skewed advice of flatterers and relatives, who told him only what he wished to hear. More personalist rulers are toppled by elites than by popular revolutions, especially in situations of economic or military distress. While they may last longer than other kinds of authoritarians, 80 percent of them are booted out of office eventually.[4]

Mobutu's fall from power is symptomatic. By 1990, twenty-five years of kleptocracy and violent behavior had turned elites and the population against him. He took one step forward and three back on his reluctant journey toward democratization. When his American backers grew ambivalent, he hired the lobbyists Roger Stone and Paul Manafort in a futile attempt to save his reputation. "Something died in him from that moment on," said Mobutu's former aide Honoré Ngbanda of Mobutu's awakening to how much he was hated by his people. Mobutu retreated to his compound in Gbadolite, with magicians and marabout healers for company. A 1996 trip to Switzerland for treatment of prostate cancer provided a window for military action by rebel leader Laurent Kabila, prompting Mobutu's 1997 departure to Morocco, where he died a few months later. Charismatic in life, he commands attention from the grave: "Mobutu is the star of the cemetery" said the caretaker of Rabat's European Cemetary in 2017.[5]

Democratic heads of state often see their departures from office as an opportunity to build on their leadership legacy. The authoritarian regards the end of being adulated by followers and controlling everything and everyone as an existential threat. Laura Fermi observed that without his audiences, Mussolini was merely an empty "shell." This is true of every ruler in this book, including those in power today. Strongmen will do *anything* to stay in office, even starting wars or deepening involvement in doomed conflicts, as when Mussolini sent troops to the Eastern Front in 1942. Political scientists call this phenomenon "gambling for resurrection," and almost all autocrats lose the wager.[6]

—

EVEN IN THEIR DEATHS, which came one day apart in April 1945, Mussolini's and Hitler's fates were intertwined. For years each had enabled the other, but the start of World War II gave the Führer the upper hand. In February 1939, in his supreme wisdom as head of the ministries of war, army, navy, colonies, and air force, Il Duce signed the Pact of Steel alliance with Germany, even though Italy needed years to replenish finances and military equipment exhausted by years of combat. In mid-August 1939, he dispatched his foreign minister, Galeazzo Ciano, to Germany to convince Nazi foreign minister Joachim von Ribbentrop and Hitler to call off the war. The encounter did not go well. "The decision to fight is implacable," Ciano reported back to his father-in-law. "During the dinner hour not a word is exchanged." As a last resort, Mussolini declared that Italy would be a "non-belligerent" country. Ignoring the counsel of his generals and Hitler's increasingly angry messages, Mussolini spent the next nine months in denial, passing hours each day with Clara Petacci and other lovers.[7]

The success of Hitler's blitzkrieg in France changed the Italian leader's mind, as did reports from cowed underlings that told him what he wanted to hear about Italy's military capacities. On June 10, 1940, Mussolini announced Italy's mobilization. On June 11, the first Allied bombs hit Italian cities, starting years of civilian suffering. Huge numbers of Italians evacuated to the countryside, and those who remained spent time in cellars and other improvised bomb shelters. Focused on the glories of foreign conquest, Mussolini had never bothered to develop adequate anti-aircraft defenses to protect his people. "You may be powerful, but you're not immortal. You too will die one day," Lina Romani warned Mussolini in a letter from Trent a few days after the bombardments began.[8]

The Italian military fought tenaciously given their lack of adequate provisions and weapons, but they could not overcome Italy's inability to fight a multifront war. A misguided strategy that diverted troops from Africa to the Balkans and Russia made it easier for the Allies to liberate East Africa. In May 1941, Emperor Haile Selassie returned to his Ethiopian throne, and in 1942–1943, the Allies also took Libya, ending Fascism's imperial dream. As Italy became a liability, Hitler treated Mussolini imperiously, haranguing him for hours at their meetings. Mussolini, in turn, blamed his people for being "cowards."[9]

The year 1942 was the turning point on the home front. Having to endure air raids, hunger, and desperation, more Italians lost their fear of the regime. In Turin, workers organized large-scale strikes, the first in sixteen years. Communist networks revived and Christian Democrats organized Catholic resistance from inside the Vatican. Mussolini had promised to tame corruption in Italy, but twenty years later, Fascism had become a symbol for many Italians of "racketeering, exploitation of the weak, injustice, immorality," as an informer reported in 1942. Even Mussolini's daughter Edda acknowledged reality after seeing starving children in Palermo: "I have been in Albania and Russia, but I have never seen suffering and pain on this scale," she wrote indignantly to her father that year. In 1942, a record number of people were also arrested for insulting Il Duce, and in 1943, far fewer Italians wrote to ask for his photograph. By then, Mussolini barely appeared in public, fueling rumors he was sick or dead. When he spoke on the radio, people were not sure it was him. His image, once so indelible, had lost its impact.[10]

"Seldom in history has the overthrow of a government been more overdue and less prepared for than that of 25 July 1943 in Italy," wrote Friedrich-Karl von Plehwe, military attaché at the German embassy in

Rome, of Mussolini's ouster by his Grand Council (which had not met since 1939). The Allies had landed in Sicily weeks before, and Il Duce had lost all legitimacy for many of the men on that council, who had been hired and fired by him many times. Minister of National Education Giuseppe Bottai, a Mussolini loyalist since the squadrist days, had reached his limit when the dictator called him in 1941 and curtly ordered him to the Greek front:

> I put down the receiver, mechanically. I gaze ahead of me into the void. My fourth war arrives in this dehumanized way from my Leader. . . . Something that's been beating in my heart for more than twenty years suddenly stops: a Love, a faith, a devotion. Now I am alone, without my Leader.[11]

Two years later, Bottai was among the Grand Council members who voted 19–7 on the night of July 24 to depose Il Duce and extricate Italy from an impossible situation. Unable to comprehend this insurrection by his subordinates, Mussolini came to work the next day as though nothing had happened. Summoned by the king, who now ruled alongside Marshal Pietro Badoglio, he was taken to the Ponza penal colony and ultimately to a lodge in the Gran Sasso mountains.

For twenty years, Italian state radio had broadcast Mussolini's propaganda. At 10:47 p.m. that July 25, it told listeners that his rule had finally ended. A collective shout could be heard in every city and town center, and parents woke up their children to tell them the news. Mussolini sculptures were smashed and pictures of him tossed from windows. People made bonfires out of their Fascist uniforms and party cards, and a Roman tram circulated with a banner that read, "the tragic carnival is over." Fascist loyalists, overcome with grief and dread, hid at home. Carlo Ciseri, who had been mesmerized by Mussolini as a youth in 1920, was "overcome with a kind of vertigo that left me stunned and confused and prevented me from speaking" when he got the news at his British POW camp in Kenya. Throughout the summer of 1943, as the Allies advanced up the peninsula, the country lived in limbo, its military still fighting in the Axis although Il Duce was no longer in power.[12]

Mussolini's second act started with Marshal Pietro Badoglio's surrender to the Allies on September 8. As the king and Badoglio went south to set up the kingdom of Italy in Allied-liberated territory, 800,000 Italian military men serving in Italy and abroad, now considered by the Germans to have betrayed the Axis, were deported to concentration camps throughout the Reich. Four days later, commandos led by SS officer Otto Skorzeny rescued Mussolini and reunited him with his family in Germany. Nazi aides' courtesy did not fool Il Duce's wife Rachele: the Germans were in charge now.[13]

"Half of Italy is German, half is English, and there is no longer an Italian Italy," wrote the partisan Emmanuele Artom on September 9 as Hitler installed Mussolini at the head of a German client state, the Republic of Salò. As civil war exploded between Nazi-backed Italian Fascists and Allied-backed partisans, Italy's labor, food supply, and military were subordinated to the needs of the German war machine.[14] Years of Italian Fascist anti-Semitic propaganda and legislation, including a 1938 census of Italian Jews, helped Italians and Germans to hunt down Jews and expropriate their assets. Italian engineers drove the trains that took Jews to the border to be deported or to Trieste to be exterminated in the Risiera di San Sabbia camp, where SS official Franz Suchomel, formerly of Sobibor and Treblinka, now plied his trade. Of the almost 9,000 Jews deported from Italian territories between 1943 and 1945, just 12 percent came home. Many non-Jewish Italians, clergy included, sheltered Jews in homes, factories, and monasteries. A phone call from one of her father's Christian employees let eleven-year-old Anna Saxon's family escape the October 1943 Nazi roundup in Rome's Jewish ghetto.[15]

That month, Europe's largest resistance movement took shape. Fighters flowed in from over fifty nations, swelling from a core of 9,000 partisans to more than 250,000 by April 1945. Libyans and other survivors of Italian imperial oppression took up arms against the Fascists, as did escaped Allied POWs and Russian partisans. An estimated 44,000 resistance fighters died.[16] For Italians, joining the resistance reactivated codes of honor and humanitarian principles that Fascism had scorned. Their ranks included career military men like General Quirino Armellino and Italian Jews like Primo Levi, detained as a partisan before his deportation to Auschwitz. The Communist commando Ilio Barontini had trained with the Red Army in Russia and the Maoists in Manchuria and then fought in Spain and with Ethiopian guerrillas. Now he returned home and became "Commander Dario" of a resistance unit in Emilia-Romagna. The partisan Ada Gobetti, whose publisher husband Piero Gobetti had died in 1926 after being beaten by Fascists, saw the resistance as the recovery of "a bond of solidarity, founded not on a community of blood, country, or intellectual tradition, but on a simple human relationship, the feeling of being at one with many."[17]

For Mussolini, who had been used to the many feeling communion with the One, these years of diminished power in Salò were difficult. An SS vehicle was part of his escort, and the Germans recorded his conversations. His writings during the period, published in summer 1944 in the *Corriere della sera*, display the authoritarian's capacity to blame others for the messes he causes. "It's not surprising that people destroy the idols of their own creation. Perhaps it is the only way to bring them [the idols] down to human proportions," he wrote of his fall from power, as though his repression and incompetency had nothing to do with his fate. From prison, one former idolizer, Tullio Cianetti, (a Fascist minister punished for voting to remove Mussolini in 1943) acknowledged that he had been too infatuated with "Mussolinian miracle working" and too blinded by the cult of "the man who knows, foresees and achieves everything" to see how the the dictator was leading Italy to disaster.[18]

Mussolini was mortal enough to the Communist partisans who captured him and his lover Petacci on April 27, 1945, and shot them the next day. On April 29, their bodies were taken to Milan's Piazza Loreto, where someone with a sense of gallows humor placed a scepter in Mussolini's hands. "No one had ever looked at the Italians the way he had when he was alive," wrote Curzio Malaparte of Il Duce's gaze that had captivated so many. Now Italians paid him back for his betrayal of their trust, urinating on his corpse and beating it until the famous face was almost unrecognizable. To end the spectacle and allow more people to see he was really dead, the bodies of Mussolini and Petacci, along with those of other Fascist officials, were suspended from a gas station before being taken to the morgue.[19]

Even in death, Mussolini's body continued to call to some Italians. In 1946, it went missing for three weeks after some Fascists stole it from its unmarked grave. After that, the state kept the location of his corpse (now missing a leg) secret even from his family. In 1957, Mussolini was brought home to his birthplace, Predappio, for reburial. There to meet him was his wife Rachele, who had outlasted all of his lovers and knew him better than anyone in the world, which is probably why she never prayed at the temple of his greatness. "My husband appeared to be a lion, but instead he was a rather sad and small man," she told a journalist in 1946.[20]

—

MANY PEOPLE HAD PREDICTED that Hitler might kill himself one day. The palm reader Josef Ranald, who met him in 1932, foresaw suicidal tendencies and a "violent end." The Führer seemed confident and unstoppable, though, at the outset of World War II. He is "the sole master of the circus ring," the writer André Gide observed after the fall of France to the Nazis in June 1940. "Soon the very people he is crushing will be obliged, while cursing him, to admire him."[21]

Yet Germans found it challenging to continue to admire Hitler as the war went on. The Nazis' 1941 invasion of Russia led to a protracted two-front war, and the Stalingrad defeat of 1942–1943 shook the doctrine of Nazi military and racial superiority. Between 1942 and 1945, 390,000 Allied bombings cost half a million lives in 130 towns and cities. Germans also lacked food and clothing. Women wore their dead husbands' and brothers' garments, and workers from the East labored with rags around their feet. Even 111,000 pairs of shoes and 155,000 coats, collected from victims of the gas chambers at Auschwitz and Majdanek, could not meet the demand.[22]

Like all strongmen, the Führer lacked empathy. The turn in Germany's fortunes brought out the "truly terrifying weakness of his character" that General Walter Warlimont had seen during setbacks in the 1940 occupation of Norway. Hitler's speeches, once his source of emotional connection with Germans, now disappointed with their lack of warmth and reassurance. Letters to him and requests for his autograph declined drastically, and criticism of him escalated, leading to record numbers of prosecutions for anti-Hitler remarks in 1942.[23]

Mussolini assuaged his anxieties with sex, and Hitler relied on dozens of drugs prescribed by his physician, Dr. Theodor Morell. These did nothing to improve his capacity to assess reality. General Franz Halder worried that Hitler's "chronic tendency to underrate enemy capabilities is gradually assuming grotesque proportions." A woman in a Schweinfurt bomb shelter predicted he would "leave us all in the mess and put a bullet through his head." The July 20, 1944, assassination attempt brought a wave of Führer affection, but his disappearance from the scene after that decreased confidence. "The Führer was sent to us from God, though not in order to save Germany, but to ruin it" was one German's judgment of the outcome of Hitler's national project.[24]

In January 1945, the Red Army reached Germany (the Western Allies arrived in March), and the liberation of the concentration camps began. In Auschwitz-Birkenau, women who could still walk took tablecloths from SS camp offices to make "liberation dresses"—a first step to reclaiming their identity. That month Hitler moved into his Berlin bunker and left Germans to their fate. Like Mussolini, he blamed his own people for the unfolding catastrophe. But he also felt they should be obliterated due to their unworthiness. "Let it perish and be annihilated by some stronger power. . . . I shall shed no tears for the German nation," Hitler had stated in 1941, speaking of the eventuality of defeat, his scorn for his people evident. His March 1945 Nero Decree mandated the destruction of vital military and transport infrastructure, orders that his architect Albert Speer, now minister of Armaments and War Production, worked to countermand.[25]

On Hitler's birthday, April 20, the Soviets bombed Berlin as the Allies surrounded the capital. Days later, the fashion house of Annemarie Heise received a request for a couture dress, which was delivered under fire to the Führerbunker. Eva Braun wore it with Ferragamo black suede shoes at her wedding on April 29, the same day that Hitler heard the news of Il Duce's death and macabre display. On April 30, he and Braun took cyanide, and he shot himself in the head. Fulfilling his desires that his death not become a "spectacle," aides incinerated their bodies in the bunker's garden. Hitler escaped Mussolini's public humiliation, but his ashes, taken by the Red Army, ended up the property of the Communists he had so hated.[26]

The absence of a body deprived Germans of the cathartic verification of death the Italians had with Mussolini. Some of his followers preferred to believe he had escaped to Argentina. Tens of thousands of others, driven by military codes of honor or by a mix of nihilism and shame, killed themselves in 1945. They included Magda and Joseph Goebbels; 10 to 20 percent of German generals and admirals; and myriad NSDAP members and civil servants. In July 1945, as Germany lay in ruins, US Army intelligence officers interviewed Hitler's sister Paula. "I must honestly confess that I would have preferred it if he had followed his original ambition and become an architect," she stated, speaking for millions.[27]

—

ALL STRONGMEN BELIEVE they have been touched by divine providence, but Franco's ending might suggest he had a special dispensation. Dying of illness at eighty-two years old in his own country after more than three decades of repressing his people, Franco appeared to have mastered the authoritarian playbook. His first survival move had been declining to join the Axis in World War II. This separated his destiny from that of Hitler and Mussolini and made his political rehabilitation as a Cold War client possible. Franco also led a less complicated life than his sex, drug, and expansion-addicted fellow fascists. He put all his attention into securing his authority at home and persecuting the left. "Franco's political strategy is simple as a spear," wrote the historian Salvador de Madariaga. "There is no action of his that is not directed towards his consolidation of power. . . . The only thing Franco believes in is Franco himself."[28]

The Spaniard's legitimacy as a ruler rested on the idea that he brought peace to Spain from the civil war onward, saving it from leftist apocalypse. His real success, though, was creating silence around memories of his violence. If you had been a leftist combatant in the past and wanted to avoid persecution in the present, then "it was more important to forget than to remember," as one Republican veteran stated. The slave-labor-built Valley of the Fallen memorial complex, inaugurated in 1959 as a site of "national reconciliation" (it contained the graves of Nationalist and Republican fighters), symbolized a memory politics that was codified in the 1977 "Pact of Silence" amnesty for perpetrators after Franco's death.[29]

Franco shaped decades of Spain's history, but he could not turn back time. In 1969, he appointed Prince Juan Carlos I as his successor while he continued in power. He declined slowly from Parkinson's disease and other ailments, and in 1975 his body settled into its crypt in the Valley of the Fallen. Other bodies, thrown into unmarked mass graves all over Spain by Nationalist troops during the civil war, then called out to their loved ones. Or so it seemed to people in villages like Arnedo, who hired diggers to exhume the corpses of family members for reburial. These semi-clandestine grassroots initiatives started an accounting of the fates of more than 100,000 people that continues today as Spanish archaeologists excavate mass graves and restore the remains of Franco's victims to their families.[30]

The family of Catalina Muñoz was among these. Muñoz, a thirty-seven-year-old mother of four had her youngest, nine-month-old Martin, in her arms when the Nationalists came for her in August 1936. She still had his baby rattle in her pocket when they shot her in September and left her in a mass grave in the Palencia zone. Her son Martin grew up with his aunt, and when his leftist father returned from seventeen years in prison, his mother was never discussed. The baby rattle was discovered with Muñoz's skeleton by a team of archaeologists in 2011, but when they tracked down the almost eighty-year-old Martin, he initially did not want to hear about her. His sister Lucia and daughter Martina, contacted by an *El Pais* journalist, took charge of recovering Muñoz's remains and arranging for her reburial in Cevico de la Torre cemetery next to her husband. On June 23, 2019, Martin was present when the Association for the Recovery of the Historical Memory of Palencia and the Aranzadi Society paid homage to Muñoz. Those gathered to honor her shook baby rattles as Martin's was restored to him. "*Qué tiempos aquellos* (what times those were)," he said softly, holding this symbol of an interrupted mother-son love.[31]

Four months later came Franco's reckoning. The Socialist Party had long sought to have his body removed from the Valley of the Fallen, arguing that it did not belong in a site maintained by public funds. In October 2019, years of litigation with Franco's family and the Francisco Franco Foundation culminated in the transfer of his remains to a cemetery near the El Pardo palace. Franco's supporters claimed the move would "reopen old rifts in Spanish society." Instead, it closed a historical period still tinged with the stardust of Franco's cult of power. The Valley of the Fallen is being transformed into a site of historical education, as mandated by the 2007 Memory Law. As excavations of graves continue and thousands of humble objects of devotion and pride flow from the dead to the living—wedding rings, lapel pins, a baby rattle—the full toll of Franco's dictatorship on Spanish society may one day be known.[32]

PINOCHET HAD ALWAYS MODELED HIMSELF on Franco. He partially succeeded in following the Spaniard's path: he, too, died in his native land of natural causes, avoiding exile or execution. Yet the Chilean had a far more complicated end. He lost power in stages. His ejection from political power by the October 1988 plebiscite was followed by his 1998 arrest in London and the exposure of his corruption in the early 2000s. All of this shocked him. Hearing only what he wished to hear, Pinochet dismissed signs in the 1980s that many in the US government saw him as an anachronism. When American ambassador to Chile Harry Barnes broke precedent by meeting with the opposition, Pinochet banned Barnes from the presidential palace, as though that would solve the problem. Above all, the Chilean leader underestimated his people's determination to end his rule and restore democracy.[33]

During the 1988 plebiscite campaign (this vote on whether he should continue in office had been mandated by the 1980 constitution), Pinochet toured the country, giving out deeds to new homes to win over the poor. Yet this was no democratic election. The offices of the opposition campaign were firebombed, volunteers beaten, rallies forcibly dissolved, and thousands arrested. His television ads relied on the old scare tactics. They showed a man drowning in rising water, a mother and child fleeing an armed mob, and even Allende, resurrected from the grave and clutching a rifle. Pinochet played on fears of leftist anarchy as he sent Chileans a chilling message: vote for me or else.[34]

This threatening atmosphere made the opposition's success at mobilizing civil society all the more remarkable. Crucially, anti-Pinochet parties put aside their differences, and over a dozen of them united in one coalition, the *Concertación*. The junta had thrown away voter lists after the coup, but the National Endowment for Democracy and Civic Crusade, helped by $2.2 million of American aid, registered 7.4 million Chileans and trained 120,000 poll watchers. Activists went door-to-door to convince people their vote would matter, and a Tribunal of Jurists was established to ratify a parallel vote count.[35] The opposition's carefully conceived positive campaign acknowledged the "desire for care and solidarity" that came out of earlier mass demonstrations. The NO+ slogan of the CADA collective returned as a March for Joy held in September 1988 drew hundreds of thousands. Television spots that featured ordinary people daring to feel hope for Chile struck a chord.[36]

The choice of the moderate Christian Democrat leader Patricio Aylwin as the opposition candidate helped to restore trust in the political process. With his baggy sweaters and serene manner, the law professor projected a nonthreatening civilian masculinity. He also reassured conservatives that neoliberal economic policies would not be reversed. Other opposition figures played more confrontational roles. In December 1987, Socialist leader Ricardo Lagos broke a taboo by accusing Pinochet on television of "torture, assassination and human rights violations," telling the nervous interviewers who tried to quiet him, "I speak for 15 years of silence." New publications like *La Época* revealed the "hidden history" of military violence, and the junta-allied newspaper *El Mercurio* started to cover human rights to regain an audience that had declined to a 13 percent share. By the time the plebiscite arrived, Pinochet no longer had a monopoly on public narratives of his actions as a leader.[37]

The dictator's defeat on October 5, 1988, made headlines around the world, but the 54.7 percent to 43 percent vote meant that Chile started its journey to democracy as a divided nation. Pinochet's exit package let him stay on as head of the armed forces until 1998 and then become a senator for life, a position that carried immunity from prosecution. He spent his last year in office working to limit the power of the new democracy, for example by stacking the Chilean Supreme Court to make sure loyalist justices had a majority. Yet Pinochet couldn't stop the measures Aylwin's government took in the early 1990s to address the dictatorship's injustices. Victims' families got reparations payments, hundreds of political prisoners were pardoned, and exiles received repatriation assistance. By 1994, 50,000 of 200,000 Chilean exiles had returned home.[38]

Prosecution of Pinochet's perpetrators took longer. The military's claim that Pinochet's 1978 amnesty prevented criminal justice proceedings regarding actions taken during the peak years of terror saved former DINA torturers like Ingrid Olderock from prison. She felt secure enough to have an "I love my dogs" bumper sticker on her car in 1996. But others, most notably former DINA head Manuel Contreras, served time. His first jail term in 1995–2001 for Orlando Letelier's 1976 murder was followed by hundreds of years' worth of sentences. Paul Schäfer of the neo-Nazi Colonia Dignidad went to prison in 2005. By 2007, dozens of army generals and close to 500 officers and former DINA agents had been prosecuted, a number that increased to 800 by 2015.[39]

The final volume of Pinochet's memoirs, published in 1994, gives a sense of how he experienced the end of the dictatorship. Photographs of him with admirers, flattery from foreign luminaries like Kissinger, and mentions of Caesar and Napoleon emphasize his place in history beyond "electoral contingencies." A darker tone takes over as he depicts the plebiscite as a "transnational" conspiracy by Fidel Castro and American officials and as a Nazi-style "Night of the Long Knives" plot, with "Mr. Harry Barnes Jr." in the role of Hitler. For strongmen like Pinochet, leaving office is like a plunge into a psychological abyss, and the Chilean leader's references to *la vorágine plebiscitaria* (the chasm of the plebiscite) express a sense of being annihilated.[40]

The year 1998 was a watershed year. In London, where Pinochet had gone for medical treatment, he was placed under house arrest for crimes against humanity. Spanish National Court judge Baltasar Garzón, who grew up under Franco, initiated the charges. Garzón applied the principle of universal jurisdiction in requesting Pinochet's extradition to stand trial in Spain. The House of Lords set legal precedent in denying Pinochet immunity, but the British Home Office let him return home on grounds of ill health. As soon as the plane landed in Santiago in 2000, Pinochet performed a strongman miracle, getting out of his wheelchair, suddenly recovered, to enjoy a welcome ceremony.[41]

Yet the news of the former dictator's arrest had set the wheels of justice in motion. Months earlier, Chilean Communist Party head Gladys Marín had filed the first suit that named Pinochet personally, accusing him of genocide, kidnapping, and other human rights violations.

In London, Cristina Godoy-Navarrete, who had endured rape and violence by DINA agents as a student, was one of four former prisoners who requested that charges be filed against Pinochet for kidnapping and torture. This meant telling her children for the first time what had happened to her. Pinochet was stripped of his immunity, and cases were eventually opened against him for his role in the Caravan of Death and Operation Condor. Multiple indictments followed, although a dubious diagnosis of dementia by military doctors allowed him to avoid standing trial.[42]

As Pinochet's violence was exposed, so was his corruption. In 2004 came the discovery of secret Riggs Bank accounts and in 2005 revelations of kickbacks he received on the arms deals he made with Britain and other countries, these illicit profits secured in offshore accounts. The resulting charges against him and his family included tax evasion, misuse of public funds, money-laundering, and more.[43]

Unlike legions of his lackeys, Pinochet never went to prison. He died in December 2006 with hundreds of cases open against him and zero convictions. "Death got him before justice," reflected the writer and artist Pedro Lemebel in a blistering *La Nación* essay on Pinochet's passing. At the funeral, Francisco Cuadrado Prats, grandson of the murdered general Carlos Prats, spat on Pinochet's coffin. Augusto Pinochet Molina, grandson of the dictator, praised his namesake and was removed from the military the next day.[44]

"Time, alas, is on the side of death and oblivion," writes the Chilean exile Ariel Dorfman, but continuing judicial reckonings have kept alive the memory of Pinochet's crimes. Chileans followed the 2013–2016 Operation Condor trial, held in Buenos Aires and livestreamed in Santiago, Asunción, La Paz, and Montevideo. In the courtroom, people held up faded pictures of their disappeared loved ones to the defendants through the glass security wall.[45] Pinochet thought he would follow Franco in exiting the scene in glory with his secrets still his own. Instead, once he lost power, he faced human rights activists, investigative journalists, and judges specializing in international law, all of whom would be the strongman's nemeses in the twenty-first century.

—

GADDAFI THOUGHT HE HAD MASTERED the transition to the new authoritarian era. He outdid Franco in his willingness to ally with his former enemies if his survival required it. He partnered with the West as he rode the crest of the post-9/11 anti-Islamist crusade. He had no intention of being forced into exile, like Mobutu and Amin, or meeting the fate of Sadaam Hussein, who was pulled out of a hole in the ground by American soldiers and executed by his own people after being found guilty of crimes against humanity.

In the mid- and late 2000s, to forestall rising domestic opposition, Gaddafi experimented with some liberalization. His son Saif al-Islam, who had a PhD from the London School of Economics, became the emblem of a new Libya. Saif al-Islam started an anti-torture campaign and a "Reform and Repent" program for Islamist prisoners (one hundred were freed in 2006). His Al Ghad media group, which included the Libya Press news agency, the Al Libia television network, and several newspapers, touched on issues of corruption. Like Pinochet, Gaddafi found domestic reform dangerous. By the end of 2010, he had shut down his son's experiments and arrested many Al Ghad employees.[46]

Through it all, Gaddafi's resentment of the West remained unchanged. In 2003 he had agreed to pay $1.5 billion to families of victims of the 1988 Scotland and 1989 Niger terrorist attacks. In 2009, though, his government falsely claimed it could not pay back the "loan" it took to fund this compensation. Gaddafi demanded that Western oil companies pay Libya's reparations or suffer "serious consequences." Those that caved to his extortion effectively paid his penance for killing their fellow citizens.[47] When Gaddafi was invited to speak that same year at the UN General Assembly, he used his debut to deliver a tirade against Western imperialism. Trump, too, saw Gaddafi's visit to New York as an opportunity. In 2009, he had sought out the Libyan dictator unsuccessfully to fund a project billed as "Mediterranean waterfront and construction." Knowing Gaddafi was having trouble finding a place to pitch the gigantic tent he used as lodging, Trump rented the Libyan his Bedford, New York, estate. When neighbors blocked the deal, Trump claimed he had "screwed" the Libyan out of his $200,000 deposit. The incident sums up the way both foreign elites and Gaddafi benefited from Libya's rapprochement with the West: they earned money, while he prolonged his time in power.[48]

"Some people will die and people will forget about them but the result will be that right will triumph, good will triumph, progress will triumph": this was Gaddafi's philosophy. But his scorn for his people and disregard for the bonds of love and memory came back to bite him in 2011. Libya's revolution started among women who had protested for years outside the Benghazi courthouse, demanding information about their family members who had disappeared in Abu Salim prison. The February 15 arrest of human rights lawyer Fathi Terbil, the man who represented *them*, proved to be one injustice too many. Fueled by the Arab Spring successes in Tunisia and Egypt, dozens of protestors grew to hundreds on February 16 and then to thousands for the February 17 Day of Rage. When government forces fired on this peaceful demonstration, a local campaign against human rights injustices turned into a movement to bring down a regime.[49]

Gaddafi had promised Libyans freedom from exploitation, but by 2011, millions associated him with misery and tyranny. Already suffocated by corruption, the Libyan economy also suffered from a decline in oil prices after the 2008 recession. Unemployed young men formed the initial core of an insurgency that expanded to include hard-up middle-class Libyans. Women sheltered and fed rebels, smuggled weapons, and worked as journalists, but were mostly kept away from armed struggle, despite their military training—a taste of the gender politics to come as Islamists gained power.[50]

By February 20, the revolution had spread from the east to Tripolitania, adding many defectors from the armed forces. The Gaddafi-allied Warfalla tribe had always had its dissenters, like the officers of the 1993 coup whose memory was honored in an insurgent Brigade 93. Now tribal elder Akram Al-Warfalli sent a message to Gaddafi on *Al Jazeera* in late February: "We tell the brother, well he's no longer a brother, we tell him to leave the country."[51]

Exile was inconceivable to Gaddafi, who at first was stunned by events so at odds with the state propaganda about his popularity that he had come to believe. "All my people love me," he told CNN's Christine Amanpour early in the conflict. "They will die to protect me." As the uprising intensified, his shock turned to rage. Consistent with the strongman mentality, he saw the revolution as a personal betrayal. "I am not going to leave this land," he told Libyans on February 22, vowing to "cleanse Libya . . . house by house, alley by alley, and individual by individual." Gaddafi here sounded like Franco, and in March he compared his siege on Benghazi to the Spaniard's taking of Madrid.[52]

As in the Italian resistance, exiles returned to fight the man who had changed their lives forever. Anwar Haraga had moved to Manchester with his fiancée upon his release in 2000 after eleven years in Abu Salim prison. In August 2011, he participated in the siege of the Libyan capital, fighting with the Tripoli Brigade. Anwar Fekini, a Sorbonne-educated lawyer, also returned to Libya, to coordinate resistance efforts against Gaddafi. He carried with him the spirit of his warrior grandfather Mohamed Fekini, who had fought the Fascists in the 1920s, and the reformist hopes of his uncle, Mohieddin Fekini, prime minister during the monarchy.[53]

The existence of hundreds of insurgent groups, some of which did not accept the transitional NTC government's authority, made for a chaotic environment. So did NATO military interventions undertaken without a clear transition plan. Berlusconi came out against proposed NATO actions in February, seeing no defined path for Libya's future (and no substitute for Libyan oil), but Italy joined the air strikes that began in March. By August, with Gaddafi's stronghold of Tripoli surrounded, Libyan elites also turned against him. Abdessalam Jalloud, who had been with Gaddafi since his coup-plotting days, now called on Libyans to "disown this tyrant." He warned that Gaddafi, unlike Hitler, would not kill himself.[54]

Gaddafi's death resembled Hussein's and Mussolini's rather than the Führer's. On October 20, NATO bombs destroyed much of Gaddafi's convoy as he tried to reach his native village. National Liberation Army fighters found him hiding in a sewage pipe and dragged him out of the earth. "What did I do to you?" Gaddafi cried as he was beaten and shot multiple times. His body was taken to a cold storage room in Misrata for display to the public. Some Libyans drove hundreds of miles to see with their own eyes that he was dead.[55]

For Soraya, who spent years captive in Gaddafi's compound, seeing his body on television brought relief and bitterness. "I had wanted him to live. . . . I wanted him to account for his actions." Her ordeal hardly ended with his passing, since she was raped by both pro-Gaddafi and anti-Gaddafi fighters. As investigations by the UN Human Rights Council and Libyan psychologist Seham Sergiwa found, the regime's culture of sexual violence continued during the civil war. Rape became part of a policy of revenge and intimidation. Rising Islamist influence also led to rollbacks of female freedoms. Three days after Gaddafi's death, the National Transition Council government chair Mustafa Abdul Jalil announced Libya's liberation—and a new legislative framework based on Sharia law that loosened restrictions on polygamy. "I guess we all expected a lot more," the psychotherapist Samar Auassoud reflected in 2018. She and other women had hoped that ending dictatorship would bring greater gender equality—or at least a Libya where one could live without fear.[56]

Hisham Matar, whose family was torn apart by Gaddafi's violence, had waited years for that day to come. In February 2011, his relatives were released from Abu Salim, except for his father, Jaballa Matar, whose fate was still unknown. In 2012, a year after Gaddafi died, Matar returned to the country he had left decades earlier. He did not find out what happened to his father, but he saw his uncle Mahmoud. "I kept a place in my mind, where I was still able to love and forgive everyone," Mahmoud told him, explaining how he survived twenty-one years in prison. "They never succeeded to take that from me."[57]

———

"*SIC TRANSIT GLORIA MUNDI*" ("So passes the glory of the world"), said Berlusconi upon hearing that Gaddafi had died.[58] Less than a month later, on November 15, 2011, it was Berlusconi's turn to leave office, having been asked to resign by President Giorgio Napolitano at a critical moment in the eurozone crisis. It was a strangely low-key ending for such a commanding personality, who had twenty indictments and seven convictions to his name (all overturned). The "technocratic" government that replaced him, led by former EU Commissioner Mario Monti, an economist, rebuked Berlusconi's preference for loyalty over expertise.

Seventy-five years old when he stepped down, Berlusconi had represented for his fans a model of aging while retaining masculine power. His disclosures of his plastic surgeries, like the "California lifting" he had at a Swiss clinic, increased his emotional appeal for both men and women. His boasts about his virility angered critics who saw his machismo as part of his authoritarian governing style, but delighted his admirers. "He lost his wife but not his votes," said commentator Beppe Severgnini in 2009 of the consequences of his compulsion to have young female bodies at his disposal.[59]

"I was the star of the last two international summits: everyone wants to take a picture with me because I am a tycoon and not a politician," Berlusconi boasted in December 2010. In fact, his personality cult left Forza Italia no space to develop a political identity independent of him, and no respite from his endless judicial woes, scandals, and loyalty tests. Protection of Berlusconi "from real or imagined attacks had become more important than long-term and wide-ranging reform," political scientist Giovanni Orsina concludes.[60]

By February 2011, the sense of political stasis and dissatisfaction with Berlusconi had reached a critical point. Millions filled the streets of thirty

Italian cities that month calling for his resignation. Among Italians aged twenty-five to thirty-four, who were vocal about the need for a different leader, participation in protest movements had increased since 2006 from 28.3 percent to 41.7 percent. Berlusconi's April 2011 trial for sex with the underage El Mahroug was a media spectacle, with 110 accredited reporters and 200 witnesses present. Thirty-three individuals who had attended his sex parties were in the courtroom, including George Clooney, who had departed after dinner, but not before Berlusconi proudly showed the American actor his "Putin bed." The Italian leader framed the charges as more judicial persecution and leftist slander, but the old talking points no longer worked when underage sex was on the table.[61]

The eurozone crisis prompted Berlusconi's removal, but years of his sexist behavior, corruption, and alliances with autocrats contributed to his loss of credibility among European leaders and financial and political elites. Italy was spared the fates of Greece, Portugal, and Spain due in part to Italians' robust saving habits, but the country's $2.6 trillion sovereign debt surpassed the capabilities of EU and other financial rescue mechanisms. Berlusconi did not want to implement the austerity measures being pushed by the EU and the IMF. When Italian ten-year bonds rose in October to a threshold of unsustainability, though, the Italian financial establishment issued an ultimatum: reform or resign.[62]

The coup de grâce to Berlusconi's reputation came when reporters at an October 23 emergency summit asked Merkel and Sarkozy if they believed that Italy would meet its obligations. The normally diplomatic German chancellor rolled her eyes, the French president smirked, and the room exploded in laughter, as Berlusconi stood by. In 2009, Ambassador Spogli had warned Secretary of State Clinton that Berlusconi's transformation into a "mouthpiece" of Putin made him an ineffective leader and unreliable ally. Now the cost to his country of his behavior and character was evident. When Napolitano summoned Berlusconi to the presidential palace three weeks later, the Italian president made it clear that the request for the prime minister's resignation could not be refused.[63]

It is a testament to the power of Berlusconi's personality cult and media machine that his forced resignation did not initially lose him his core voters. Rather, as was the case with Trump's 2019 impeachment, it reinforced his supporters' loyalty to him by playing into his cult of victimhood. When Forza Italia was revived as a party for the 2013 elections, it lost to the center-left by less than 1 percent. Later that year the hammer fell. Berlusconi was banned for running for office until 2018 as part of his convictions for tax fraud, sex with a minor, wiretapping, and bribery. In 2017, Berlusconi gave Putin a duvet cover adorned with their faces, but by then he was no longer useful to the Russian president, who had found a far more powerful partner to promote his agendas.[64]

Berlusconi avoided prison, but some of his closest collaborators ended up behind bars or under house arrest. Since he was over seventy, he was allowed to substitute a year of community service, which he served at a Milan eldercare facility. In 2019, judges decided that his collaborator Emilio Fede, then eighty-eight years old, could serve his four-year and seven-month sentence for procurement under house arrest. Marcello Dell'Utri, his close associate for decades, was less fortunate. In 2014, when the Supreme Court upheld his 2004 conviction for the crime of Mafia association, Dell'Utri fled to Lebanon to escape imprisonment, but was apprehended. His seven-year prison term ends in 2021.[65]

Unlike Pinochet, Berlusconi did not write an official memoir. But the theme of his persecution recurs in the extensive interviews he did in 2014–2015 with journalist Alan Friedman. He described his legal troubles as the result of "a judicial coup" and commented that he felt "invisible," having been largely absent from television. As soon as his ban on political activity ended in 2018, the eighty-one-year-old was back in front of the cameras, campaigning for Forza Italia and joking about giving Gaddafi tips on oral sex. The election that year confirmed the seismic shifts in the national political landscape since his 2011 departure from office. Beppe Grillo's Five Star Movement and Matteo Salvini's League formed Europe's first all-populist government, having gotten the votes of almost half the electorate. The center-left received just 18 percent and

Forza Italia barely 14 percent. But Berlusconi managed to keep a foot in politics through his election to the European Parliament in 2019.[66]

Master of the television age, Berlusconi has little place in the Internet era. When the Italian leader left office in 2011, the activist and theorist Franco "Bifo" Berardi had warned that someone "younger and colder" could prevail as leader of the "populist army." That person is forty-six-year-old League leader Salvini, who uses social media with the same skill as Berlusconi used television. This twenty-first-century strongman tweets about eating and drinking only national products, poses shirtless, admires Putin, and kisses his rosary at strategic moments. Salvini also recalls past authoritarian leaders in his violent language and open racism. Berlusconi penned up migrants, among the very first to do so in Europe; but in 2017, as minister of the interior, Salvini echoed Franco and Gaddafi as he called for "mass cleansings, street by street, neighborhood by neighborhood" of immigrants.[67]

IN MARCH 2015, BERLUSCONI had proposed to "transform Forza Italia into the Republican Party." That same month, Trump set up an exploratory committee for a presidential campaign that accelerated the Republican Party's transformation into a version of Forza Italia. The GOP's authoritarian drift predated Trump. Yet by 2020, the party had become the tool of a personalist leader whose priorities were staying in office to avoid prosecution, maintaining his personality cult, advancing Putin's foreign policy goals, and mainstreaming the far right. Studies conducted by Pippa Norris and other political scientists rank the GOP among the most extremist parties in the West in terms of its rejection of liberal democratic values. Its positions on immigration, crusades against racial and gender equality and LGBTQ+ rights, and attitudes toward ethnic and religious minorities have placed it close to the platforms of the parties of sitting autocrats like Erdoğan and Modi.[68]

With access to nuclear weapons and command of the world's most powerful military, Trump has been a far more dangerous and disruptive leader than Berlusconi. Yet Berlusconi's decade in power merits attention as a cautionary tale for America, Brazil, and other nations now under antidemocratic assault. The Italian prime minister operated in an open society but gradually eroded support for government accountability, mutual tolerance, respect for freedom of expression, and other bedrock democratic values. By 2009, he had merged his party with the far-right AN to form the People of Freedom coalition, which governed Italy on an anti-immigrant, pro–White Christian platform until his ouster in 2011. Italy may have remained a nominal democracy, but Berlusconi turned government into a vehicle for accumulating more personal wealth and power on the model of the illiberal leaders he so admired.

CONCLUSION

WHEN AUTOCRATS FALL FROM POWER, their people often outwardly repudiate them and banish their memory. They use images of having lived in a state of unreality, forced to act out one man's destructive fantasy. An Italian journalist recalled Fascism as "the history of a dream," although many would term it a twenty-year-long nightmare of violence and fear. For the ruler's collaborators, such images minimize responsibility for enabling the leader's destructive agendas. It is convenient as well as cathartic for the nation when the leader dies. Since he claimed a unique ability to rule the nation, he can be blamed for its sorry fate, assigned all responsibility.[1]

In fact, strongmen do not vanish with their exits from power, but instead remain as traces within the body of their people. The muscle memory to salute and sing the songs can be hard to shake. The mother of Norbert Steinhauser, a museum director in the German town of Friedrichshafen, held his father's hand during their early postwar Sunday walks to make sure he did not "Heil Hitler" out of habit. "A dictator can remain after his death, not just in the minds and bodies of his victims, but in others too," reflected the Chilean graphic artist Guillo in 2018. Undoing the effects of the leader's oppressive presence and policies takes years, especially when his symbols, burial sites, and buildings live on. The philosopher Ortega y Gasset catalogued such ruins as "slough, residiuum, corpse, skeleton, or fossil."[2]

The Foro Mussolini sports complex (today the Foro Italico) in Rome, with its blackshirt-themed mosaics and Il Duce slogans, represents one outcome: the time capsule. Architectural preservationists and a far right full of Fascist nostalgia both cheered its restoration, completed in 2000. In 2014, center-left prime minister Matteo Renzi announced Rome's bid for the 2024 Olympics from the site. He stood under the painting *The Apotheosis of Fascism* (Luigi Montanarini, 1936), which features Mussolini as a savior figure—an apt comment on the way the the dictator continues to haunt Italy. Pinochet's lavish library, the fruit of collecting made possible in part by his illegal earnings, is a Santiago tourist attraction. His country estate Los Boldos, however, fell into a state of disrepair. It became a marijuana plantation, even though his ashes are scattered there.[3]

The strongman's stadiums, highways, and airports, which his admirers see as proof that he brought the nation to greatness, cannot cover over the catastrophic loss that results from his rule. Expropriated assets, raided companies, interrupted schooling, disappeared parents, kidnapped children, and massacred communities leave voids that cannot be filled. As the anti-Fascist Carlo Rosselli testified in court in 1930:

> I had a home: they destroyed it. I had a newspaper: they suppressed it. I had a professorship: I had to abandon it. I had, as I still have today, ideas, dignity, and ideals: to defend them, I had to go to prison. I had teachers and friends—Amendola, Matteotti, Gobetti—they killed them.[4]

Seven years later, Mussolini took Rosselli's life from him too.

As for the institutions the strongman uses to get and keep his power, they often become irrelevant or discredited after he leaves office. Mussolini's Fascist Party, Hitler's NSDAP, and Mobutu's Popular Movement of the Revolution were all dissolved. The same is true for the civil service and professions. Gaddafi left Libyan state bureaucracies rife with corruption and nepotism, and journalists' skills were stunted from years of producing propaganda. Valuing loyalty over expertise and allowing violence to become an end in itself can result in a deprofessionalized and demoralized military, especially if misguided wars end in defeat. The mass suicides of German officers in 1945 are one outcome. The Chilean army retained some power as long as Pinochet remained commander in chief. It was decimated, though, when dozens of generals and 1,300 lesser officials were prosecuted for human rights violations in the 2000s. "I am still trying to understand what happened to our institution, how officials I knew and respected came to commit the acts they did," said a Chilean officer who retired just before the coup.[5]

Strongman states, helped by their foreign backers, obscure the profound chaos and destruction they cause. Instead, they perpetuate the notion that authoritarianism bests democracy in terms of efficiency and economic growth.[6] Certainly, some categories of people prosper under authoritarian rule. Leaders help their cronies and financial elites concentrate capital and privatize public goods. Yet business in general is often devastated by such predation. Fascist states went after the assets of Jews and other enemies; anti-colonial military regimes expelled foreigners (Mobutu, Gaddafi, and Amin had to invite some of them back to save their economies); and new authoritarians like Putin and Erdoğan take over profitable businesses, some built up over decades. By exacerbating economic inequality, plundering state assets, favoring ideology over expertise, and killing, imprisoning, and forcing into exile large numbers of talented people, strongmen impoverish the societies they rule.

Pinochet is one example. His reputation has long depended on the notion that the neoliberal reforms he permitted saved the country from becoming another Cuba. This is a counterfactual argument, which also disregards the catastrophic bank failures of the early 1980s, the corruption that came with privatization, and the economic, political, and human costs of his coup. Putin is another case. Claims that his autocracy spurred economic growth discount factors outside his control, like rising oil prices. They also ignore the enormous waste and loss to state revenues caused by his corruption and his exfiltration of assets.[7]

The drive to accumulate and control bodies, territory, and wealth is a hallmark of strongman rule. The leader needs these possessions as much as he needs food and sleep. The rituals and pageantry of authoritarian rule, from rallies for the masses to the elite gatherings staged at private spaces like Hitler's Berghof retreat, Mobutu's Gbadolite palaces, and Trump's Mar-a-Lago resort in Florida, play to his bottomless need for control and adoration. Of course, having it all is never enough for men who live in a secret state of dread at losing everything. Even as the strongman proclaims his infallibility, he is pursued by the demon of fear. He's wary of the people he represses; of foreign patrons and international forces who may sanction him or arrange for his ouster; of individuals who might prosecute him; of elites who can turn on him; and of enemies who wish to remove him from the face of the earth. Fear is why such rulers use blackmail and clientelism to tie people to them, why they throw on a cloak of masculine invincibility, and why they seek out other strongmen as partners who will legitimate their authoritarian worldview. Many despots build palaces and bunkers to store their loot, and when their hubris and mismanagement bring about crises, hide in them to escape their people.

To oppose authoritarians effectively, we must have a clear-eyed view of how they manage to get into power and stay there. The strongman brand of charisma, equal parts seduction and threat, attracts many followers by celebrating male authority. The autocrat bolsters patriarchal authority when it is seen as under threat, as in Italy in the 1920s, Germany and Spain in the 1930s, Russia and Italy in the 1990s, and America in 2016. That male model of authoritarian power, built on virile display and "man to man" diplomacy, may give way in the future as female-led authoritarian states emerge. Women are prominent within the European far right, starting with Marine Le Pen, head of France's

National Rally party. Trump markets his daughter Ivanka as a future leader, repeatedly inserting her into head-of-state group photos, as at the 2019 meeting of the Group of Twenty organization. Yet a female-led rightist state would pose no threat to authoritarianism's appeal as a legitimating force of corruption, misogyny, and, in many countries, White racial domination.[8]

The strongman's rogue nature also draws people to him. He proclaims law-and-order rule, yet enables lawlessness. This paradox becomes official policy as government evolves into a criminal enterprise, Hitler's Germany being one example and Putin's Russia another. For many, it is intoxicating to be able to commit criminal acts with impunity and participate in the collective work of undoing one political order and creating another. This is why some collaborators of defunct rulers remain unrepentant even when the scope of the horror they participated in becomes clear, like the Chilean torturer Ingrid Olderock, with her gruesome "I love dogs" bumper sticker. The special psychological climate that strongmen create among their people—the thrill of transgression mixed with the comfort of submitting to his power—endows life with energy, purpose, and drama.

Understanding how strongmen triumph and stay in power for so long also means abandoning some cherished notions about national identity— for example, that Germans are the most cultured people or that Chileans are unlike their violent Latin American neighbors. Few wanted to hear Gobetti's message to Italians in the early 1920s that "Fascism is the autobiography of the nation." Likewise, many Americans dismissed the notion that Trump's racism and his obsession with celebrity and profit above all else might help him win the election because they reflect enduring traits of American society. "Every country gets the gangster it deserves," a former partisan's comment about Italy under Mussolini, may seem harsh to some and true to others.[9]

"Those who determine our destiny are not really better than ourselves; they are neither more intelligent nor stronger nor more enlightened," concluded the journalist Oriana Fallaci, who spent many hours with autocrats. The strongman's trick is to seem exceptional and yet to embody the national everyman, with all of his endearing flaws. Mussolini struck the novelist Elsa Morante as "a mediocre man, crude, uncultured" and as such "the perfect exemplar and mirror of today's Italian people." Berlusconi made Italians feel good about breaking the rules, as Trump would do for Americans. Turkish admirers describe Erdoğan as a member of their extended family. "There is a little piece of Putin in everyone," says the Nobel Prize–winning author Svetlana Alexievich, no fan of the Russian leader.[10]

The familiarity of these personages, marketed by their personality cults and populist ideologies as "one of us," is also why many people don't see them as dangerous early on. Although we often hear that strongmen are genius strategists, few, if any, of them had a master plan for their rule. Their real talents are those of the street fighter and the con man rather than the chess master: quickness at making the most of the opportunities offered to them, skill at getting people to bond with them and believe their fictions, and a willingness to do anything necessary to get the absolute authority they crave. Most of them ended up with more power than they ever imagined.

The leader's centrality in the lives of his acolytes makes his utter scorn for them more poignant. Curzio Malaparte's 1931 comment about Hitler's relationship with his most faithful collaborators proved prescient:

> He channels his brutality into humbling their pride, crushing
> their freedom of conscience, diminishing their individual mer-
> its and transforming his supporters into flunkeys stripped of
> all dignity. Like all dictators, Hitler loves only those whom he
> can despise.[11]

This universal principle is why the strongman is so quick to blame his own people. It is all their fault, rulers from the fascists to Gaddafi say as the enemy bombs fall, the rebels advance, or the prosecutors close in. Their people lacked the audacity and toughness to wear the cloak of greatness he offered to them. "The Italian race is a race of sheep. Eighteen years are not enough to transform it," Mussolini complained to Galeazzo Ciano in January 1940, months before he recklessly entered the war that caused millions of deaths and ended his regime. "Even Michelangelo needed marble in order to make his statues. If he had only had clay, he would simply have been a potter."[12]

To counter authoritarianism, we must prioritize accountability and transparency in government. At the heart of strongman rule is the claim that he and his agents are above the law, above judgment, and not beholden to the truth. Accountability also matters as a measure of open societies because the old yardstick—elections—is less reliable. New authoritarian states often simulate democracy, and nominal democracies governed by personalist rulers often act like autocracies. In Trump's America, as in Berlusconi's Italy, the legal and the illegal, fact and fiction, celebrity and politics blend together until nothing means anything anymore and everything is "a confidence game." The corrosive effects of the shift away from standards of accountability and truth were evident in the reaction of CBS News journalist Norah O'Donnell to Trump's January 2020 State of the Union speech. Although the speech contained multiple false statements about economic growth during his presidency, O'Donnell hailed it as a triumph by "the reality TV president . . . a master showman at his best."[13]

Anti-corruption efforts should encompass education about the merits of transparency and accountability to encourage workplace and governmental cultures that deter people from engaging in corruption in the first place. Prosecution can be unpopular and play into the victimhood cult of leaders and their allies. Prevention is far better. We can encourage elites to form alliances with anti-corruption forces, as Transparency International does around the world. We can also support civic and nonprofit organizations that work for community justice and accountability at both the local and national levels. Pressure campaigns on banks, law firms, and other enablers of authoritarian corruption can fuel a reconsideration of the practice of working for autocrats for the revenue it brings. The media, always so quick to cover every utterance and action of the strongman, must also tell the stories of those who courageously denounce corruption, from Giacomo Matteotti to Boris Nemtsov to those risking their lives today. We should also hear more about efforts to incentivize anti-corruption behaviors. The Mo Ibrahim Foundation awards a prize of $5 million, paid out over ten years, to democratically elected African heads of state who strengthen the rule of law and human rights in their countries.[14]

Democracy needs heroes more than ever and compelling narratives that make the case for the merits and advantages of open societies. Liberal values don't have to seem "tepid and boring," the philosopher Martha Nussbaum argues, if compassion and love are recognized as fundamental to the democratic model of politics. Too often, we have left the work of shaping emotions—including patriotism, our love for our country—to democracy's enemies. Writing in June 2020, George Packer found lessons in the political corruption, failures of leadership, and other societal ills the coronavirus pandemic exposed in America: "that in a democracy being a citizen is essential work, that the alternative to solidarity is death." Around the world, it has often taken the decline or eclipse of freedom to make that message resonate.[15]

AMERICA HAS PLAYED AN OUTSIZED ROLE in the success of authoritarianism around the world, starting with the US banks and media outlets that supported Mussolini's dictatorship in the 1920s. Although American backing of strongmen was most visible in the age of military coups, the US continues to prop up authoritarians. Lawyers and wealth managers help to keep them in power by securing the money they loot from their nations in offshore accounts. From 2015 through 2019, both directly and as a subcontractor, the law firm Greenberg Traurig worked for Orbán and Erdoğan. Rudolph Giuliani, Trump's personal lawyer and private envoy, previously worked for Greenberg Traurig, handling the Turkish president's affairs abroad.[16]

American public relations and lobbying companies have covered up authoritarians' violence while touting their countries as business and tourist opportunities. Ketchum represented Putin from 2006 to 2014 and lobbied successfully for him to be *TIME*'s 2007 Man of the Year. Trump has shared Ballard Partners with Erdoğan, who has five other American lobbying and public relations firms working for him. In 2017, Trump's national security adviser Michael Flynn was simultaneously on Erdoğan's payroll as a foreign agent representing the Turkish president's interests in America. All of these firms and individuals enjoy the benefits of democracy while assisting despots to destroy it for millions abroad.[17]

Given America's entanglements with the history of authoritarianism, some may see Trump's ascent to power as divine justice. A nation that never endured dictatorship or foreign occupation now has firsthand experience of the authoritarian playbook. A great privilege of life under democracies—taking freedom for granted—becomes a weakness when that freedom is under assault. As in the past, the novelty of the strongman's approach to politics threw even seasoned observers off course. President George W. Bush had no frame of reference for Trump's 2017 inaugural address and described it as "weird shit," although it was perfectly normal in the context of authoritarian history. Like Italians and Germans in the 1920s and 1930s and some Chileans after the 1973 coup, many Americans believed that the man espousing lies and extremist politics would calm down and abide by democratic norms and institutions once he took power. The former *New York Times* journalist Clyde Haberman was more candid than most when he tweeted in March 2020:

> Thinking this morning about my naïveté in November 2016.
> We all knew that Trump was a hideous character, but I thought
> the Presidency would change him, that he would be elevated by
> the office. Couldn't have been more wrong.[18]

By the time many recognize the scope of the danger at hand, the costs of the head of state's destructive character and style of governance are often all too evident.

Trump's responses to the coronavirus outbreak and the anti-racist protests in 2020 have been emblematic. In the crucial early weeks of the coronavirus outbreak, the president sidelined the government's Centers for Disease Control and other experts and unleashed a barrage of misinformation. He called COVID-19 no worse than the flu, peddled unproven or deadly cures, and obstructed mass testing. More tests would result in more reported cases, which would harm his claims of competency and delay the relaunch of the American economy, jeopardizing his reelection. Trump went to lengths to create a sense of normality, refusing to wear protective gear in public, although he is a noted germaphobe. The thousands who heeded his call and gathered, unmasked, at indoor rallies in Tulsa, Phoenix, and other cities in June became fodder for his propaganda machine, letting him pose as a virile leader untouchable even by disease. By then, America had had the world's highest infection rate for several months running.[19]

In keeping with traditions of authoritarian corruption, the Trump administration also used resources allocated for relief related to the pandemic to reward allies and consolidate patronage networks. Phunware, a data firm employed by the Trump reelection campaign, received $2.85 million from the $2 trillion stimulus fund, or fourteen times the average payout. Divide-and-rule tactics pitted states against each other in a war for medical equipment. Trump favored Republican governors and anyone who paid him public homage, and he sought to lessen public confidence in other officials. "If you have a governor that's failing, we're going to protect you," he said at an April 2020 press briefing. Congressman Adam Schiff put it differently, summarizing the president's approach this way: "Governors basically pay fealty to him, praise him, or they'll suffer consequences."[20]

The authoritarian model of leadership Schiff describes also guided Trump's response to the protests. On Friday, May 29, 2020, when demonstrators breached temporary fences near the White House lawn, the Secret Service rushed Trump to a secure bunker on the White House grounds. When Trump emerged an hour later, plans were underway to turn Washington, DC, into something resembling a military occupation zone. Over the weekend, Lakota and Black Hawk helicopters buzzed crowds of protesters, and 5,000 National Guard troops poured into the capital. Tens of thousands of ammunition rounds came with them, to be used, if necessary, against the American people. The security forces of the FBI, the DOJ, the Bureau of Prisons, and other agencies also participated in the operation. Many heavily armed personnel had no clearly recognizable uniform insignia, which for some observers recalled Putin's use of unmarked "Little Green Men" troops during Russia's 2014 annexation of Crimea.[21]

A strongman's fear and loathing of his people come through most clearly when his power is threatened, and so it was with Trump. On Monday, June 1, accompanied by an entourage of White men, including Secretary of Defense Mark Esper, the president walked to the Rose Garden and denounced "professional anarchists, violent mobs, arsonists . . . Antifa" and other "terrorists" involved in the protests. He warned local and state officials that if they did not end the unrest, "then I will deploy the United States military and quickly solve the problem for them." As a demonstration, while he spoke security forces used tear gas, flash-bang shells, and mounted police to clear protesters from Lafayette Square park, just in front of the White House. He then walked to St. John's Church and posed for photographs, holding a Bible like a prop.[22]

Trump's propaganda stunt and his handling of the protests further tarnished his reputation, leading some long-standing allies to take their distance. Evangelical leader Pat Robertson, a staunch Trump ally (and supporter of Mobutu and other dictators), denounced the president's law-and-order rhetoric as callous and dangerous. Trump's former defense secretary, General James Mattis, warned that Trump was a threat to democracy. Yet nothing deterred Trump from escalating such tactics in July 2020 on protesters in Portland and other cities. Preventive arrests and the sight of protesters being forced into unmarked vans recalled the actions of Erdoğan, Pinochet, and other autocrats against their enemies.[23]

"If you don't dominate, you are wasting your time," Trump said on that day, expressing a philosophy of life common to authoritarians. His behavior in those days seemed all too familiar to Americans with firsthand experience of how autocrats act when their power is threatened. "Saddam. Bashar. Qaddafi. They all did this," tweeted Marc Polymeropoulos, who ran CIA operations in Europe and Asia, of Trump's use of force on protesters. Former ambassador Robert Ford and other diplomats were reminded of Gaddafi's last-stand vow during the Libyan revolution to hunt down and kill every last dissenter.[24]

Such comparisons, however, also bring to mind another lesson of history: never to underestimate the strongman's tenacity and his will to do whatever it takes to stay in power. Current and former CIA analysts and officers, trained to spot signs of democratic disintegration, cautioned that polarization and use of force against protesters have often heralded an authoritarian crackdown. "This is what happens in countries before a collapse," said former analyst Gail Helt. "I know this playbook," warned former CIA undercover officer Rep. Abigail Spanberger (D-VA) of the escalating tensions in America. Emergency actions hold special appeal for a leader whose competency and popularity ratings are in decline.[25]

Propaganda takes on a special importance at such moments, and those who serve the leader must work overtime to compensate for the waning of his charismatic powers. On June 8, 2020, White House press secretary Kayleigh McEnany held a briefing for reporters. Outside, things looked dim for the president. Over 100,000 Americans had died of coronavirus (of a total 405,000 deaths globally), and infections were still spiking. Unemployment was up (the 6.2 million Americans out of work in February had risen to 20.5 million in May), and Trump's approval ratings were down to 38 percent—he had lost another 7 points since May. Inside the

White House, though, the magical thinking that has sustained so many authoritarian states in the past prevailed. "Good morning ladies and gentlemen," said McEnany to the journalists. "The transition to national greatness has officially begun."[26]

THE CEASELESS LYING AND CORRUPTION and the cynical disregard for human life that marks strongman rule can lead to despair. This makes it all the more important to know the history of resistance to repressive governance. Time and again people have shown great resolve and courage and risked their lives to keep alive the hope that a different society can be created. This process may start with the rejection of the emotional training every leader invests in to encourage cruelty and discourage solidarity among his people. "Keep your heart a desert," said Mussolini to a journalist who asked him the secret of his success, noting that friendships get in the way of the exercise of power. That sentiment summed up all that was wrong with Fascism for the young filmmaker Alberto Lattuada, who grew up under the dictatorship. In 1941, he delivered a devastating diagnosis:

> The absence of love brought many tragedies that might have
> been averted. Instead of the golden rain of love, a black cloak of
> indifference fell upon the people. And thus people have lost *the
> eyes of love* and can no longer see clearly. . . . Here are the origins
> of the disintegration of all values and the destruction and steril-
> ization of conscience.[27]

Almost eighty years later, a college student in Moscow echoed this sentiment. In 2019, Yegor Zhukov, who had campaigned for a seat in Moscow's city council, was accused by Putin's government of "extremism" for advocating nonviolent protest and for calling the Russian leader a "madman." In his court testimony, Zhukov highlighted the hypocrisy of Putin's claim to be the defender of Christianity and traditional values.

He pointed out the Russian leader's corruption and his aim of "dehumanizing us in one another's eyes." For Zhukov, Christianity means loving your neighbor and taking up "the burdens of the world," precepts that he believes should also guide secular governance. "Love is trust, empathy, humanity, mutual aid, and care. A society built on such love is a strong society—probably the strongest of all possible societies." Zhukov was sentenced to three months' probation, rather than the four years of prison the prosecution wanted, but he is banned from posting online for three years. Putin knows that Zhukov is the voice of Russia's future—a future without Putin—and the advocate of a model of politics and ethics diametrically opposed to his own.[28]

Opening the heart to others and viewing them with compassion has time and again led to effective electoral pushback against strongman rule. The Chilean opposition's "joy is on the way" 1988 campaign that drove Pinochet out of office and the "radical love" platform that lifted Ekram Imamoğlu to victory in 2019 as Istanbul's mayor both mobilized sentiments of optimism, solidarity, and community. Reaching out to those who still support the strongman but inside may be wavering, as Imamoğlu did, can also yield results. Such individuals may feel ashamed and unwilling to admit their errors of judgment unless they are approached with the right spirit of openness, at the right time.[29]

An economic downturn, a losing war, exhaustion from state thievery and violence, or a mishandled public health crisis can make evidence of the strongman's malfeasance and incompetence difficult to ignore. No other type of ruler is so transparent about prioritizing self-preservation over the public good and so lacking in the human qualities that define ethical leadership—the ability to feel empathy for others and act on their behalf. As one country after another has discovered, the strongman is at his worst as a leader when he is most needed by his country.

There are two paths people can take when faced with the proliferation of polarization and hatred in their societies. They can dig their trenches deeper, or they can reach across the lines to stop a new cycle of destruction, knowing that solidarity, love, and dialogue are what the strongman most fears. History shows the importance of keeping hope and faith in humanity and of supporting those who struggle for freedom in our own time. We can carry with us the stories of those who lived and died over a century of democracy's destruction and resurrection. They are precious counsel for us today.

EPILOGUE TO THE
PAPERBACK EDITION

THE CONFLICTS DESCRIBED IN THIS BOOK between authoritarians and those who resist them have intensified over the last year. As of early 2021, over half of the world's population lives under some form of illiberal rule. In Poland, Hungary, India, and elsewhere, extremist ideologies, anti-Semitism, Islamophobia, and adherence to conspiracy theories increasingly shape government policies. Established autocracies such as China have also become more repressive, as the jailing of resisters in Hong Kong and the persecution of Uyghur Muslims in Xinjiang indicate.[1] As for military coups, while they happen less often in the twenty-first century, Myanmar had one in February 2021. It highlights a larger "democratic fatigue and authoritarian nostalgia" in Southeast Asia.[2]

In Western Europe, far-right movements and parties, some with affinities to historic fascism, have gained traction. In France, Marine Le Pen, head of the National Rally party, has become a competitive candidate in the 2022 presidential election. In Italy, the Brothers of Italy party, led by Giorgia Meloni, has an 18.9 percent potential voter share, bringing its level of support close to that of the center-left Democratic Party (20.9 percent). In Germany, displays of Nazi symbols and anti-Semitic attacks accompany a surge in extremist crimes. The far right talking point that

White people are being "replaced" by non-Whites has also gained adherents. Mussolini had warned Italians of the apocalyptic consequences of demographic shifts a century ago, proposing Fascism as the remedy.[3]

Certainly, the wrenching effects of the COVID-19 pandemic have accelerated authoritarian ascents and democratic decline. One-third of all countries, democracies included, have passed emergency measures (increased surveillance of citizens, restrictions on freedoms of movement and assembly, and more) without time limits, giving rise to a new term: pandemic backsliding. In Turkey, Venezuela, and elsewhere, authoritarians have used the pandemic as an opportunity to ramp up their persecution of dissenters and journalists. They blame immigrants and other targeted groups for spreading the virus in their countries—the better to turn attention away from their own incompetence.[4]

One year into the pandemic, the toll of the strongman style of rule is tragically evident. When the leader and his allies are focused on "cultivating their image and staying in power," as Akanksha Singh finds is happening in Modi's India; when experts are sidelined in favor of ideologues, as in Bolsonaro's Brazil; when none of the head of state's advisers have the courage to tell him how destructive his policies are for the nation, the results can be devastating. Mass sickness and death are compounded by the awful realization that the head of state has little interest in public welfare. "It is what it is," Trump said in September 2020 upon learning of the deaths of 1,000 Americans per day from COVID-19, his chilling statement conveying the strongman's lack of empathy. The former president staged effective political theater around his own bout with coronavirus in October 2020. His balcony performance after he returned from being treated at Walter Reed Hospital reminded many of Il Duce. Trump has "God-tier genetics," a self-described "MAGA life coach," Brenden Dilley, told his radio audience, displaying an adulation for the leader's special body that has marked acolytes of strongmen for a century. Yet Trump's personal victory over the disease could not help him escape the taint of his government's negligence where the health of millions of others was concerned. In the month before the November 2020 presidential election, twenty-five states set weekly death records, and a total of 228,000 Americans had died to that point. The massive human loss and cascading economic woes brought by the pandemic likely contributed to Trump's loss to Joe Biden.[5]

The deepening global health crisis made the surge of protests against illiberal governments and abuses of power in 2020 all the more striking. The new wave of activism, which is "historically unprecedented in frequency, scope and size," built on momentum from 2019: demonstrations against economic inequality in Chile (the largest since the 1980s anti-Pinochet protests), mobilizations in Hong Kong against a bill that would allow extraditions to mainland China, and mass protests in 112 other countries. The pandemic did not prevent an estimated 15 to 26 million people from taking part in Black Lives Matter events in America over the summer of 2020. It also did not deter hundreds of thousands from protesting in August against Belarus president Alexander Lukashenko's manipulation of election results to remain in power. As crowds marched to his presidential palace, Lukashenko surveyed them from his helicopter, clad in body armor, then brandished an AK-47 rifle when he landed. Meant to convey dominance, the macho performance reminds us that strongmen who realize that their repression cannot contain the people's desire for freedom may be overcome with dread.[6]

That is a lesson for Putin as well. The Russian president's formal lock on power, secured by his 2020 amendment of the constitution, has been accompanied by more, not less, violence against those who expose his corruption. His treatment of Alexei Navalny is a case in point. In August 2020, after being poisoned with a Novichok nerve agent, Navalny received permission to be transported to Germany for treatment. The Kremlin likely hoped he would go into exile, as so many in the past have done to survive authoritarian regimes. That was never an option for Navalny, an intense nationalist with his own history of xenophobic remarks. When he returned to Russia in January 2021, he was immediately arrested and, in February, sentenced to 2½ years in prison for breaking the terms of a 2014 suspended sentence. Poisoning someone and then locking them up for not reporting to parole authorities while they are recovering from the poisoning sums up the operation of autocratic "justice."[7]

That is why Navalny's actions resonate with millions, from the video his anti-corruption foundation released that shows the latest fruits of Putin's system of kleptocracy—a Black Sea mansion that reportedly cost $1.3 billion to build—to Navalny's hunger strike in the IK-2 penal colony. His testimony at his Moscow sentencing, which denounced the "thieving little man in his bunker" who is too cowardly to engage in debates or face his opponents in free elections, showed a hard-won familiarity with the strongman who clings to power. The steady erosion of support for Putin among younger Russians indicates a disaffection that will likely grow. In a February 2021 Levada poll, 48 percent of respondents aged eighteen to twenty-four felt that the country was going in the wrong direction. The increased volume of disinformation that Putin directs at foreign and domestic populations is a sign that he is applying the authoritarian tools of rule with an ever-heavier hand. The Russian "firehose of falsehood" has lately become a water cannon.[8]

—

IN THE UNITED STATES, long a supporter of both foreign autocracies and open societies, the struggle between illiberalism and democracy has become a central theme of American politics and a source of grave divisions in society. Four years of an authoritarian-style presidency cemented the GOP's abandonment of consensus politics and the norms and customs of democracy. The widening gap between the rhetoric, values, and methods of Democrats and Republicans poses difficult questions. What happens in a bipartisan system when one of two parties turns toward autocracy? What is the fate of a country in which right-wing extremist incidents are surging, as elsewhere in the world, but sales of guns to civilians have also reached record levels?[9]

The dramatic events that followed Trump's loss in the 2020 election, culminating in the January 6, 2021, armed assault on the Capitol, offer clues to the challenges American democracy will face in the coming years. When major press outlets, Fox News included, called the election for Biden on November 7 and Trump refused to accept the results, a state of exception was created that lasted until Biden's January 20, 2021, inauguration. Seeing this period through the lens of authoritarian history gives clarity and context to what, for America, was uncharted territory. Trump's behavior in these months built on the desperate acts autocrats have always engaged in to avoid having to leave office. The purges of the inner sanctum, starting with the November 9 firing of defense secretary Mark Esper, and the pardons of unscrupulous individuals like General Michael Flynn set the stage for dangerous developments by creating a circle of hard-core loyalists willing to do anything to keep their leader in the White House.

For Flynn and others, that meant a military intervention to facilitate a rerun of the election, which was why Esper, who had resisted deploying active-duty troops against Black Lives Matter protesters, had to go. "I serve the country in deference to the Constitution," Esper had noted tellingly in his resignation letter. Days later, the chairman of the Joint Chiefs of Staff, General Mark Milley, declared that the military did not take an oath to any individual, "king or queen, or tyrant or dictator," but only to the Constitution. On December 1, a week before he was pardoned, Flynn approvingly tweeted an ad from a group called the We the People Convention that asked Trump to suspend the Constitution so the military could oversee a new election. Flynn's efforts to drum up Republican support for martial law apparently alarmed ten former defense secretaries enough for them to issue an unusual collective warning: military involvement in elections "would take us into dangerous, unlawful, and unconstitutional territory."[10]

As he explored a military option, Trump also attempted the favorite twenty-first-century despot trick of electoral manipulation, alleging extensive voter fraud and pressuring state officials, such as Georgia's secretary of state Brad Raffensperger, to "find votes" sufficient to overturn the results. Unfortunately, four years of rigged election talk and Trump's personality cult primed his supporters to accept his claim that he, and not Biden, had won the election. The Big Lie had traction because of the many thousands of small lies told by Trump and his GOP and media allies about Democrats' supposed criminality, rampant fraud, and trickery in American elections, not to mention the president's victimization by his enemies.[11]

The judiciary proved a harder sell. At least eighty-six Republican and Democratic judges rejected Trump's efforts to overturn state election results. Nor did most state election officials cooperate. Raffensperger, for example, taped his call with Trump, which was then leaked to the press, exposing the president's machinations. By the end of 2020, with the armed forces and electoral options looking less viable, Trump's inner circle focused on the event that could seal Trump's fate: the Electoral College certification of Biden's victory on January 6 and a "Stop the Steal" rally, months in the planning, to be held near the Capitol that day. "Big protest in D.C. on January 6," Trump tweeted on December 19. "Be there, will be wild!"[12]

Like all shock events, January 6 will take years to digest and investigate. Only the 9/11 terrorist attacks rival January 6's importance in recent American history. As an act of domestic terror, it connects to a tradition of far-right extremism in America that is currently "metastasizing," in the words of FBI director Christopher Wray. Yet it can also be seen as a coup attempt (technically, a self-coup) by a sitting president who sought to interrupt the democratic process to remain in power illegally. Trump was not merely the instigator of the assault (the House convicted him of this charge at his February 2021 impeachment trial), but also its main intended beneficiary.[13]

We still don't know the full story of how Trump insiders (Roger Stone and Steve Bannon among them) and GOP elites organized and funded the January 6 rally and created the proper psychological and political atmosphere for an intervention—whatever that was going to mean. Skilled propagandists like Alex Jones did their part, and the far-right corners of the Internet lit up with chatter as the day of the fateful Electoral College meeting approached. "Be ready to fight. Congress needs to hear glass breaking, doors being kicked in," said a commentator who came to the FBI's attention, as did a map of the Capitol complex and its connecting tunnels that circulated on January 5. That day, Bannon told listeners of his podcast, "All hell will break loose tomorrow. It will be quite extraordinarily different. All I can say is strap in."[14]

Those who attended the January 6 rally heard the familiar talking points about election fraud and the need to "take back the country," but the heightened stakes of the day lent an urgency to Rudy Giuliani's call for "trial by combat" and Trump's apocalyptic warning, "If you don't fight like hell, you won't have a country anymore." An authoritarian's followers can become especially volatile if they feel he is endangered. Storming the Capitol was not just an act of populist rage, but also a last-ditch operation to rescue their leader. The film shown at the rally paid homage to Trump's personality cult, and a close-up of his face lingered on screen as his supporters streamed to the Capitol, becoming the latest people to commit violence on the strongman's behalf.[15]

An image of Trump from a film shown at the Jan. 6 rally, Washington, DC.
ZUMA PRESS INC./ZUMA PRESS/AGEFOTOSTOCK

As some armed individuals charged the Capitol, others stood down to let operations proceed. The Pentagon's more than 3-hour delay in approving reinforcements for the beleaguered Capitol Police has been called a "security lapse," but such nonaction can be strategic. For counterterrorism expert Malcolm Nance, it was as though "the entire national security apparatus was deliberately turned off," a situation that facilitated the rioters' breach of the Capitol. Video footage of the attack conveys the "grisly, grunting, intimate violence" that left 140 Capitol Police injured and led to the deaths of three others—two by suicide days later. Three rioters also died.[16] As for Trump, he watched the assault on television. The video he tweeted (and later removed) to call off the rioters, hours into the assault, sums up how the authoritarian manipulates his followers, professing care for them to keep their loyalty, while renewing their hatred for his enemies. "I know your pain, I know you're hurt. . . . This was a fraudulent election, but we can't play into the hands of these people. We have to have peace. So go home, we love you, you're very special."[17]

It may be tempting to think of the estimated 800 individuals who stormed the Capitol as outliers: scruffy anti-government militia types, fascist-worshipping Proud Boys, and others who fit the "extremist" stereotype. Individuals from those categories took part in the January 6 assault, but so did dozens of retired and active-duty law enforcement, military, and government personnel, as well as fifty-seven state and local GOP elected officials. The coup designation matters because January 6 was, in part, an inside job. It exposed the consequences of years of tolerating the presence of far-right extremists inside state institutions. The Capitol assault also revealed how the Trump presidency radicalized ordinary Americans. A February 2021 study by Robert A. Pape and Keven Ruby of 193 people charged with breaching the Capitol grounds or building found that 89 percent had no affiliation with militant organizations, and 40 percent were business owners or white-collar workers: accountants, CEOs, computer programmers, doctors, and more. These "middle-aged, middle-class insurrectionists" may have had "a lot to lose," as Pape and Ruby conclude, but they engaged in political violence as a means of subverting the democratic system—a tactic that strongmen have always championed.[18]

January 6 could have cost the GOP some of its supporters, given the pro–law enforcement sentiments of Trump's base. Yet the party and its media allies quickly closed ranks to rewrite history, blaming the left for the violence to whitewash the right's crimes. Tucker Carlson told millions of Fox News viewers that the rioters had no guns, and Trump asserted that they were "hugging and kissing the police and the guards." By April 2021, more than half of the Republicans polled by Reuters/Ipsos agreed that January 6 was the work of "violent left-wing protesters trying to make Trump look bad."[19]

The Capitol assault and Trump's second impeachment trial in February 2021 also led to a further tightening of the GOP's authoritarian-style party discipline, creating a dangerous climate for anyone who showed independence from the leader—even when the individual in question was no longer in office. Republicans who broke with the party line and voted to impeach Trump, such as Rep. Peter Meijer of Michigan, had to buy body armor. "Our expectation is that somebody may try to kill us," said Meijer in an interview. It's not surprising that Democrats find little bipartisan resolve for an independent probe of the events of January 6 or that former vice-president Mike Pence, who escaped a mob that wanted to hang him for allowing the certification of Biden's victory, remains silent about his experience. The GOP no longer seems to recognize the right of Democratic *or* Republican lawmakers to exercise their constitutional duties without fearing for their lives. As of May 2021, threats against members of Congress are up 107 percent compared with 2020.[20]

Whether or not Trump runs for office in 2024, the time-tested methods of autocracy—electoral manipulation, voter suppression, the criminalization of protest, political violence, and disinformation—are now part of the way the GOP conducts its business as a far-right party. After January 6, nothing is off the table: extremists might well view the failed coup as a trial run. "That's what we fucking need to have, 30,000 guns up here," said one rioter that day, frustrated that he was not entering the Capitol more rapidly. "Next trip," someone answered him.[21]

That's why Biden's assertive advocacy of democracy at home and abroad is so important. "Democracy requires consensus. I'm running as a proud Democrat, but I will govern as an American president," he had asserted on the campaign trail. As president he has passed sweeping measures intended to benefit Americans across the political spectrum, such as the $1.9 trillion COVID relief bill. With bipartisan governance in tatters in Congress, Biden has chosen to talk past GOP politicians directly to the American people, channeling "the spirit of being able to work together," just as İmamoğlu did when he beat Erdoğan's candidate in the 2019 Istanbul mayoral race. Biden's communication strategy counters the strongman's mania for nonstop attention: he speaks sparingly, appears on television only when necessary, and tweets with restraint. His blunt denunciations of Putin as a "killer"; his emphasis on transparency and ethics in government, as embodied in his Accountability 2021 initiative; and his choice of a woman of color, Kamala Harris, as vice-president—all of this reverses maybe: "undoes" the authoritarian playbook Trump followed faithfully.[22]

"I predict to you, your children and grandchildren are going to be doing their doctoral theses on the issue of who succeeded—autocracy or democracy?" said Biden at his first press conference in March 2021. "We've got to prove democracy works." Authoritarian history shows that while democracies have often failed, so have autocracies, which fall victim to systemic dysfunction and the rapacious nature of those who govern them. The story of the strongman, rife with tragedy, also offers lessons in hope and resiliency. It urges us to invest in democracy and protect it rather than take our freedoms for granted. The costs of not doing so are far too great.[23]

ABBREVIATIONS

AKP	Justice and Development Party
AN	National Alliance
CADA	Art Actions Collective
CBPUS	Customs and Border Protection
CEMA	Women's Centers Foundation
CIA	Central Intelligence Agency
DINA	Directorate of National Intelligence
EU	European Union
FPMR	Manuel Rodriguez Patriotic Front
FSB	Federal Security Service
GOP	Republican Party
ICEUS	Immigration and Customs Enforcement Agency
IMF	International Monetary Fund
KGB	Committee for State Security
MIR	Revolutionary Movement of the Left
MSI	Italian Social Movement
NATO	North Atlantic Treaty Organization
NFSL	National Front for the Salvation of Libya
NSDAP	National Socialist German Workers' Party
NTC	National Transition Council
OVRA	Organization for Vigilance and Repression of Anti-Fascism
PCI	Italian Communist Party
PNF	National Fascist Party

PSI   Italian Socialist Party
Rai   Italian Radio Television
RCC   Revolutionary Command Council
SA   Stormtroopers
SS   Protection Squadron
UN   United Nations

NOTES

INTRODUCTION

1. Rob Evans, Luke Harding, and John Hooper, "WikiLeaks Cables: Berlusconi 'Profited from Secret Deals' with Putin," *Guardian*, December 2, 2010; "Silvio e Patrizia, tutte le registrazioni," *L'Espresso*, July 20, 2009: http://espresso.repubblica.it/palazzo/2009/07/20/news/silvio-e-patrizia-tutte-le-registrazioni-br-1.28772?refresh_ce.

2. Mikhail Zygar, *All the Kremlin's Men. Inside the Court of Vladimir Putin* (New York: Public Affairs, 2016), 121–23; Michael Crowley, "Is Putin Playing Trump Like He Did Berlusconi?" *Politico*, August 18, 2016; Jason Horowitz, "A Prime Minister Cut Down to Size," *New York Times*, December 31, 2003.

3. Ronald Spogli, "Italy-Russia Relations: The View from Rome" cable to Hillary Clinton, secretary of state, January 26, 2009, at: https://wikileaks.org/plusd/cables/09ROME97_a .html. Also Ronald Spogli, "Scenesetter for your December 3 Visit to Rome," cable to Condoleezza Rice, secretary of state, November 19, 2008, in Guardian Staff, "US Embassy Cables: Italian MP Named as Berlusconi's Bagman by US," *Guardian*, December 2, 2010: https://www.theguardian.com/world/us-embassy-cables-documents/179002.

4. Evans, Harding, Hooper, "WikiLeaks Cables"; Matt Trueman, "Satirical Play Gives New Head of State Putin the Berlusconi Treatment," *Guardian*, March 5, 2012. Varvara Faer directed *BerlusPutin*. The South Stream pipeline project was canceled in 2014 due to EU objections.

5. David Runciman, *How Democracy Ends* (London: Profile Books, 2018), 87–93; Basharat Peet, *A Question of Order. India, Turkey, and the Return of Strongmen* (New York: Columbia Global Reports, 2017); Sergei Guriev and Daniel Treisman, "How Modern Dictators Survive: An Informational Theory of the New Authoritarianism," NBER Working Paper 21136 (April 2015). Freedom House recorded fewer democracies in Europe and Eurasia in 2020 than at any point since they began to issue reports on the health of global democracy in 1995. Zselyke Csaky, *Dropping the Democratic Façade*, Freedom House Nations in Transit 2020 report: https://freedomhouse.org/sites/default/files/2020-05/NIT_2020_FINAL_05062020.pdf.

6. Dr. Li Wenliang passed away five weeks later of coronavirus. Li Yuan, "Widespread Outcry in China over Death of Coronavirus Doctor," *New York Times*, February 7, 2020; Lisandra Paraguassu and Anthony Boudle, "While Bolsonaro Ignores Warnings, Coronavirus Spreads in Brazil," Reuters, March 24, 2020; Economist Staff, "Diseases like Covid-19 Are Deadlier in Non-Democracies," *Economist*, February 18, 2020; Zeynep Tufekci, "How the Coronavirus Revealed Authoritarianism's Fatal Flaw," *Atlantic*, February 22, 2020; Florian Bieber, "Authoritarianism in the Time of Coronavirus," *Foreign Policy*, March 30, 2020; Orna Herr, "How Is Chinese Censorship Affecting Reporting of the Coronavirus?" *Index on Censorship*, February 5, 2020.

7. Robert Darnton, *Censors at Work: How States Shaped Literature* (New York: W. W. Norton, 2014), 14.

8. Frank Dikötter, *How to Be a Dictator. The Cult of Personality in the Twentieth Century* (London: Bloomsbury, 2019); E. A. Rees, "Leader Cults: Varieties, Preconditions and Functions," in *The Leader Cult in Communist Dictatorships*, ed. Balázs Apor, Jan C. Behrends, Polly Jones, and E. A. Rees (New York: Palgrave Macmillan, 2004), 3–26; David D. Roberts, *Fascist Interactions. Proposals for a New Approach to Fascism and Its Era* (New York: Berghahn, 2016), 202–19; Howard W. French, "Anatomy of Autocracy: Mobutu's Era," *New York Times*, May 17, 1997.

9. Owen Worth, *Morbid Symptoms: The Global Rise of the Far-Right* (London: Zed Books, 2019); Cas Mudde, *The Far Right Today* (Oxford: Polity Press, 2019).

10. Cas Mudde, *Populism: A Very Short Introduction* (New York: Oxford University Press, 2017); Jan-Werner Müller, *What Is Populism?* (Philadelphia: University of Pennsylvania Press, 2016); Pippa Norris, *Cultural Backlash: Trump, Brexit, and Authoritarian Populism* (Cambridge, UK: Cambridge University Press, 2019); Roger Eatwell and Matthew Goodwin, *National Populism. The Revolt against Liberal Democracy* (New York: Penguin Random House, 2018); Federico Finchelstein, *From Fascism to Populism in History* (Berkeley: University of California Press, 2017).

11. Eva Hartog, "Is Stalin Making a Comeback in Russia?" *Atlantic*, May 28, 2019; Timofey Neshitov, "The Comeback of a Soviet Dictator," *Der Spiegel*, August 8, 2019. Putin banned mention of the 1939 Molotov-Ribbentrop pact so as not to tarnish Stalin's Great Patriotic War against the Nazis. Vladimir Luzgin was convicted in 2016 for posting an article on Vkontatke saying the USSR and Germany attacked Poland together. The historian Yury Dmitriev has been in and out of prison since December 2016 for exposing Soviet-era executions and mass graves (his latest imprisonment is due to false charges of sex crimes): Perseus Strategies, *The Kremlin's Political Prisoners. Advancing a Political Agenda By Crushing Dissent*, May 2019, 1, 71. https://www.perseus-strategies.com/wp-content/uploads/2019/04/The-Kremlins-Political-Prisoners-May-2019.pdf.

12. Berlusconi, interview with Boris Johnson and Nicholas Farrell, *Spectator*, September 11, 2003; Vassili Golod, "Austria's Kurz Wants 'Axis of Willing' against Illegal Migration," *Politico* (EU edition), June 13, 2018; Chris Baynes, "Brazil's Far-Right President Bolsonaro Falsely Claims Nazism Was a 'Leftist' Movement," *Independent*, April 4, 2019. Historically grounded works include Sheri Berman, *Democracy and Dictatorship in Europe from the Ancien Régime to the Present Day* (New York: Oxford University Press, 2019); Federico Finchelstein, *A Brief History of Fascist Lies* (Berkeley: University of California Press, 2020); Gavriel D. Rosenfeld, *Hi Hitler! How the Nazi Past Is Being Normalized in Contemporary Culture* (Cambridge, UK: Cambridge University Press, 2015).

13. Fareed Zakaria, "The Rise of Illiberal Democracy," *Foreign Affairs*, 76, no. 6 (1997): 22–43, and his *The Future of Freedom: Illiberal Democracy at Home and Abroad* (New York: W. W. Norton, 2003); Paul Lendval, *Orbán: Hungary's Strongman* (New York:

Oxford University Press, 2018). On varieties of authoritarianism, Natasha Ezrow, "Authoritarianism in the 21st Century," and Erica Frantz, "Authoritarian Politics: Trends and Debates," in *Politics and Governance*, 6, no. 2 (2018), 83–86 and 87–89; Erica Frantz, *Authoritarianism: What Everyone Needs to Know* (New York: Oxford University Press, 2018); Juan Linz, *Totalitarian and Authoritarian Regimes* (1975; rev. ed., Boulder: Lynne Riennes, 2000); Milan Svolik, *The Politics of Authoritarian Rule* (Cambridge, UK: Cambridge University Press, 2012); Marlies Glasius, "What Authoritarianism Is . . . and Is Not: A Practice Perspective," *International Affairs*, 94, no. 3 (2018): 513–33.

14. Daron Acemoglu, Thierry Verdier, and James A Robinson, "Kleptocracy and Divide-and-Rule: A Model of Personal Rule" *Journal of the European Economic Association*, 2, nos. 2–3 (2004): 162–92; Erica Frantz and Natasha Ezrow, *The Politics of Dictatorship Institutions and Outcomes in Authoritarian Regimes* (Boulder; Lynne Rienner, 2011); Barbara Geddes, *How Dictatorships Work. Power, Personalization, and Collapse* (Cambridge, UK: Cambridge University Press, 2018); Bruce Bueno de Mesquita, James D. Morrow, Randolph M. Siverson, and Alastair Smith, *The Logic of Political Survival* (Cambridge, MA: MIT Press, 2003).

15. For other discussions of dictators' toolkits: Bruce Bueno de Mesquita and Alastair Smith, *The Dictator's Handbook: Why Bad Behavior Is Almost Always Good Politics* (New York: Public Affairs, 2011); Erica Frantz and Andrea Kendall-Taylor, "A Dictator's Toolkit: Understanding how Co-optation Affects Repression in Dictatorships," *Journal of Peace Research*, 51, no. 3 (March 2014): 332–46; Barry Rubin, *Modern Dictators. Third World Coup Makers, Strongmen, and Populist Tyrants* (New York: McGraw-Hill, 1987), 294–321.

16. Reuters Staff, "Philippine Leader Says Once Threw Man from Helicopter, Would Do It Again," Reuters, December 29, 2016; Trump, in "Remarks by President Trump and President Erdoğan of Turkey before Bilateral Meeting," at https://www.whitehouse.gov/briefings-statements/remarks-president-trump-president-erdogan-turkey-bilateral-meeting-2/; Douglas C. Canterbury, *Neoextractionism and Capitalist Development* (London: Routledge, 2018), 158–211.

17. Ariel Malka, Yphtach Lelkes, Bert N. Bakker, Eliyahu Spivack, "Who Is Open to Authoritarian Governance within Western Democracies?" *Perspectives on Politics*, forthcoming; Karen Stenner, *The Authoritarian Dynamic* (Cambridge, UK: Cambridge University Press, 2005); Steven Levitsky and Daniel Ziblatt, *How Democracies Die* (New York: Crown Books, 2018), 102–12; Marc J. Hetherington and Jonathan D. Weiler, *Authoritarianism and Polarization in American Politics* (Cambridge, UK: Cambridge University Press, 2009); Fathali M. Moghaddam, *Threat to Democracy: The Appeal of Authoritarianism in an Age of Uncertainty* (Washington, DC: American Psychological Association, 2019); Kate Manne, *Down Girl: The Logic of Misogyny* (New York: Oxford University Press, 2018); Peter Beinert, "The New Authoritarians Are Waging War on Women," *Atlantic*, January/February 2019; Jason Stanley, *How Fascism Works. The Politics of Us and Them* (New York: Random House, 2018), 127–40.

18. Jacques Bainville, *Les Dictateurs* (Paris: Denoël et Steele, 1935), 11. Bainville is warning against underestimating Mussolini in this manner. Ernest Becker, *The Birth and Death of Meaning* (New York: Free Press, 1971), 161; Francesca Dallago and Michele Roccato, "Right-Wing Authoritarianism: Big Five and Perceived Threat to Safety," *European Journal of Personality*, 24, no. 2 (2010): 106–22.

19. Oliver Hahl, Minjae Kim, and Ezra W. Zuckerman Sivan, "The Authentic Appeal of the Lying Demagogue: Proclaiming the Deeper Truth about Political Illegitimacy," *American Sociological Review* 83, no. 1 (2018): 1 33; Jennifer Kavanagh and Michael D.

Rich, *Truth Decay: An Initial Exploration of the Diminishing Role of Facts and Analysis in American Public Life*, RAND Corporation Report, 2018: https://www.rand.org/pubs/research_reports/RR2314.html; Sophia Rosenfeld, *Democracy and Truth. A Short History* (Philadelphia: University of Pennsylvania Press, 2018).

20. Mario Celentano, in Christopher Duggan, *Fascism and the Mafia* (New Haven: Yale University Press, 1989), 101.

21. Ali Vitali, "Trump Says He Could 'Shoot Somebody' and Still Maintain Support," NBC News.com, January 23, 2016; Rodrigo Duterte, in Adrian Chen, "When a Populist Demagogue Takes Power," *New Yorker*, November 21, 2016.

22. Walter Benjamin, *Illuminations*, ed. Hannah Arendt, trans. Harry Zohn (New York: Schocken Books, 1968), 257; Giorgio Agamben, *State of Exception*, trans. Kevin Attell (Chicago: University of Chicago Press, 2005).

23. Curzio Malaparte, *Tecnica del colpo di Stato* (Florence: Vallecchi, 1994), 227, 240.

24. Ian Kershaw, *The "Hitler Myth". Image and Reality in the Third Reich* (Oxford: Oxford University Press, 1987); Association for Diplomatic Studies and Training, Oral History Collection (ADST), Brandon Grove, ambassador to Zaire 1984–1987, interviewed by Thomas Stern, November 1994 at: https://adst.org/2016/09/kleptocracy-and-anti-communism-when-mobutu-ruled-zaire/; George Seldes, *Sawdust Caesar. The Untold History of Mussolini and Fascism* (New York: Harper and Brothers, 1935), 367; Brian D. Taylor, *The Code of Putinism* (New York: Oxford University Press, 2019), 2; Dean Haycock, *Tyrannical Minds. Psychological Profiling, Narcissism, and Dictatorship* (New York: Pegasus Books, 2019); Jerrold Post, *Leaders and Their Followers in a Dangerous World. The Psychology of Political Behavior* (Ithaca, NY: Cornell University Press, 2004).

25. Daron Acemoglu and Murat Ucer, "The Ups and Downs of Turkish Growth, 2002–2015: Political Dynamics, the European Union and the Institutional Slide," National Bureau of Economic Research Working Paper no. 21608 (October 2015); Maggie Haberman and Russ Buettner, "In Business and in Governing, Trump Seeks Victory in Chaos," *New York Times*, January 20, 2019; Philip Rucker and Carol Leonnig, *A Very Stable Genius: Donald J. Trump's Testing of America* (New York: Penguin, 2020); Mansour O. El-Kikhia, *Libya's Qaddafi. The Politics of Contradiction* (Gainesville: University Press of Florida, 1997), 88–89; Dr. David Barkham, in Haycock, *Tyrannical Minds*, 152.

26. Jon Lee Anderson, "King of Kings. The Last Days of Muammar Gaddafi," *New Yorker*, November 7, 2011.

27. Archie Brown, *The Myth of the Strong Leader. Political Leadership in the Modern Age* (New York: Basic Books, 2014); Benjamin F. Jones and Benjamin A. Olken, "Do Leaders Matter? Leadership and Growth since World War II," *Quarterly Journal of Economics* 120, no. 3 (2005): 835–64; Vance Serchuk, "The Myth of Authoritarian Competence," *Atlantic*, September 24, 2018; Acemoglu, Verdier, Robinson, "Kleptocracy."

28. Charlie Chaplin, in Alain Joubert, *Le moustache d'Adolf Hitler, et autres essais* (Paris: Gallimard, 2016), 16–17.

29. Max Weber, *Economy and Society. An Outline of Interpretive Sociology*, ed. Guenther Roth and Claus Wittich, vol. 1 (Berkeley: University of California Press, 1978), 241; Brown, *Myth of the Strong Leader*, 4–6; Kershaw, *"Hitler Myth,"* 8–11.

30. Bueno de Mesquita, Morrow, Siverson, and Smith, *Logic*; Jennifer Gandhi, *Political Institutions under Dictatorship* (Cambridge, UK: Cambridge University Press, 2008), 73–106.

31. Raj M. Desai, Anders Olofsgård, and Tarik M. Yousef, "The Logic of Authoritarian Bargains: A Test of a Structural Model," Brookings Global Economy and Development

Working Paper no. 3 (2007); Guriev and Treisman, "Modern Dictators"; Acemoglu, Verdier, Robinson, "Kleptocracy," 169–172.

32. David Enrich, *Dark Towers: Deutsche Bank, Donald Trump, and an Epic Trail of Destruction* (New York: Custom House, 2020); Gabriel Zucman, *The Hidden Wealth of Nations. The Scourge of Tax Havens*, trans. Teresa Laven-der Fagan (Chicago: University of Chicago Press, 2015); Brian Klaas, *The Despot's Accomplice: How the West Is Aiding and Abetting the Decline of Democracy* (New York: Oxford University Press, 2016).

33. Joseph Szlavik, in Richard Leiby, "Fall of the House of von Kloberg," *Washington Post*, July 31, 2005; Pamela Brogan, *The Torturers' Lobby. How Human Rights-Abusing Nations Are Represented in Washington*, The Center for Public Integrity Report, 1992: https://cloudfront -files-1.publicintegrity.org/legacy_projects/pdf_reports/THETORTURERSLOBBY .pdf; *Spin Doctors to the Autocrats: European PR Firms Whitewash Repressive Regimes*, Corporate Europe Observatory report, January 20, 2015: https://corporateeurope.org/sites/ default/files/20150120_spindoctors_mr.pdf; Neal M. Rosendorf, *Franco Sells Spain to America. Hollywood Tourism and PR as Postwar Spanish Soft Power* (New York: Palgrave, 2014).

34. Shawn Wen, "Eight Women in Love," *N+1*, October 17, 2016; Rose Styron, "Special Report on Chile," in Amnesty International, *Special Report on Torture* (New York: Farrar, Straus and Giroux, 1975), 257; Hannah Arendt, *Origins of Totalitarianism* (New York: Meridian Press, 1958) and her *Eichmann in Jerusalem* (New York: Viking Press, 1964).

35. Gabriele Herz, *The Women's Camp in Moringen. A Memoir of Imprisonment in Nazi Germany 1936–1937*, ed. Jane Caplan (New York: Berghahn, 2006), 90, 113–14.

ONE: FASCIST TAKEOVERS

1. Elena Bianchini Braglia, *Donna Rachele* (Milan: Mursia, 2007), 62; Laura Fermi, *Mussolini* (Chicago: University of Chicago Press, 1961); Mimmo Franzinelli, *Il Duce e le donne. Avventure e passioni extraconiugali di Mussolini* (Milan: Mondadori, 2013).

2. The offending article was Mussolini, "Dalla neutralità assoluta alla neutralità attiva ed operante," *Avanti!* October 18, 1914; Renzo De Felice, *Mussolini il rivoluzionario, 1883–1920* (Turin: Einaudi, 1965); Richard Bosworth, *Mussolini* (London: Bloomsbury, 2011), 66–103; Franzinelli, *Il Duce*, 24–28.

3. Enzo Traverso, *The Origins of Nazi Violence*, trans. Janet Lloyd (New York: The New Press, 2003), and his *Fire and Blood. The European Civil War 1914–1945*, trans. David Fernbach (London: Verso, 2016).

4. Fermi, *Mussolini*, 73; Mussolini, "Trincerocrazia," *Il Popolo d'Italia*, December 15, 1917; Sven Reichardt, *Faschistische Kampfbünde: Gewalt und Gemeinschaft im italienischen Squadrismus und in der deutschen SA* (Vienna and Cologne: Böhlau-Verlag Gmbh, 2009).

5. Mussolini, "Stato anti-stato e fascismo," *Gerarchia*, June 25, 1922; Robert Paxton, *The Anatomy of Fascism* (New York: Vintage, 2005), 3–54.

6. Susan Pedersen, *The Guardians. World War One and the Crisis of Empire* (New York: Oxford University Press, 2017).

7. Marc Reynebeau, "'Je ne sais quoi': Reflections on the Study of Charisma," in *Charismatic Leadership and Social Movements*, ed. Jan Willem Stutje (New York: Berghahn, 2012), 155–63; first and third quotes from Heinrich Class, 1920, in Lothar Machtan, *The Hidden Hitler*, trans. John Brownjohn (New York: Basic Books, 2001), 122–23; Ojetti, 1921, in Christopher Duggan, *Fascist Voices. An Intimate History of Mussolini's Italy* (New York: Oxford University Press, 2013), 48.

8. Richard Evans, *The Coming of the Third Reich* (New York: Penguin, 2003); Wolfgang Schivelbusch, *The Culture of Defeat: On National Trauma, Mourning, and Recovery* (New York: Picador, 2001), 189–288; H. James Burgwyn, *The Legend of the Mutilated Victory. Italy, the Great War and the Paris Peace Conference, 1915–1919* (Westport, CT: Praeger, 1993).

9. Kersten Knipp, *Die Kommune der Faschisten Gabriele D'Annunzio, die Republik von Fiume und die Extreme des 20. Jahrhundert* (Stuttgart: WBG Theiss, 2019).

10. Mario Piazzesi, in Duggan, *Fascist Voices*, 43; Mimmo Franzinelli, *Squadristi. Protagonisti e techniche della violenza fascista, 1919–1922* (Milan: Mondadori, 2003).

11. Jacqueline Reich, *The Maciste Films of Italian Cinema* (Bloomington: Indiana University Press, 2015); Giuseppe Bastianini, *Uomini cose fatti. Memorie di un ambasciatore* (Milan: Vitagliano, 1959), 6; Giorgio Pini, *Filo diretto con Palazzo Venezia* (Bologna: Cappelli, 1950), 23; Carlo Ciseri, in Duggan, *Fascist Voices*, 8.

12. Benito Mussolini, "Il fascismo e i problemi della politica estera italiana," speech given in Trieste, February 6, 1921, in *Opera Omnia*, ed. Edoardo and Duilio Susmel (Florence: La Fenice, 1951–1980), 44 vols., XVI/150–160; Mussolini, "Stato anti-Stato e fascismo."

13. Giulia Albanese, *La marcia su Roma* (Rome: Laterza, 2006); Mauro Canali, *La scoperta dell'Italia. Il Fascismo raccontato dai corrispondenti americani* (Venice: Marsilio, 2017).

14. Mussolini, "Forza e consenso," *Gerarchia*, March 1923; Rachele Ferrario, *Margherita Sarfatti: La regina dell'arte nell'Italia fascista* (Milan: Mondadori, 2015); Denis Mack Smith, *Mussolini* (New York: Alfred A. Knopf, 1982), 56–58, 62–74; Clara Elisabetta Mattei. "Austerity and Repressive Politics: Italian Economists in the Early Years of the Fascist Government," *The European Journal of the History of Economic Thought*, 24, no. 5 (2017): 998–1026.

15. Fermi, *Mussolini*, 229; Mauro Canali, "The Matteotti Murder and the Origins of Mussolini's Totalitarian Dictatorship," *Journal of Modern Italian Studies* 14, no. 2 (2009): 143–67.

16. Canali, "Matteotti Murder."

17. Canali, "Matteotti Murder"; Mack Smith, *Mussolini*, 74–79; Duggan, *Fascist Voices*, 50.

18. G. A. Borgese, *Goliath: The March of Fascism* (New York: Viking, 1937), 263; Canali, "Matteotti Murder"; Rosa B. to Mussolini, December 31, 1923, in *Caro Duce. Lettere di donne italiane a Mussolini 1922–1943* (Milan: Rizzoli, 1989), 114; Ugo Ojetti, in Fermi, *Mussolini*, 238.

19. Fermi, *Mussolini*, 237; Giorgio Amendola in Mack Smith, *Mussolini*, 85; Mussolini, "Discorso del 3 gennaio," in Mussolini, *Opera Omnia*, XI/235–241.

20. Francesco Nitti, letter of March 5, 1925, to King Vittorio Emanuele III, in Santi Fedele, "Francesco Saverio Nitti dal lungo esilio al rientro in Italia," *Humanities* 1, no. 1 (2012), 2.

21. Canali, "Matteotti Murder"; Gian Giacomo Migone, *The United States and Italy. The Rise of American Finance in Europe* (Cambridge, UK: Cambridge University Press, 2015), 90–94, 150–64.

22. Wolfgang Schieder, *Adolf Hitler. Politischer Zauberlehrling Mussolinis* (Berlin: De Gruyter Oldenbourg, 2017).

23. Sefton Delmer, *Trail Sinister. An Autobiography, Volume One* (London: Secker and Warburg, 1961), 188–89; Benjamin Carter Hett, *Burning the Reichstag* (New York: Oxford University Press, 2014); Richard J. Evans, "The Conspiracists," *London Review of Books* 36, no. 9 (2014).

24. Neil Gregor, "Hitler," in *Mental Maps in the Era of Two World Wars*, ed. Steven Casey and Jonathan Wright (New York: Palgrave Macmillan, 2008), 196; August Kubizek, *The Young Hitler I Knew*, trans. E. V. Anderson (Boston: Houghton Mifflin, 1955), 14;

Volker Ulrich, *Hitler: Ascent 1889–1939* (New York: Knopf, 2016); Joachim Fest, *Hitler* (New York: Mariner Books, 2002).

25. Hitler, speech in Salzburg, August 1920, in Gregor, "Hitler,"189; Hitler, "Rathenau und Sancho Pansa," *Völkischer Beobachter*, March 13, 1921; Hitler, *Mein Kampf*, trans. Ralph Manheim (Boston: Houghton Mifflin, 1999), 562; Joseph Goebbels, July 12, 1925, in *Die Tagebücher von Joseph Goebbels. Sämtliche Fragmente: Aufzeichnungen 1923–1941*, ed. Elke Fröhlich (Munich: K.G. Saur Verlag, 1998–2006), vol. 1, 326–27.

26. Daniel Siemens, *Stormtroopers. A New History of Hitler's Brownshirts* (New Haven: Yale University Press, 2017); Reichardt, *Faschistische.*

27. Daniel Kalder, *The Infernal Library: On Dictators, the Books They Wrote, and Other Catastrophes of Literacy* (New York: Henry Holt, 2018), 128.

28. Major Giuseppe Renzetti met with Hitler forty-two times between 1929 and 1942. Renzo De Felice, *Mussolini e Hitler. I rapporti segreti, 1922–1933* (Rome: Laterza, 2013); Schieder, *Hitler*, 40–43, 54–57; Christian Goeschels, *Mussolini and Hitler: The Forging of the Fascist Alliance* (New Haven: Yale University Press, 2018), 17–36; Mack Smith, *Mussolini*, 172–73.

29. Claudia Schmölders, *Hitler's Face. The Biography of an Image* (Philadelphia: University of Pennsylvania Press, 2006), 69–99; Lutz Koepnik, "Face Time with Hitler," in *Visualizing Fascism: The Twentieth-Century Rise of the Global Right*, ed. Julia Adeney Thomas and Geoff Eley (Durham: Duke University Press, 2020), 111–33.

30. Eugen Dollmann, in Machtan, *Hitler*, 134; Hitler to Mussolini, June 8, 1931, in De Felice, *Mussolini e Hitler*, 229; Kalder, *Library*, 134–38; P. F. Beck to Hitler, April 25, 1932, in *Letters to Hitler*, ed. Henrik Eberle, trans. Steven Rendall (New York: Polity Press, 2012), 50–52.

31. Evans, *Coming of the Third Reich*; Fritz Thyssen, *I Paid Hitler* (New York: Farrar and Rinehart, 1941), 111.

32. Renzetti, January 23, 1933, report to Mussolini, in De Felice, *Mussolini e Hitler*, 249; Hett, *Reichstag Fire*; Borgese, *Goliath*, 375.

33. Enrique Moradiellos, *Franco: Anatomy of a Dictator* (London: I.B. Tauris, 2018); Paul Preston, *Franco: A Biography* (New York: Basic Books, 1994); Stanley G. Payne and Jesus Palacios, *Franco: A Personal and Political Biography* (Madison: University of Wisconsin Press, 2018).

34. Bruce W. Farcau, *The Coup. Tactics in the Seizure of Power* (Westport, CT: Praeger, 1994), 115–20; Julian Casanova, *A Short History of the Spanish Civil War* (London: I.B.Tauris, 2013), 6–11.

35. Franco, in Preston, *Franco*, 105; Moradiellos, *Franco*, 33; Geoff Jensen, *Franco: Soldier, Commander, Dictator* (Dulles, VA: Potomac Books, 2005), 57–70; Manuel Villatoro, "'La Baraka': la misteriosa 'benedición mora' que salvó a Francisco Franco de una sangrienta muerte en el Rif," *ABC*, October 18, 2018.

36. Casanova, *Short History*. The center-left earned 34.3 percent vs. 33.2 percent for the center-right.

37. Paul Preston, "Franco as Military Leader," *Transactions of the Royal Historical Society* 4 (1994), 27–28; Ismael Saz, "Fascism and Empire: Fascist Italy against Republican Spain," *Mediterranean Historical Review*, 13, nos. 1–2 (1998), 126; Ángel Viñas and Carlos Collado Seidel, "Franco's Request to the Third Reich for Military Assistance," *Contemporary European History* 11, no. 2 (2002), 207–8; Helen Graham, *The Spanish Civil War. A Very Short Introduction* (New York: Oxford University Press, 2005), 38–39.

38. General Amado Balmes died by accidental gunshot on the eve of the coup. Generals Joaquín Fanjul and Manuel Goded were executed by Republicans.

39. NSA Archive, FBI report, January 21, 1982, mentions the meeting of Pinochet and Delle Chiaie in the context of the terrorist activities of the Pinochet regime: https://nsarchive2.gwu.edu//NSAEBB/NSAEBB8/docs/doc02.pdf.

Two: MILITARY COUPS

1. President Richard Nixon, in R. W. Apple, "Nixon, Greeting Mobutu, Lauds the Congo," *New York Times*, May 8, 1970; Sean Kelly, *America's Tyrant. The CIA and Mobutu of Zaire* (Washington, DC: American University Press, 1993).

2. Malcolm X, in Robin D. G. Kelly, "A Poetics of Anticolonialism," in Aimé Cesaire, *Discourse on Colonialism* (New York: Monthly Review Press, 2000), 8. Spain retained the Moroccan cities of Ceuta and Melilla. Jan C. Jansen and Jürgen Osterhammel, *Decolonization: A Short History*, trans. Jeremiah Riemer (Princeton, NJ: Princeton University Press, 2017); Todd Shepard, *Voices of Decolonization: A Brief History with Documents* (New York: Bedford/St. Martins, 2014).

3. Dirk Vandevalle, *A History of Modern Libya* (Cambridge, UK: Cambridge University Press, 2012), 78–82; Josh Keating, "Trained in the USA," *Foreign Policy*, March 28, 2012.

4. Naumihal Singh, *Seizing Power. The Strategic Logic of Military Coups* (Baltimore: Johns Hopkins University Press, 2014), 3. The 75 percent of democratic failures were in areas with populations of more than 100,000; Farcau, *The Coup*, 54.

5. Singh, *Seizing Power*, 3.

6. Gaddafi, radio address, September 1, 1969, in Alison Pargeter, *Libya: The Rise and Fall of Gaddafi* (New Haven: Yale University Press, 2012), 59–60; ADST, George Lane, principal officer of US Libyan embassy, Benghazi branch office, interview with Richard Nethercutt, 1990: https://adst.org/2013/08/qaddafi-the-man-and-his-rise-to-power/.

7. Gaddafi attended the Army School of Education in Beaconsfield. Michael Cockerell, "Lieutenant Gaddafi in Swinging London," *Standpoint Magazine*, January/February 2012.

8. Mohamed Fekini to General Rodolfo Graziani, letters of June 4 and June 10, 1922. Eight other tribal chiefs signed the former letter. In Angelo Del Boca, *Mohamed Fekini and the Fight to Free Libya* (New York: Palgrave Macmillan, 2011), 115–18.

9. Ali Ahmida, *Forgotten Voices. Power and Agency in Colonial and Postcolonial Libya* (New York: Routledge, 2005); Hisham Matar, *The Return: Fathers, Sons and the Land in Between* (New York: Random House, 2016), 131–40; Stephanie Malia Hom, *Empire's Mobius Strip. Historical Echoes in Italy's Crisis of Migration and Detention* (Ithaca, NY: Cornell University Press, 2019), 83–89.

10. Vandevalle, *Modern Libya*, 50–53; Muhammad T. Jerary, "Damages Caused by the Italian Fascist Colonization of Libya," in *Italian Colonialism*, ed. Ruth Ben-Ghiat and Mia Fuller (New York: Palgrave Macmillan, 2005), 203–8; Anna Baldinetti, *The Origins of the Libyan Nation. Colonial Legacy, Exile and the Emergence of the Nation-State* (New York: Routledge, 2010).

11. Saskia van Genugten, *Libya in Western Foreign Policies, 1911–2011* (New York: Palgrave Macmillan, 2016), 59–80; Stephen Blackwell, "Saving the King: Anglo-American Strategy and British Counter-Subversion Operations in Libya, 1953–59," *Middle Eastern Studies* 39, no. 1 (2003), 14–15.

12. Matar, *Return*, 29–30; Daniel Kawczyinski, *Seeking Gaddafi: Libya, the West, and the Arab Spring* (London: Biteback Publishing, 2011), 18–19; ADST, George Lane interview; Ronald Bruce St. John, *Libya: From Colony to Revolution* (London: Oneworld Publications, 2017), 139–40.

13. Vandewalle, *Modern Libya*, 78; Pargeter, *Libya*, 72–76.

14. Joel Fishman, "The Postwar Career of Nazi Ideologue Johann von Leers, aka Omar Amin, the 'First Ranking German' in Nasser's Egypt," *Jewish Political Studies Review* 26, nos. 3–4 (2014): 54–72; van Genugten, *Libya*, 81–104; Arturo Varvelli, *L'Italia e l'ascesa di Gheddafi. La cacciata degli italiani, le armi e il petrolio (1969–1974)* (Milan: Baldini Castoldi Dalai, 2009), 210–22.

15. Muammar Gaddafi, *Escape to Hell and Other Stories* (Toronto: Hushion House, 1998), 64; Pargeter, *Gaddafi's Libya*, 76–80; Gaddafi, in Ruth First Papers, RF/2/21/10: "Answers to questions submitted by Ruth First to Colonel Muammar Gaddafi, Tripoli, Friday 2 July 1971," 5: https://sas-space.sas.ac.uk/3598/1/RF_2_21_10.pdf.

16. Transcript of call in Jon Lee Anderson, "The Dictator," *New Yorker*, October 19, 1998; Ana Maria, interview in José Yglesias, *Chile's Days of Terror. Eyewitness Accounts of the Military Coup*, ed. Judy White (New York: Pathfinder Press, 1974), 76.

17. Patrice McSherry, *Predatory States: Operation Condor and Covert War in Latin America* (Lanham, MD: Rowman & Littlefield, 2005); Patricia Mayorga, *Il condor nero. L'internazionale fascista e i rapporti segreti con il regime di Pinochet* (Milan: Sperling & Kupfer, 2003); Anna Cento Bull and Galadriel Ravelli, "The Pinochet Regime and the Trans-Nationalization of Italian Neo-Fascism," in Robert Leeson, ed., *Hayek: A Collaborative Bibliography. Part XIII: "Fascism" and Liberalism in the (Austrian) Classical Tradition* (New York: Palgrave Macmillan, 2018), 361–93.

18. Oscar Guardiola-Rivera, *Story of a Death Foretold. The Coup against Salvador Allende, September 11, 1973* (London: Bloomsbury Press, 2013), 44–45, 76–95; Maria José Henríquez Uzal, *Viva la verdadera Amistad! Franco y Allende, 1970–1973* (Santiago: Editorial Unversitaria, 2014); ADST, Samuel F. Hart, economist, US embassy, Santiago, 1971–1975, interview with Charles Stuart Kennedy, June 12, 1992, at https://adst.org/2013/09/chiles-coup-against-salvador-allende-and-the-truth-behind-missing/.

19. Nixon to White House Chief of Staff H. R. Haldeman, January 18, 1972, Nixon Tapes, Conversation 650–013: http://nixontapeaudio.org/chile/650–013.pdf.

20. Guardiola-Rivera, *Death Foretold*, 178–215; Henry Kissinger, *Years of Upheaval* (Boston: Little, Brown, 1982), 376; Richard Helms, in NSA Archive, Kornbluh, "Chile and the United States," CIA, Notes on Meeting with the President on Chile, September 15, 1970: https://nsarchive2.gwu.edu/NSAEBB/NSAEBB8/docs/doc26.pdf; Henry Kissinger to Nixon and H. R. Haldeman, June 11, 1971, Nixon Tapes, Conversation 517–004: http://nixontapeaudio.org/chile/517–004.pdf.

21. Ambassador Edward Korry, 1970 cable to Washington DC, in David Stout, "Edward Korry, 81, Is Dead: Falsely Tied to Chile Coup," *New York Times*, January 30, 2003. Korry detested Allende but was kept out of coup plotting due to Nixon's distrust of him.

22. Jonathan Kandel, "Chilean Officers Tell How They Began to Plan the Take-Over Last November," *New York Times*, September 27, 1973; CIA officer, in Kristian C. Gustafson, "CIA Machinations in Chile. Reexamining the Record," at: https://www.cia.gov/library/center-for-the-study-of-intelligence/csi-publications/csi-studies/studies/vol47no3/article03.html; John R. Bawden, *The Pinochet Generation. The Chilean Military in the Twentieth Century* (Tuscaloosa: University of Alabama Press, 2016), 96–134; Mónica González, *La Conjura. Los mil y un dias del golpe* (Santiago: Ediciones B Chile, 2000).

23. Jack Devine, "What Really Happened in Chile," *Foreign Affairs* 93, no.4 (2014): 26–35; Senator Maria Elena Carrera, in Thomas Wright and Rody Oñate, *Flight from Chile. Voices from Exile* (Albuquerque: University of New Mexico Press, 1998), 15; Bawden,

Pinochet Generation, 128–131; Heraldo Muñoz, *The Dictator's Shadow: Life Under Augusto Pinochet* (New York: Basic Books, 2008), 22–44; González, *Conjura*.

24. Muñoz, *Dictator's Shadow*, 21; Mario González, in Wright and Oñate, *Flight*, 31–36.

25. Muñoz, *Dictator's Shadow*, 22–31, Juan Cristóbal Peña, *La secreta vida literaria de Augusto Pinochet* (Santiago: Random House Mondadori, 2013), 81–88; Mary Helen Spooner, *Soldiers in a Narrow World. The Pinochet Regime in Chile* (Berkeley: University of California Press, 1999), 18–24.

26. Patricio, in Yglesias, *Terror*, 113–14.

27. Jurandir Antonio Xavier, in Yglesias, *Terror*, 123; Mark Ensalaco, *Chile under Pinochet: Recovering the Truth* (Philadelphia: University of Pennsylvania Press, 1999), 69–97; Pablo Policzer, *The Rise and Fall of Repression in Chile* (Notre Dame, IN: University of Notre Dame Press, 2009).

28. Eduardo Frei, quoted in Steve J. Stern, *Battling for Hearts and Minds. Memory Struggles in Pinochet's Chile, 1973–1988* (Durham, NC: Duke University Press, 2006), 26; Associated Press, "Chile: Six People Sentenced for 1982 Murder of Former President," *Guardian*, January 30, 2019.

29. Pinochet, in Genaro Arriagada, *Pinochet. The Politics of Power* (Boston: Unwin Hyman, 1988), 9, 16; Gerretsen, interview with Melissa Gutierrez,"Chas Gerretsen, el fotógrafo tras la imagine más terrorifica de Pinochet: 'El era un monstruo,'" *The Clinic Online*, September 2, 2013; Carlos Huneeus, *The Pinochet Regime*, trans. Lake Sagaris (Boulder: Lynne Rienner, 2007), 70–81.

THREE: NEW AUTHORITARIAN ASCENTS

1. Silvio Berlusconi, videomessage, January 26 1994, transcription in Gian Antonio Stella and Sergio Rizzo, *Cosi parlò il cavaliere* (Milan: Rizzoli 2011), 120–22; Alexander Stille, *The Sack of Rome: How a Beautiful European Country with a Fabled History and a Storied Culture Was Taken Over by a Man Named Silvio Berlusconi* (New York: Penguin Press, 2006), 151–57; Massimo Ragnedda, "Censorship and Media Ownership in Italy in the Era of Berlusconi," *Global Media Journal: Mediterranean Edition* 9, no. 1 (2014), 13.

2. Yascha Mounk, 'How Authoritarians Manipulate Elections," *Atlantic*, May 8, 2019; Nic Cheeseman and Brian Klaas, *How to Rig an Election* (New Haven: Yale University Press, 2019).

3. Mark Bray, *Antifa: The Anti-Fascist Handbook* (New York: Melville House, 2017), 54–64; Paul Hockenos, *Free to Hate. The Rise of the Right in Post-Communist Europe* (New York: Routledge, 1993); Post, *Leaders*, 162–71.

4. Gregory Crouch, "Three to Watch: Populists of the Hard Right," and Mark Hunter, "Europe's Reborn Right," both in *New York Times Magazine*, April 21, 1996; Stephen Kinzer, "Germany's New Right Wears a 3-Piece Suit," *New York Times*, May 28, 1995; Paul Ginsborg, *Silvio Berlusconi. Television, Power, and Patrimony* (New York: Verso, 2004), 66.

5. Margaret Quigley, "The European New Right and U.S. Politics," in *Trumping Democracy. From Reagan to the Alt-Right*, ed. Chip Berlet (New York: Routledge, 2020), 54–60; Piero Ignazi, *Postfascisti? Dal Movimento sociale italiano ad Alleanza Nazionale* (Bologna: Il Mulino, 1994).

6. Berlusconi, in Giovanni Ruggeri and Mario Guarino, *Berlusconi. Inchiesta sul signor TV* (Milan: Kaos 1994), 271. The Christian Democrat Party provided every prime minister, 1946 to 1983 and 1986 to 1992.

7. Berlusconi and Francesco Borelli, in Alan Friedman, *My Way. Berlusconi in His Own Words* (London: Biteback Publishing, 2015), 90, 107.

8. On Dell'Utri, whose 2004 conviction was confirmed by the Italian Supreme Court in 2014, Stille, *Sack of Rome*, 37–51.

9. Ginsborg, *Berlusconi*, 3–6.

10. Stille, *Sack of Rome*, 16; Ginsborg, *Berlusconi*, 33; Ragnedda, "Censorship," 15.

11. Friedman, *My Way*, 97–98; Gianfranco Pasquino, "The Five Faces of Silvio Berlusconi: The Knight of Anti-Politics," *Modern Italy* 12, no. 1 (2007): 39–54; Cristian Vaccari, "The Features, Impact, and Legacy of Berlusconi's Campaigning Language and Style," *Modern Italy* 20, no. 1 (2015); 25–39; Stille, *Sack of Rome*, 162–69; Dell'Utri, in Ruggeri and Guarino, *Berlusconi*, 270.

12. Gianni Agnelli, in Friedman, *My Way*, 97.

13. Experience of the author in Rome, 1994; Gianfranco Fini, interview with Alberto Statera, "Il migliore resta Mussolini," *La Stampa*, April 1, 1994; Ignazi, *Postfascisti?*; Ginsborg, *Berlusconi*, 68. AN got 13.5 percent and the League 8.4 percent in the 1994 election.

14. Vittorio Sgarbi, July 14 and 16, 1994, in Ginsborg, *Berlusconi*, 83, 67; Elisabetta Rubini, "Le vicende giudiziarie di Silvio B.: è andato così," in *Berlusconismo. Analisi di un fenomeno*, ed. Paul Ginsborg and Enrica Asquer (Rome: Laterza, 2011); Cristina Dallara, "Powerful Resistance against a Long-Running Personal Crusade: The Impact of Silvio Berlusconi on the Italian Judicial System," *Modern Italy*, 20, no. 1 (2015), 64; Alberto Vannucci, "The Controversial Legacy of 'Mani Pulite': A Critical Analysis of Italian Corruption and Anti-Corruption Policies," *Bulletin of Italian Politics* 1, no. 2 (2009), 251.

15. Berlusconi, in Stille, *Sack of Rome*, 17–18.

16. Fiona Hill and Clifford Gaddy, *Mr. Putin. Operative in the Kremlin* (Washington, DC: Brookings Institution Press, 2013), 153–89; Julie A. Cassidy and Emily D. Johnson, "A Personality Cult for the Postmodern Age," in Helena Goscilo, ed., *Putin as Celebrity and Cultural Icon* (New York: Routledge, 2013), 40.

17. Putin, in Masha Gessen, *The Man without a Face: The Unlikely Rise of Vladimir Putin* (New York: Riverhead Books, 2012), 68; Hill and Gaddy, *Putin*, 181–83.

18. Singh, *Seizing Power*, 195–221; Gessen, *Man without a Face*, 101–29.

19. Joke in David Stuckler and Sanjay Basu, *The Body Economic: Why Austerity Kills* (New York: Basic Books, 2013), 32; Timothy Heleniak, "Population Trends," in Stephen K. Wegren, ed., *Putin's Russia: Past Imperfect, Future Uncertain* (Lanham, MD: Rowman & Littlefield, 2016), 153–60; Masha Gessen, "The Dying Russians," *New York Review of Books*, September 2, 2014; Karen Dawisha, *Putin's Kleptocracy: Who Owns Russia?* (New York: Simon and Schuster, 2015), 13–35.

20. Hill and Gaddy, *Putin*, 147–65; Dawisha, *Putin's Kleptocracy*, 104–62.

21. As FSB head, Putin had also proved his worth by forcing the resignation of Russian prosecutor general Yuri Skuratov, who was investigating Yeltsin's family and inner circle for corruption. The FSB had film shown on television of Skuratov having sex with two prostitutes. David Satter, "How Putin Became President," *The American Interest*, May 19, 2016; ADST, Thomas Pickering, ambassador to Russia, 1993–1996, interviewed by Charles Stuart Kennedy, April 2003: https://adst.org/?s=Putin.

22. Zhenya Molchanova and Lt. Colonel Ivan Timoshenko, in Natalya Shulyakovskaya and Catherine Belton, "Public Sees Madness in the Kremlin," *Moscow Times*, August 10, 1999; "'Who Is Putin?' How Russia Reacted to Leader's Rise to Power, 20 Years Ago," *Moscow Times*, August 9, 2019; Boris Nemtsov, in Andrei Zolotov, "President Draws Criticism from All Political Camps," *Moscow Times*, August 10, 1999; Tobias Rup-

precht, "Formula Pinochet: Chilean Lessons for Russian Liberal Reformers during the Soviet Collapse, 1970–2000," *Journal of Contemporary History*, 51, no. 1 (2016): 165–86.

23. Putin, August 16, 1999, speech to Duma, in Dawisha, *Putin's Kleptocracy*, 202–3; Gessen, *Man without a Face*, 22–42; Amy Knight, *Orders to Kill. The Putin Regime and Political Murder* (New York: Thomas Dunne Books, 2017), 79–99; David Satter, *Darkness at Dawn: The Rise of the Russian Criminal State* (New Haven: Yale University Press, 2004), 63–71.

24. Knight, *Orders*, 93–98; Dawisha, *Putin's Kleptocracy*, 243–51.

25. Kissinger, quoted in Ian Traynor, "Putin Urged to Apply the Pinochet Stick," *Guardian*, March 30, 2000; José Pinera, "A Chilean Model for Russia," *Foreign Policy* 79, no. 5 (2000): 62–73; Rupprecht, "Formula Pinochet"; "Russia at the Turn of the Millenium," December 31, 1999, essay attributed to Putin, in Hill and Gaddy, *Putin*, 40; Dawisha, *Putin's Kleptocracy*, 7; Masha Gessen, *The Future Is History: How Totalitarianism Reclaimed Russia* (New York: Riverhead Books, 2017), on how the process unfolded.

26. George W. Bush, in Michael Wolff, *Fire and Fury. Inside the Trump White House* (New York: Henry Holt, 2018), 44; Donald Trump, "The Inaugural Address," January 20, 2017, at: https://www.whitehouse.gov/briefings-statements/the-inaugural-address/.

27. Sarah Kendzior, *Hiding in Plain Sight. The Invention of Donald Trump* (New York: Flatiron Books, 2020); Wayne Barrett, *Trump: The Deals and the Downfall* (New York: HarperCollins, 1992); David Barstow, Susanne Craig, and Russ Buettner, "Trump Engaged in Suspect Tax Schemes as He Reaped Riches from his Father," *New York Times*, October 2, 2018; Michael Rothfeld and Alexandra Berzon, "Donald Trump and the Mob," *Wall Street Journal*, September 1, 2016; David Cay Johnson, "Just What Were Donald Trump's Ties to the Mob?" *Politico*, May 22, 2016; Christopher Knaus, "Trump's Bid for Sydney Casino 30 Years Ago Rejected Due to 'Mafia Connections,'" *Guardian*, August 15, 2017; David A. Fahrenthold and Jonathan O'Connell, "How Donald Trump Inflated His Net Worth to Lenders and Investors," *Washington Post*, March 28, 2019.

28. Mike McIntire, Megan Twohey, and Mark Mazzetti, "How a Lawyer, a Felon and a Russian General Chased a Moscow Trump Tower Deal," *New York Times*, November 29, 2018; Franklin Foer, "Russian-Style Kleptocracy Is Infiltrating America," *Atlantic*, March 2019; Christina Maza, "Former Trump Associate Felix Sater Accused of Laundering Millions," *Newsweek*, March 26, 2019; Robby Browne, Corcoran Group broker, in Jacob Bernstein, "Trump Tower, a Home for Celebrities and Charlatans," *New York Times*, August 12, 2017; Brett Samuels, "Trump Says He'll Meet with Dictators If It's Good for the US," *Hill*, November 12, 2019; Greg Price, "Ivanka Trump Sat in Vladimir Putin's Chair and Spun Around, President's Former Associate Says," *Newsweek*, May 17, 2018; Vicky Ward, *Kushner, Inc. Greed. Ambition, Corruption* (New York: St. Martin's Press, 2019), 38; Anita Kumar, "Buyers Tied to Russia, Former Soviet Republics Paid $109 Million in Cash for Trump Properties," *McClatchy*, June 19, 2018.

29. Emma Green, "It Was Cultural Anxiety That Drove White, Working-Class Voters to Trump," *Atlantic*, May 9, 2017; Trump, in Politico Staff, "Full Text: Donald Trump 2016 RNC Draft Speech Transcript," *Politico*, July 21, 2016; German Lopez, "Trump's Long History of Racism from the 1970s to 2019," *Vox*, July 15, 2019; *USA Today*, "Trump Nation," 2016 interviews with Trump supporters from all 50 states: https://www.usatoday.com/pages/interactives/trump-nation/#/?_k=9nqnw0.

30. Thomas E. Mann and Norman J. Ornstein, "Let's Just Say It: The Republicans Are the Problem," *Washington Post*, April 27, 2012; Hetherington and Weiler, *Authoritarianism*; Tim Alberta, *American Carnage* (New York: HarperCollins, 2019).

31. Berlet, ed., *Trumping Democracy*; Alberta, *American Carnage*, 110–17; Brian Rosenwald,

Talk Radio's America. How an Industry Took Over a Political Party That Took Over the United States (Cambridge, MA: Harvard University Press, 2019); Guardiola-Rivera, *Death Foretold*, 238.

32. Sessions and Trump in Eli Stokol, "Sen. Jeff Sessions endorses Trump," *Politico*, February 28, 2016. Nancy McLean, *Democracy in Chains: The Deep History of the Radical Right's Stealth Plan for America* (New York: Viking, 2017), 154–68; Sahil Chinoy, "What Happened to America's Political Center of Gravity?" *New York Times*, June 26, 2019, which discusses results from the Manifesto Project that covers over 1,000 parties in 50 countries since 1945: https://manifesto-project.wzb.eu/; Pippa Norris, "Measuring Populism Worldwide," Harvard Kennedy School Faculty Research Working Paper No. RWP20-002, February 2020. Link to results and Global Party Survey dataset at: https://www.hks.harvard.edu/publications/measuring-populism -worldwide.

33. Nicholas Farrell, "'I'm Fascinated by Mussolini,'" *Spectator USA*, March 14, 2018; Jane Mayer, "New Evidence Emerges of Steve Bannon and Cambridge Analytica's Role in Brexit," *New Yorker*, November 18, 2018.

34. Ward, *Kushner,* 82; Wolff, *Fire and Fury*, 41, 77, 193; Nahal Toosi and Isaac Arnsdorf, "Kissinger, Longtime Putin Confidant, Sidles Up to Trump," *Politico*, December 24, 2016.

35. Jeff Horowitz and Chad Day, "AP Exclusive: Before Trump Job, Manafort Worked to Aid Putin," *AP News*, March 22, 2017; Betsy Swan and Tim Mak, "Top Trump Aide Led the 'Torturers' Lobby,'" *Daily Beast*, November 6, 2017; Tom McCarthy, "Paul Manafort: How Decades of Serving Dictators Led to Role as Trump's Go-To Guy," *Guardian*, October 30, 2017; Jack Anderson and Dale Van Atta, "Mobutu in Search of an Image Boost," *Washington Post*, September 25, 1989; Brogan, "The Torturers' Lobby," 1, 6, 31, 51–60.

36. Trump, tweet of June 18, 2013, at: https://twitter.com/realdonaldtrump/status/347191 326112112640?lang=en; Tina Nguyen, "Eric Trump Reportedly Bragged about Access to $100 Million in Russian Money," *Vanity Fair*, May 8, 2017; Donald Trump Jr. comment in David Remnick, "Trump and Putin: A Love Story," *New Yorker*, August 3, 2016; Craig Unger, *House of Trump, House of Putin* (New York: Dutton, 2019); Michael Isikoff and David Corn, *Russian Roulette: The Inside Story of Putin's War on America and the Election of Donald Trump* (New York: Twelve, 2018).

37. Nick Corasaniti and Maggie Haberman, "Trump Suggests 'Second Amendment People' Could Act against Hillary Clinton," *New York Times*, August 8, 2016; Eric Bradner, "Conway: Trump Offered 'Alternative Facts' on Crowd Size," CNN.com, January 23, 2017.

38. Ruth Ben-Ghiat, "Trump and Bannon's Coup," CNN.com, February 1, 2017; Bannon, in Philip Rucker and Robert Costa, "Bannon Vows a Daily Fight for 'Deconstruction of the Administrative State,'" *Washington Post*, February 23, 2017; Conor Friedersdorf, "The Radical Anti-Conservatism of Stephen Bannon," *Atlantic*, August 25, 2016; Kellyanne Conway, tweet, January 28, 2017: https://twitter.com/KellyannePolls/ status/825358733945475073.

Four: A Greater Nation

1. Herr S., in Charlotte Beradt, *The Third Reich of Dreams*, trans. Adriane Gottwald (Chicago: Quadrangle Books, 1966), 5–7.

2. Tilman Allert, *The Hitler Salute. On the Meaning of a Gesture* (New York: Picador, 2009); Kershaw, *"Hitler Myth,"* 60.

3. Allert, *Hitler Salute*, 38–39, 60, 68; Wendy Lower, *Hitler's Furies: German Women in the Nazi Killing Fields* (New York: Houghton Mifflin, 2013), 22.

4. Gaddafi adopted a different Muslim calendar than the rest of the Arab world. Mussolini, "Discorso sull' Ascensione," May 26, 1927, in *Scritti e discorsi* 66: 77.

5. Paulo Pachá, "Why the Brazilian Far Right Loves the European Middle Ages," *Pacific Standard*, March 12, 2019; Matthew Gabriel, "Islamophobes Want to Recreate the Crusades. But They Don't Understand Them at All," *Washington Post*, June 6, 2017; Aristotle Kallis, *Fascist Ideology: Territory and Expansionism in Italy and Germany, 1922–1945* (New York: Routledge, 2000); Soner Cagaptay, *Erdogan's Empire: Turkey and the Politics of the Middle East* (London: I.B. Tauris, 2019).

6. Alexander Reid Ross, "Hitler in Brasilia: The U.S. Evangelicals and Nazi Political Theory behind Brazil's President in Waiting," *Haaretz*, October 28, 2018; John G. Dunlop, "Aleksandr Dugin's Foundation of Geopolitics," *Demokratizatskiya* 23, no. 1 (2004): 41–58. General Golbery do Couto e Silva published the influential book *Brazil's Geopolitics* in 1966 while he headed the Brazilian dictatorship's national intelligence services.

7. David Aliano, *Mussolini's National Project in Argentina* (Madison, NJ: Farleigh Dickinson Press, 2012); Aristotle Rama Lakshmi, "Narendra Modi Urges the Indian Diaspora to Become an Extension of Foreign Policy," *Guardian*, March 2, 2015; Jenny Hill, "Turkey Election: Expats Play Decisive Role in Erdogan Vote," BBC.com, June 21, 2018.

8. Matar, *Return*, 92; Tim Noonan, "Hoop Dreams of a Stateless Player," *Asia Times*, May 9, 2019.

9. Matar, *Return*, 4; Iván Jakisć and Luis Caro, in Wright and Oñate, *Flight*, 122, 125–30.

10. Steven J. Ross, *Hitler in Los Angeles. How Jews Foiled Nazi Plots against Hollywood and America* (New York: Bloomsbury, 2017).

11. Bawden, *Pinochet Generation*, 149; Sarah Sanders, in Kate Sullivan, "God 'wanted Donald Trump to become President,'" CNN.com, January 31, 2019; Jeff Sharlet, "'He's the Chosen One to Run America': Inside the Cult of Trump, His Rallies Are Church and He Is the Gospel," *Vanity Fair*, June 18, 2020.

12. Mussolini, "Discorso sull' Ascensione"; Benito Mussolini, preface to Riccardo Korherr, *Regresso delle nascite: Morte dei popoli* (Rome: Unione Editoriale d'Italia, 1928), 10, 19.

13. Victoria de Grazia, *How Fascism Ruled Women* (Berkeley: University of California Press, 1992); Duggan, *Fascist Voices*, 145–46; Alessandra Gissi, "Reproduction," in *The Politics of Everyday Life in Fascist Italy. Outside the State?* ed. Josh Arthurs, Michael Ebner, and Kate Ferris (New York: Palgrave Macmillan, 2017), 99–122.

14. Duggan, *Fascist Voices*, 274–82; Raymond Jones, *Adwa: African Victory in an Age of Empire* (Cambridge, MA: Harvard University Press, 2011); Aram Mattioli, *Experimentierfeld der Gewalt: der Abessinienkrieg und seine internationale Bedeutung, 1935–1941* (Zürich: Orell Füssli, 2005).

15. Ben-Ghiat, *Fascist Modernities: Italy, 1922–1945* (Berkeley: University of California Press, 2001), 123–70; Mia Fuller, *Moderns Abroad. Architecture, Cities, and Italian Imperialism* (New York: Routledge, 2006); Lorenzo Benadusi, *The Enemy of the New Man: Homosexuality in Fascist Italy*, trans. Suzanne Dingee and Jennifer Pudney (Madison: University of Wisconsin Press, 2012); Maura Hametz, "Borderlands," in *Everyday Life*, ed. Arthurs, Ebner, Ferris, 151–78.

16. "Come coprire i vuoti," *Vita universitaria*, October 5, 1938; Michele Sarfatti, *The Jews in Mussolini's Italy: From Equality to Persecution* (Madison: University of Wisconsin Press, 2006); Marie-Anne Matard-Bonnard, *L'Italia fascista e la persecuzione degli ebrei* (Bologna: Mulino, 2007); for legal aspects, Michael Livingston, *The Fascists and the Jews of*

Italy: Mussolini's Race Laws, 1938–1945 (Cambridge, UK: Cambridge University Press, 2014).

17. Angela Saini, *Superior: The Return of Race Science* (Boston: Beacon, 2019), gives an overview. Hans Weinert, *Biologische Grundlagen für Rassenkunde und Rassenhygiene* (Stuttgart: Ferdinand Enke Verlag, 1934), in Roberto Esposito, *Bios: Biopolitcs and Philosophy*, trans. Timothy Campbell (Minneapolis: University of Minnesota Press, 2008), 113, 110–43; Michael Burleigh and Wolfgang Wipperman, *The Racial State. Germany, 1933–1945* (Cambridge, UK: Cambridge University Press, 1991); Henry Friedlander, "The Exclusion and Murder of the Disabled," in *Social Outsiders in Nazi Germany*, ed. Robert Gellately and Nathan Stoltzfus (Princeton, NJ: Princeton University Press, 2018), 145–64.

18. Clarence Lusane, *Hitler's Black Victims. The Historical Experiences of Afro-Germans, European Blacks, Africans, and African-Americans in the Nazi Era* (New York: Routledge, 2002), 137–41; Hitler, *Mein Kampf*, 644.

19. The 1935 Nuremberg Laws encompassed the Law for the Protection of German Blood and German Honor and the Reich Citizenship Law and their supplementary decrees. Sheila Fitzpatrick and Alf Lüdtke, "Energizing the Everyday. On the Making of Social Bonds in Nazism and Stalinism," in *Beyond Totalitarianism: Stalinism and Nazism Compared*, ed. Michael Geyer and Sheila Fitzpatrick (New York: Cambridge University Press, 2009), 276–79; Arnold Schoenberg, *Letters*, ed. Erwin Stein (Berkeley: University of California Press, 1987), 192; David Cesarani, *Final Solution. The Fate of the Jews, 1933–1949* (New York: St. Martins Press, 2016), 158–9, 216–21. Ten thousand Jews returned to Germany by 1935, most because they could not support themselves abroad or had expired visas: Jane Caplan, "Introduction" to Herz, *Moringen*, 8–9.

20. Mosse, "Introduction," xxxviii, and Ilse McKee, "Skepticism and Participation," 278, in George Mosse, *Nazi Culture. A Documentary History* (New York: Schocken Books, 1966); Friedrich C. Tubach, *German Voices: Memories of Life during Hitler's Third Reich* (Berkeley: University of California Press, 2011), 25–26; Claudia Koonz, *The Nazi Conscience* (Cambridge, MA: Belknap Press, 2003); Melita Maschmann, *Account Rendered. A Dossier on my Former Self*, trans. Geoffrey Strachan (New York: Abelard-Shuman, 1965), 36.

21. Letter from Dr. Erich Oberdorfer, Vienna, March 16, 1938, in *Letters to Hitler*, ed. Eberle, 160.

22. Augusto Pinochet, *El Dia Decisivo: 11 de Septiembre de 1973* (Santiago: Andres Bello, 1979), 156; Augusto Pinochet, *Camino Recorrido. Memorias de un Soldado* (Santiago: Instituto Geográfico Militar de Chile, 1991), 2: 29–30; Pinochet, speech of March 11, 1974, in Stern, *Battling*, 68; Giselle Munizaga and Carlos Ochsenius, *El discurso publico de Pinochet* (Buenos Aires: Consejo Latinoamericano de Ciencias Sociales, 1983), 40–42; Jack B. Kubisch, November 16, 1973 memo to Kissinger, in Bawden, *Pinochet Generation*, 143.

23. Foreign Affairs Minister Admiral Ismael Huerta, address to the United Nations General Assembly, October 9, 1973, in Laurence Birns, ed., *The End of Chilean Democracy: An IDOC Dossier on the Coup and Its Aftermath* (New York: Seabury Press, 1974), 46.

24. Gason Acuna, director of government information, in Stern, *Battling*, 61; Luis Hernán Errázuriz and Gonzalo Leiva Quijada, *El Golpe Estético. Dictadura Militar en Chile 1973–1989* (Santiago: Ocholibros, 2012), 13–43.

25. Mario Rinvolucri, "Faculty Purge at Austral University," in Birns, ed., *Chilean Democracy*, 122–25; Marc Cooper, *Pinochet and Me. A Chilean Anti-Memoir* (New York. Verso, 2000), 65; Jonathan Kandell, "A Wide Anti-Marxist Purge in Chile Is Shaking the

Universities," *New York Times*, November 14, 1973, reported that 6,000 out of 16,000 students and 100 professors had already been removed at the University of Concepción alone.

26. Muñoz, *Dictator's Shadow*, 52–54; Huneeus, *Pinochet*, 57–59; Errázuriz and Leiva Quijada, *Golpe Estético*; Alejandra Matus, *Doña Lucia. La biografía no autorizada* (Santiago: Ediciones B, 2013), 212–18; Stern, *Battling*, 68–73.

27. Galadriel Ravelli, "Far-Right Militants and Sanctuaries in the Cold War: The Transnational Trajectories of Italian Neo-Fascism." PhD dissertation, University of Bath, 2017, 178–94.

28. Cooper, *Pinochet*, 106; Clara Han, *Life in Debt. Times of Care and Violence in Neoliberal Chile* (Berkeley: University of California Press, 2012), 6; ADST, Charlotte Roe, political officer, US embassy, Santiago, 1985–1989, and Harry Barnes, US ambassador to Chile, 1985–1989, interviewed by Charles Stuart Kennedy, January 2005: https://adst.org/2014/11/chiles-1988–plebiscite-and-the-end-of-pinochets-dictatorship/.

29. Gaddafi, radio address, July 21, 1970, in Angelo Del Boca, *Gli italiani in Libia. Dal fascismo a Gheddafi* (Milan: Mondadori, 1994), 270–271.

30. Gaddafi, *The Green Book*, in Muammar Gaddafi, *My Vision. Conversations and Frank Exchanges of Views with Edmond Jouve*, trans. Angela Parfitt (London: John Blake, 2005), 150; Vandewalle, *Libya*, 87; van Genugten, *Libya*, 85; Kevin Dunn, *Imagining the Congo. The International Relations of Identity* (New York: Palgrave Macmillan, 2003), 105–38.

31. ADST, Harold G. Josif, deputy chief of mission, US embassy in Tripoli, interviewed by Charles Stuart Kennedy, October 1999, at: https://adst.org/2016/09/sudden-rise-muammar-qaddafi-hostile-libya/; June 11, 1970, cable from American embassy in Tripoli, in St. John, *Libya*, 142.

32. Chiara Loschi, "La comunità degli italiani nella Libia indipendente," in *Rovesci della fortuna. La minoranza italiana in Libia dalla seconda guerra mondiale all'espulsione (1940–1970)*, ed. Francesca Di Giulio and Federico Cresti (Ariccia: Aracne, 2016), 101–18; Plinio Maggi, in Antonino Cimino, "Italiani espulsi dalla Libia," tesi di laurea, Università di Palermo, 2010, 36; Gaddafi, in Pargeter, *Libya*, 71.

33. New York Times Staff, "Property of Italians and Jews Confiscated by Libya Regime," *New York Times*, July 22, 1970; ADST, George Lane interview; van Genugten, *Libya*, 90–104; Benjamin Smith, "Oil Wealth and Regime Survival in the Developing World, 1960–1999," *American Journal of Political Science*, 48, no. 2 (2004): 232–46.

34. Lisa Anderson, *The State and Social Transformation in Tunisia and Libya, 1830–1980* (Princeton, NJ: Princeton University Press, 1986), 266; Gaddafi, *Green Book*, in *My Vision*, 153–58; El-Kikhia, *Libya's Qaddafi*.

35. Gaddafi, 2006, in Selwyn Duke, "Islam Is Taking Over Europe—'Without Swords, without Guns, without Conquest,'" *Observer*, January 25, 2017.

36. Katalin Novák, minister for family and youth affairs, in Valerie Hopkins, "Hungary Chides the Childless as 'Not Normal' as Birth Rate Tops Agenda," *Financial Times*, September 5, 2019.

37. Marcello Dell'Utri, June 2002 statement of the Forza Italia program, in Gabriele Turi, "I 'think tank' di destra," in Ginsborg and Asquer, *Berlusconismo*, 31; Silvio Berlusconi, *Una storia italiana* (Milan: Mondadori, 2001), frontispiece, 42–59, 78.

38. Berlusconi, January 15, 2000, in Giovanni Orsina, *Berlusconism and Italy: A Historical Interpretation* (New York: Palgrave Macmillan, 2014), 69; Gustavo Zagrebelsky, "La neolingua dell'età berlusconiana," in Ginzburg and Asquer, *Berlusconismo*, 225–28.

39. Orsina, *Berlusconism*, 96–97; David Wiley, "Berlusconi Says 'I Am Like Jesus,'" BBC

News, February 13, 2006; Renato Schifani, in Marco Travaglio, "Il caso Schifani comincia ora," *Micromega* 4 (2008).

40. Berlusconi, interview with Johnson and Farrell.

41. Berlusconi, on "Porta a porta," August 2002, in Stella and Rizzo, *Così parlò*, 125; Berlusconi, April 10, 2008, in Malcolm Moore, "Berlusconi Says Immigrants Are 'an Army of Evil,'" *Telegraph*, April 16, 2008; migration figures and ISTAT results in Barbara Faedda, "'We Are Not Racists, But We Do Not Want Immigrants.' How Italy Uses Immigration Law to Marginalize Immigrants and Create a [New] National Identity," in *Migrant Marginality: A Transnational Perspective*, ed. Philip Kretsedemas, Jorge Capetillo-Ponce, and Glenn Jacobs (New York: Routledge, 2014): 119, 121. Detention increased to a six-month maximum in 2009.

42. Carlo Giovanardi, in Milena Marchesi, "Reproducing Italians: Contested Biopolitics in the Age of 'Replacement Anxiety,'" *Anthropology & Medicine* 19, no. 2 (2012): 175; Hom, *Empire's Mobius Strip*, 118–38.

43. In 2000–2006, 10 percent of illegal migrant entries were by sea, 20 percent were by land, and 70 percent were "overstays" by those in Italy: David Forgacs, "Coasts, Blockades, and the Free Movement of People," in *Italian Mobilities*, ed. Ruth Ben-Ghiat and Stephanie Malia Hom (New York: Routledge, 2015), 181; van Genugten, *Libya*, 143–44; Emidio Diodato and Federico Niglia, *Berlusconi "The Diplomat." Populism and Foreign Policy in Italy* (New York: Palgrave MacMillan, 2019), 124.

44. Putin, in transcript of the September 19, 2013, meeting of the Valdai International Discussion Club: http://en.kremlin.ru/events/president/news/19243; Putin, "Russia at the Turn of the Millenium," in Hill and Gaddy, *Putin*, 61.

45. Putin's December 2013 address to the nation, in Hill and Gaddy, *Putin*, 255–56.

46. Josh Hersh, "How Putin Is Using the Orthodox Church to Build His Power," *Vice*, March 26, 2018; Hill and Gaddy, *Putin*, 66–67; "Russia: New Wave of Anti-LGBY Persecution," *Human Rights Watch*, February 15, 2019; Jeff Sharlet, "Inside the Iron Closet: What It's Like to Be Gay in Putin's Russia," *GQ*, February 4, 2014; Masha Gessen, "How LGBT Couples in Russia Decide Whether to Leave the Country," *New Yorker*, June 11, 2019.

47. Heleniak, "Population Trends," 153–59, and Louise Shelley, "Crime and Corruption," 195, both in *Putin's Russia*, ed. Wegren; Dawisha, *Putin's Kleptocracy*, 313–15.

48. Linda Robinson et al., *Modern Political Warfare. Current Practices and Possible Responses*, RAND Corporation Report, 2018, xvi–xvii, 41–124; BBC Staff, "'Russian Trolls' Promoted California Independence," BBC.com, November 4, 2017; Mansur Mirovalev, "What's Behind Russian Support for World's Separatist Movements," NBCNews.com, July 23, 2016; Alex Finley, John Sipher, and Asha Rangappa, "Why the 2020 Election Will Be a Mess: It's Just Too Easy for Putin," *Just Security*, February 19, 2020.

49. Margherita Sarfatti, *Dux* (Milan: Mondadori, 1926), 303; Brian Murphy and Paul A. Specht, "'Send Her Back,' Crowd Chants at Rep. Ilhan Omar at Trump Campaign Rally in NC," *News & Observer*, July 17, 2019; Susan Richard, in Kristen Inbody and Phil Drake, "Trump Rally Crowd Jazzed before Campaign Event in Billings, Montana," *Great Falls Tribune*, September 6, 2018.

50. State Sen. Sylvia Allen (R-AZ) warned in July 2019 of the "browning of America." Video: https://twitter.com/nowthisnews/status/1154898693671157760; Louis Nelson, "Rep. King: 'I Meant Exactly What I Said' with 'Babies' Tweet," *Politico*, March 13, 2017.

51. William H. Frey, The US Will Become 'Minority White' in 2045, Census Projects, Brookings, March 14, 2018: https://www.brookings.edu/blog/the-avenue/2018/03/14/

the-us-will-become-minority-white-in-2045–census-projects/; Trump, in Peter Baker, "Trump Declares a National Emergency and Provokes a Constitutional Clash," *New York Times*, February 15, 2019; Damien Paletta, Mike DeBonis, and John Wagner, "Trump Declares National Emergency on Southern Border in Bid to Build Wall," *Washington Post*, February 15, 2019.

52. Dan Diamond, "The Religious Activists on the Rise inside Trump's Health Department," *Politico*, January 22, 2018; Andrew Whitehead and Samuel Perry, *Taking America Back for God: Christian Nationalism in the United States* (New York: Oxford University Press, 2020). Trump administration members on the board of directors of Opus Dei's Catholic Information Center include Attorney General William Barr and White House lawyer Pat Cipollone. Larry Kudlow was converted to Catholicism from Judaism by former CIC head Father John McClosky: Joan Walsh, "William Barr Is Neck-Deep in Extremist Catholic Institutions," *Nation*, October 15, 2019; Alison Kodjak, "New Rule Protects Health Care Workers Who Refuse Care for Religious Reasons," NPR, May 2, 2019; Stephen Miller, interviewed by Chris Wallace, Fox News, July 20, 2019; Andy Kroll, "Internal Emails Reveal How Stephen Miller Leads an Extremist Network to Push Trump's Anti-Immigrant Agenda," *Rolling Stone*, December 11, 2019.

53. William Barr, quotes from remarks at the Grand Lodge Fraternal Order of Police's 64th National Biennal Conference," New Orleans, LA, August 12, 2019, https://www.justice.gov/opa/speech/attorney-general-william-p-barr-delivers-remarks-grand-lodge-fraternal-order-polices-64th and November 15, 2019, speech to the Federalist Society, https://www.c-span.org/video/?466450–1/attorney-general-barr-federalist-society-convention; Charlie Savage, "Barr Bridges the Reagan Revolution and Trump on Executive Power," *New York Times*, November 18, 2019; Tamsin Shaw, "William Barr: The Carl Schmitt of Our Time," *New York Review of Books*, January 15, 2020; Betsy Woodruff Swan, "DOJ Seeks New Emergency Powers amid Coronavirus Pandemic," *Politico*, March 21, 2020; Quinta Jurecic and Benjamin Wittes, "Three Plausible—and Troubling—Reasons Why Barr Tried to Force Berman Out," *Atlantic*, June 22, 2020.

54. Nick Danforth, "Turkey's New Maps Are Reclaiming the Ottoman Empire," *Foreign Policy*, October 23, 2016; Gonul Tol, "Turkey's Bid for Religious Leadership," *Foreign Affairs*, January 10, 2019; Tahar Ben Jelloun, "Il piano neo-ottomano di Erdogan: imporsi in Libia per tornare in Maghreb," *La Stampa*, February 6, 2020; Natasha Turak, "Turkey's Erdogan Threatens to Release Millions of Refugees into Europe over Criticism of Syria Offensive," CNBC, October 10, 2019.

55. Acemoglu and Ucer, "Ups and Downs"; "Erdoganomics," *Economist*, February 4, 2016; Zeynep Tufekci, *Twitter and Teargas: The Power and Fragility of Networked Protest* (New Haven: Yale University Press, 2017).

56. M. Hakan Yavuz and Bayram Balci, eds., *Turkey's July 15th Coup: What Happened and Why* (Salt Lake City: University of Utah Press, 2018).

57. Maximilian Popp, "Revisiting Turkey's Failed Coup Attempt," *Der Spiegel*, July 6, 2017; Christiaan Triebert, "'We've Shot Four People. Everything's Fine. The Turkish Coup through the Eyes of its Plotters," *Bellingcat*, July 24, 2016.

58. Carlotta Gall, "Spurning Erdogan's Vision, Turks Leave in Droves, Draining Money and Talent," *New York Times*, January 2, 2019; Mehul Srivastava, "Turkish Economy Turns in Worst Performance since 2009," *Financial Times*, December 12, 2016; Simon Tisdall, "Erdogan Is on a Lonely Path to Ruin. Will He Take Turkey Down with Him?" *Guardian*, July 20, 2019. Figures on assets seized through March 2019: https://turkeypurge.com; Stockholm Center for Freedom, "Turkey Has Detained More than 282,000 and Arrested 94,000 since the 2016 Failed Coup," July 15, 2020: https://

stockholmcf.org/turkey-has-detained-more-than-282000-arrested-94000-since-2016
-failed-coup/.

59. Onur Ant, "Erdogan's Approval Rating Soars after Coup Attempt," *Bloomberg*, August 11, 2016; Ed Finn, "The Power of Social Media. Erdogan's Smart Use of a Smartphone," CNN.com, July 18, 2016.

60. Hürriyet Daily News Staff, "Erdogan Voice Message Surprises Turkey Mobile Users on Failed Coup Anniversary," *Hürriyet Daily News*, July 16, 2017; Tom Stevenson, "Bleak Burial: Turkey's Traitors' Cemetery," DW.com, August 1, 2016; Ishaan Tharoor, "Turkey's Erdogan Turned a Failed Coup into His Path to Greater Power," *Washington Post*, July 17, 2017.

61. Erdoğan, January 2019 speech, in Lorenzo Vidino, "Erdogan's Long Arm in Europe," *Foreign Policy*, May 7, 2019; Bekir Agirdir, in Gall, "Spurning Erdogan's Vision"; Erdoğan, speech of July 15, 2019, in Tisdall, "Erdogan Is on a Lonely Path."

FIVE: PROPAGANDA

1. Oriana Fallaci, *Interview with History*, trans. John Shepley (Boston: Houghton Mifflin, 1976), 40–41; Henry Kissinger, *White House Years* (Boston: Little, Brown, 1979), 1409.

2. Gaddafi interview in Fallaci, "Italians Are Our Brothers," *New York Times Magazine*, December 16, 1979.

3. Joseph Goebbels, in David Welch, *The Third Reich: Politics and Propaganda* (New York: Routledge, 1993), 22.

4. The classic study is Marc Bloch, *Royal Touch: Sacred Monarchy and Scrofula in England and France* (Toronto: McGill-Queen's University Press, 1973); Traverso, *Fire*, 94–98; Giorgio Bertellini, *Divo/Duce. Promoting Film Stardom and Political Leadership in 1920s America* (Berkeley: University of California Press, 2019); Stephen Gundle, Christopher Duggan, and Giuliana Pieri, eds., *The Cult of the Duce* (Manchester: Manchester University Press, 2015), 72–92; Dikötter, *Dictator*.

5. Simonetta Falasca-Zamponi, *Fascist Spectacle* (Berkeley: University of California Press, 1997), Nicholas O'Shaughnessy, *Selling Hitler. Propaganda and the Nazi Brand* (London: Hurst, 2016).

6. Jacques Ellul, *Propaganda. The Formation of Men's Attitudes* (New York: Vintage Books, 1973), 10.

7. Sohini Mitter, "Inside the New Modi App: Instagram-like Stories, Live Events, Exclusive Content, and More," *YourStory*, October 7, 2019; Varsha Jain, Meetu Chawla, B. E. Ganesh, and Christopher Pich, "Exploring and Consolidating the Brand Personality Elements of the Political Leader," *Spanish Journal of Marketing*, 22, no. 3 (2018): 295–318.

8. Gaetano Polverelli to Mussolini, 1933 letter in Archivio Centrale dello Stato (ACS), Ministro della Cultura Popolare (MCP), b.155, f.10; Ruth Ben-Ghiat, "Fascist Italy and Nazi Germany: The Dynamics of an Uneasy Relationship," in *Art, Culture, and Media under the Third Reich*, ed. Richard Etlin (Chicago: University of Chicago Press, 2002), 257–86; Virginia Higginbotham, *Spanish Film under Franco* (Austin: University of Texas Press, 1988), 7.

9. Nina Tumarkin, *Lenin Lives! The Lenin Cult in Soviet Russia* (Cambridge, MA: Harvard University Press, 1997); Dikötter, *Dictator*; Jan Plamper, *The Stalin Cult. A Study in the Alchemy of Power* (New Haven: Yale University Press, 2012); Ben-Ghiat, *Fascist Modernities*.

10. Pamela Constable and Arturo Valenzuela, *A Nation of Enemies. Chile under Pinochet* (New York: W. W. Norton, 1993), 155.

11. Gaetano Salvemini, "Mussolini's Battle of Wheat," *Political Science Quarterly* 46, no. 1 (1931): 38.

12. Ellen Nakashima, "U.S. Department of Justice Admits Error but Won't Correct Report

Linking Terrorism to Immigration," *Washington Post*, March 1, 2019; Pia Orrenius and Madeline Zavodny, "Do Immigrants Threaten US Public Safety?" *Journal on Migration and Human Security* 7, no. 3 (2019): 52–61.

13. Eliza Apperly, "Why Europe's Far Right Is Targeting Gender Studies," *Atlantic*, June 15, 2019.

14. Federico Fellini, "Notes on Censorship" (1958), on Fascist and Christian Democratic censorship, in *Fellini on Fellini*, trans. Isabel Quigley (New York: Delacorte Press, 1976), 84, 86.

15. Author interview with Guillo; see his graphic history of the regime, *Pinochet Illustrado* (Santiago: Editorial Genus, 2008); Randall Bytwerk, *Bending Spines: The Propagandas of Nazi Germany and the German Democratic Republic* (East Lansing: Michigan State University Press, 2004), 155–69; Ruth Ben-Ghiat, *Italian Fascism's Empire Cinema* (Bloomington: Indiana University Press, 2015), 4; Stephen Burt Wiley, "Transnation: Chilean Television Infrastructure and Policy as National Space, 1969–1996," PhD dissertation, University of Illinois Champagne-Urbana, 1999, 121.

16. Ben-Ghiat, *Empire Cinema*. Communists also used mobile cinemas, as did the French and the British in their colonies.

17. Seldes, *Sawdust Caesar*, 375; Bertellini, *Divo/Duce*.

18. Isituto Luce (IL), Archivio Cinematografico (AC), "Mussolini si cimenta nella trebbiatura del grano," Giornale Luce B0707, July 3, 1935, which documents his June 27 visit to Sabaudia; Bertellini, *Divo/Duce*; Alessandra Antola Swan, "The Iconic Body: Mussolini Unclothed," *Modern Italy* 21, no. 4 (2016): 361–81.

19. Gaetano Salvemini, *Mussolini diplomatico* (Bari: Laterza, 1952), 384; Bertellini, *Divo/Duce*; Migone, *United States*; John Diggins, *Mussolini and Fascism: The View from America* (1972) (Princeton, NJ: Princeton University Press, 2015); Pierluigi Erbaggio, "Writing Mussolini: Il Duce's American Biographies on Paper and on Screen," PhD dissertation, University of Michigan, 2016.

20. David Kertzer, *The Pope and Mussolini: The Secret History of Pius XI and the Rise of Fascism in Europe* (New York: Random House, 2014); Gundle, Duggan, Pieri, eds., *The Cult of the Duce*; Duggan, *Fascist Voices*, 102; Mack Smith, *Mussolini*, 103; letter from Margherita V., May 8, 1936, in *Caro Duce*, 51.

21. *Corriere della sera*, November 3, 1936, in Duggan, *Fascist Voices*, 230.

22. Luigi Albertini, in Mack Smith, *Mussolini*, 58; Guido Bonsaver, *Censorship and Literature in Fascist Italy* (Toronto: University of Toronto Press, 2007), 27–32.

23. Mussolini, "Il giornalismo come missione," speech of October 10, 1928, in *Scritti e discorsi*, vol. VI, 250–51; Seldes, *Sawdust Caesar*, 312; MCP press directive of September 21, 1939, in Giancarlo Ottaviano, ed., *Le veline di Mussolini* (Viterbo: Stampa Alternativa, 2008), 11.

24. Goebbels, in Welch, *Third Reich*, 43–48; Nicholas O'Shaughnessy, *Marketing the Third Reich: Persuasion, Packaging, and Propaganda* (New York: Routledge, 2018), 214.

25. Peter Longerich, *Goebbels: A Biography* (New York: Random House, 2015); Hitler, *Mein Kampf*, 178–86; letters of Werner M, November 10, 1933, M. von Keyden-Plötz, March 1934, Curt Rudolf Kempe, April 4, 1935, in *Letters to Hitler*, ed. Eberle, 81–83, 91–92, 144–45; Kershaw, *"Hitler Cult."*

26. O'Shaughnessy, *Marketing*, 197–201; Welch, *Third Reich*, 38–43; Heidi Tworek, *News from Germany. The Competition to Control Wireless Communications, 1900–1945* (Cambridge, MA: Harvard University Press, 2019).

27. Italo Calvino, "The Duce's Portraits," *New Yorker*, January 6, 2003; Bainville, *Les dictateurs*, 287; Janet Flannery, in Michael Munn, *Hitler and the Nazi Cult of Film and Fame*

(New York: Skyhorse, 2013), 70–73; Traverso, *Fire*, 180–96; Schmölders, *Hitler's Face*; Otto Strasser, cited in F. W. Lambertson, "Hitler, the Orator: A Study in Mob Psychology," *Quarterly Journal of Speech* 28 (1942): 126–27.

28. Tubach, *German Voices*, 53; Lower, *Furies*, 26.

29. Welch, *Third Reich*, 43; Fermi, *Mussolini*, 193; Clara Petacci, *Mussolini Segreto. Diari, 1932–1938*, ed. Mauro Sutturo (Milan: RCS Libri, 2009), entry of October 23, 1937, location 801 (Kindle edition).

30. IL, AC, "Adunata!" October 8, 1935, Giornale Luce B0761; Ruth Ben-Ghiat, "Five Faces of Fascism," in *Visualizing Fascism*, ed. Thomas and Eley, 94–110.

31. O'Shaughnessy, *Marketing*, 200–201; ACS, Ministero dell'interno (MI), Direzione Generale Pubblica Sicurezza (DGPS), Divisione Polizia Politica (1927–1943), b.132, K111, reports from Genoa, June 13, 1937; Milan, January 12, 1938; April 7, 9, 1938; May 8, 31, 1938.

32. Arendt, *Origins*, 474.

33. Theodor Adorno, "Television and the Patterns of Mass Culture," in *Mass Culture. The Popular Arts in America*, ed. Bernard Rosenberg and David Manning White (New York: The Free Press, 1957), 479.

34. Francisco Franco, *Discursos y mensajes del Jefe del Estado 1955–1959* (Madrid: Dirección General de Información Publicacions Españolas, 1960), 122; Manuel Palacio, "Early Spanish Television and the Paradoxes of a Dictator General," *Historical Journal of Film, Radio, and Television* 25, no. 4 (2005): 599–617.

35. Richard Gunther, José Ramón Montero, and José Ignacio Wert, "Media and Politics in Spain: From Dictatorship to Democracy," Working Paper 176, Institut de Ciències Politiques i Socials (1999), 8–9; Luis González Seara, *La España de los años 70* (Madrid: Ed. Moneda y Crédito, 1972), 781; Higginbotham, *Spanish Film*, 7.

36. Rosendorf, *Franco*; Antonio Cazorla Sánchez, *Fear and Progress. Ordinary Lives in Franco's Spain, 1939–1975* (Oxford: Blackwell, 2010), 14–15.

37. Cento Bull and Ravelli, "Pinochet Regime"; Peter Kornbluh, *The Pinochet File: A Declassified Dossier on Atrocity and Accountability* (New York: The New Press, 2003), 232–33; Mayorga, *Il condor nero*; Spooner, *Soldiers*, 97.

38. Muñoz, *Dictator's Shadow*, 53; Stern, *Battling*, 60–62; Munizaga and Ochsenius, *El discurso*, 17–22; Wiley, "Transnation," 23.

39. Gabriel García Márquez tells Littín's story in *Clandestine in Chile. The Adventures of Miguel Littín*, trans. Asa Zatz (New York: Henry Holt, 1986), 16; Ariel Dorfman, *Homeland Security Ate My Speech* (New York: OR Books, 2017), 184–85.

40. Vandewalle, *Libya*, 99–104.

41. Drew O. McDaniel, "Libya," in Douglas A. Boyd, *Broadcasting in the Arab World* (Ames: University of Iowa Press, 1999), 231–36; Abdallah Rached, in Fatima El-Issawi, *Libya Media Transition. Heading to the Unknown*, London School of Economics Polis Report (2013), 27: http://eprints.lse.ac.uk/59906/1/El-Issawi_Libya-media-transition_2013_pub.pdf.

42. Boyd, *Broadcasting*, 130. Televised trials started in Iraq under Abd Al-Karim Qasim, who took power via military coup in 1958 and ruled until 1963.

43. L.S., interview with author. The University of Tripoli was renamed Al-Fateh University.

44. Gaddafi, *Green Book*, in Gaddafi, *My Vision*, 131; Pargeter, *Libya*, 100–102. Peter Bouckaert, Human Rights Watch researcher, worked with the late *Guardian* reporter Tim Heatherington to bring security services footage of this and other executions to safety after Gaddafi's fall: Ian Black, "Gaddafi's Terror Exposed in Lost Picture Archive," *Guardian*, July 18, 2011.

45. L.S., interview with author.

46. "'You Have a Terribly Homosexual Face': Brazil's President Launches Attack on Journalist," *Independent*, December 21, 2019; Colby Itkowitz, "Trump Attacks Rep. Cummings's District, Calling It a 'Disgusting, Rat and Rodent-Infested Mess,'" *Washington Post*, July 27, 2019; Matthew Daly, "House Dems Back Subpoenas for Ivanka, Jared Private Emails," AP News, July 25, 2019; Joel Simon, "Muzzling the Media: How the New Autocrats Threaten Press Freedom," *World Policy Journal* 23, no. 2 (2006): 51–61.

47. Gábor Polyak, "How Hungary Shrunk the Media," *Mérték Media Monitor*, February 14, 2019, at European Centre for Press and Media Freedom: https://www.ecpmf.eu/news/threats/how-hungary-shrunk-the-media.

48. Ronald J. Deibert, "The Road to Unfreedom: Three Painful Truths about Social Media," *Journal of Democracy* 30, no. 1 (2019): 25–39; Adrian Shahbaz, *Freedom on the Net 2018: The Rise of Digital Authoritarianism.* Freedom House report, https://freedomhouse.org/report/freedom-net/2018/rise-digital-authoritarianism; Jason Schwartz, "Trump's 'Fake News' Mantra a Hit with Despots," *Politico*, December 8, 2017; Elana Beiser, *Hundreds of Journalists Jailed Globally Becomes the New Normal*, Committee to Protect Journalists, December 13, 2018: https://cpj.org/reports/2018/12/journalists-jailed-imprisoned-turkey-china-egypt-saudi-arabia/.

49. Yakov Smirnoff, in Randall Wood and Carmine DeLuca, *Dictator's Handbook: A Practical Manual for the Aspiring Tyrant* (Newfoundland: Gull Pond Books, 2012), 167; Masha Lipman, "The Media," in *Putin's Russia*, ed. Wegren, 127–150; Ruben Enikolopov, Maria Petrova, and Ekaterina Zhuravskaya, "Media and Political Persuasion: Evidence from Russia," *American Economic Review* 101, no. 7 (2011): 3253–85.

50. Peter Pomerantsev and Michael Weiss, *The Menace of Unreality: How the Kremlin Weaponizes Information, Culture and Money*, The Interpreter Project, Institute of Modern Russia, 2014: https://imrussia.org/media/pdf/Research/Michael_Weiss_and_Peter_Pomerantsev__The_Menace_of_Unreality.pdf; Robinson et al., *Modern Political Warfare*, 66–68: https://www.rand.org/pubs/research_reports/RR1772.html; Lily Hay Newman, "Russia Takes a Big Step Towards Internet Isolation," *Wired*, January 5, 2020. As of March 2020, RT had just over 3 million Twitter followers (combined world and UK channels) to CNN's 55 million (combined US and international) and BBC's 37 million (combined world and UK channels). Economist Staff, "Russians Are Shunning State-Controlled TV for YouTube," *Economist*, March 7, 2019.

51. Robinson et al., *Political Warfare*, 56–71; David E. Sanger, "Russian Hackers Appear to Shift Focus to the U.S. Power Grid," *New York Times*, July 27, 2018; Molly K. McKew, "Putin's Real Long Game," *Politico*, January 1, 2017; Alina Polyakova and Chris Meserole, *Exporting Digital Authoritarianism: The Russian and Chinese Models*, Brookings Institute Foreign Policy Brief, August 2019: https://www.brookings.edu/research/exporting-digital-authoritarianism/.

52. Yuri Levada, in Helena Goscilo, "The Ultimate Celebrity. VVP as VIP Objet d'Art," in *Celebrity and Glamour in Contemporary Russia. Shocking Chic*, ed. Helena Goscilo and Vlad Strukov (New York: Routledge, 2011), 41; Peter Pomerantsev, *Nothing Is True and Everything Is Possible: The Surreal Heart of the New Russia* (New York: Public Affairs, 2015).

53. Ingo Beckendorf, "Russia: Putin Satire as 'Extremist Material' on Prohibition List," European Centre for Press and Media Freedom Newsletter, November 5, 2017; Sergey Shvakin, in Marc Bennetts, "Russia Passes Law to Jail People for 15 Days for 'Disrespecting' Government," *Guardian*, March 6, 2019; BBC Staff, "Russia Laws Ban 'Disrespect' of Government and 'Fake News,'" BBC.com, March 7, 2019.

54. Ragnedda, "Censorship," 15; Ruben Durante, Paolo Pinotti, and Andrea Tesei, "The Political Legacy of Entertainment TV," *American Economic Review* 109, no. 7 (2019): 2497–2530.

55. Paolo Guzzanti, *Mignottocrazia. La sera andavamo a ministre* (Rome: Aliberti, 2010); Jeffrey Edward Green, *Eyes of the People. Democracy in an Age of Spectatorship* (New York: Oxford University Press, 2010); Thomas Meyer, *Media Democracy. How the Media Colonize Politics* (Cambridge, UK: Polity Press, 2002), 65–70.

56. Aram Mattioli, *"Viva Mussolini!" Die Aufwertung des Faschismus im Italien Berlusconis* (Paderborn: Ferdinand Schöningh, 2010); Sara Mondini and Carlo Semenza, "Research Report: How Berlusconi Keeps His Face," *Cortex* 42, no. 3 (2006): 332–35; Berlusconi, September 9, 2009, in Stella and Rizzo, *Così parlò*, 67; Sarfatti, *Dux*, 297, for the original "Fortuna c'e Mussolini"; "Berlusconi via satellite su maxi-schermo a Rimini," *La Repubblica*, March 13, 1994; Pasquino, "Five Faces."

57. Ragnedda, "Censorship," 18; Stille, *Sack of Rome*, 294–312; Monica Boria, "Silenced Humor on RAI TV: Daniele Luzzatti, Sabrina Guzzanti & Co," in *Resisting the Tide. Cultures of Opposition under Berlusconi (2001–2006)*, ed. Daniele Albertazzi, Nina Rothenberg, Charlotte Ross, and Clodagh Brook (New York: Continuum, 2011), 97–109.

58. Justin Wise, "Trump: What You're Seeing and Reading in the News 'Is Not What's Happening,'" *Hill*, July 24, 2018.

59. McKay Coppins, "The Billion-Dollar Disinformation Campaign to Reelect the President," *Atlantic*, February 10, 2020; Glenn Kessler, Salvador Rizzo, and Meg Kelly, "President Trump Made 16,241 False or Misleading Claims in His First Three Years," *Washington Post*, January 20, 2020; Michiko Kakutani, *The Death of Truth. Notes on Falsehood in the Age of Trump* (New York: Penguin, 2018); Yochai Benkler, Robert Faris, and Hal Roberts. *Network Propaganda: Manipulation, Disinformation, and Radicalization in American Politics* (New York: Oxford University Press, 2018).

60. Quote in Andrew Marantz, "The Man Behind Trump's Facebook Juggernaut," *New Yorker*, March 2, 2020.

61. Oliver Darcy, "Comey Writes in Memo He Laughed When Trump Floated the Idea of Jailing Journalists," CNN.com, April 20, 2018; Josh Dawsey, "Trump Asked China's Xi to Help Him Win Reelection, According to Bolton Book," *Washington Post*, June 17, 2020, quoting John Bolton's *The Room Where It Happened* (New York: Simon and Schuster, 2020); Guy Snodgrass, former chief speechwriter of Defense Secretary James Mattis, regarding a 2019 meeting with Trump at the Pentagon, tweet from June 17, 2020: https://twitter.com/GuySnodgrass/status/1273359990905024513; Mallory Shelbourne, "Trump: 'They're Not Going to Take Away My Social Media,'" *Hill*, July 11, 2017; Lauren Egan, "The Fake News Is Creating Violence," NBCNews.com, November 2, 2018; Jim Acosta, *Enemy of the People: A Dangerous Time to Tell the Truth in America* (New York: Harper Collins, 2019).

62. Tali Arbel, "Trump Bump? NYT Adds Subscribers, Grows Digital Revenue," AP, February 6, 2019; "The Washington Post Announces Plans to Expand Its Investigative Journalism," *Washington Post*, June 20, 2019; "The New York Times Adds to Investigative Muscle with Three New Hires," *New York Times*, March 16, 2017; Katie Rogers, "White House Hosts Conservative Internet Activists at a 'Social Media Summit,'" *New York Times*, July 11, 2019; Alex Kaplan, "Trump Keeps Amplifying Far-Right Racist Katie Hopkins, Who Called for a 'Final Solution' for Muslims," *Media Matters*, August 26, 2019; Katharine Schwab, "Trump Tweets 2020 Campaign Logo Linked to Alt-Right and White Supremacist Groups," *Fast Company*, August 29, 2019; David Niewert, *Alt-*

America: The Rise of the Radical Right in the Age of Trump (New York: Verso, 2017). The now-deleted tweet is reproduced in Anthony Smith, "Donald Trump's Star of David Hillary Clinton Meme Was Created by White Supremacists," *Mic*, July 3, 2016.

63. Michael D. Shear, Maggie Haberman, Nicholas Confessore, Karen Yourish, Larry Buchanan, and Keith Collins, "How Trump Reshaped the Presidency in Over 11,000 Tweets," *New York Times*, November 2, 2019; Michael Wilner, "'We All Found Out by Tweet': Trump's Golan Heights Surprise," McClatchy, March 21, 2019.

64. Oliver Darcy, "'I Want to Quit': Fox News Employees Say Their Network's Russia Coverage Was 'an Embarrassment,'" CNN.com, October 31, 2017; Matthew Gertz, "I've Studied Trump's Feedback Loop for Months. It's Crazier Than You Think," *Politico*, January 5, 2018; Sean Illing, "How Fox News Evolved into a Propaganda Operation," *Vox*, March 22, 2019; Robert Costa, Sarah Ellison, and Jose Dawsey, "Hannity's Rising Role in Trump's World: 'He Basically Has a Desk in the Place,'" *Washington Post*, April 17, 2018.

SIX: VIRILITY

1. Michela C., letter of December 14, 1925, in *Caro Duce*, 81.

2. Fermi, *Mussolini*, 66; Franzinelli, *Il Duce*; Roberto Olla, *Il Duce and His Women: Mussolini's Rise to Power* (Richmond: Alma Books, 2011); Duggan, *Fascist Voices*, 216–37; Richard Bosworth, *Claretta: Mussolini's Last Lover* (New Haven: Yale University Press, 2017).

3. Duterte, in Chen, "Populist Demagogue"; Berlusconi, in Franco Vanni, "In discoteca col Cavaliere fino all'alba," *La Repubblica*, October 6, 2008; Sarfatti, *Dux*, 312.

4. Federico Boni, *Il Superleader. Fenomenologia mediatica di Silvio Berlusconi* (Rome: Meltemi, 2008), 11; Ben Dreyfuss, "Stormy Daniels Confirmed She Spanked Trump with a Magazine," *Mother Jones*, March 25, 2018.

5. Claudine Haroche, "Anthropology of Virility: The Fear of Powerlessness," in *A History of Virility*, ed. Alain Corbin, Jean-Jacques Courtine, and Georges Vigarello (New York: Columbia University Press, 2016), 403–15; Beinart, "New Authoritarians"; Berlusconi, in Angelo Bocconeti, "Stupri, gaffe del premier," *Secolo XIX*, January 26, 2009; Alfred Rosenberg, 1930, in Mosse, *Nazi Culture*, 40.

6. Valerie Sperling, *Sex, Politics, and Putin. Political Legitimacy in Russia* (New York: Oxford University Press, 2014); Marc Bennetts, "Putin Poses with Bikers as Thousands Take to Streets," *The Times*, August 12, 2019; Gessen, *Man without a Face*, 43–70; Taylor, *Code of Putinism*, 28–29; Galeotti, "Fear Gives Putin More Power Than He Deserves."

7. Hitler, in Goeschels, *Mussolini and Hitler*, 42; Ruth Ben-Ghiat, "Trump's Twinship with Orbán Shows 'Illiberal Democracy' Has a Home in the US," *Guardian*, May 16, 2019.

8. James Anthony Mangan, ed., *Shaping the Superman. The Fascist Body as Political Icon* (London: Frank Cass, 1999); Calvino, "Duce's Portraits"; Duggan, "The Internalization of the Cult of the Duce: The Evidence of Diaries and Letters," in *Cult of the Duce*, ed. Gundle, Duggan, Pieri, 129–43.

9. Mafiki Yav Marie, in Chris McGreal, "Women Seek Abolition of 'Family Code' as Most Hated Legacy of Regime," *Irish Times*, April 15, 1997.

10. Kamau Mutunga, "'My View, Sir, Is That Marriage Does Not Exist in Nature,'" *Daily Nation*, December 5, 2012; Jay Nordlinger, *Children of Monsters: An Inquiry into the Sons and Daughters of Dictators* (New York: Encounter Books, 2017), 200; Wen, "Eight Women."

11. Former Pinochet minister, in Matus, *Doña Lucia*, 223; Claudia Farfán and Fernando Vega, *La familia. Historia privada de los Pinochet* (Santiago: Random House Mondadori, 2009); Juan Cristóbal Peña, "Manuel Contreras, 'El Mamo' Por un Camino de Som-

bras," in *Los Malos*, ed. Leila Guerriero (Santiago: Ediciones Diego Portales, 2015), 21–23.

12. Lyudmila Putina, in Vladimir Putin, *First Person: An Astonishingly Frank Self-Portrait by Russia's President Vladimir Putin*, with Nataliya Gevorkyan, Natalya Timakova, Andrei Kolesnikov, trans. Catherine A. Fitzpatrick (New York: Public Affairs, 2000), 149–50; Etakerina Sokirianskaia, "Vladimir Putin Has One Reliable Set of Allies," *Guardian*, March 22, 2017; Janet Elise Johnson and Alexandra Novitskaya, "Gender and Politics," in *Putin's Russia*, ed. Wegren, 215–32; Misha Friedman, "Babushkas for Putin," *New York Times*, March 15, 2018.

13. Angela Merkel, in George Packer, "The Quiet German," *New Yorker*, November 24, 2014; Dan Kedmey, "Berlusconi Stunned into Silence over Alleged Merkel Insult," *TIME*, May 21, 2014.

14. Alessandro Amadori, *Madre Silvio. Perché la psicologia profonda di Berlusconi è più femminile che maschile* (Milano: Mind Edizioni, 2011); Bolsonaro's hospital video: https://www.youtube.com/watch?v=OkENgrM0VEM; Mariana Simões, "Brazil's Polarizing New President, Jair Bolsonaro, in His Own Words," *New York Times*, October 28, 2018; Ed Pilkington, "Feel the Love, Feel the Hate—My Week in the Cauldron of Trump's Wild Rallies," *Guardian*, November 1, 2018; Christian Carraway of Greenville, NC, in Peter Nicholas, "It Makes Us Want to Support Him More," *Atlantic*, July 18, 2019; BBC Staff, "Trump on Kim Jong-un: 'We Fell in Love,'" BBC.com, September 30, 2018.

15. Indro Montanelli, "Mussolini e noi" (1936), quoted in Oreste del Buono, ed., *Eia, Eia, alalà: La stampa italiana sotto il fascismo* (Milan: Feltrinelli, 1971), 310–11.

16. Emil Ludwig, *Talks with Mussolini*, trans. Eden and Cedar Paul (Boston: Little, Brown, 1933), 193; Fermi, *Mussolini*, 66.

17. Fermi, *Mussolini*, 124–25; Franzinelli, *Il Duce*, 11–66, 81–104; Olla, *Duce*, 123–68.

18. Franzinelli, *Il Duce*, 122; Olla, *Duce*, 256–59.

19. Fermi, *Mussolini*, 66; Duggan, *Fascist Voices*, 216–19; Cederna, preface to *Caro Duce*, 9; Olla, *Duce*, 353–86; Franzinelli, *Il Duce*, 204–19; Bosworth, *Claretta*; Petacci, *Mussolini segreto*.

20. Bosworth, *Claretta*; Petacci, *Mussolini segreto*; Franzinelli, *Il Duce*, 4, 120; Romano Mussolini, *Il Duce Mio Padre* (Milan: Rizzoli, 2004), 41.

21. Papini, *Maschilità*, *Quaderni della Voce*, series III, no. 25 (1915); Filippo Tommaso Marinetti, "Manifeste du Futurisme," *Le Figaro*, February 20, 1909; Stéphane Audoin-Rouzeau, "The Great War and the History of Virility," in *Virility*, ed. Corbin, Courtine, Vigorello, 391–98. For similar fears among German veterans, Klaus Theweleit, *Male Fantasies*, Vol. 1: *Women, Floods, Bodies, Histories* (Minneapolis: University of Minnesota Press, 1987).

22. Giorgio Amendola, *Un'isola* (Milan: Rizzoli, 1980), 30; Johann Chapoutot, "Fascist Virility," in *Virility*, ed. Corbin, Courtine, Vigarello, 491–514.

23. Fermi, *Mussolini*, 281; Ben-Ghiat, *Empire Cinema*, 10–13, 124–46; Lorenzo Benadusi, "Masculinity," in *Everyday Life*, ed. Arthurs, Ebner, Ferris, 51–76; Ara Merjian, "Fascist Revolution, Futurist Spin: Renato Bertelli's Continuous Profile of Mussolini and the Face of Fascist Time," *Oxford Art Journal* 42, no. 3 (2019): 307–33.

24. Hitler, in Garry O'Connor, *The Butcher of Poland. Hitler's Lawyer Hans Frank* (Stroud: History Press, 2013), 76.

25. Heike B. Görtemaker, *Eva Braun. Life with Hitler* (New York: Knopf, 2011), 48; Munn, *Hitler*, 2–3.

26. Machtan, *Hitler*; Siemens, *Stormtroopers*, 172–75; Theodor Adorno, Else Frenkel-Brunswik, Daniel Levinson, and R. Nevitt Sanford, *The Authoritarian Personality* (New

York: Harper and Row, 1950); Robert Beachy, *Gay Berlin: Birthplace of a Modern Identity* (New York: Knopf, 2014), 244.

27. Karl Larkin, "It's True—Adolf Hitler Was a Woman!" *Weekly World News*, 27, no. 30 (1992); Rudolph Hess, in Machtan, *Hitler*, 144; Michael Fry, *Hitler's Wonderland* (London: J. Murray, 1934), 106.

28. Eva Braun, in Guido Knopp, *Hitler's Women* (New York: Routledge, 2003), 19; Görtemaker, *Eva Braun*; Munn, *Hitler*.

29. Hans Frank in O'Connor, *Butcher*, 153; Siemens, *Stormtroopers*, 172–75; Traverso, *Fire*, 211–18.

30. Gaddafi, in Annick Cojean, *Gaddafi's Harem* (New York: Grove Press, 2013), epitaph.

31. Maria Graeff-Wassink, "The Militarization of Women and 'Feminism' in Libya," in *Women Soldiers: Images and Realities*, ed. Elisabetta Addis, Valeria E. Russo, and Lorenza Sebesta (Basingstoke: Palgrave Macmillan, 1994), 137–49; Alison Rogers, "Revolutionary Nuns or Totalitarian Pawns: Evaluating Libyan State Feminism after Mu'ammar Gaddafi," in *Women's Movements in Post-"Arab Spring" North Africa*, ed. Fatima Sadiqi (New York: Palgrave Macmillan, 2016), 177–93.

32. Soraya, in Cojean, *Harem*, 75, 78. Soraya told the story of Gaddafi's system of sexual abuse to French journalist Annick Cojean after his regime collapsed in 2011. Staff, "Gaddafi Formed Special Department to Find Prostitutes," *Deccan Herald*, September 24, 2013; Vivienne Walt, "Gaddafi's Ghost: How a Tyrant Haunts Libya a Year after his Death," *TIME*, October 19, 2012; Marie Colvin, "Viagra-Munching Gaddafi Bedded Five a Day," *Sunday Times*, November 14, 2011; L.S., interview with author.

33. Condoleezza Rice, *No Higher Honor. A Memoir of My Years in Washington* (New York: Crown Publishing, 2011), 703; L.S., interview with author.

34. Cojean, *Harem*.

35. Soraya, in Cojean, *Harem*, 75; L.S., interview with author.

36. L.S., account of an early 1980s assembly of female students in eastern Libya and its consequences, interview with author; Soraya in Cojean, *Harem*, 27, 57, 61.

37. Annalisa Merelli, "What Happens When You Elect a Sexist to Run Your Country? Ask Italian Women," *Quartz*, October 19, 2016; Elisa Giomi, "Da 'Drive in' alla 'Makeover Television.' Modelli femminili e di rapporto fra i sessi nella TV berlusconiana (e non)," *Studi culturali*, IX, no. 1 (2012): 3–28.

38. Stille, *Sack of Rome*, 86.

39. Staff, "Acerto (Prc): una vergogna Emilio Fede a un concorso di miss a Pescara," www.6aprile.it, September 17, 2011; Staff, "Per il meteo Fede arruola Miss Italia," *Il Tempo*, September 3, 2003; Piero Colaprico, Giuseppe D'Avanzo, and Emilio Randacio, "Fede: 'Dormirete a casa mia': I provini per le ragazze del Cavaliere," *La Repubblica*, August 13, 2011; United Nations Convention on the Elimination of All Forms of Discrimination against Women, "Concluding Observations," 2011 session, 5–6: https://www2.ohchr.org/english/bodies/cedaw/docs/co/CEDAW-C-ITA-CO-6.pdf.

40. Berlusconi's March 25, 2006, molestation of the policewoman is on video here: https://www.youtube.com/watch?v=_2xHB1FmWpk, accessed April 20, 2020. Other two episodes in Merelli, "What Happens When You Elect a Sexist?"

41. Amalia Signorelli, "Le ambigue pari opportunità e il nuovo maschilismo," in *Berlusconismo*, ed. Ginsborg and Asquer, 207–22. Letizia Moratti, 2001–2006, and Mariastella Gelmini, 2008–2011, were education ministers.

42. Berlusconi, speech of January 15, 2000, in Orsina, *Berlusconism*, 69; Berlusconi, speech to Federcasalinghe, June 9, 1994, in Stella and Rizzo, *Così parlò*, 49; Stille, *Sack of Rome*, 89–90.

43. Evgenia Peretz, "La Dolce Viagra," *Vanity Fair*, May 31, 2011; Rachel Donadio, "Premier's Roving Eye Enrages Wife, but Not His Public," *New York Times*, April 29, 2009; Boni, *Il Superleader*, 167–70.

44. Mussolini's lover Giulia Alliata di Montereale influenced the choice of Alberto Varano as prefect of Palermo in June 1943: Franzinelli, *Il Duce*, 110; Peretz, "La Dolce Viagra"; Vittoria Brambilla, who had starred in Berlusconi's TV shows, became a parliamentarian, and Barbara Matera, who had been on TV and run for Miss Italy, became a Europarliamentarian. Guzzanti, *Mignottocrazia*; Staff, "Profile: Karima El Mahroug," BBC News, June 24, 2013.

45. Paolo Berizzi, interview with Karima El-Mahroug, *La Repubblica*, January 14, 2011; Guzzanti, *Mignottocrazia*; Staff, "Ruby, due nuove ragazze dal pm. 'Un incubo quelle notti ad Arcore,'" *Il Gazzettino*, April 13, 2011; Colaprico, D'Avanzo, Randacio, "Fede."

46. Staff, "Ruby"; "Woman Describes Berlusconi's 'Bunga Bunga' Parties," *USA Today*, May 17, 2013.

47. Berizzi, El Mahroug interview; Chiara Danese, in Francesco Oggiano, "Chiara Danese: 'Come si vive quando tutti ti considerano una prostituta,'" *Vanity Fair*, December 11, 2018.

48. Jane Timm, "Trump on Hot Mic: 'When You're a Star . . . You Can Do Anything to Women,'" NBC News, October 7, 2016; Tessa Stuart, "A Timeline of Donald Trump's Creepiness While He Owned Miss Universe," *Rolling Stone*, October 12, 2016; Jeffrey Toobin, "Trump's Miss Universe Gambit," *New Yorker*, February 19, 2018; Jazz Egger, in Nina Burleigh, *Golden Handcuffs. The Secret History of Trump's Women* (New York: Gallery Books, 2018), 183, 199–208.

49. Michael Snyder, "During the Trump Era, Will Men Finally Start Acting Like Men Again?" *Infowars*, January 25, 2017; Trump tweet, November 27, 2019, at: https://twitter.com/realDonaldTrump/status/1199718185865535490.

50. Compare the current DOJ Office on Violence against Women website page: https://www.justice.gov/ovw/domestic-violence, with the one from April 9, 2018: https://web.archive.org/web/20180409111243/https:/www.justice.gov/ovw/domestic-violence; Maya Oppenheim, "Trump Administration 'Rolling Back Women's Rights by 50 Years' by Changing Definitions of Domestic Violence and Sexual Assault," *Independent*, January 24, 2019.

51. Eric Ortiz and Tyler Kingkade, "Betsy DeVos Releases Final Changes to Campus Sexual Assault Policies," NBC News, May 6, 2020; Philip Rucker, Robert Costa, Josh Dawsey, and Ashley Parker, "Defending Kavanaugh, Trump Laments #MeToo as 'Very Dangerous' for Powerful Men," *Washington Post*, September 26, 2018; Ryan Teague Beckwith, "President Trump Is Defending Kavanaugh the Same Way He Defended Himself and Other Men," *TIME*, September 20, 2018.

52. Tim Dickinson, "A History of Sex and Abuse in the Trump Administration," *Rolling Stone*, February 23, 2018; Jacey Fortin, "Trump's History of Defending Men Accused of Hurting Women," *New York Times*, February 11, 2018; Justin Elliott, "Trump Administration Hires Official Whom Five Students Accused of Sexual Assault," *ProPublica*, May 3, 2017; David Nakamura, "Formal and Casual White House Photos Show Distance between Trump and Increasingly Diverse Nation," *Washington Post*, April 4, 2019; Jennifer Jacobs and Daniel Flatley, "Trump's Protocol Chief Is Quitting Just Before the G-20 Summit," *Bloomberg*, June 26, 2019.

53. Trump, in Kate Briquelet, "How Did Trump and Clinton Pal Jeffrey Epstein Escape #MeToo?" *Daily Beast*, June 22, 2018; Lucia Graves and Sam Morris, "The Trump Allegations," *Guardian*, November 29, 2017; Alva Johnson, "Former Trump Campaign

Staffer Accuses President of Sexual Assault," *Fortune*, February 25, 2019; Burleigh, *Handcuffs*; Nicole Hong, Michael Rothfeld, Rebecca Davis O'Brien, and Rebecca Ballhaus, "Donald Trump Played Central Role in Hush Payoffs to Stormy Daniels and Karen McDougal," *Wall Street Journal*, November 9, 2018.

SEVEN: CORRUPTION

1. Mobutu Sese Seko, May 20, 1976, in Keith B. Richburg, "Mobutu: A Rich Man in Poor Standing," *Washington Post*, October 3, 1991; Rep. Stephen Solarz, in Léonce Ndikumana and James K. Boyce, "Congo's Odious Debt: External Borrowing and Capital Flight in Zaire," *Development and Change* 29, no. 2 (1998): 208; David Smith, "Where Concorde Once Flew: The Story of President Mobutu's 'African Versailles,'" *Guardian*, February 10, 2015; James Brooke, "Mobutu's Village Basks in His Glory," *New York Times*, September 29, 1988; Michela Wrong, *In the Footsteps of Mr. Kurtz. Living on the Brink of Disaster in the Congo* (London: Fourth Estate, 2000), 213–31; Adam Zagorin, "Leaving Fire in his Wake: Mobutu Sese Seko," *TIME*, February 22, 1983.

2. Acemoglu, Verdier, Robinson, "Kleptocracy"; Frantz and Ezrow, *Politics of Dictatorship*, 23; Thomas Turner and Crawford Young, *The Rise and Decline of the Zairian State* (Madison: University of Wisconsin Press, 1985).

3. Jean Nzuga Karl-i-Bond, *Mobutu, ou l'incarnation du Mal Zaïrois* (London: Rex Collings, 1982); Blaine Harden, "Mobutu Is Unchallenged 'Messiah' of Zaire," *Washington Post*, November 10, 1987.

4. Zaire was among the world's top exporters of copper, diamonds, and cobalt during Mobutu's rule. Ndikumana and Boyce, "Odious Debt," 208–12; Kelly, *America's Tyrant*, 200; Anderson and Van Atta, "Mobutu in Search of an Image Boost"; Vanessa Ogle, "'Funk Money': The End of Empires, the Expansion of Tax Havens, and Decolonization as an Economic and Financial Event," forthcoming in *Past and Present* (2020).

5. Rasma Karklins, *The System Made Me Do It. Corruption in Post-Communist Societies* (New York: Routledge, 2005), 4–5, 25; Oskar Kurer, "Definitions of Corruption," in *The Routledge Handbook of Political Corruption*, ed. Paul M. Heywood (London: Routledge, 2015), 30–39. Already in the 1970s, 15 to 20 percent of Zaire's operating budget went to Mobutu directly. Ndikumana and Boyce, "Odious Debt," 206.

6. Gandhi, *Political Institutions*, 73–105; Desai, Olofsgård, Yousef, "Authoritarian Bargains."

7. Daron Acemoglu, "Countries Fail the Same Way Businesses Do, Gradually and Then Suddenly," *Foreign Affairs*, June 15, 2020.

8. Devlin Barrett, Adam Entous, Ellen Nakashima, and Sari Horwitz, "Special Counsel Is Investigating Trump for Possible Obstruction of Justice, Officials Say," *Washington Post*, June 14, 2017.

9. Nadia Popovich, Livia Albeck-Ripka, and Kendra Pierre-Louis, "95 Environmental Rules Being Rolled Back under Trump," *New York Times*, December 21, 2019 (updated May 20, 2020); for updates see the Drilled News Climate & COVID-19 Policy Tracker: https://www.drillednews.com/post/the-climate-covid-19-policy-tracker; Evan Osnos, "Trump vs. the 'Deep State,'" *New Yorker*, May 21, 2018; Vanessa Barbara, "Where Do You Turn When the Anti-Corruption Crusaders Are Dirty?" *New York Times*, July 5, 2019; Danielle Brant and Phillippe Watanabe, "Sob Bolsonaro, multas ambientais caem 34% para meno nivel em 24 anos," *Folha de S. Puolo*, March 9, 2020.

10. Pompeo, in Jennifer Hansler, "Pompeo: Melting Sea Ice Presents New 'Opportunities for Trade,'" CNN.com, May 7, 2019. Under the guise of countering Chinese and Rus-

sian influence in the Arctic, the US offered Greenland a $12.1 million aid package: Martin Selsoe Sorensen, "U.S. Aid for Greeland Prompts Praise and Suspicion in Denmark," *New York Times*, April 24, 2020; Nina Martyris, "Buying Greenland? That's Nothing to Gabriel García Márquez," NPR.com, August 24, 2019.

11. Acemoglu, Verdier, Robinson, "Kleptocracy"; Wrong, *Footsteps*; Mack Smith, *Mussolini*, 175; Cliff Sims, *Team of Vipers: My 500 Extraordinary Days in the Trump White House* (New York: Thomas Dunne, 2019), 320.

12. Karl H. von Weigand, "Hitler Foresees His End," *Cosmopolitan*, April 1939; El-Kikhia, *Qaddafi*, 5; Maggie Haberman and Russ Buettner, "In Business and in Governing, Trump Seeks Victory in Chaos," *New York Times*, January 20, 2019; Michael Morell, "I Ran the CIA. Now I'm Endorsing Hillary Clinton," *New York Times*, August 5, 2016.

13. Nordlinger, *Children*, 131–47, 197–205; Farfán and Vega, *La familia*; Michael Wolff, *Fire and Fury*, 27.

14. Mauro Canali and Clemente Volpini, *Mussolini e i ladri del regime* (Milan: Mondadori, 2019), 147, 151; Ward, *Kushner, Inc.*; Andrea Bernstein, *American Oligarchs. The Kushners, the Trumps, and the Marriage of Money and Power* (New York: W. W. Norton, 2020); Kendzior, *Hiding in Plain Sight*; "EU Pursues Orbán Son in Law Case Despite Hungary Ending Probe," *Politico* (EU edition), November 8, 2018; Lawrence Norman, "EU Fraud Office Finds Irregularities in Projects Linked to Hungarian Leader's Son-in-Law," *Wall Street Journal*, January 12, 2018; Alexander Christie-Miller, "Erdogan's Son in Law linked to 'Isis Oil Trade,'" *Times*, December 5, 2015.

15. Mussolini, "Discorso sull' Ascensione"; Mattei, "Austerity."

16. James Dodds, British consul general in Palermo, in Duggan, *Fascist Voices*, 145; Seldes, *Sawdust Caesar*, 196–200; Salvatore Lupo, *Il fascismo. La politica in un regime totalitario* (Rome: Donzelli, 2000); Vittorio Coco, "Una carriera emergente in terra di mafia," in *Il fascismo dalle mani sporche. Dittatura, corruzione, affarismo*, ed. Paolo Giovannini and Marco Palla (Rome: Laterza, 2019), 141–62.

17. Canali and Volpini, *Mussolini e i ladri*, 45–46, 116–24; Ilaria Pavan, *Tra indifferenza e odio. Le conseguenze economiche delle leggi razziali in italia, 1938–1970* (Milan: Mondadori, 2019).

18. Emilio De Bono, in MacGregor Knox, "Mussolini and Hitler: Charisma, Regime, and National Catastrophe," in *Political Leadership, Nations and Charisma*, ed. Vivian Ibrahim and Margit Wunsch (New York: Routledge, 2012), 105. Mussolini reshuffled his cabinet in 1924, 1929, 1932, 1935, 1939, and 1943.

19. Mussolini, telegram to prefect of Milan, June 2, 1930, in Benito Mussolini, *Corrispondenza inedita*, ed. Duilio Susmel (Milan: Edizioni del Borghese, 1972), 114; Mack Smith, *Mussolini*, 127–30.

20. Canali and Volpini, *Mussolini e i ladri*, 183–204; Michela C. to Mussolini, December 14, 1925, in *Caro Duce*, 81; Romano Mussolini, *Il Duce*, 140.

21. Police report of January 31, 1935, in Kershaw, *"Hitler Myth,"* 98; Kalder, *Library*, 136; Hitler, in Richard Evans, "Corruption and Plunder in the Third Reich," blog post at: https://www.richardjevans.com/lectures/corruption-plunder-third-reich/.

22. Jane Caplan, *Government without Administration* (Oxford: Clarendon Press, 1988); Knox, "Mussolini and Hitler," 105; Arendt, *Origins*, 396–409; António Costa Pinto, "Ruling Elites, Political Institutions and Decision-Making in Fascist-Era Dictatorships: Comparative Perspectives," in *Rethinking the Nature of Fascism. Comparative Perspectives*, ed. António Costa Pinto (New York: Palgrave Macmillan, 2011), 204–7; Alexander De Grand, *Fascist Italy and Nazi Germany. The "Fascist" Style of Rule* (New

York: Routledge, 2004), 34–35; Otto Dietrich, *The Hitler I Knew. Memoirs of the Third Reich's Press Chief* (New York: Skyhorse, 2014), 92.

23. On "little dictators," Fathali M. Moghaddam, *The Psychology of Dictatorship* (Washington, DC: American Psychological Association, 2013), 77; Kershaw, *"Hitler Myth,"* 96–104; Evans, "Corruption and Plunder." In 1935, the government shut down Die Katakombe. Finck spent six weeks in Esterwegen camp and was banned from performing in public for a year.

24. Götz Aly, *Hitler's Beneficiaries* (New York: Metropolitan Books, 2007); Kershaw, *"Hitler Myth,"* 83; Evans, "Corruption and Plunder."

25. Frantz and Ezrow, *Politics of Dictatorship*, 18–46; Huneeus, *Pinochet*, 1–3.

26. Constable and Valenzuela, *Enemies*, 118–22.

27. Former prosecutor, in Constable and Valenzuela, *Enemies*, 115, and 116–36 on the domestication of the judiciary.

28. Spooner, *Soldiers*, 86–87, 102–3, 150; Pinochet also created a new lieutenant general rank and sped up the clock for promotions to general; Huneeus, *Pinochet*, 91–95; Cristóbal Peña, *La secreta vida*, 29; Anderson, "The Dictator."

29. Arriagada, *Pinochet*, 30; Erin Carlyle, "Meet Chemicals Billionaire Julio Ponce Lerou, Former Son-in-Law of the Chilean Dictator," *Forbes*, June 19, 2013; Timothy L. O'Brien and Larry Rohter, "The Pinochet Money Trail," *New York Times*, December 12, 2004; "Swiss Lead International Inquiry into Assets of Pinochet Family," *Irish Times*, February 15, 1999.

30. González, *Conjura*; Stern, *Battling*, 57–58; Angélica Thumala Olave, "The Richness of Ordinary Life: Religious Justification among Chile's Business Elite," *Religion* 40, no. 1 (2010): 14–26; Huneeus, *Pinochet*, 162–68; Márquez, *Clandestine*, 29–30.

31. Jonathan Franklin, "Pinochet's Widow under Investigation on Suspicion of Swindling Millions," *Guardian*, August 18, 2016; Nicholas O'Shaughnessy, "Pinochet's Lost Millions: The UK Connection," *Independent*, August 23, 2009; David Leigh and Rob Evans, "Revealed: BAE's Secret (GB Pound)1m to Pinochet," *Guardian* (joint investigation with *La Tercera*), September 15, 2005; Farfán and Vega, *Familia*, 109–46; Huneeus, *Pinochet*, 457–59.

32. Michael Ross, "What Have We Learned about the Resource Curse?" *Annual Review of Political Science* 18 (2015): 239–59; Jørgen Juel Andersen and Silje Aslaksen, "Oil and Political Survival," *Journal of Development Economics* 100, no.1 (2013): 89–106; Bueno de Mesquita and Smith, *Dictators' Playbook*; Smith, "Oil Wealth and Regime Survival."

33. ADST, Josif interview; van Genugten, *Libya*, 93–101; Anderson, *State and Social Transfomation*, 262.

34. Pargeter, *Gaddafi*, 72–80; El-Kikhia, *Qaddafi*, 84–92; Arendt, *Origins*, 400.

35. *New York Times* Wikileaks Archive, cable from Elizabeth Fritschle, political/economic chief, US Liaisons Office, Department of State, May 10 2006: https://archive.nytimes .com/www.nytimes.com/interactive/2010/11/28/world/20101128–cables-viewer .html#report/libya-06TRIPOLI198.

36. Jessica Donati and Marie-Louise Gumuchian, "Special Report: The Gaddafi Oil Papers," Reuters, December 23, 2011; Jaber Emhemed Masaud Shariha, Bambang Supriyono, M. Mardiyono, Andy Fefta Wijaya, and Soesilo Zauhar, "Corruption in the Regime's Apparatus and State Institutions in Libya during Gaddafi's Rule," *International Refereed Journal of Engineering and Science* 3, no. 11 (2014): 1–3.

37. Vandewalle, *Libya*, 173–94; "Libya Documents: A Programme to Enhance the International Reputation of Libya," *Guardian*, March 4, 2011; Kevin Bogardus, "PR Firm Books $1.2 Million from Gadhafi's Libya," *Hill*, July 18, 2011; Kawczynski, *Gad-*

dafi, 191–213; "Libya's Top 5 Corruption Scandals," Transparency International blog, July 28, 2014, at https://blog.transparency.org/2014/07/28/libyas-top-5–corruption -scandals-2/; van Genugten, *Libya*, 127–46.

38. John Markoff, "U.S. Group Reaches Deal to Provide Laptops to All Libyan Schoolchildren," *New York Times*, October 11, 2006; James S. Henry, "Gaddafi's Fellow Travellers," *Forbes*, August 26, 2011; Rajiv Syal and Jeevan Vasagar, "Anthony Gidden's Trip to See Gaddafi Vetted by Libyan Intelligence Chief," *Guardian*, March 4, 2011; *Delivered into Enemy Hands. U.S.-Led Rendition of Opponents to Gaddafi's Libya*, Human Rights Watch Report, 2012: https://www.hrw.org/sites/default/files/report_pdf/libya0912_web_0.pdf.

39. Anderson, "King of Kings"; Edwin Durgy, "Did Muammar Gaddafi Die the Richest Man in the World?" *Forbes*, October 25, 2011. *Forbes* did not rank Gaddafi as the richest man because most of his wealth was in accounts in the name of the government of Libya—another example of the melding of state and individual finances under personalist rule.

40. Guriev and Treisman, "Modern Dictators"; Bálint Magyar, *The Post-Communist Mafia State* (Budapest: Central European University Press, 2015); Anders Aslund, *Russia's Crony Capitalism: The Path from Market Economy to Kleptocracy* (New Haven: Yale University Press, 2019).

41. Leighann Spencer and Ali Yildiz, *The Erosion of Property Rights in Turkey*, Platform Peace & Justice, 2020, at: http://www.platformpj.org/wp-content/uploads/EROSION -OF-PROPERTY-RIGHTS-IN-TURKEY-1.pdf.

42. J. C. Sharfman, *The Despot's Guide of Wealth Management* (Ithaca, NY: Cornell University Press, 2017); Zucman, *Hidden Wealth*; Alexander Cooley, John Heathershaw, and J. C. Sharfman, "Laundering Cash, Whitewashing Reputations," *Journal of Democracy* 29, no. 1 (2018): 39–53; Luke Harding, "Revealed: The $2bn Offshore Trail That Leads to Vladimir Putin," *Guardian*, April 3, 2016; Jacob Rund, "House Passes Beneficial Ownership Disclosure Bill," *Bloomberg Law*, October 22, 2019; Foer, "Russian-Style Kleptocracy."

43. Hill and Gaddy, *Putin*, 216; Karklins, *System*, 36; Aslund, *Crony Capitalism*; Staff, "Richest 3% Russians Hold 90% Country's Financial Assets," *Moscow Times*, April 12, 2019.

44. The 2012 Magnitsky Act allowed the US to withhold visas and freeze assets of Russian officials involved in human rights violations. Shelley, "Crime and Corruption," 194, 200–201; Dawisha, *Putin's Kleptocracy*, 317–18. A 2013 amnesty freed 10,000 businesspeople. Owen Matthews, "Putin's Russia: Exile Businessmen," *Newsweek*, August 14, 2010; James Marson and Thomas Grove, "In Russia, the Corporate Raiders Are Often Cops," *Wall Street Journal*, August 7, 2018.

45. Anders Aslund, "Vladimir Putin Is Russia's Biggest Oligarch," *Washington Post*, June 5, 2019; Vanand Meliksetian, "A Watershed Moment for Gazprom," Oilprice.com, June 15, 2019: https://oilprice.com/Energy/Natural-Gas/A-Watershed-Moment-For -Gazprom.html; Dawisha, *Putin's Kleptocracy*, 326–31; on the Sberbank report, Leonid Bershidsky, "A Fired Analyst Got Too Close to Gazprom's Truth," *Bloomberg Opinion*, May 23, 2018.

46. Aslund, "Vladimir Putin Is Russia's Biggest Oligarch"; Nguyen, "Eric Trump Reportedly Bragged about Access to $100 Million in Russian Money." Eric Trump omitted mention of the $2 billion loaned by Deutsche Bank to the Trump Organization over almost two decades: Enrich, *Dark Towers*.

47. Rubini, "Le vicende giudiziarie," 138; Vannucci, "Controversial Legacy", Dallara,

"Powerful resistance"; Amedeo Benedetti, *Il linguaggio e la retorica della nuova politica italiana: Silvio Berlusconi e Forza Italia* (Genoa: Erga, 2004), 11–12.

48. Vannucci, "Controversial Legacy," 251; Berlusconi, in Stella and Rizzi, *Cosi parlò*, 25.
49. Berlusconi, in Ginsborg, *Berlusconi*, 84; Pierfranco Pellizzetti, *Fenomenologia di Berlusconi* (Rome: Manifestolibri, 2009), 56; Orsina, *Berlusconism*, 96; Vannucci, "Controversial Legacy."
50. Vannucci, "Controversial Legacy," 235.
51. Stratfor, "Italy's Interests in Libya," *Forbes*, March 31, 2011.
52. Putin, in Hill and Gaddy, *Putin*, 166–67, also 280–84; Zygar, *Kremlin's Men*, 32–33, 36–37, 112–13, 118–23; Todd H. Hall, *Emotional Diplomacy* (Ithaca, NY: Cornell University Press, 2015), 94–100; Caroline Wyatt, "Bush and Putin: Best of Friends," BBC News, June 16, 2001.
53. Diodato and Niglia, *Berlusconi*, 91; Maurizio Carbone, "Russia's Trojan Horse in Europe? Italy and the War in Georgia," *Italian Politics*, 24 (2008): 138–40; Taylor, *Code of Putinism*; Angela Stent, *Putin's World: Russia against the West and with the Rest* (New York: Twelve, 2019); Mark Galeotti, *We Need to Talk about Putin: How the West Gets Him Wrong* (London: Ebury Press, 2019*)*.
54. Diodato and Niglia, *Berlusconi*, 55–56, 105; Friedman, *My Way*, 138–43.
55. Carbone, "Trojan Horse"; *La Stampa* Staff, "Gaffe di Berslusconi che mima un mitra. Putin: 'Si, mi piacciono le belle donne,'" *La Stampa*, April 18, 2008; Spogli, 'Italy-Russia Relations" and "Scenesetter"; Michael Scherer, "Silvio Berlusconi, A Small Man," *TIME*, December 3, 2010. Spogli's concerns were echoed by his successor, Ambassador David Thorne, in "Italy: Scandals Taking Toll on Berlusconi's Personal and Political Health," October 27, 2009: https://www.theguardian.com/world/us-embassy-cables-documents/231600.
56. Olivia Nuzzi, "What Hope Hicks Knows," *New York*, March 18, 2018.
57. Philip Bump, "Nearly a Third of the Days He's Been President, Trump Has Visited a Trump-Branded Property," *Washington Post*, December 30, 2019; David Fahrenthold, Josh Dawsey, Jonathan O'Connell, and Michelle Ye Hee Lee, "When Trump Visits His Clubs, Government Agencies and Republicans Pay to Be Where He Is," *Washington Post*, June 20, 2019; David Leonhardt and Ian Prasad Philbrick, "Trump's Corruption: The Definitive List," *New York Times*, October 28, 2018.
58. Osnos, "'Deep State'"; Ashley Parker, Philip Rucker, and Josh Dawsey, "'Ready, Shoot, Aim': President Trump's Loyalty Tests Cause Hiring Headaches," *Washington Post*, April 29, 2018; Karklins, *System*, 153; Julia Ioffe, "Trump Is Waging War on America's Diplomats," *GQ*, December 3, 2019.
59. Conway, in Aaron Blake, "'Blah, Blah, Blah': This 2-Week-Old Kellyanne Conway Clip Looks a Lot Worse Today," *Washington Post*, June 13, 2019; Margaret Taylor, "I Vetted the State Department Whip Guy," *Lawfare*, July 1, 2019; Andrew Desiderio, "House Oversight Threatens to Subpoena Kellyanne Conway," *Politico*, June 23, 2019.
60. Osnos, "'Deep State'"; Kathryn Dunn Tenpas et al., *Tracking Turnover in the Trump Administration*, Brookings Report, April 2019; Anonymous, "I Am Part of the Resistance Inside the Trump Adminstration," *New York Times*, September 5, 2018; Rucker and Leonnig, *Stable Genius*; Alexander Nazaryan, *The Best People: Trump's Cabinet and the Siege on Washington* (New York: Hachette, 2019); Bob Woodward, *Fear: Trump in the White House* (New York: Simon and Schuster, 2018).
61. Dan Spinelli, "Report: Barr Protected Turkish Bank from Prosecution to Appease Erdogan," *Mother Jones*, February 15, 2020; Ambassador Thorne, "Italy: Scandals Taking Toll," referred to Valentini as Berlusconi's "bagman."

62. David Graham, "The Unchecked Corruption of Trump's Cabinet," *Atlantic*, May 20, 2019; Osnos, "'Deep State'"; Dan Alexander, "Lies, China, and Putin: Solving the Mystery of Wilbur Ross's Missing Fortune," *Forbes*, June 18, 2019; Steven Mufson, "Wilbur Ross Owned Stock in a Company with Close Ties to Putin Associates. Now He's Facing Questions about What He Did with It," *Washington Post*, June 20, 2018.

63. Alan Rappeport, "Mnuchin Defends Plan to Lift Sanctions on Russian Oligarch's Companies," *New York Times*, January 10, 2019; Christina Maza, "Sanctioned Russian Oligarich's Company to Invest Millions in New Aluminum Plant in Mitch McConnell's State," *Newsweek*, April 15, 2019; Tom Porter, "Russia State Media Mocked Trump by Calling Him 'Our Donald Ivanovych' and Complained US Politicians Had Lost Their Minds over Attempts to Impeach Him," *Business Insider*, November 7, 2019; Brendan Cole, "Trump's Praise of Putin Mocked on Russian TV with 'Señorita' Mashup," *Newsweek*, August 29, 2019.

64. James Comey, "How Trump Co-Opts Leaders Like Bill Barr," *New York Times*, May 1, 2019.

EIGHT: VIOLENCE

1. Cristina Godoy-Navarrete, in Kim Sengupta, "Victims of Pinochet's Secret Police Prepare to Reveal Details of Rape and Torture," *Independent*, November 9, 1998.

2. Styron, "Special Report on Chile," 258; Jean Améry, *Beyond the Mind's Limits. Contemplations by a Survivor on Auschwitz and Its Realities* (New York: Schocken Books, 1986), 39, 36, 24; Wolfgang Sofsky, *The Order of Terror. The Concentration Camp*, trans. William Templer (Princeton, NJ: Princeton University Press, 1997), 16–27.

3. Hannah Arendt, *On Violence* (New York: Harcourt, Brace and World, 1969), 56.

4. Styron, "Special Report on Chile," 247; Tubach, *German Voices*, 47.

5. Rubin, *Modern Dictators*, 298.

6. José Ortega y Gasset, *Man and People*, trans. Willard R. Trask (New York: W. W. Norton, 1957), 196; Michael Ebner, *Ordinary Violence in Mussolini's Italy* (Cambridge, UK: Cambridge University Press, 2010), 177–78; Mosse, *Nazi Culture*, xxxix; Eugen Nerdinger, in Annette Dumbach and Jud Newborn, *Sophie Scholl and the White Rose* (London: Oneworld Publications, 2018), 165–66.

7. Fitzpatrick and Lüdtke, "Energizing," 278. In Würzburg, public cooperation led to 64 percent of Gestapo cases opened on questions of "racial defilement" and "friendship with Jews": Darius Rejali, *Torture and Democracy* (Princeton, NJ: Princeton University Press, 2009), 494.

8. Timothy Snyder, *Black Earth. The Holocaust as History and Warning* (New York: Tim Duggan Books, 2015), 82–83; United Nations War Crimes Commission (UNWCC), PAG-3/2.0, reg no. 4551/Gr/It/35, microfilm p. 1340; also reg. no. 7054/Gr/It/88, microfilm 1589, and reg. no. 6804/Gr/It/76 charge no. 485/45, microfilm 1536.

9. Arendt, *Origins*; Isabel Hull, *Absolute Destruction: Military Culture and the Practices of War in Imperial Germany* (Ithaca, NY: Cornell University Press, 2006); Adam Hochschild, *King Leopold's Ghost: A Story of Greed, Terror, and Heroism in Colonial Africa* (New York: Houghton Mifflin, 1999); Andrea Pitzer, *One Dark Night: A Global History of Concentration Camps* (Boston: Little, Brown, 2017).

10. Douglas Porch, *Counterinsurgency: Exposing the Myths of the New Way of War* (Cambridge, UK: Cambridge University Press, 2013); Rejali, *Torture*, 167–224 on electric shock devices, 108–119 on bathtubs; Perseus Strategies, *The Kremlin's Political Prisoners*.

11. Mussolini, "Stato anti-Stato e fascismo"; Anonymous torturer, in John Perry, *Torture: Religious Ethics and National Security* (Princeton, NJ: Princeton University Press, 2005), 92.

12. Mussolini, "Fascismo," *Enciclopedia Treccani* (Milan: Istituto Trecccani, 1932) at: http://www.treccani.it/enciclopedia/fascismo_%28Enciclopedia-Italiana%29/.

13. Ruth Ben-Ghiat, "A Lesser Evil? Italian Fascism in/and the Totalitarian Equation," in *The Lesser Evil. Moral Approaches to Genocide Practices*, ed. Helmut Dubiel and Gabriel Motzkin (New York: Routledge, 2004), 137–53; Mimmo Franzinelli, *Il tribunale del Duce. La giustizia fascista e le sue vittime (1927–1943)* (Milano: Le Scie, 2017); Ebner, *Violence*, 11, 60–64, 188–91.

14. Marshal Pietro Badoglio to General Graziani, June 20, 1930, in Giorgio Rochat, *Guerre italiane in Libia e in Etiopia. Studi militari 1921–1939* (Treviso: Pagus, 1991), 61; Hom, *Empire's Mobius Strip*, 89–108; Ahmida, *Forgotten Voices*; Jamlila Sa'īd Sulaymān, in Katrina Yeaw, "Women, Resistance, and the Creation of New Gendered Frontiers in the Making of Modern Libya, 1890–1980," PhD dissertation, Georgetown University, 2017, 269–71. The population declined from 110,000 to 40,000, and 300,000 animals died. Between 85,000 and 110,000 people were interned. Knud Holmboe, *Desert Encounter. An Adventurous Journey through Italian Africa*, trans. Helga Holbek (London: George G. Harrap, 1936), 203, 103.

15. Mussolini, to General Emilio De Bono, March 8, 1935, in Mussolini, *Corrispondenza inedita*, 149–51; Bruce Strang, ed., *Collision of Empires: Italy's Invasion of Ethiopia and Its International Impact* (New York: Routledge, 2013); Mattioli, *Experimentierfeld*.

16. Emperor Haile Selassie, *League of Nations Official Journal*, Special Supplement 151, Records of the Sixteenth Ordinary Session of the Assembly, Plenary Meeting, June 30, 1936, 22–25; Thomas Mann, *Diaries 1918–1939* (New York: Harry N. Abrams, 1982), entry of 1935, 246–47.

17. Dana Renga, Elizabeth Leake, and Piero Garofalo, *Internal Exile in Fascist Italy* (Bloomington: Indiana University Press, 2019); Ebner, *Violence*, 103–38; www.campifascisti.it for a list of camps and Italian government agencies that administered them; Vito Ailara and Massimo Caserta, *I relegati libici a Ustica dal 1911 al 1934* (Ustica: Centro Studi Isola di Ustica, 2012); Hom, *Empire's Mobius Strip*, 48–50. Many inmates were sent to Ponza when Ustica closed in 1932.

18. Aldo Pavia and Antonella Tiburzi, "I campi di concentramento italiani 1926–1940": http://www.storiaxxisecolo.it/deportazione/deportazionecampid.html.

19. Gianfranco Goretti and Tommaso Giartosio, *La città e l'isola: Omosessuali al confino nell'Italia fascista* (Rome: Donzelli, 2006), 154; Ebner, *Violence*, 196.

20. Mussolini, in Galeazzo Ciano, *Diario 1937–43* (Milan: Rizzoli, 1990), entry of July 10, 1938, 156; Dina M. to Mussolini, December 1938, in *Caro Duce*, 49–50; "Come coprire i vuoti"; Gherardo Casini, "Bonifica della cultura italiana," *L'Orto* (January 1938).

21. Mussolini, in Petacci, *Mussolini segreto*, entries of October 9 and 11, 1938, locations 6254–6258, 6275–6278 (Kindle edition).

22. Renzetti to Mussolini, July 14, 1934, in De Felice, *Mussolini e Hitler*, 302.

23. Hannah Arendt, "Social Science Techniques and the Study of Concentration Camps," *Jewish Social Studies* 12, no. 1 (1950): 58–59; Rejali, *Torture*, 499; Geoffrey Megargee and Martin Dean, eds., *Encyclopedia of Camps and Ghettos, 1933–1945* (Washington, DC: United States Holocaust Memorial Museum, 2009); Caplan, "Introduction," 1–18; Nicholas Wachsmann, *KL. A History of the Nazi Concentration Camps* (New York: Farrar Straus and Giroux, 2016).

24. Pitzer, *Dark Night*, 166–75; Rejali, *Torture*, 92–104.

25. Victor Klemperer, *I Will Bear Witness: A Diary of the Nazi Years 1933–1941*, trans. Martin Chalmers (New York: Knopf, 1999); Cesarani, *Final Solution*, 158–59, 216–21; Caplan, "Introduction," in Herz, *Moringen*, 8–9. In January 1933, the German Jewish popula-

tion was 523,000. By 1939, 304,000 of them had left, 100,000 fleeing after the 1938 Kristallnacht pogrom.

26. Tubach, *German Voices*, 88–89; Goebbels, in Cesarani, *Final Solution*, 181–99.

27. The phrase "radical cleansing" is from a 1938 division commanders' manual, in Jensen, *Franco*, 78; Javier Rodrigo, "Exploitation, Fascist Violence, and Social Cleansing: An Exploration of Franco's Concentration Camps from a Comparative Perspective," *European Review of History* 19, no. 4 (2012): 553–73.

28. Paul Preston, "Franco and Hitler: The Myth of Hendaye, 1940," *Contemporary European History* 1, no. 1 (1992): 1–16; Wayne H. Bowen, *Spain during World War Two* (Columbia: University of Missouri Press, 2006).

29. UNWCC, 341/Y/It10 no.R/I/10, October 14 1944, 1078 Rab, 1079 Monigo. Hom, *Empire's Mobius Strip*, 110–12; Alessandra Kersevan, *I lager italiani. Pulizia etnica e campi di concentramento fascisti per civili jugoslavi 1941–1943* (Rome: Nutrimenti, 2008).

30. Schmitt, in Traverso, *Fire*, 73–74; Mark Mazower, *Dark Continent: Europe's Twentieth Century* (New York: Vintage, 2009), 143–47.

31. Hitler, August 22, 1939, order, in Timothy Snyder, *Bloodlands: Europe between Hitler and Stalin* (New York: Basic Books, 2012), 121; Omer Bartov, *Hitler's Army: Soldiers, Nazis, and War in the Third Reich* (New York: Oxford University Press, 1992); Friedrich M., letter September 13, 1939, in Tubach, *German Voices*, 203–4; Jan Gross, *Neighbors. The Destruction of the Jewish Community in Jedwabne, Poland* (Princeton, NJ: Princeton University Press, 2001).

32. Snyder, *Bloodlands*, ix–x; High Command of the German Armed Forces (OKH), "Guidelines for the Behavior of Troops in Russia," May 1941, in Martin Kitchen, *A World in Flames* (New York: Routledge, 1990), 72; Traverso, *Fire*, 104–11; Bartov, *Hitler's Army*, 83; Mark Edele and Michael Geyer, "States of Exception. The Nazi-Soviet War as a System of Violence, 1939–1945," in *Beyond Totalitarianism*, ed. Fitzpatrick and Lüdtke, 345–95.

33. Evans, "Corruption and Plunder"; Aly, *Hitler's Beneficiaries*; O'Connor, *Butcher*.

34. Herman Voss, "The Posen Diaries of the Anatomist Herman Voss," in *Cleansing the Fatherland. Nazi Medicine and Racial Hygiene*, ed. Götz Aly, Peter Chroust, and Christian Pross (Baltimore: Johns Hopkins University Press, 1994), entries of September 30, 1941, and April 27, 1942, 135, 141.

35. Christa Schroeder, in Lower, *Furies*, 5, also 6–8, 21, 36–37.

36. Sofsky, *Order*, 23, 37–38; Raul Hilberg, in Claude Lanzmann, *Shoah. The Complete Text of the Acclaimed Holocaust Film* (New York: Da Capo Press, 1995), 61.

37. Walter Rauff, report of June 5, 1942, in Kate Millett, *The Politics of Cruelty. An Essay on the Literature of Political Imprisonment* (New York: W. W. Norton, 1994), 68. Statistics from "Gas Chambers," at http://auschwitz.org/en/history/auschwitz-and-shoah/gas-chambers.

38. Doris Reiprich, 1984 interview, in May Optiz, Katharina Oguntoye, and Dagmar Schulaz, *Showing Our Colors. Afro-German Women Speak Out* (Amherst: University of Massachusetts Press 1992), 66; Voss, entry of June 2, 1941, and Aly, "Medicine against the Useless," both in *Cleansing*, ed. Aly, Chroust, Pross, 105–6 and 22–98; Friedlander, "Exclusion and Murder." Nurses trained for euthanasia also worked in the camps: Lower, *Furies*, 38. Death figures: https://www.ushmm.org/learn/students/learning-materials-and-resources/mentally-and-physically-handicapped-victims-of-the-nazi-era/euthanasia-killings.

39. Primo Levi, *Survival in Auschwitz* (New York: Touchstone Books, 1996), 29, 88; Sofsky, *Order*, 82–93.

40. Nieves Ayress, in Archivio Chile, Centro de Estudios Miguel Enríquez, "El testimonio de Nieves Ayress Moreno se levanta con la fuerza de la Verdad fruente a los cobardes che niegan la tortura en Chile": http://www.archivochile.com/Derechos_humanos/testimo/hhddtestimo0006.pdf; Temma Kaplan, *Taking Back the Streets. Women, Youth, and Direct Democracy* (Berkeley: University of California Press, 2004), 15–39; Jorge Ramos, "This Is How Pinochet Tortured Me," *The Scholar and Feminist Online*, 2, no. 1 (2003).

41. Ecuador and Peru joined Operation Condor later and had more marginal roles. Osni Geraldo Gomes, in Yglesias, ed., *Terror*, 43–50; McSherry, *Predatory States*. In 1983–1984, the School of the Americas relocated to Fort Benning, Georgia.

42. Author interview with S.

43. Ravelli, "Far Right Militants"; Matteo Albanese and Pablo Del Hierro, *Transnational Fascism in the Twentieth Century: Spain, Italy and the Global Neofascist Network* (London: Bloomsbury Academic, 2016); Gerald Steinbach, *Nazis on the Run. How Hitler's Henchmen Fled Europe* (New York: Oxford University Press, 2011), 209–10. Colonia Dignidad also hosted an army chemical weapons facility.

44. Quotes from Olderock and Alejandra Holzapfel, in Alejandra Matus, "Ingrid Olderock," in *Los Malos*, ed. Guerriero, 144, 148.

45. Laurence Birns, "The Demise of a Constitutional Society," *New York Review of Books*, November 1, 1973; Jack Chang, "Downstairs From Her Glittering Chilean Salon, There Was a Torture Chamber," McClatchy, August 3, 2008; Ravelli, "Far Right Militants," 178–94.

46. General Carlos Prats González, *Una vida por la legalidad* (México: Fondo de Cultura Económica, 1975), entry of September 21, 1973, 92; Alejandro Carrió, *Los crímenes del Cóndor. El caso Prats y la trama de conspiraciones entre los servicios de inteligencia del Cono Sur* (Buenos Aires: Editorial Sudamericana, 2005).

47. Cristóbal Peña, "Contreras," 39–40; Karen De Young, David Montgomery, Missy Ryan, Ishaan Tharoor, and Jia Lynn Yang, "This Was Not an Accident. This Was a Bomb," *Washington Post*, September 20, 2016; Guardiola-Rivera, *Death Foretold*, 387–95.

48. Cristóbal Peña, "Contreras"; NSA Archive, "Chile and the United States," October 6, 1987, memo from George P. Shultz to President Ronald Reagan: https://nsarchive2.gwu.edu/NSAEBB/NSAEBB532-The-Letelier-Moffitt-Assassination-Papers/.

49. Sheila Cassidy, "Tortured in Chile," *Index on Censorship* 5, no. 2 (1976): 67–73; Israel Bórquez, in Constable and Valenzuela, *Enemies*, 131, 129–30 on the amnesty; Stern, *Battling*.

50. Ayress, in Archivio Chile, "El testimonio de Nieves Ayress Moreno."

51. Faisal Zagallai was shot by a former Green Beret working indirectly for the Libyans. Nadine Dahan, "How Khashoggi Case Brings Back Bad Memories for Libyan Exiles," *Middle East Eye*, October 15, 2018; Matar, *Return*; CIA, *Libya under Gaddafi: A Pattern of Aggression*, 1986 report: https://www.cia.gov/library/readingroom/docs/CIA-RDP91B00874R000200060007-8.pdf.

52. Kawczynski, *Gaddafi*, 41, 88–111; L.S., interview with author; Gaddafi, in Pargeter, *Libya*, 95; Vandewalle, *Libya*, 118–22.

53. Corri Zoli, Sahar Azar, and Shani Ross, *Patterns of Conduct. Libyan Regime Support for and Involvement in Acts of Terrorism*, UNHRC Commission of Inquiry into Human Rights Violations in Libya, 2011: https://papers.ssrn.com/sol3/papers.cfm?abstract_id=2004546.

54. State Department report on Gaddafi's terrorism, in *New York Times*, January 9, 1986; Seymour Hersh, "Target Qaddafi," *New York Times*, February 22, 1987; Abu Farsan, quoted in Human Rights Watch, *Delivered*, 21, 111–16; van Genugten, *Libya*, 105–25.

55. Patrick J. McDonnell, "Notorious Libyan Prison Now a Symbol of Kadafi Era," *Los Angeles Times*, October 1, 2011; Matar, *Return*, 222, 226–30; Evan Hill, "Libya Survivor Describes 1996 Prison Massacre," *Al Jazeera*, October 21, 2011; Gaddafi, in Pargeter, *Gaddafi*, 105.

56. Tolga's testimony in Rachel Goldberg, "Kidnapped, Escaped, and Survived to Tell the Tale: How Erdogan's Regime Tried to Make Us Disappear," *Haaretz*, December 11, 2018; Erdoğan, in Alexa Liautaud, "Turkey's Spy Agency Has Secretly Abducted 80 Turkish Citizens Living Abroad," *Vice News*, April, 10, 2018; Rick Gladstone, "Turkish Secret Agents Seized 80 People in 18 Countries, Official Says," *New York Times*, April 5, 2019; Vidino, "Erdogan's Long Arm."

57. Gurlev, Treisman, "Modern Dictators"; Simon, "Muzzling the Media"; Stockholm Center for Freedom, "Turkey Has Detained More than 282,000."

58. Putin, February 1, 2000, in Knight, *Orders*, 145, 132–37 on Anna Politkovskaya.

59. Knight, *Orders*, 257–78.

60. Armin Rosen, "Inside Russia's Prison System," *Atlantic*, October 18, 2012; Marc Bennetts, "Putin's Gulag," *Politico*, December 7, 2016; "Russia Admits Slave Labor Used at Pussy Riot Penal Colony," *Moscow Times*, December 25, 2018; Eli Lake, "What Is Vladimir Putin Afraid Of?" *Bloomberg*, April 30, 2019; Perseus Strategies, *The Kremlin's Political Prisoners*.

61. "Poison in the System," *Buzzfeed*, June 12, 2017; Knight, *Orders*, , 145–87 on Litvinenko, 278–81 on Vladimir Kara-Murza, 303 for Leonid Marynyuk quote, October 2016; Tom Peck, "Vladimir Kara-Murza, a Twice Poisoned Russian Dissident, Says 'If It Happens a Third Time, That'll Be It,'" *Independent*, March 18, 2017.

62. Trump and Bill O'Reilly, in Knight, *Orders*, 280; Trump had also aired this view in a 2015 interview with Joe Scarborough, on MSNBC's *Morning Joe*. See Philip Bump, "Trump Isn't Fazed by Vladimir Putin's Journalist-Murdering," *Washington Post*, December 18, 2015.

63. Ayal Feinberg, Regina Branton, and Valerie Martinez-Ebers, "Counties That Hosted a 2016 Trump Rally Saw a 226 Percent Increase in Hate Crimes," *Washington Post*, March 22, 2019; Jeremy Diamond, "Trump on Protester: 'I'd Like to Punch Him in the Face,'" CNN.com, February 23, 2016; FBI statistics on hate crimes at: https://www.fbi.gov/news/pressrel/press-releases/fbi-releases-2017–hate-crime-statistics.

64. Figures from US Immigration and Customs Enforcement, Fiscal Year 2018, ICE Enforcement and Removal Operations Report: https://www.ice.gov/doclib/about/offices/ero/pdf/eroFY2018Report.pdf; tweet by Hispanic Caucus, August 25, 2019: https://twitter.com/HispanicCaucus/status/1165690934820036609; Julie Hirschfeld David and Michael D. Shear, *Border Wars. Inside Trump's Assault on Immigration* (New York: Simon and Schuster, 2019).

65. John Fritze, "Trump Used Words Like 'Invasion' and 'Killer' to Discuss Immigration at Rallies 500 Times: USA Today Analysis," *USA Today*, August 9, 2019; Julia Carrie Wong, "Trump Referred to Immigrant 'Invasion' in 2000 FB Ads, Analysis Reveals," *New York Times*, August 5, 2019; Philip Rucker, "'How Do You Stop These People?': Trump's Anti-Immigrant Rhetoric Looms over El Paso Massacre," *Washington Post*, August 4, 2019.

66. Jason Zengerle, "How America Got to 'Zero Tolerance' on Immigration: The Inside Story," *New York Times Magazine*, July 16, 2019; Jennifer Jacobs and Justin Sink, "White House Looked into Ways to Block Migrant Children from Going to School," *Bloomberg*, August 17, 2019; Caitlin Dickerson, "'There Is a Stench': Soiled Clothes and No Baths for Migrant Children at a Texas Center," *New York Times*, June 21, 2019; Michael Edi-

son Hayden, "Miller Dismisses DACA in Emails, Mirroring Anti-Immigrant Extremists' Views," Hatewatch, Southern Poverty Law Center, January 14, 2020: https://www
.splcenter.org/hatewatch/2020/01/14/miller-dismisses-daca-emails-mirroring-anti
-immigrant-extremists-views.

67. Melissa Nann Burke, "Bethany: Migrant Children Still Being Separated from Parents at the Border," *Detroit News*, February 7, 2019; E. Kay Trimberger, "Separating Children of Immigrants and Unethical Adoptions," *Psychology Today*, July 18, 2018; Maria Sacchetti, "ACLU: U.S. Has Taken Nearly 1000 Child Migrants from Their Parents Since Judge Ordered Stop to Border Separations," *Washington Post*, July 30, 2019; AP, "The U.S. Has Held a Record 69,550 Children in Government Custody in 2019," NBCNews.com, November 12, 2019. The Dick and Betsy DeVos Foundation gave $343,000 in grants to Bethany, 2001–2015, and the Richard and Helen DeVos Foundation, run by DeVos's father-in-law, gave $750,000. Kathyrn Joyce, *The Child Catchers: Rescue, Trafficking, and the New Gospel of Adoption* (New York: Public Affairs, 2013); Jane Chambers, "Chile's Stolen Children," BBC, September 26, 2019.

68. Caitlin Dickerson and Zolan Kanno-Youngs, "Border Patrol Will Deploy Elite Tactical Agents to Sanctuary Cities," *New York Times*, February 14, 2020; Maya Srikrishnan, "Border Report: The Link between Border Enforcement and Corruption," *Voice of San Diego*, October 14, 2019; Ben Penn, "Human Trafficking Victims Blocked from Visas by Trump Wage Boss," *Bloomberg*, June 24, 2019; Franklin Foer, "How Trump Radicalized ICE," *Atlantic*, September 2018; Jenn Budd, interview with author.

69. James Sargent, Elinor Aspegren, Elizabeth Lawrence, and Olivia Sanchez, "Chilling First-Hand Reports of Migrant Detention Centers Highlight Smell of 'Urine, Feces,' Overcrowded Conditions," *USA Today*, July 17, 2019; Cynthia Pompa, "Kids Keep Dying in CBP Detention Centers, and DHS Won't Take Accountability," ACLU.org, June 24, 2019: https://www.aclu.org/blog/immigrants-rights/immigrants-rights-and
-detention/immigrant-kids-keep-dying-cbp-detention.

70. Sargent et al., "Chilling"; Jessica Bursztynsky, "The US Won't Provide Flu Vaccines to Migrant Families in Detention Camps," CNBC, August 20, 2019; Sam Levin, "Caged Alone 24 Hours a Day, Denied Medicine: Lawsuit Claims 'Torture' in Migrant Jails," *Guardian*, August 19, 2019; Mihir Zaveri, "El Paso Immigrant Center Is Dangerously Overcrowded, Authorities Warn," *New York Times*, May 31, 2019; Guardian Staff, "Texas Migrant Detention Facilities 'Dangerously Overcrowded'—US Government Report," *Guardian*, July 2, 2019; DHS Office of Inspector General report, released July 2, 2019, is at: https://www.oig.dhs.gov/sites/default/files/assets/2019–07/OIG-19-51–
Jul19.pdf.

71. Ken Klippenstein, "Saudi-Linked Lobby Group Pitched Film to Humanize Child Detention Camp," *The Young Turks*, September 6, 2019; Aaron Rupar, "Trump Turns Shooting Migrants into a Punchline at Florida Rally," *Vox*, May 9, 2019.

NINE: RESISTANCE

1. Georg Elser, in Chris Bowlby, "The Man Who Missed Killing Hitler by 13 Minutes," BBC, April 5, 2015; Roger Moorhouse, *Killing Hitler: The Plots, the Assassins, and the Dictator Who Cheated Death* (New York: Bantam Books, 2006), 49–78; Joachim Fest, *Plotting Hitler's Death. The Story of German Resistance* (New York: Metropolitan Books, 1996). Three other people died of their injuries, bringing the death toll to eight.

2. Mussolini, *My Autobiography* (New York: Charles Scribner's Sons, 1928), 237; Gárcia Márquez, *Clandestine*, 36–37; Will Stewart, "Vladimir Putin Assassination Attempt 'Foiled,'" *Telegraph*, March 15, 2008.

3. Maria Castro, in Wright and Oñate, *Flight*, 89.

4. Guillo, in Natalia Pinazola, "El humor que desnudó a Pinochet," BBC Mundo, July 22, 2008; Guillo, interview with author.

5. Maria Stephan and Erica Chenoweth, *Why Civil Resistance Works* (New York: Columbia University Press, 2012).

6. Mischa Gabowitsch, *Protest in Putin's Russia* (Cambridge, UK: Polity Press, 2017), 8–9; Marwan Kraidy, "Public Space, Street Art, and Communication in the Arab Uprisings," in *Bullets and Bulletins. Media and Politics in the Wake of the Arab Uprisings*, ed. Mohamed Zayani and Suzi Mirgani (New York: Oxford University Press, 2016), 116–21; Gárcia Márquez, *Clandestine*, 47–48.

7. Renato Gomez, in Constable and Valenzuela, *Enemies*, 165.

8. Duggan, *Fascist Voices*, 165; Moorhouse, *Killing Hitler*, 59; Gissi, "Reproduction"; Maria Bucur, "Policing the Womb 2.0," *Public Seminar*, February 28, 2019.

9. Dorfman, *Homeland Security*, 98–100; Leonardo Sciascia, *Le parrocchie del Regelpetra* (1956) (Milan: Adelphi, 1991), 43; Matar, *Return*, 151; Hill, "Libya Survivor Describes 1996 Prison Massacre"; Paul Preston, "The Crimes of Franco," in *Looking Back at the Spanish Civil War*, ed. Jim Jump (London: Lawrence and Wishart, 2010), 181–82.

10. Dietrich Von Hildebrand, with John Crosby, *My Battle against Hitler: Defiance in the Shadow of the Third Reich* (New York: Image Books, 2016), 173; Eduardo Saavedra, in White and Oñate, *Flight*, 97.

11. Natalia Ginzburg, "Chiarezza," *Italia libera*, December 31, 1944.

12. Quote from Carlo Rosselli from Alberto Tarchiani, "L'impresa di Lipari," in *No al fascismo*, ed. Ernesto Rossi (Turin: Einaudi, 1963), 119; Caroline Moorhead, *A Bold and Dangerous Family: The Remarkable Story of an Italian Mother, Her Two Sons, and Their Fight against Fascism* (New York: HarperCollins, 2017), 221–35, Francesco Cannata cable, 230; Isabelle Richet, *Women, Anti-Fascism, and Mussolini's Italy. The Life of Marion Cave Rosselli* (London: I.B. Tauris, 2018), 94–115; Stanislao Pugliese, *Carlo Rosselli. Socialist Heretic and Antifascist Exile* (Cambridge: MA: Harvard University Press, 1999).

13. Ebner, *Violence*, 74–102, 78 for May 1, 1930, propaganda campaign.

14. Stanislao Pugliese, ed., *Fascism and Anti-Fascism* (Manchester: Manchester University Press, 2001), 167; H. Stuart Hughes, *The United States and Italy* (Cambridge, MA: Harvard University Press, 1953), 102–5; Richet, *Women*, 87, 157; Pugliese, *Rosselli*, 84–120, 189–94.

15. George Orwell, *Homage to Catalonia* (New York: Harcourt Brace and World, 1952), 47; Bray, *Antifa*, 31–32.

16. Rosselli, *Oggi in Spagna, domani in italia* (Turin: Einaudi, 1967), 70–75; Mussolini, in Yvon de Begnac, *Palazzo Venezia: storia di un regime* (Rome: La Rocca, 1950), 613; Pugliese, *Rosselli*, 220.

17. Political Police reports, January 12, April 7, April 9, May 8, May 31, 1938, all in ACS, MI, DGPS, DPP, b.132, f.K11; Giulia Veronesi, "Chi siamo," *Campo di Marte*, September 1, 1938.

18. Ben-Ghiat, *Empire Cinema*, 243–66.

19. White Rose, quote from first letter, 1942, in Dumbach and Newborn, *White Rose*, 187; Christiane Moll, "Acts of Resistance: The White Rose in the Light of New Archival Evidence," in *Resistance against the Third Reich 1933–1990*, ed. Michael Geyer and John W. Boyer (Chicago: University of Chicago Press, 1994), 173–200.

20. First quote by Hans Scholl, second by Sophie Scholl, in Moll, "Resistance," 181.

21. White Rose, first and second letters, Dumbach and Newborn, *White Rose*, 189, 190.

22. Dumbach and Newborn, *White Rose*, 183; Hans Scholl, interrogated by the Gestapo, in

Moll, "Resistance," 192; George Axelsson, "Nazi Slur Stirred Students' Revolt," *New York Times*, April 18, 1943.

23. Moorhouse, *Killing Hitler*, 79–114; 248, 260–69.

24. Klemens von Klemperer, "'What Is the Law That Lies behind These Words?' Antigone's Question and the German Resistance against Hitler," and Alfred G. Frei, "'In the End I Just Said O.K.': Political and Moral Dimensions of Escape Aid at the Swiss Border," both in *Resistance*, ed. Geyer and Boyer, 141–50, 75–88; Freya von Moltke and Helmuth James von Moltke, *Last Letters: the Prison Correspondence, 1944–1945*, eds. Dorothea von Moltke and Johannes von Moltke (New York: New York Review of Books, 2019); Mark Roseman, *Lives Reclaimed: A Story of Rescue and Resistance in Nazi Germany* (New York: Metropolitan Books, 2019).

25. May 4, 1939, letter to the Württemberg officials, *Nazi Culture*, 252; Richard Steigmann-Gall, *The Holy Reich. Nazi Conceptions of Christianity, 1919–1945* (Cambridge, UK: Cambridge University Press, 2003); Claudia Koonz, "Ethical Dilemmas and Nazi Eugenics: Single-Issue Dissent in Religious Contexts," in *Resistance*, eds. Geyer and Boyer, 15–38.

26. "Text of the State Department Report on Libya under Qaddafi," *New York Times*, January 9, 1986.

27. Muñoz, *Dictator's Shadow*, 160–81.

28. Pinochet, in Muñoz, *Dictator's Shadow*, 173–74. One FPMR fighter sustained leg wounds and was treated at an underground clinic; the others were unharmed.

29. Muñoz, *Dictator's Shadow*, 177; CIA, "Chile: Pinochet under Pressure," 1984 report: https://www.cia.gov/library/readingroom/docs/DOC_0000451427.pdf.

30. ADST, Barnes interview; Arriagada, *Pinochet*, 40–45; Ensalaco, *Chile*, 125–55.

31. Arriagada, *Pinochet*, 49–55.

32. Rodolfo Seguel, in Constable and Valenzuela, *Enemies*, 242–43; Cooper, *Pinochet*, 71; CIA, "Chile: Pinochet under Pressure," 1–2.

33. Hunees, *Pinochet Regime*, 376–80; Constable and Valenzuela, *Enemies*, 122–23.

34. Constable and Valenzuela, *Enemies*, 260–68; Stern, *Battling*.

35. Fernando Balcells, in Robert Neustadt, *Cada Día: La Creación de un arte social* (Santiago: Editorial Cuarto Propio, 2001), 73. CADA was composed of sociologist Balcells, writer Diamela Eltit, poet Raúl Zurita, and visual artists Juan Castillo and Lotty Rosenfeld.

36. Matus, *Doña Lucia*, 207–10; Anderson; "The Dictator"; arrest figures in Arriagada, *Pinochet*, 63; Elliot Abrams, in Tom Gjelten, "Augusto Pinochet: Villain to Some, Hero to Others," NPR, December 10, 2006; CIA, "Chile: Pinochet under Pressure," 5.

37. Among seventy leadership positions in the Revolutionary Committees in 1993, the Warfalla tribe held twenty-four and the Gaddafi tribe forty-two: El-Kikhia, *Qaddafi*, 160–63; Pargeter, *Libya*, 158–63.

38. Ross, "What Have We Learned about the Resource Curse?"; Lisa Anderson, "Qadhdhafi and His Opposition," *Middle East Journal* 40, no. 2 (1986), 225–28, reports an average of three overthrow attempts a year and up to ten in the early 1980s; CIA, "Libya: Qadhafi's Domestic and International Position"; Herbert H. Denton, "Libyan Officers Try to Murder Qaddafi, U.S. Sources Say," *Washington Post*, April 12, 1985; L.S., interview with author; ADST, Josif interview.

39. CIA, "Libyan Opposition Groups: Much Sound, Little Fury," 1987 report, 2; Alfred Hackensberger, "The Desolate Wasteland of Gaddafi's Education System," Qantara.de, January 13, 2012.

40. CIA, "Libyan Opposition Groups," 5–12.

41. "USA/Chad: Target Gaddafi," *Africa Confidential* 30, no. 1 (1989): 1–2; Matar, *Return*, 111.
42. Patrick Tucker, "One of the World's Top Protest Apps Was Just Blocked in Russia," *Defense One*, April 12, 2017; Deibert, "Road to Unfreedom"; Charles Arthur, "Turkish Protestors Using Encryption Software to Evade Censors," *Guardian*, June 4, 2013; Ellen Ioanes, "Hong Kong Protesters Use 'Pokemon Go' and Tinder to Organize as Police Crack Down on Protests," *Business Insider*, August 7, 2019.
43. Enikolopov, Makarin, and Petrova, "Social Media"; Tufekci, *Twitter*; Clay Shirky, "The Political Power of Social Media," *Foreign Policy* (January-February 2011); Diana Matar, "Narratives and the Syrian Uprising," in *Bullets*, ed. Ziyani and Mirgani, 89–106; "Masked Men Raid Office of Russian Opposition Leader Sobol," *Radio Free Europe Liberty*, August 10, 2019, with video: https://www.rferl.org/a/russia-lyubov-sobol-opposition/30103137.html; Natalia Vasilyeva, "Russian Police Raid Opposition Activists' Homes in 43 Cities," AP, September 12, 2019; Will Vernon, BBC, September 13, 2019, retweet of Novosibirsk activist Sergei Boyko's photo of his drone: https://twitter.com/BBCWillVernon/status/1172456679675432960.
44. Christopher Mele, "Russia Bans a Not-So-Manly Image of Putin," *New York Times*, April 6, 2017; Constable and Valenzuela, *Enemies*, 178.
45. Ellen Ioanes and Reuters, "Hong Kong Protestors Are Forming a Human Chain 30 Years After the Baltic Way Democratic Protests," *Business Insider*, August 23, 2019.
46. "Russian Calendar Girls in Putin Birthday Battle," BBC News, October 8, 2010; Miriam Elder, "Russian Journalism Students Hit Back with Rival Anti-Putin Calendar," *Guardian*, October 7, 2010; Sperling, *Sex*.
47. Sarah Oates, *Revolution Stalled: The Political Limits of the Internet in the Post-Soviet Sphere* (Oxford: Oxford University Press, 2013); Alfred B. Evans, Jr., "Civil Society and Protest," in *Putin's Russia*, ed. Wegren, 103–25; Gabowitsch, *Protest*, 181. The Voina performance protested the new "tandem government" that made Putin's then-protégé Medvedev president and allowed Putin, as prime minister, to continue to control the government.
48. Kira Sokolova, in Gabowitsch, *Protest*, 46–51, also 2–10, 27; Enikolopov, Makarin, and Petrova, "Social Media."
49. Pussy Riot, in Gabowitsch, *Protest*, 164–73, also 16–17, 34–36; Eliot Bornstein, *Pussy Riot: Speaking Punk to Power* (London: Bloomsbury, 2020).
50. Yegor Zhukov, in Evan Gershkovich, "Trying to Maintain Momentum as Election Approaches, Moscow Protests Again," *Moscow Times*, August 31, 2019; Marc Bennetts, "Russia Passes Law to Jail People for 15 Days for 'Disrespecting Government,'" *Guardian*, March 6, 2019; Lake, "What Is Vladimir Putin Afraid Of?"
51. Francesca Ebel, "Russian Protestors Aided by Digital Tools, Self-Organizing," AP, September 6, 2019; Gershkovich, "Trying to Maintain Momentum"; Lucian Kim, "'The Government Is Very Afraid': Meet Moscow's New Opposition Leader, Lyubov Sobol," NPR, August 21, 2019.
52. Sabina Guzzanti, in Boria, "Silenced Humor," 103. The talk show host and satirist Daniele Luttazzi had his RAI television show *Satyricon* canceled in 2001.
53. Ginsborg, *Berlusconi*, 163–66; Dallara, "Powerful Resistance."
54. Paolo Ceri, "Challenging from the Grass Roots: The Girotondi and the No Global Movement," in *Resisting*, ed. Albertazzi et al., 83–93; Ginsborg, *Berlusconi*, 169–74.
55. Cristian Vaccari, "Web Challenges to Berlusconi," in *Resisting*, ed. Albertazzi et al., 140–43. Beppe Grillo, "L'etat c'est moi!" August 29, 2005 blog post: https://web.archive.org/web/20050830182506/http://www.beppegrillo.it/.

56. Orsina, *Berlusconism*, 123–33; Nanni Moretti, in Ceri, "Challenging," 92, James Newell, "Italy during the Berlusconi Years," 19–31, and Brooks and Ross, "Splinters of Resistance," 231–40, all in *Resisting*, ed. Albertazzi et al.

57. "Una manifestazione nazionale per chiedere le dimissioni di Berlusconi," Facebook page and text of appeal here: https://www.facebook.com/pg/no.berlusconi.day/about/; Lorenzo Coretti and Daniele Pica, "The Rise and Fall of Collective Identity in Networked Movements: Communication Protocols, Facebook, and Anti-Berlusconi Protest," *Information, Communication and Society* 18, no. 8 (2015): 951–67.

58. Cinzia Padovani, "Berlusconi's Italy: The Media between Structure and Agency," *Modern Italy* 20, no. 1 (2015), 49. Another TG1 anchor, Elisa Anzaldo, resigned from TG1 in 2011. Nadia Urbinati, Michela Marzano, and Barbara Spinelli, "Contro il machismo di Berlusconi," *La Repubblica*, October 22, 2009.

59. Gloria Steinem, in Diana Bruk, "Here's the Full Transcript of Gloria Steinem's Historic Women's March Speech," Elle.com, January 21, 2017; Dana Fisher, *American Resistance: From the Women's March to the Blue Wave* (New York: Columbia University Press, 2019); Jan-Werner Müller, "Reviving Civil Disobedience," *Project Syndicate*, December 21, 2018; Marie Berry and Erica Chenoweth, "Who Made the Women's March?" and Doug McAdam, "Putting Donald Trump in Historical Perspective," in *The Resistance. The Dawn of the Anti-Trump Opposition Movement*, ed. David S. Meyer and Sidney Tarrow (New York: Oxford University Press, 2018), 75–89 and 27–53.

60. Teresa Shook of Hawaii created a Facebook page on November 9, 2016. Other pages quickly followed, including one by Bob Bland, a fashion designer who served on the march's organizing committee with Vanessa Wruble, Tamika D. Mallory, Carmen Perez, and Linda Sarsour; another 273 marches, involving over 2 million more people, were held in eighty foreign countries.

61. Colleen Shalby, "A record Number of Women Are Running for Office. This Election Cycle, They Didn't Wait for an Invite," *Los Angeles Times*, October 10, 2018; Fisher, *American Resistance*.

62. Chris Mooney, "Historians Say the March for Science Is 'Pretty Unprecedented,'" *Washington Post*, April 22, 2017; James Doubek, "Thousands Protest at Airports Nationwide against Trump's Immigration Order," NPR, January 29, 2017; Jillian Stampfer, "More Than 1,200 Comcast Employees Are Walking Off Their Jobs to Protest Trump Immigration Ban," *Geekwire*, February 2, 2017; Tierney McAfee, "'Not My Presidents Day': Thousands Protest President Trump in Rallies across U.S.," *TIME*, February 20, 2017; Michael C. Dorf and Michael S. Chu, "Lawyers as Activists: From the Airport to the Courtroom," in *Resistance*, ed. Meyer and Tarrow, 127–42.

63. Megan E. Brooker, "Indivisible: Invigorating and Redirecting the Grassroots," in *Resistance*, ed. Meyer and Tarrow, 162–86; Nadia Prupis, "Groups Nationwide Create Campaign of 'United Resistance' to Trump," *Common Dreams*, January 10, 2017. For United Resistance's current partners: http://www.unstoppabletogether.org.

64. Erica Chenoweth and Jeremy Pressman, "In July, the Trump-Era Wave of Protests Started Taking a Back Seat to Campaign Rallies," *Washington Post*, October 19, 2018; Maria J. Stephan, "An Inside-Outside Strategy for Defending the US Republic," *Open Democracy*, January 27, 2017; Meyer and Tarrow, "Introduction," in *Resistance*, ed. Meyer and Tarrow, 1–26; Molly Ball, "Trench Lawfare: Inside the Battles to Save Democracy from the Trump Administration," *TIME*, June 25, 2020; Greg Sargent, "A Blueprint for Resistance to Trump Has Emerged. Here's What It Looks Like," *Washington Post*, February 10, 2019.

65. Daniel Hemel and Eric Posner, "The Strongest Pushback against the President Came

from His Own Branch of Government," *New York Times*, April 23, 2019; Elaina Plott, "Ignoring Trump's Orders, Hoping He'll Forget," *Atlantic*, May 15, 2019; J. W. Verret, "The Mueller Report Was My Tipping Point," *Atlantic*, April 23, 2019; Maria J. Stephan, "Staying True to Yourself in the Age of Trump: A How-To Guide for Federal Employees," *Washington Post*, February 10, 2017; Anonymous, *A Warning* (New York: Twelve, 2019).

66. Black Lives Matter website, accessed June 26, 2020: https://blacklivesmatter.com/about; Jelani Cobb, "An American Spring of Reckoning," *New Yorker*, June 14, 2020.

67. Amanda Barroso and Rachel Minkin, "Recent Protest Attendees Are More Racially and Ethnically Diverse, Younger Than Americans Overall," FactTank, June 24, 2020, summarize the results of the Pew Research Survey, original link here: https://www.pewresearch.org/fact-tank/2020/06/24/recent-protest-attendees-are-more-racially-and-ethnically-diverse-younger-than-americans-overall/. Event and crowd statistics from Jeremy Pressman and Erica Chenoweth, Crowd Counting Consortium: https://sites.google.com/view/crowdcountingconsortium/home.

68. "Hischfield Davis and Shear, *Border Wars*, 329–37; Jeremy Scahill, "The Counterinsurgency Paradigm; How US Politics Have Become Paramilitarized," *Intercept*, November 25, 2018; Tanvi Misra, "Militarization of Local Police Isn't Making Anyone Safer," *CityLab*, August 30, 2018; Susie Cagle, "'Protestors as Terrorists': Growing Number of States Turn Anti-Pipeline Activism into a Crime," *Guardian*, July 8, 2019. The International Center for Not-for-Profit Law tracks the status of state bills against protest: http://www.icnl.org/usprotestlawtracker/.

69. Danielle Schulkin, "White Supremacist Infiltration of US Police Forces: Fact-Checking National Security Advisor O'Brien," *Just Security*, June 1, 2020; The Plain View Project description and database can be accessed here: https://www.plainviewproject.org/. Will Carless and Michael Corey, "To Protect and Slur," June 14, 2019, report, Center for Investigative Reporting: https://www.revealnews.org/article/inside-hate-groups-on-facebook-police-officers-trade-racist-memes-conspiracy-theories-and-islamophobia/.

70. Trump tweet of June 9, 2020: https://twitter.com/realDonaldTrump/status/1270333484528214018; Betsy Woodruff Swan, "Trump Says He's Naming Antifa a 'Terrorist Organization.' Can He Do That?" *Politico*, May 31, 2020; Department of Justice, "Attorney General William P. Barr's Statement on Riots and Domestic Terrorism," May 31, 2020: https://www.justice.gov/opa/pr/attorney-general-william-p-barrs-statement-riots-and-domestic-terrorism; Barr, "Memo for all Heads of Department Components and US Attorneys," June 26, 2020, obtained by *Huffington Post* justice reporter Ryan Reilly: https://twitter.com/ryanjreilly/status/1276641618574131200; Ruth Ben-Ghiat, "How Journalists Become Objects of Hate," CNN.com, June 11, 2020.

71. In 2019, Trump threatened NBC with a Federal Communications Commission investigation or other "retribution," leading Alec Baldwin, who plays Trump on the show, to worry for his family's safety. Ellen Cranley, "Trump Seemingly Threatens 'SNL' with Federal Investigation over Critical Sketch," *Business Insider*, March 17, 2019; Kate Lyons, "Alec Baldwin Fears for Family's Safety after Trump 'Retribution' Threats," *Guardian*, February 21, 2019; Rob Rogers, "I Was Fired for Making Fun of Trump," *New York Times*, June 15, 2018; "SVA Gets Politically Charged for 'Art As Witness,'" October 4, 2018: https://sva.edu/features/sva-gets-politically-charged-for-art-as-witnesrob.

72. Author interview with Robin Bell.

73. Ates Ilyas Bassoy (whose 2019 campaign manual *Radical Love* inspired the strategy), in Carlotta Gall, "How a Message of Unity and Mistakes by Erdogan Tipped the Istanbul Election," *New York Times*, June 26, 2019; Suleyman Celebri, Imamoğlu aide, in Ali

Kucukgocmen and Organ Coskun, "Losing Its Luster—How Erdogan's Party Campaign Put Off Istanbul Voters," Reuters, April 5, 2019.

74. Ekrem Imamoğlu, "How I Won the Race for Mayor of Istanbul—And How I'll Win Again," *Washington Post*, June 4, 2019; Kucukgocmen and Coskun, "Luster"; Gall, "Unity"; Melvyn Ingleby, "A Turkish Opposition Leader Is Fighting Erdogan with 'Radical Love,'" *Atlantic*, June 14, 2019.

75. Imamoğlu, "How I Won the Race"; Ingleby, "Opposition Leader"; Kucukgocmen and Coskun, "Luster"; Gall, "Unity."

76. Imamoğlu, "How I Won the Race"; Ingleby, "Opposition Leader."

TEN: ENDINGS

1. Gaddafi, in "Gaddafi Defiant as State Teeters," *Al Jazeera*, February 23, 2011.

2. Post, *Leaders*, 68; Constable and Valenzuela, *Enemies*, 319, on Pinochet's egg and tomato reception when he left the 1990 inauguration of Patricio Aylwin.

3. Trump, in Eliana Johnson and Daniel Lippman, "Trump's 'Truly Bizarre' Visit to Mt. Vernon," *Politico*, April 10, 2019; Taylor, *Code of Putinism*, 34–35; Stanislav Belkovsky, in "Putin's Revenge," PBS, *Frontline*, July 13, 2018, transcript: https://www.pbs.org/wgbh/frontline/film/putins-way/transcript/.

4. Barbara Geddes, Joseph Wright, and Erica Frantz, "Autocratic Breakdowns and Regime Transitions: A New Data Set," *Perspectives on Politics* 12, no. 2 (2014), 325; Klaas, *Despot's Accomplice*, 123–33; Mussolini, in Seldes, *Sawdust Caesar*, 367; Desai, Olofsgård, Yousef, "Authoritarian Bargains," 7; Henk E. Goemans, Kristian Skrede Gleditsch, and Giacomo Chiozza, "Introducing Archigos: A Dataset of Leaders," *Journal of Peace Research* 46, no. 269 (2009): 269–83; Frantz and Ezrow, *Politics of Dictatorship*, 2–3.

5. Wrong, *Footsteps*, 215, Kelly, *America's Tyrant*, 250–57; Abu Fida, caretaker of Rabat European Cemetery, in "20 Years Later, Mobutu's Body Still in Moroccan Burial Place," *Daily Nation*, September 7, 2017; Anderson and Van Atta, "Mobutu."

6. Fermi, *Mussolini*, 193; Geddes, Wright, Frantz, "Autocratic Breakdowns," 314.

7. Ciano, *Diario*, entries of August 11–12 and 25, 1939, 326–27, 334; Goeschels, *Mussolini and Hitler*, 154–89.

8. Braglia, *Donna Rachele*, 207; Lina Romani, letter, June 15, 1940, in *Caro Duce*, 145–46.

9. James J. Sadkovitch, "The Italo-Greek War in Context: Italian Priorities and Axis Diplomacy," *Journal of Contemporary History* 28, no. 3 (1993): 439–64; Mussolini, in Duggan, *Fascist Voices*, 340–41.

10. Duggan, *Fascist Voices*, 168, 230, 379–83; Maria Pia di Bella, "A Duce's Trajectory," in *The Death of the Father. An Anthropology of the End in Political Authority*, ed. John Borneman (New York: Berghahn, 2004), 45–46.

11. Friedrich-Karl von Plehwe, *The End of an Alliance. Rome's Defection from the Axis in 1943* (New York: Oxford University Press, 1971), 103; Giuseppe Bottai, *Diario, 1935–1944* (Milan: Rizzoli, 1982), entries of January 17 and 21, 1941, 246–47.

12. Duggan, *Fascist Voices*, 386–93; von Plehwe, *End of an Alliance*, 39–48; Goeschels, *Mussolini and Hitler*, 248–49.

13. Braglia, *Donna Rachele*, 240–48.

14. Emanuele Artom, *Diario di un partigiano ebreo: Gennaio 1940–febbraio 1944* (Turin: Bollati Boringhieri, 2008), entry of September 9, 1943, 55; Claudio Pavone, *A Civil War: A History of the Italian Resistance* (New York: Verso, 2013); Goeschels, *Mussolini and Hitler*, 254–90.

15. Simon Levis Sullam, *The Italian Executioners. The Genocide of the Jews of Italy* (Princeton, NJ: Princeton University Press, 2018), 50–58; Anna Saxon, interview with author;

Duggan, *Fascist Voices*, 305–18. The Risiera di San Sabbia was part of the German-annexed Adriatic Littoral zone. On the seizure of Jewish assets, Pavan, *Tra indifferenza e odio*; Valerio Antonelli, Raffaele D'Alessio, Roberto Rossi, and Warwick Funnell, "Accounting and the Banality of Evil: Expropriation of Jewish Property in Fascist Italy (1939–1945)," *Accounting, Auditing and Accountability Journal* 31, no. 8 (2018): 2165–91.

16. Wu Ming, "Partigiani migranti. La Resistenza internazionalista contro il fascismo italiano," January 15, 2019: https://www.wumingfoundation.com/giap/2019/01/partigiani -migranti/.

17. Ada Gobetti, *Diario partigiano* (Turin: Einaudi, 1972), 15; Nicolas Virtue, "'Ha detto male di Garibaldi,'" in *The Concept of Resistance in Italy*, ed. Maria Laura Mosco and Pietro Pirani (Lanham, MD: Rowman and Littlefield, 2017), 153–70; Elio Barontini, *Ilio Barontini. Fuoriscito, internazionalista e partigiano* (Rome: Edizioni Robin, 2013).

18. Mussolini, *Storia di un anno. Il tempo del bastone e della carota* (Milan: Mondadori, 1945), 145; Kalder, *Library*, 110–12; Tullio Cianetti, in Duggan, *Fascist Voices*, 236.

19. Sergio Luzzatto, *Il corpo del Duce: Un cadavere tra immaginazione, storia e memoria* (Turin: Einaudi, 1998); Bello, "Duce's Journey"; Margaret Schwartz, *Dead Matter: The Meaning of Iconic Corpses* (Minneapolis: University of Minnesota Press, 2015); Curzio Malaparte, *Mussolini. Il grande imbecille* (Milan: Luni Editrice, 1999), 90.

20. Rachele Mussolini, interview with Bruno D'Agostini, February 12–15, 1946, in Braglia, *Donna Rachele*, 275.

21. André Gide, July 7, 1940, in O'Connor, *Butcher*, 141–42; Josef Ranald, *How to Know People by Their Hands* (New York: Modern Age Books, 1938), 123.

22. Kershaw, *"Hitler Myth,"* 169–99, 202; Traverso, *Fire*, 112–18; 199; Irene Guenther, *Nazi Chic* (New York: Berg, 2004), 220–223, 229, 252.

23. General Walter Warlimont, in Laurence Rees, *Hitler's Charisma* (New York: Pantheon Press, 2012), 200; Kershaw, *"Hitler Myth,"* 182–87.

24. Kershaw, *"Hitler Myth,"* 200–25 (Schweinfurt and Stuttgart quotes, 200, 221); Post, *Leaders*, 52–53; General Franz Halder, in Rees, *Hitler's Charisma*, 265.

25. Cesarani, *Final Solution*, 746–59; Guenther, *Nazi Chic*, 261; Hitler, in Moorhouse, *Killing Hitler*, 285, on Speer, 291–92; Martin Kitchen, *Albert Speer, Hitler's Architect* (New Haven: Yale University Press, 2017), 265–67.

26. Guenther, *Nazi Chic*, 263; Longerich, *Goebbels*, 686–87; Anton Joachimsthaler, *Hitlers Ende: Legenden und Dokumente* (Munich: Verlag Harbig, 2003).

27. Christian Goeschels, *Suicide in Nazi Germany* (New York: Oxford University Press, 2009), 149–72; "Suicides: Nazis Go Down to Defeat in a Wave of Selbstmord," *Life Magazine*, May 14, 1945; Paula Hitler, in Haycock, *Tyrannical Minds*, 266.

28. Preston, "Franco and Hitler"; Sánchez, *Fear*, 23–24; Rosendorf, *Franco*; Salvador de Madariaga, *España. Ensayo de historia contemporanea* (Madrid: Espasa-Calpe, 1979), 511.

29. Nazario Lazano, in Sánchez, *Fear*, 33. The 1977 amnesty, which was part of the negotiated process of democratization, also removed the subject of civil war repression from public discourse.

30. Zoé de Kerangst, "Beyond Local Memories: Exhumations of Francoism's Victims as Counter-Discourse during the Spanish Transition to Democracy," in *The Twentieth Century in European Memory*, ed. Tea Sinbæk Andersen and Barbara Törnquist-Plewa (Leiden: Brill, 2017), 104–21; Alfredo González-Ruibal, *An Archeology of the Contemporary Era* (New York: Routledge, 2019).

31. Martin Diaz, in Nuño Dominguez, "Un sonajero une a una madre fusilada y su hijo 83 años despues," *El Pais*, June 23, 2019; Almudena Álvarez/Efe, "Martín recupera el sonajero que llevaba su madre cuando fue asesinada en la Guerra Civil hace 83 años," *El*

Periódico, June 22, 2019; González-Ruibal, *Archeology*. González-Ruibal was part of the team of archaeologists who exhumed Catarina Muñoz's remains.

32. Raphael Minder, "Franco's Remains Are Exhumed and Reburied after Bitter Battle," *New York Times*, October 24, 2019; Carlos E. Cué, "Los restos de Franco saldrán del Valle de los Caidos antes del 25 de octubre," *El Pais*, October 12, 2019.

33. Spooner, *Soldiers*, 151–52; Constable and Valenzuela, *Enemies*, 289–91, 296–300; ADST, Harry Barnes, Elizabeth Barnes, and George Jones (Deputy Chief of Mission, US embassy, Santiago), interviewed by Charles Stuart Kennedy, Jones in 1996 and the Barneses in 2001: https://adst.org/2016/06/chile-burn-victims-case-containment-vs-human-rights-pinochet/; ADST, Roe and Barnes, interviewed by Kennedy.

34. Constable and Valenzuela, *Enemies*, 300–5. The Vicariate of Solidarity recorded 1,780 arrests in January 1988 alone. Huneeus, *Pinochet*, 407–9; Stern, *Battling*, 358–60; 1987 CIA report: "Pinochet and the Military: An Intelligence Assessment": https://www.cia .gov/library/readingroom/docs/DOC_0000451568.pdf.

35. Constable and Valenzuela, *Enemies*, 300–10; Mark Palmer, *Breaking the Real Axis of Evil. How to Oust the World's Last Dictators by 2025* (Lanham, MD.: Rowman and Littlefield, 2005), 110–25; Huneeus, *Pinochet*, 409–10.

36. Stern, *Battling*, 360–70.

37. Stern, *Battling*, 354.

38. Pinochet also passed measures to prevent future purges of his civil service and folded his secret police into army intelligence to prevent prying into human rights violations.

39. Matus, "Ingrid Olderock,"145; Peña, "Contreras," 43–55; Muñoz, *Dictator's Shadow*, 274–79, 283 for conviction statistics; Elizabeth Liras, "Human Rights in Chile: The Long Road to Truth Justice and Reconciliation," in *After Pinochet: The Chilean Road to Democracy and the Market*, ed. Silvia Borzutsky and Lois Hecht Oppenheim (Gainesville: University Press of Florida, 2006), 3–25.

40. Pinochet, *Camino Recorrido*, vol. 3, part 2, 159, 204, 220.

41. Ingrid Wuerth, "Pinochet's Legacy Reassessed," *American Journal of International Law* 106, no. 73 (2012): 731–68; Mary E. Black, "Diagnosing Pinochet Syndrome," *British Medical Journal* 332, no. 7534 (2006): 185.

42. Sengupta, "Victims"; Liras, "Human Rights," 13.

43. Huneeus, *Pinochet*, 456–60; Leigh and Evans, "Revealed"; Farfán and Vega, *La Familia*, 109–46; Muñoz, *Dictator's Shadow*, 283–96.

44. Muñoz, *Dictator's Shadow*, 301; Cristóbal Edwards, "Pinochet's Long Goodbye," *TIME*, December 15, 2006; Pedro Lemebel, "Farewell, Meatbag: On the Death of Pinochet," NACLA.org, April 10, 2008, at: https://nacla.org/article/farewell-meatbag -death-pinochet; originally published as "Las exequias del fiambre," in *La Nación*, December 17, 2006.

45. Dorfman, *Homeland Security*, 102; Francesca Lessa, "Operation Condor on Trial: Justice for Transnational Human Rights Crimes in South America," *Journal of Latin American Studies* 51, no. 2 (2019): 413; Lorenzo Tondo, "Italian Court Jails 24 over South American Operation Condor," *Guardian*, July 8, 2019.

46. Ian Black, "Libya Power Struggle Results in Arrest of Journalists," BBC, November 8, 2010; van Genugten, *Libya*, 127–46; Vandewalle, *Libya*, 173–203; Carola Richter, "Libyan Broadcasting under al-Qadhafi: The Politics of Pseudo-Liberalization," in *National Broadcasting and State Policy in Arab Countries*, ed. Tourya Guaaybess (New York: Palgrave Macmillan, 2013), 150–65.

47. Eric Lichtblau, David Rohde, and James Risen, "Shady Dealings Helped Qaddafi Build Fortune and Regime," *New York Times*, March 24, 2011, write that industry

officials "declined to identify" which companies paid Gaddafi's reparations bill. David Rose, "The Lockerbie Deal," *Vanity Fair*, January 26, 2011; *New York Times* Wikileaks Archive, February 4, 2009, cable from Gene A. Cretz, ambassador to Libya: https://archive.nytimes.com/www.nytimes.com/interactive/2010/11/28/world/20101128–cables-viewer.html#report/libya-09TRIPOLI99.

48. David Wagner and Aram Roston, "Donald and the Dictator," *Buzzfeed*, June 7, 2016. Gaddafi's public relations firm Brown Lloyd James was the intermediary.

49. Gaddafi, in Pargeter, *Gaddafi*, 105; Mahmoud Cherif Bassiouni, *Libya from Repression to Revolution. A Record of Armed Conflict and International Law Violations, 2011–2013* (Leiden: Martin Ninjhus Publishers, 2013), 123–96; van Genugten, *Libya*, 148–63; Ali Abdullatif Ahmida, "Social Origins of Dictatorship and the Challenge for Democracy," *Journal of the Middle East and Africa* 3, no. 1 (2012): 70–81.

50. Anne Barnard, "Libya's War-Tested Women Hope to Keep New Power," *New York Times*, September 12, 2011.

51. Akram Al-Warfalli, in "Gaddafi's Son in Civil War Warning," *Al Jazeera*, February 21, 2011; Wolfgang Lacher, "Families, Tribes, and Cities in the Libyan Revolution," *Middle East Policy Council* 18, no. 4 (2011): 140–54.

52. Gaddafi, in Christine Amanpour, "'My People Love Me': Moammar Gaddafi Denies Demonstrations against Him Anywhere in Libya," ABCNews.com, February 28, 2011; Gaddafi, in Haycock, *Tyrannical Minds*, 155; Gaddafi, in Michael Tomasky, "Gaddafi's Speech," *Guardian*, March 17, 2011; Jerrold M. Post, "Qaddafi under Siege," *Foreign Policy*, March 15, 2011; "Gaddafi: 'Voy a entrar en Bengasi como Franco entró en Madrid,'" *La Razón*, March 18, 2011.

53. Amandla Thomas-Johnson and Simon Hooper, "'Sorted' by MI5: How UK Govt Sent British-Libyans to Fight Gaddafi," *Middle East Eye*, January 29, 2019; Hill, "Libya Survivor," Al Jazeera, October 21, 2011.

54. Nick Squires, "Libya: Colonel Gaddafi 'not brave enough to do a Hitler,'" *Daily Telegraph*, August 20, 2011; Bassiouni, *Libya*, 197–288.

55. Damien McElroy, "Colonel Gaddafi Died after Being Stabbed with Bayonet, Says Report," *Telegraph*, October 17, 2012; Peter Beaumont and Chris Stephen, "Gaddafi's Last Words as He Begged for Mercy: 'What Did I Do to You?'" *Guardian*, October 22, 2011; Anderson, "King of Kings"; Rania El Gamal, "Libya Ends Public Showing of Gaddafi's Body," Reuters, October 24, 2011.

56. Bassiouni, *Libya*, 529, 554, 630, 662, 741, 799; Soraya, in Cojean, *Harem*, 7; Sara Sidner and Amir Ahmed, "Psychologist: Proof of Hundreds of Rape Cases during Libya's War," CNN, May 23, 2011. Polygamy was legal under Gaddafi, but the husband needed approval of his first wife to take other wives. Now no female permission was needed. Sergiwa, who provided her investigation data to the International Criminal Court, was elected to Parliament in 2014. In 2019, she was kidnapped and has not been found. Samar Auassoud, in "Libyan Women"; Karlos Zurutuza, "Libyan Women Lose Hope in the Revolution," DW.com, December 12, 2018.

57. Matar, *Return*, 222.

58. "Berlusconi: 'sic transit Gloria mundi,'" *Corriere della sera*, October 20, 2011; van Genugten, *Libya*, 153–54.

59. Beppe Severgnini, "Il Cavaliere spiegato di posteri. Dieci motivi per 20 anni di 'regno,'" *Corriere della sera*, October 27, 2010; Urbinati, Marzano, Spinelli, "Contro il machismo"; Boni, *Il superleader*.

60. Orsina, *Berlusconismo*, 133; Berlusconi, in Filippo Ceccarelli, "'Io star e tycoon': Va in scena il falò delle vanità," *La Repubblica*, December 6, 2010.

61. Padovani, "Berlusconi's Italy," 50; Friedman, *My Way*, 158–59; Tom Kington, "George Clooney Called as Witness in Silvio Berlusconi Trial," *Guardian*, October 19, 2012.

62. Andrea Benvenuti, "Between Myth and Reality: The Euro Crisis and the Downfall of Silvio Berlusconi," *Journal of Modern Italian Studies* 22, no. 4 (2017), 512–29.

63. Benvenuti, "Myth and Reality"; Spogli, "Italy-Russia Relations"; Evans, Harding, and Hooper, "WikiLeaks Cables." For Berlusconi's view of these events, Friedman, *My Way*, 211–51.

64. BBC Staff, "The Many Trials of Silvio Berlusconi Explained," BBC, May 6, 2014; Rubini, "Le vicende giudiziarie." Forza Italia got 29.4 percent versus 29.8 percent for the center-left; Christopher Brennan, "Italy's Berlusconi Gives Putin Duvet Cover with Their Picture on It as Birthday Gift," *Daily News*, October 9, 2017.

65. Editorial Staff, "Emilio Fede, condannato a 4 anni e 7 mesi non va in carcere: 'Enorme sofferenza,'" *Milano Today*, October 12, 2019; Ed Vulliamy, "Berlusconi Ally Marcello Dell'Utri Caught in Lebanon after Fleeing Italy," *Guardian*, April 12, 2014; BBC, "The Many Trials."

66. Friedman, *My Way*, 259; Bill Emmott, "The Bunga Bunga Party Returns to Italy," *Project Syndicate*, January 4, 2018; Barbie Latza Nadeau, "Cracking Oral Sex Jokes, Power Pervert Berlusconi Mounts a Comeback While Italy Laughs at Weinstein Victims," *Daily Beast*, October 15, 2017.

67. Franco "Bifo" Berardi, Facebook post of November 15, 2011, in *Skizo-Mails* (Dijon: Les Presses du Reél, 2012), 96–97; Redazione ANSA, "Matteo Salvini, pulizie di masse," ANSA, February 19, 2017.

68. Ben Berkowitz and Everett Rosenfeld, "Donald Trump Forms Presidential Exploratory Committee," CNBC, March 18, 2015; Berlusconi, in Friedman, *My Way*, 272–73; Norris, "Measuring Populism Worldwide"; Manifesto Project: https://manifesto-project .wzb.eu/; Ben Walker, "How Do Trump's Republicans Compare to the Rest of the World's Political Parties?" *New Statesman*, June 6, 2020, with an interactive chart.

Conclusion

1. Ludovico Greco, in Duggan, *Fascist Voices*, 281.

2. Author interview with Guillo; Allert, *Hitler Salute*, 93–94; Ortega y Gasset, *Man and People*, 198; González-Ruibal, *Archeology*.

3. Ruth Ben-Ghiat, "Why Are So Many Fascist Monuments Still Standing?" *New Yorker*, October 5, 2017; Tom Philipps, "Pinochet Retreat Turns into Marijuana Plantation," *Guardian*, July 7, 2011.

4. Rosselli, in Richet, *Women*, 130. Rosselli's statement came during his testimony for Giovanni Bassanesi, who crashed on the Swiss side of the Italian-Swiss border after dropping anti-Fascist messages over Milan and stood trial in Lugano in 1930. Rosselli partly financed Bassanesi's flight.

5. Retired Chilean officer, in Spooner, *Soldiers*, 14; Hunees, *Pinochet*, 459; Bartov, *Hitler's Army*; Jaber et al., "Corruption"; El Issawi, "Libya Media," 33; Geddes, Wright, Franz, "Autocratic Breakdown," 321.

6. A study of 184 countries from 1960 to 2010 suggests that growth under democracies is "significant and sizeable": Daron Acemoglu, Suresh Naidu, Pascual Restrepo, and James A. Robinson, "Democracy Does Cause Growth," *Journal of Political Economy* 127, no. 1 (2019): 47.

7. Han, *Life in Debt*; Erik Meyersson, "Political Man on Horseback: Coups and Development," Stockholm Institute for Transition Economics, paper, April 5, 2016, at: https://www.hhs.se/en/research/institutes/site/publications/2015–political-man-on

-horseback/; Michael McFaul and Kathryn Stoner-Weiss, "The Myth of the Authoritarian Model: How Putin's Crackdown Holds Russia Back," *Foreign Affairs* 87, no. 1 (2008): 68–80, 82–84.

8. Edna Bonhomme, "The Disturbing Rise of 'Femonationalism,'" *N+1*, May 7, 2019; Michaela Köttig, Renate Bitzan, and Andrea Petö, eds., *Gender and Far Right Politics in Europe* (New York: Palgrave Macmillan, 2017).

9. Piero Gobetti, *La rivoluzione liberale. Saggio sulla politica della lotta in Italia* (Fano: Aras Edizioni, 2016); Piero Rachetto, "Fascismo," in *Poesie della Resistenza* (Turin: Voci Nuove, 1973), 13; Jon Blitzer, "A Scholar of Fascism Sees Similarities in Trump," *New Yorker*, November 4, 2016.

10. Fallaci, *Interview*, 12; Elsa Morante, "Pagine di diario, 1945," in *Paragone letteratura*, 39, no. 7, new series (1988): 3–16; Svetlana Alexievich, in Rachel Donadio, "The Laureate of Russian Misery," *New York Times*, May 21, 2016; Yalcin Akdogan, *Political Leadership and Erdogan* (Cambridge, UK: Cambridge Scholars Publishing, 2018), 40.

11. Malaparte, *Tecnica*, 240; Post, *Leaders*, 191–92.

12. Mussolini, in Ciano, *Diario*, entry of January 29, 1940, 391.

13. Guriev and Treisman, "Modern Dictators"; Marlies, "Authoritarianism"; New York Times Staff, "Fact-Checking Trump's 2020 State of the Union Address and the Democratic Response," *New York Times*, February 5, 2020; Norah O'Donnell, tweet of February 4, 2020: https://twitter.com/norahodonnell/status/1224897706415529986?lang=en;fa.

14. Karklins, *System*, 155–68. On the Ibrahim Prize for Achievement in African Leadership: https://mo.ibrahim.foundation/prize.

15. Martha Nussbaum, *Political Emotions. Why Love Matters for Justice* (Cambridge, MA: Harvard University Press, 2013), 2; Ruth Ben-Ghiat, "Liberals Are Reclaiming Patriotism from the Right," CNN.com, July 2, 2017; George Packer, "We Are Living in a Failed State," *Atlantic*, June 2020.

16. Kate Ackley, "Before Trump Meeting, Hungary Hired a Powerhouse K Street Firm," *Roll Call*, May 22, 2019; Clay Fuller, *Dismantling the Authoritarian-Corruption Nexus*, American Enterprise Institute Report, July 8, 2019; Elsa Peraldi, "Kleptocracy—A Global Phenomenon, with Local Consequences," *Global Integrity* blog post, June 13, 2019: https://www.globalintegrity.org/2019/06/13/kleptocracy/.

17. Adam Klasfeld, "Boom Times for Turkey's Lobbyists in Trump's Washington," *Courthouse News*, October 31, 2019; Peter Baker and Matthew Rosenberg, "Michael Flynn Was Paid to Represent Turkey's Interests during Trump Campaign," *New York Times*, March 10, 2017; Dan Spinelli, "How Jack Abramoff's Old Lobbying Firm Became Turkey's Biggest Defender," *Mother Jones*, November 7, 2019; Brogan, "Torturers' Lobby"; Ben Judah and Nate Sibley, "The West Is Open for Dirty Business," *Foreign Policy*, October 5, 2019.

18. Tweet by Clyde Haberman, March 21, 2020: https://twitter.com/ClydeHaberman/status/1241347252821602304.

19. Dylan Scott and Rani Molla, "How the US Stacks Up to Other Countries in Confirmed Coronavirus Cases," *Vox*, April 27, 2020; Dan Mangan, "Trump Dismissed Coronavirus Pandemic Worry in January—Now Claims He Long Warned about It," CNBC, March 17, 2020; Philip Rucker, Josh Dawsey, Yasmeen Abutaleb, and Lena H. Sun, "Trump Floats Another Bogus Coronavirus Cure—And His Administration Scrambles to Stop People from Injecting Disinfectants," *Washington Post*, April 24, 2020; McKay Coppins, "Trump's Dangerously Effective Coronavirus Propaganda," *Atlantic*, March 11, 2020.

20. Stephen Gandel and Graham Kates, "Phunware, a Data Firm for Trump Campaign, Got Millions in Coronavirus Small Business Help," CBSNews.com, April 23, 2020.

Companies run by Trump and GOP donors have benefited from $600 billion allocated for taxpayer-funded loans. Ashford Hospitality Trust, a large hotel chain run by Trump donor Monty Bennett, received $96.1 million of the funds meant for small businesses. Ilma Hasan, "Trump-Tied Companies Receive Millions in Small Business Aid," OpenSecrets.org, May 1, 2020; Trump, in Amber Phillips, "What You Need to Know from Tuesday's White House Coronavirus Briefing," *Washington Post*, April 8, 2020; Rep. Adam Schiff, in Michelle Goldberg, "Trump to Governors: I'd Like You to Do Us a Favor, Though," *New York Times*, March 30, 2020; Marcy Gordon and Mary Clare Jalonick, "Treasury Chief Refusing to Disclose Recipients of Aid," AP News, June 12, 2020.

21. Matt Zapotosky, "Trump Threatens Military Action to Quell Protests, and the Law Would Let Him Do It," *Washington Post*, June 1, 2020; Thomas Gibbons-Neff, Eric Schmitt, and Helene Cooper, "Aggressive Tactics by National Guard, Ordered to Appease Trump, Wounded the Military, Too," *New York Times*, June 10, 2020; Greg Miller, "CIA Veterans Who Monitored Crackdowns Abroad See Troubling Parallels in Trump's Handling of Protests," *Washington Post*, June 2, 2020.

22. President Trump's Rose Garden speech on protests, transcript, CNN.com, June 1, 2020; Philip Rucker and Ashley Parker, "Lafayette Square Clash, Still Reverberating, Becomes an Iconic Episode in Donald Trump's Presidency," *Washington Post*, June 13, 2020.

23. Sarah Pulliam Bailey, "Televangelist Pat Robertson Blasts Trump for His Protest Response," *Washington Post*, June 2, 2020; Jeffrey Goldberg, "James Mattis Denounces President Trump, Describes Him as a Threat to the Constitution," *Atlantic*, June 3, 2020; Mike Baker, Thomas Fuller, Sergio Olmos, "Federal Agents Push into Portland Streets, Stretching Limits of Their Authority," *New York Times*, July 25, 2020.

24. Marc Polymeropoulos, in Miller, "CIA Veterans Who Monitored Crackdowns"; Ambassador Robert Ford and Ambassador Dennis Ross, in Tony Badran, "Bringing the Middle East Back Home," *Tablet*, June 7, 2020, original Tweets here: https://twitter.com/fordrs58/status/1267521267294494724 and https://twitter.com/AmbDennisRoss/status/1267608046261481477; Franklin Foer, "The Trump Regime Is Beginning to Topple," *Atlantic*, June 6, 2020.

25. Helt and Spanberger in Miller, "CIA Veterans"; Spanberger Tweet here: https://twitter.com/RepSpanberger/status/1267649988831690756.

26. Jessie Yeung, Steve George, and Emma Reynolds, "June 8 Coronavirus News," CNN, June 9, 2020; Rakesh Kochhar, "Unemployment Rose Higher in Three Months of COVID-19 Than It Did in Two Years of the Great Recession," Facttank, Pew Research Center, June 11, 2020; Jennifer Agiesta, "CNN Poll: Trump Losing Ground to Biden Amid Chaotic Week," CNN, June 8, 2020; White House, "Press Briefing by Press Secretary Kayleigh McEnany, June 8, 2020: https://www.whitehouse.gov/briefings-statements/press-briefing-press-secretary-kayleigh-mcenany-060820/.

27. Mussolini, in Mack Smith, *Mussolini*, 57; Alberto Lattuada, *Occhio quadrato* (1941), in *Alberto Lattuada fotografo*, ed. Piero Berengo Gardin (Florence: Alinari, 1982), 15.

28. Masha Gessen, "A Powerful Statement of Resistance from a College Student on Trial in Moscow," *New Yorker*, December 7, 2019.

29. Franklin Foer, "Cory Booker's Theory of Love," *Atlantic*, December 17, 2018; Arlie Russel Hochschild, *Strangers in Their Own Land: Anger and Mourning on the American Right* (New York: The New Press, 2016); Duggan, *Fascist Voices*, 383, on this syndrome among Fascist supporters; Bassoy, in Gall, "Message of Unity"; Peter Wehner, on Trump supporters: "To indict him would be to indict themselves." Interviewed by Brian Stelter on "Reliable Sources," CNN, October 13, 2019: https://www.cnn.com/videos/tv/2019/10/13/exp-former-bush-aide-trump-is-mentally-not-well.cnn.

EPILOGUE TO THE PAPERBACK EDITION

1. V-Dem Institute, "Autocratization Turns Viral. Democracy Report 2021": https://www.v-dem.net/files/25/DR%202021.pdf; Joe Mulhall and Safya Khan-Ruf, eds., "State of Hate: Far-Right Extremism in Europe 2021": https://www.amadeu-antonio-stiftung.de/wp-content/uploads/2021/02/ESOH-LOCKED-FINAL.pdf; "India: Government Policies, Actions Target Minorities," Human Rights Watch Report, February 19, 2021; Lindsay Maizland, "China's Repression of Uyghurs in Xinjiang," Council on Foreign Relations, March 2, 2021; Shibani Mahtani, Timothy McLaughlin, and Theodora Yu, "With Mass Detentions, Every Prominent Hong Kong Activist Is Either in Jail or Exile," *Washington Post*, February 28, 2021.

2. Richard Javad Heydarian, in Hannah Beech, "Myanmar Coup Puts the Seal on Autocracy's Rise in Southeast Asia," *New York Times*, April 12, 2021.

3. Angeline Benoit, "France's Le Pen Gains Ground for 2022 Elections, Poll Shows," Bloomberg, April 11, 2021; Nando Pagnoncelli, "Il PD a un punto dalla Lega e Fratelli d'Italia supera i 5 stelle: Sondaggio," *Corriere della sera*, May 1, 2021; Frank Jansen, "Straftaten ohne Ende im Jahr der Pandemie," *Der Tagesspiegel*, May 4, 2021.

4. On "pandemic backsliding": V-Dem Institute, "Autocratization Turns Viral"; "Turkey: Covid-19 Pandemic Used to Strengthen Autocratic Rule," Human Rights Watch, January 13, 2021; Ana Vanessa Herrero, Anthony Faiola, and Mariana Zuñiga, "Coronavirus Explodes in Venezuela, Maduro's Government Blames 'Biological Weapon': The Country's Returning Refugees," *Washington Post*, July 19, 2020; Louis Fishman, "As Coronavirus Cases Spike in Turkey, So Does Anti-Semitism," *Haaretz*, March 19, 2020.

5. Quote from Akanksha Singh, "Modi has offered little more than hollow words amid India's horrifying Covid crisis," CNN, May 2, 2021; Trump, in Devan Cole and Tara Subramaniam, "Trump on Covid Death Toll: 'It Is What It Is,'" CNN.com, September 3, 2020; Tina Nguyen, "'God-Tier Genetics': A Stunned MAGA World Offers Blame, Adulation after Trump's Diagnosis," *Politico*, October 2, 2020; Tommy Beer, "November's Grim Covid-19 Totals: More Than 4.3 Million Infections and 37,000 Americans Killed," Forbes, December 1, 2020; Miranda Bryant, "US Shatters Daily Coronavirus Record with Nearly 90,000 Infections," *Guardian*, October 30, 2020.

6. Samuel J. Brannen, Christian S. Haig, and Katherine Schmidt, *The Age of Mass Protests: Understanding an Escalating Global Trend*, Center for Strategic and International Studies Report, March 2, 2020; Amanda Taub, "'Chile Woke Up': Dictatorship's Legacy of Inequality Triggers Mass Protests," *New York Times*, November 3, 2019; Larry Buchanan, Quoctrung Bui, and Jugal K. Patel, "Black Lives Matter May Be the Largest Movement in U.S. History," *New York Times*, July 3, 2020; Vladislav Davidzon, "Lukashenko Mistakes Protesters' Principles for Weakness," *Foreign Policy*, August 24, 2020.

7. Madeline Roache, "'His Fight Is in Russia': Why Navalny Flew Home Straight into Putin's Clutches," *TIME*, January 18, 2021; Terrell Jermaine Starr, "We Need To Have a Talk about Alexei Navalny," *Washington Post*, March 1, 2021.

8. Alexei Navalny, "Vladimir the Poisoner of Underpants," *New York Times*, February 3, 2021; "Putin's Palace. History of World's Largest Bribe," January 16, 2021: https://www.youtube.com/watch?v=ipAnwilMncI; Tom Balmforth, "Putin Approval Rating Holds Steady Despite Navalny Crackdown: Poll," Reuters, February 4, 2021; Christopher Paul and Miriam Matthews, *The Russian 'Firehose of Falsehood' Propaganda Model*, RAND report, April 14, 2016: https://www.rand.org/pubs/perspectives/PE198.html.

9. FBI Director Christopher A. Wray, quoted in Devlin Barrett and Matt Zapotosky, "FBI Director Says Domestic Terrorism Cases 'Metastasizing' throughout U.S., as Cases Soar," *Washington Post*, March 2, 2021; Robert O'Harrow Jr., Andrew Ba Tran, and Derek Hawkins, "The Rise of Domestic Extremism in America," *Washington Post*, April 12, 2021; Lois Beckett, "Americans Have Bought Record 17M Guns in Year of Unrest, Analysis Finds," *Guardian*, October 30, 2020.

10. General Mark Esper, quoted in Julian Borger, "Mark Esper Fired as Pentagon Chief," *Guardian*, November 9, 2020; General Mark Milley, quoted in James Walker, "Top General Says Military Doesn't Take an Oath to Any Individual amid Pentagon Shakeup," *Newsweek*, November 13, 2020; Ashton Carter, Dick Cheney, William Cohen, Mark Esper, Robert Gates, Chuck Nagel, James Mattis, Leon Panetta, William Perry, and Donald Rumsfeld, "All 10 Living Former Defense Secretaries: Involving the Military in Election Disputes Would Cross into Dangerous Territory," *Washington Post*, January 3, 2021; Justin Vallejo, "Michael Flynn Calls for Trump to Suspend the Constitution and Declare Martial Law to Re-Run Election," *Independent*, December 3, 2020.

11. Michael Warren, "Georgia's Secretary of State Remains under Enormous Political Pressure from His Fellow Republicans," CNN.com, January 4, 2021; Dan Glaun, "Threats Against Election Officials Piled Up as Trump Refused to Concede," Frontline, PBS. org, November 17, 2020.

12. Rosalind S. Helderman and Elise Viebeck, "'The Last Wall': How Dozens of Judges across the Political Spectrum Rejected Trump's Efforts to Overturn The Election," *Washington Post*, December 12, 2020; Amy Gardner and Paulina Firozi, "Here's the Full Transcript and Audio of the Call between Trump and Raffensperger," *Washington Post*, January 5, 2021; Trump tweet quoted in Dan Barry and Sheera Frenkel, "'Be There. Will Be Wild!': Trump All but Circled the Date," *New York Times*, January 6, 2021.

13. Eric Tucker and Mary Claire Jalonick, "FBI Chief Warns 'Domestic Terrorism' Growing in the US," AP, March 2, 2021.

14. Will Steakin et al., "Longtime Trump Advisors Connected to Groups behind Rally That Led to Capitol Attack," ABC News, January 15, 2021; Bannon, quoted in Adele M. Stan, "Insurrectionist in Chief: How Steve Bannon Led the Vanguard of the Capitol Riots," *New Republic*, March 10, 2021; Anna Massoglia, "Trump Political Operation Paid More Than 3.5 Million to Jan. 6 Organizers," Propublica.org, February 10, 2021; Devlin Barrett, Spencer S. Hsu, and Aaron C. David, "'Be Ready to Fight': FBI Probe of U.S. Capitol Riot Finds Evidence Detailing Coordination of Assault," *Washington Post*, January 30, 2021.

15. Rudy Giuliani quote from Reuters Staff, "'Let's Have Trial by Combat' over Election—Giuliani," Reuters, January 6, 2021; Trump quotes from Brian Naylor, "Read Trump's Jan. 6 Speech, A Key Part of Impeachment Trial," NPR.org, February 10, 2021.

16. Luke Broadwater, "Capitol Police Told to Hold Back on Riot Response on Jan. 6, Report Finds," *New York Times*, April 13, 2021; Eric Tucker and Mary Clare Jalonick, "General: Pentagon Hesitated on Sending Guard to Capitol Riot," AP News, March 3, 2021; James Poniewozik, "Impeachment Video Reveals a True American Horror Story," *New York Times*, February 10, 2021; Malcolm Nance, in Ruth Ben-Ghiat, "Lucid Interview: Malcolm Nance," April 14, 2021: https://lucid.substack.com/p/lucid-interview-malcolm-nance.

17. CBS Baltimore Staff, "'We Love You, You're Very Special.': Trump Tweets Message, Later Removed, To Rioters Storming the U.S. Capitol," CBS Baltimore, January 6, 2021.

18. Dan Barry, Mike McIntire, and Matthew Rosenberg, "'The President Wants Us Here': The Mob That Stormed the Capitol," *New York Times*, January 8, 2020; Christopher Mathias, "57 GOP State and Local Officials Were at the Capitol Insurrection," Huffpost, February 13, 2021; Olivia Rubin, "Number of Capitol Riot Arrests of Military, Law Enforcement and Government Personnel Rises to 52," ABC News, April 23, 2021; Robert A. Pape and Keven Ruby, "The Capitol Rioters Aren't Like Other Extremists," *Atlantic*, February 2, 2021.

19. Ben Leonard, "Ron Johnson Says He Didn't Feel Threatened Jan. 6. If BLM or Antifa Stormed Capitol, He 'Might Have.'" *Politico*, March 13, 2021; Colby Itkowitz, "Trump Falsely Claims Jan. 6 Rioters Were 'Hugging and Kissing' Police," *Washington Post*, March 26, 2021; Lee Moran, "Tucker Carlson Goes Full Revisionist on the U.S. Capitol Riot," Huffpost, April 7, 2021; Glenn Thrush, "More Than Half of Republicans Blame the Jan. 6 Capitol Attack on 'Left-Wing' Rioters, a New Poll Finds," *New York Times*, April 5, 2021.

20. Rebecca Morin, "Peter Meijer, Republican Who Voted for Impeachment, Says He's Buying Body Armor Due to Threats," *USA Today*, January 14, 2021; Karoun Demirjian, "Trump's Grip on GOP Looms as Support Falters for Independent Probe of Capitol Riot," *Washington Post*, April 18, 2021; Elizabeth Crisp, "Mike Pence Keeps Quiet as His Safety During Capitol Riot Becomes a Focal Point in Trump's Trial," *Newsweek*, February 12, 2021; Zachary Cohen, "US Capitol Police Says Threats against Members of Congress up 107% Compared to 2020," CNN.com, May 7, 2021.

21. Rioter quote from "Trump Impeachment: Rep. Raskin's Video Montage of Capitol Insurrection," February 9, 2021: https://www.youtube.com/watch?v=2KVUB4L1LyI.

22. Peter W. Stevenson, "How Biden's Definition of Bipartisanship Has Quickly Evolved," *Washington Post*, April 13, 2021; Anna Chernova, Zahra Ullah, and Rob Picheta, "Russia Reacts Angrily after Biden Calls Putin a 'Killer,'" CNN.com, March 18, 2021.

23. Joe Biden, "Remarks by President Biden in Press Conference," March 25, 2021: https://www.whitehouse.gov/briefing-room/speeches-remarks/2021/03/25/remarks-by-president-biden-in-press-conference/.

SELECTED BIBLIOGRAPHY

Interviews
Guillo Bastías, Santiago, November 9, 2018.
Robin Bell, New York, March 11, 2018.
Jenn Budd, telephone interview, August 4, 2019.
L.S., email interview, February–April 2019.
S., Santiago, November 8, 2018.
Anna Saxon, New York, June 17, 2016.

Archival Sources
Archivio Centrale dello Stato, Rome
Archivio Chile, Centro de Estudios Miguel Enríquez (digital)
Association for Diplomatic History and Training, Oral History Collections (digital)
CIA, Freedom of Information Act Electronic Reading Room (digital)
Istituto Luce, Archivio Cinematografico (digital)
National Security Agency Archive (digital)
New York Times Wikileaks Archive (digital)
The Nixon Tapes, www.nixontapes.org (digital)
Richard Nixon Presidential Library and Museum, Yorba Linda, CA
Ruth First Papers (digital)
United Nations Archives, New York

Journal Articles, Reports, and Theses
Acemoglu, Daron. "Countries Fail the Same Way Businesses Do, Gradually and Then Suddenly." *Foreign Affairs*, June 15, 2020.
Acemoglu, Daron, Suresh Naidu, Pascual Restrepo, and James A. Robinson. "Democracy Does Cause Growth." *Journal of Political Economy* 127, no. 1 (2019): 47–100.
Acemoglu, Daron, and Murat Ucer. "The Ups and Downs of Turkish Growth, 2002–2015:

Political Dynamics, the European Union and the Institutional Slide." Working Paper no. 21608. Cambridge, MA: National Bureau of Economic Research, October 2015.

Acemoglu, Daron, Thierry Verdier, and James A. Robinson. "Kleptocracy and Divide-and-Rule: A Model of Personal Rule." *Journal of the European Economic Association* 2, nos. 2–3 (2004): 162–92.

Ahmida, Ali Abdullatif. "Social Origins of Dictatorship and the Challenge for Democracy." *Journal of the Middle East and Africa* 3, no. 1 (2012): 70–81.

Andersen, Jørgen Juel, and Silje Aslaksen. "Oil and Political Survival." *Journal of Development Economics* 100, no. 1 (2013): 89–106.

Anderson, Lisa. "Qadhdhafi and His Opposition." *Middle East Journal* 40, no. 2 (1986): 225–37.

Antonelli, Valerio, Raffaele D'Alessio, Roberto Rossi, and Warwick Funnell. "Accounting and the Banality of Evil: Expropriation of Jewish Property in Fascist Italy (1939–1945)." *Accounting, Auditing and Accountability Journal* 31, no. 8 (2018): 2165–91.

Arendt, Hannah. "Social Science Techniques and the Study of Concentration Camps." *Jewish Social Studies* 12, no.1 (1950): 49–64.

Beckendorf, Ingo. "Russia: Putin Satire as 'Extremist Material' on Prohibition List," European Centre for Press and Media Freedom. November 5, 2017. https://www.ecpmf.eu/archive/news/legal/russia-putin-satire-as-extremist-material-on-prohibition-list.html.

Beiser, Elana. *Hundreds of Journalists Jailed Globally Becomes the New Normal.* Committee to Protect Journalists, December 13, 2018. https://cpj.org/reports/2018/12/journalists-jailed-imprisoned-turkey-china-egypt-saudi-arabia/.

Benvenuti, Andrea. "Between Myth and Reality: The Euro Crisis and the Downfall of Silvio Berlusconi." *Journal of Modern Italian Studies* 22, no. 4 (2017): 512–29.

Black, Mary E. "Diagnosing Pinochet Syndrome." *British Medical Journal* 332, no. 7534 (2006): 185.

Blackwell, Stephen. "Saving the King: Anglo-American Strategy and British Counter-Subversion Operations in Libya, 1953–59." *Middle Eastern Studies* 39, no. 1 (2003): 1–18.

Brogan, Pamela. *The Torturers' Lobby. How Human Rights-Abusing Nations Are Represented in Washington.* Washington, DC: The Center for Public Integrity, 1992. https://cloudfront-files-1.publicintegrity.org/legacy_projects/pdf_reports/THETORTURERSLOBBY.pdf.

Bucur, Maria. "Policing the Womb 2.0." *Public Seminar.* February 2019.

Canali, Mauro. "The Matteotti Murder and the Origins of Mussolini's Totalitarian Dictatorship." *Journal of Modern Italian Studies* 14, no. 2 (2009): 143–67.

Carbone, Maurizio. "Russia's Trojan Horse in Europe? Italy and the War in Georgia." *Italian Politics* 24 (2008): 135–51.

Casini, Gherardo. "Bonifica della cultura italiana." *L'Orto.* January 1938.

Cassidy, Sheila. "Tortured in Chile." *Index on Censorship* 5, no. 2 (1976): 67–73.

Cimino, Antonino. "Italiani espulsi dalla Libia." Tesi di laurea, Università di Palermo, 2010.

"Come coprire i vuoti." *Vita Universitaria.* October 5, 1938.

Cooley, Alexander, John Heathershaw, and J. C. Sharman. "Laundering Cash, Whitewashing Reputations." *Journal of Democracy* 29, no. 1 (2018): 39–53.

Coretti, Lorenzo, and Daniele Pica. "The Rise and Fall of Collective Identity in Networked Movements: Communication Protocols, Facebook, and Anti-Berlusconi Protest." *Information, Communication and Society* 18, no. 8 (2015): 951–67.

Corporate Europe Observatory. *Spin Doctors to the Autocrats: European PR Firms Whitewash Repressive Regimes.* January 20, 2015 report. https://corporateeurope.org/sites/default/files/20150120_spindoctors_mr.pdf.

Csaky, Zselyke. *Dropping the Democratic Façade*. Freedom House Nations in Transit 2020 report. https://freedomhouse.org/sites/default/files/2020 05/NIT_2020_FINAL _05062020.pdf.

Dallago, Francesca, and Michele Roccato. "Right-Wing Authoritarianism: Big Five and Perceived Threat to Safety." *European Journal of Personality* 24, no. 2 (2010): 106–22.

Dallara, Cristina. "Powerful Resistance against a Long-Running Personal Crusade: The Impact of Silvio Berlusconi on the Italian Judicial System." *Modern Italy* 20, no. 1 (2015): 59–76.

Deibert, Ronald. "The Road to Unfreedom: Three Painful Truths about Social Media." *Journal of Democracy* 30, no. 1 (2019): 25–39.

Desai, Raj M., Anders Olofsgård, and Tarik M. Yousef. "The Logic of Authoritarian Bargains: A Test of a Structural Model." Brookings Global Economy and Development Working Paper no. 3 (January 2007).

Devine, Jack. "What Really Happened in Chile." *Foreign Affairs* 93, no. 4 (2014): 26–35.

Dunlop, John G. "Aleksandr Dugin's Foundation of Geopolitics." *Demokratizatskiya* 23, no. 1 (2004): 41–58.

Durante, Ruben, Paolo Pinotti, and Andrea Tesei. "The Political Legacy of Entertainment TV." *American Economic Review* 109, no. 7 (2019): 2497–530.

El-Issawi, Fatima. *Libya Media Transition. Heading to the Unknown*. Polis Report, London School of Economics, 2013. http://eprints.lse.ac.uk/59906/1/El-Issawi_Libya-media-transition _2013_pub.pdf.

Enikolopov, Ruben, Maria Petrova, and Ekaterina Zhuravskaya. "Media and Political Persuasion: Evidence from Russia." *American Economic Review* 101, no. 7 (2011): 3253–85.

Erbaggio, Pierluigi. "Writing Mussolini: Il Duce's American Biographies on Paper and on Screen." PhD dissertation. University of Michigan, 2016.

Evans, Richard J. "Corruption and Plunder in the Third Reich." https://www.richardjevans .com/lectures/corruption-plunder-third-reich/.

Ezrow, Natasha. "Authoritarianism in the 21st Century." *Politics and Governance* 6, no. 2 (2018): 83–86.

Fedele, Santi. "Francesco Saverio Nitti dal lungo esilio al rientro in Italia." *Humanities* 1, no. 1 (2012): 1–18.

Fishman, Joel. "The Postwar Career of Nazi Ideologue Johann von Leers, aka Omar Amin, the 'First Ranking German' in Nasser's Egypt." *Jewish Political Studies Review* 26, nos. 3–4 (2014): 54–72.

Frantz, Erica. "Authoritarian Politics: Trends and Debates." *Politics and Governance* 6, no. 2 (2018): 87–89.

Frantz, Erica, and Andrea Kendall-Taylor, "A Dictator's Toolkit: Understanding How Co-optation Affects Repression in Dictatorships." *Journal of Peace Research* 51, no. 3 (2014): 332–46.

Frey, William H. *The US Will Become 'Minority White' in 2045, Census Projects*. Brookings Institute, March 14, 2018. https://www.brookings.edu/blog/the-avenue/2018/03/14/the -us-will-become-minority-white-in-2045-census-projects/.

Fuller, Clay. *Dismantling the Authoritarian-Corruption Nexus*. American Enterprise Institute Report. July 8, 2019. https://www.aei.org/research-products/report/dismantling -authoritarian-corruption-nexus.

Geddes, Barbara, Joseph Wright, and Erica Frantz. "Autocratic Breakdowns and Regime Transitions: A New Data Set." *Perspectives on Politics* 12, no. 2 (2014): 313–31.

Giomi, Elisa. "Da 'Drive in' alla 'Makeover Television'. Modelli femminili e di rapporto fra i sessi nella TV belusconiana (e non)." *Studi culturali* 9, no. 1 (2012): 3–28.

Glasius, Marlies. "What Authoritarianism Is . . . and Is Not: A Practice Perspective." *International Affairs* 94, no. 3 (May 2018): 513–33.

Goemans, Henk E., Kristian Skrede Gleditsch, and Giacomo Chiozza. "Introducing Archigos: A Dataset of Leaders." *Journal of Peace Research* 46, no. 2 (2004): 269–83.

Gunther, Richard, José Ramón Montero, and José Ignacio Wert. "Media and Politics in Spain: From Dictatorship to Democracy." Working Paper 176. Institut de Ciències Polítiques i Socials, 1999.

Guriev, Sergei, and Daniel Treisman. "How Modern Dictators Survive: An Informational Theory of the New Authoritarianism." NBER Working Paper 21136 (April 2015).

Hahl, Oliver, Minjae Kim, and Ezra W. Zuckerman Sivan. "The Authentic Appeal of the Lying Demagogue: Proclaiming the Deeper Truth about Political Illegitimacy." *American Sociological Review* 83, no. 1 (2018): 1–33.

Herr, Orna. "How Is Chinese Censorship Affecting Reporting of the Coronavirus?" *Index on Censorship*, February 5, 2020.

Human Rights Watch. *Delivered into Enemy Hands. U.S.-Led Rendition of Opponents to Gaddafi's Libya*. Human Rights Watch Report, 2012. https://www.hrw.org/sites/default/files/report_pdf/libya0912_web_0.pdf.

Jain, Varsha, Meetu Chawla, B. E. Ganesh, and Christopher Pich. "Exploring and Consolidating the Brand Personality Elements of the Political Leader." *Spanish Journal of Marketing* 22, no. 3 (2018): 295–318.

Jones, Benjamin F., and Benjamin A. Olken. "Do Leaders Matter? Leadership and Growth since World War II." *Quarterly Journal of Economics* 120, no. 3 (2005): 835–64.

Kavanagh, Jennifer, and Michael D. Rich. *Truth Decay: An Initial Exploration of the Diminishing Role of Facts and Analysis in American Public Life*. RAND Corporation Report, 2018. https://www.rand.org/pubs/research_reports/RR2314.html.

Lacher, Wolfgang. "Families, Tribes, and Cities in the Libyan Revolution." *Middle East Policy Council* 18, no. 4 (2011): 140–54.

Lambertson, F. W. "Hitler, the Orator: A Study in Mob Psychology." *Quarterly Journal of Speech* 28, no. 2 (1942): 123–31.

Lemebel, Pedro. "Farewell, Meatbag: On the Death of Pinochet." *NACLA.org*, April 10, 2008. https://nacla.org/article/farewell-meatbag-death-pinochet.

Lessa, Francesca. "Operation Condor on Trial: Justice for Transnational Human Rights Crimes in South America." *Journal of Latin American Studies* 51, no. 2 (2019): 409–39.

Malka, Ariel, Yphtach Lelkes, Bert N. Bakker, and Eliyahu Spivack. "Who Is Open to Authoritarian Governance within Western Democracies?" *Perspectives on Politics*, forthcoming.

Marchesi, Milena. "Reproducing Italians: Contested Biopolitics in the Age of 'Replacement Anxiety'." *Anthropology & Medicine* 19, no. 2 (2012): 171–88.

Mattei, Clara Elisabetta. "Austerity and Repressive Politics: Italian Economists in the Early Years of the Fascist Government." *The European Journal of the History of Economic Thought* 24, no. 5 (October 2017): 998–1026.

McFaul, Michael, and Kathryn Stoner-Weiss. "The Myth of the Authoritarian Model: How Putin's Crackdown Holds Russia Back." *Foreign Affairs* 87, no. 1 (2008): 68–80, 82–84.

Merjian, Ara. "Fascist Revolution, Futurist Spin: Renato Berilli's Continuous Profile of Mussolini and the Face of Fascist Time." *Oxford Art Journal* 42, no. 3 (2019): 307–33.

Meyersson, Erik. "Political Man on Horseback: Coups and Development." Stockholm: Institute for Transition Economics, April 5, 2016. https://www.hhs.se/en/research/institutes/site/publications/2015-political-man-on-horseback/.

Mondini, Sara, and Carlo Semenza. "Research Report: How Berlusconi Keeps His Face." *Cortex* 42, no. 3 (2006): 332–35.

Morante, Elsa. "Pagine di diario, 1945." *Paragone letteratura* 39, no. 7, new series (1988): 3–16.

Ndikumana, Léonce, and James Boyce. "Congo's Odious Debt: External Borrowing and Capital Flight in Zaire." *Development and Change* 29, no. 2 (1998): 195–217.

Norris, Pippa. "Measuring Populism Worldwide." Harvard Kennedy School Faculty Research Working Paper No. RWP20-002, February 2020. https://www.hks.harvard.edu/publications/measuring-populism-worldwide

Ogle, Vanessa. "'Funk Money': The End of Empires, the Expansion of Tax Havens, and Decolonization as an Economic and Financial Event." *Past and Present*. Forthcoming, 2020.

Olave, Angélica Thumala. "The Richness of Ordinary Life: Religious Justification among Chile's Business Elite." *Religion* 40, no. 1 (2010): 14–26.

Orrenius, Pia, and Madeline Zavodny. "Do Immigrants Threaten US Public Safety?" *Journal on Migration and Human Security* 7, no. 3 (2019): 52–61.

Padovani, Cinzia. "Berlusconi's Italy: The Media between Structure and Agency." *Modern Italy* 20, no. 1 (2015): 41–57.

Palacio, Manuel. "Early Spanish Television and the Paradoxes of a Dictator General." *Historical Journal of Film, Radio, and Television* 25, no. 4 (2005): 599–617.

Papini, Giovanni. "Maschilità." *Quaderni della Voce*, series III, no. 25 (1915).

Pasquino, Gianfranco. "The Five Faces of Silvio Berlusconi: The Knight of Anti-Politics." *Modern Italy* 12, no. 1 (2007): 39–54.

Perseus Strategies. *The Kremlin's Political Prisoners. Advancing a Political Agenda by Crushing Dissent*. Washington, DC: May 2019 Report. https://www.perseus-strategies.com/wp-content/uploads/2019/04/The-Kremlins-Political-Prisoners-May-2019.pdf.

Polyak, Gábor. "How Hungary Shrunk the Media," *Mérték Media Monitor*, February 14, 2019, at European Centre for Press and Media Freedom. https://www.ecpmf.eu/news/threats/how-hungary-shrunk-the-media.

Polyakova, Alina, and Chris Meserole. *Exporting Digital Authoritarianism: The Russian and Chinese Models*. Brookings Institute Policy Brief, Democracy and Disorder Series, 2019, https://www.brookings.edu/research/exporting-digital-authoritarianism/: 1–22.

Pomerantsev, Peter, and Michael Weiss. *The Menace of Unreality: How the Kremlin Weaponizes Information, Culture and Money*. The Interpreter Project Report, Institute of Modern Russia, 2014. https://imrussia.org/media/pdf/Research/Michael_Weiss_and_Peter_Pomerantsev__The_Menace_of_Unreality.pdf.

Preston, Paul. "Franco and Hitler: The Myth of Hendaye, 1940." *Contemporary European History* 1, no. 1 (1992): 1–16.

Preston, Paul. "General Franco as Military Leader." *Transactions of the Royal Historical Society* 4 (1994): 21–41.

Ragnedda, Massimo. "Censorship and Media Ownership in Italy in the Era of Berlusconi." *Global Media Journal: Mediterranean Edition* 9, no. 1 (2014), 13.

Ramos, Jorge. "This Is How Pinochet Tortured Me." *The Scholar and Feminist Online* 2, no. 1 (2003).

Ravelli, Galadriel. "Far-Right Militants and Sanctuaries in the Cold War: The Transnational Trajectories of Italian Neo-Fascism." PhD dissertation. University of Bath, 2017.

Robinson, Linda, Todd C. Helmus, Raphael S. Cohen, Alireza Nader, Andrew Radin, Madeline Magnuson, and Katya Migacheva. *Modern Political Warfare. Current Practices and Possible Responses*. RAND Corporation Report, 2018. https://www.rand.org/pubs/research_reports/RR1772.html.

Rodrigo, Javier. "Exploitation, Fascist Violence and Social Cleansing: A Study of Franco's Concentration Camps from a Comparative Perspective." *European Review of History* 19, no. 4 (2012): 553–73.

Ross, Michael. "What Have We Learned about the Resource Curse?" *Annual Review of Political Science* 18 (2015): 239–59.

Rupprecht, Tobias. "Formula Pinochet: Chilean Lessons for Russian Liberal Reformers during the Soviet Collapse, 1970–2000." *Journal of Contemporary History* 51, no. 1 (2016): 165–86.

Sadkovich, James J. "The Italo-Greek War in Context: Italian Priorities and Axis Diplomacy." *Journal of Contemporary History* 28, no. 3 (1993): 439–64.

Salvemini, Gaetano. "Mussolini's Battle of Wheat." *Political Science Quarterly* 46, no. 1 (1931): 25–40.

Saz, Ismael. "Fascism and Empire: Fascist Italy against Republican Spain." *Mediterranean Historical Review* 13, nos. 1–2 (1998): 116–34.

Selassie, Haile. *League of Nations Official Journal.* Special Supplement 151. Records of the Sixteenth Ordinary Session of the Assembly, Plenary Meeting, June 30, 1936: 22–25.

Shahbaz, Adrian. *Freedom on the Net 2018: The Rise of Digital Authoritarianism.* New York: Freedom House, 2018. https://freedomhouse.org/report/freedom-net/2018/rise-digital -authoritarianism.

Sharia, Jaber Emhemed Masaud, Bambang Supriyono, M. Mardiyono, Andy Fefta Wijaya, and Soesilo Zauhar. "Corruption in the Regime's Apparatus and State Institutions in Libya during Gaddafi's Rule." *International Refereed Journal of Engineering and Science* 3, no. 11 (2014): 1–3.

Simon, Joel. "Muzzling the Media: How the New Autocrats Threaten Press Freedom." *World Policy Journal* 23, no. 2 (2006): 51–61.

Smith, Benjamin. "Oil Wealth and Regime Survival in the Developing World, 1960–1999." *American Journal of Political Science* 48, no. 2 (2004): 232–46.

Spencer, Leighann, and Ali Yildiz. *The Erosion of Property Rights in Turkey.* Platform Peace & Justice, 2020. Accessed March 18, 2020. http://www.platformpj.org/wp-content/uploads/ EROSION-OF-PROPERTY-RIGHTS-IN-TURKEY-1.pdf.

Swan, Alessandra Antola. "The Iconic Body: Mussolini Unclothed." *Modern Italy* 21, no. 4 (2016): 361–81.

Tenpas, Kathryn Dunn, Elaine Kamarck, and Nicholas W. Zeppos. *Tracking Turnover in the Trump Administration.* Washington, DC: Brookings Institution Report, 2018.

Tol, Gonul. "Turkey's Bid for Religious Leadership." *Foreign Affairs*, January 10, 2019.

Travaglio, Marco. "Il caso Schifani cominicia ora." *Micromega* 4 (2008).

Vaccari, Christian. "The Features, Impact, and Legacy of Berlusconi's Campaigning Language and Style." *Modern Italy* 20, no. 1 (2015): 25–39.

Vannucci, Alberto. "The Controversial Legacy of 'Mani Pulite': A Critical Analysis of Italian Corruption and Anti-Corruption Policies." *Bulletin of Italian Politics* 1, no. 2 (2009): 233–64.

Veronesi, Giulia. "Chi siamo." *Campo di Marte*, September 1, 1938.

Viñas, Angel, and Carlos Collado Seidel. "Franco's Request to the Third Reich for Military Assistance." *Contemporary European History* 11, no. 2 (2002): 191–210.

Wiley, Stephen Bert. "Transnation: Chilean Television Infrastructure and Policy as National Space, 1969–1996." PhD dissertation. University of Illinois at Urbana-Champaign, 1999.

Wuerth, Ingrid. "Pinochet's Legacy Reassessed." *American Journal of International Law* 106, no. 73 (2012): 731–68.

Yeaw, Katrina. "Women, Resistance, and the Creation of New Gendered Frontiers in the Making of Modern Libya, 1890–1980." PhD dissertation. Georgetown University, 2017.

Zakaria, Fareed. "The Rise of Illiberal Democracy." *Foreign Affairs* 76, no. 6 (1997): 22–43.

Zoli, Corri, Sahar Azar, and Shani Ross. *Patterns of Conduct. Libyan Regime Support for and*

Involvement in Acts of Terrorism. UNHRC Commission of Inquiry into Human Rights Violations in Libya Report, 2011.

Books

Acosta, Jim. *Enemy of the People: A Dangerous Time to Tell the Truth in America.* New York: HarperCollins, 2019.

Addis, Elisabetta, Valeria E. Russo, and Lorenza Sebesta, eds. *Women Soldiers: Images and Realities.* Basingstoke, UK: Macmillan, 1994.

Adorno, Theodor, Else Frenkel-Brunswik, Daniel Levinson, and R. Nevitt Sanford. *The Authoritarian Personality.* New York: Harper and Row, 1950.

Agamben, Giorgio. *State of Exception.* Translated by Kevin Attell. Chicago: University of Chicago Press, 2005.

Ahmida, Ali. *Forgotten Voices. Power and Agency in Colonial and Postcolonial Libya.* New York: Routledge, 2005.

Ailara, Vito, and Massimo Caserta. *I relegati libici a Ustica dal 1911 al 1934.* Ustica: Centro Studi Isola di Ustica, 2012.

Akdogan, Yalcin. *Political Leadership and Erdoğan.* Cambridge, UK: Cambridge Scholars Publishing, 2018.

Albanese, Giulia. *La Marcia su Roma.* Rome: Laterza, 2006.

Albanese, Matteo, and Pablo Del Hierro. *Transnational Fascism in the Twentieth Century: Spain, Italy and the Global Neofascist Network.* London: Bloomsbury Academic, 2016.

Alberta, Tim. *American Carnage.* New York: HarperCollins, 2019.

Albertazzi, Daniele, Nina Rothenberg, Charlotte Ross, and Clodagh Brook, eds. *Resisting the Tide. Cultures of Opposition under Berlusconi.* New York: Continuum, 2011.

Aliano, David. *Mussolini's National Project in Argentina.* Madison, NJ: Farleigh Dickinson Press, 2012.

Allert, Tilman. *The Hitler Salute. On the Meaning of a Gesture.* New York: Picador, 2009.

Aly, Götz. *Hitler's Beneficiaries.* New York: Metropolitan Books, 2007.

Aly, Götz, Peter Chroust, and Christian Pross, eds. *Cleansing the Fatherland. Nazi Medicine and Racial Hygiene.* Baltimore: Johns Hopkins University Press, 1994.

Amadori, Alessandro. *Madre Silvio. Perché la psicologia profonda di Berlusconi è più femminile che maschile.* Milano: Mind Edizioni, 2011.

Amendola, Giorgio. *Un'isola.* Milan: Rizzoli, 1980.

Améry, Jean. *Beyond the Mind's Limits. Contemplations by a Survivor on Auschwitz and Its Realities.* New York: Schocken Books, 1986.

Amnesty International. *Report on Torture.* New York: Farrar, Straus and Giroux, 1975.

Andersen, Tea Sinbæk, and Barbara Törnquist-Plewa, eds. *The Twentieth Century in European Memory.* Leiden, Neth.: Brill, 2017.

Anderson, Lisa. *The State and Social Transformation in Tunisia and Libya, 1830–1980.* Princeton, NJ: Princeton University Press, 1986.

Anonymous. *A Warning.* New York: Twelve, 2019.

Apor, Balázs, Jan C. Behrends, Polly Jones, and E. A. Rees, eds. *The Leader Cult in Communist Dictatorships.* New York: Palgrave Macmillan, 2004.

Arendt, Hannah. *Eichmann in Jerusalem.* New York: Viking Press, 1964.

Arendt, Hannah. *On Violence.* New York: Harcourt Brace and World, 1969.

Arendt, Hannah. *Origins of Totalitarianism.* New York: Meridian Press, 1958.

Arriagada, Genaro. *Pinochet. The Politics of Power.* Boston: Unwin Hyman, 1988.

Arthurs, Joshua, Michael Ebner, and Kate Ferris, eds. *The Politics of Everyday Life in Fascist Italy. Outside the State?* New York: Palgrave Macmillan, 2017.

Artom, Emanuele. *Diario di un partigiano ebreo: Gennaio 1940–febbraio 1944*. Turin: Bollati Boringhieri, 2008.

Aslund, Anders. *Russia's Crony Capitalism: The Path from Market Economy to Kleptocracy*. New Haven: Yale University Press, 2019.

Bainville, Jacques. *Les Dictateurs*. Paris: Denoël et Steele, 1935.

Baldinetti, Anna. *The Origins of the Libyan Nation. Colonial Legacy, Exile and the Emergence of the Nation-State*. New York: Routledge, 2010.

Barontini, Elio. *Ilio Barontini. Fuoriscito, internazionalista e partigiano*. Rome: Edizioni Robin, 2013.

Barrett, Wayne. *Trump: The Deals and the Downfall*. New York: HarperCollins, 1992.

Bartov, Omer. *Hitler's Army: Soldiers, Nazis, and War in the Third Reich*. New York: Oxford University Press, 1992.

Bassiouni, Mahmoud Cherif. *Libya: From Repression to Revolution. A Record of Armed Conflict and International Law Violations, 2011–2013*. Leiden, Neth.: Martin Ninjhus Publishers, 2013.

Bastianini, Giuseppe. *Uomini cose fatti. Memorie di un ambasciatore*. Milan: Vitagliano, 1959.

Bastías, Guillermo. *Pinochet Illustrado*. Santiago: Editorial Genus, 2008.

Bawden, John R. *The Pinochet Generation: The Chilean Military in the Twentieth Century*. Tuscaloosa: University of Alabama Press, 2016.

Beachy, Robert. *Gay Berlin: Birthplace of a Modern Identity*. New York: Knopf, 2014.

Becker, Ernest. *The Birth and Death of Meaning*. New York: Free Press, 1971.

Benadusi, Lorenzo. *The Enemy of the New Man: Homosexuality in Fascist Italy*. Translated by Suzanne Dingee and Jennifer Pudney. Madison: University of Wisconsin Press, 2012.

Benedetti, Amedeo. *Il linguaggio e la retorica della nuova politica italiana: Silvio Berlusconi e Forza Italia*. Genoa: Erga, 2004.

Ben-Ghiat, Ruth. *Fascist Modernities: Italy, 1922–1945*. Berkeley: University of California Press, 2001.

Ben-Ghiat, Ruth. *Italian Fascism's Empire Cinema*. Bloomington: Indiana University Press, 2015.

Ben-Ghiat, Ruth, and Mia Fuller, eds. *Italian Colonialism*. New York: Palgrave Macmillan, 2005.

Ben-Ghiat, Ruth, and Stephanie Malia Hom, eds. *Italian Mobilities*. New York: Routledge, 2015.

Benjamin, Walter. *Illuminations*. Edited by Hannah Arendt. Translated by Harry Zohn. New York: Schocken, 1968.

Benkler, Yochai, Robert Faris, and Hal Roberts. *Network Propaganda: Manipulation, Disinformation, and Radicalization in American Politics*. New York: Oxford University Press, 2018.

Beradt, Charlotte. *The Third Reich of Dreams*. Translated by Adriane Gottwald. Chicago: Quadrangle Books, 1966.

Berardi, Francesco Bifo. *Skizo-Mails*. Dijon: Les Presses du Reél, 2012.

Berlet, Chip, ed. *Trumping Democracy: From Reagan to the Alt-Right*. New York: Routledge, 2020.

Berlusconi, Silvio. *Una storia italiana*. Milan: Mondadori, 2001.

Berman, Sheri. *Democracy and Dictatorship in Europe from the Ancien Régime to the Present Day*. New York: Oxford University Press, 2019.

Bernstein, Andrea. *American Oligarchs. The Kushners, the Trumps, and the Marriage of Money and Power*. New York: W. W. Norton, 2020.

Bertellini, Giorgio. *Divo/Duce. Promoting Film Stardom and Political Leadership in 1920s America*. Berkeley: University of California Press, 2019.

Bianco, Mirella. *Gaddafi: Voice from the Desert*. London: Longman, 1975.

Birns, Lawrence. *The End of Chilean Democracy: An IDOC Dossier on the Coup and Its Aftermath*. New York: Seabury Press, 1974.

Bloch, Marc. *Royal Touch: Sacred Monarchy and Scrofula in England and France*. Toronto: McGill-Queen's University Press, 1973.

Boni, Federico. *Il Superleader. Fenomenologia mediatica di Silvio Berlusconi*. Rome: Meltemi, 2008.

Bonsaver, Guido. *Censorship and Literature in Fascist Italy*. Toronto: University of Toronto Press, 2007.

Borgese, G. A. *Goliath. The March of Fascism*. New York: Viking, 1937.

Borneman, John, ed. *The Death of the Father. An Anthropology of the End in Political Authority*. New York: Berghahn, 2004.

Bornstein, Eliot. *Pussy Riot: Speaking Punk to Power*. London: Bloomsbury, 2020.

Borzutzky, Silvia, and Lois Hecht Oppenheim, eds. *After Pinochet: The Chilean Road to Democracy and the Market*. Gainesville: University Press of Florida, 2006.

Bosworth, Richard. *Claretta: Mussolini's Last Lover*. New Haven: Yale University Press, 2017.

Bosworth, Richard. *Mussolini*. London: Bloomsbury, 2011.

Bottai, Giuseppe. *Diario, 1935–1944*. Milan: Rizzoli, 1982.

Bowen, Wayne H. *Spain during World War Two*. Columbia: University of Missouri Press, 2006.

Boyd, Douglas A. *Broadcasting in the Arab World*. Ames: University of Iowa Press, 1999.

Braglia, Elena Bianchini. *Donna Rachele*. Milan: Mursia, 2007.

Bray, Mark. *Antifa: The Anti-Fascist Handbook*. New York: Melville House, 2017.

Brown, Archie. *The Myth of the Strong Leader: Political Leadership in the Modern Age*. New York: Basic Books, 2014.

Bueno de Mesquita, Bruce, James D. Morrow, Randolph M. Siverson, and Alastair Smith. *The Logic of Political Survival*. Cambridge, MA.: MIT Press, 2003.

Bueno de Mesquita, Bruce, and Alastair Smith. *The Dictator's Handbook: Why Bad Behavior Is Almost Always Good Politics*. New York: Public Affairs, 2011.

Burgwyn, James. *The Legend of the Mutilated Victory. Italy, the Great War and the Paris Peace Conference, 1915–1919*. Westport, CT: Praeger Press, 1993.

Burleigh, Michael, and Wolfgang Wipperman. *The Racial State. Germany, 1933–1945*. Cambridge, UK: Cambridge University Press, 1991.

Burleigh, Nina. *Golden Handcuffs. The Secret History of Trump's Women*. New York: Gallery Books, 2018.

Bytwerk, Randall. *Bending Spines: The Propagandas of Nazi Germany and the German Democratic Republic*. East Lansing: Michigan State University Press, 2004.

Cagaptay, Soner. *Erdoğan's Empire: Turkey and the Politics of the Middle East*. London: I.B. Tauris, 2019.

Canali, Mauro. *La scoperta dell'Italia. Il fascismo raccontato dai corrispondenti americani*. Venice: Marsilio, 2017.

Canali, Mauro, and Clemente Volpini. *Mussolini e i ladri del regime. Gli arrichimenti illeciti del fascismo*. Milan: Mondadori, 2019.

Canterbury, Douglas C. *Neoextractivism and Capitalist Development*. New York: Routledge, 2018.

Caplan, Jane. *Government without Administration: State and Civil Service in Weimar and Nazi Germany*. Oxford: Clarendon Press, 1988.

Caro Duce. Lettere di donne italiane a Mussolini 1922–1943. Milan: Rizzoli, 1989.

Carrió, Alejandro. *Los crímenes del Cóndor. El caso Prats y la trama de conspiraciones entre los servicios de inteligencia del Cono Sur*. Buenos Aires: Editorial Sudamericana, 2005.

Casanova, Julian. *A Short History of the Spanish Civil War.* London: I.B. Tauris, 2013.

Casey, Steven, and Jonathan Wright, eds. *Mental Maps in the Era of Two World Wars.* New York: Palgrave Macmillan, 2008.

Césaire, Aimé. *Discourse on Colonialism.* New York: Monthly Review Press, 2000.

Cesarani, David. *Final Solution. The Fate of the Jews, 1933–1949.* New York: St. Martin's Press, 2016.

Cheeseman, Nicholas, and Brian Klaas. *How to Rig an Election.* New Haven: Yale University Press, 2019.

Ciano, Galeazzo. *Diario 1937–43.* Milan: Rizzoli, 1990.

Cojean, Annick. *Gaddafi's Harem.* New York: Grove Press, 2013.

Constable, Pamela, and Arturo Valenzuela. *A Nation of Enemies. Chile under Pinochet.* New York: W. W. Norton, 1993.

Cooper, Marc. *Pinochet and Me. A Chilean Anti-Memoir.* New York: Verso, 2000.

Corbin, Alain, Jean-Jacques Courtine, and Georges Vigarello, eds. *A History of Virility.* New York: Columbia University Press, 2016.

Darnton, Robert. *Censors at Work. How States Shaped Literature.* New York: W. W. Norton, 2014.

David, Julie Hirschfeld, and Michael D. Shear. *Border Wars. Inside Trump's Assault on Immigration.* New York: Simon and Schuster, 2019.

Dawisha, Karen. *Putin's Kleptocracy: Who Owns Russia?* New York: Simon and Schuster, 2015.

De Begnac, Yvon. *Palazzo Venezia: Storia di un Regime.* Rome: La Rocca, 1950.

De Felice, Renzo. *Mussolini e Hitler. I Rapporti Segreti, 1922–1933.* Rome: Laterza, 2013.

De Felice, Renzo. *Mussolini il rivoluzionario, 1883–1920.* Turin: Einaudi, 1965.

De Grand, Alexander. *Fascist Italy and Nazi Germany. The "Fascist" Style of Rule.* New York: Routledge, 2004.

De Grazia, Victoria. *How Fascism Ruled Women.* Berkeley: University of California Press, 1992.

Del Boca, Angelo. *Gli italiani in Libia. Dal fascismo a Gheddafi.* Milan: Mondadori, 1994.

Del Boca, Angelo. *Mohamed Fekini and the Fight to Free Libya.* New York: Palgrave Macmillan, 2011.

Del Buono, Oreste, ed. *Eia, Eia, alalà: La stampa italiana sotto il fascismo.* Milan: Feltrinelli, 1971.

Delmer, Sefton. *Trail Sinister. An Autobiography, Volume One.* London: Secker and Warburg, 1961.

De Madariaga, Salvador. *España. Ensayo de Historia Contemporanea.* Madrid: Espasa-Calpe, 1979.

Dietrich, Otto. *The Hitler I Knew. Memoirs of the Third Reich's Press Chief.* New York: Skyhorse, 2014.

Diggins, John Patrick. *Mussolini and Fascism: The View from America* (1972). Princeton, NJ: Princeton University Press, 2015.

Di Giulio, Francesca, and Federico Cresti, eds. *Rovesci della fortuna. La minoranza italiana in Libia dalla seconda guerra mondiale all'espulsione 1940–1970.* Ariccia, Italy: Aracne, 2016.

Dikötter, Frank. *How to Be a Dictator. The Cult of Personality in the Twentieth Century.* London: Bloomsbury, 2019.

Diodato, Emidio, and Federico Niglia. *Berlusconi 'The Diplomat': Populism and Foreign Policy in Italy.* New York: Palgrave Macmillan, 2019.

Dorfman, Ariel. *Homeland Security Ate My Speech.* New York: OR Books, 2017.

Dubiel, Helmut, and Gabriel Motzkin, eds. *The Lesser Evil: Moral Approaches to Genocide Practices*. New York: Routledge, 2004.

Duggan, Christopher. *Fascism and the Mafia*. New Haven: Yale University Press, 1989.

Duggan, Christopher. *Fascist Voices. An Intimate History of Mussolini's Italy*. New York: Oxford University Press, 2013.

Dumbach, Annette, and Jud Newborn. *Sophie Scholl and the White Rose*. London: Oneworld Publications, 2018.

Dunn, Kevin. *Imagining the Congo. The International Relations of Identity*. New York: Palgrave Macmillan, 2003.

Eatwell, Roger, and Matthew Goodwin. *National Populism. The Revolt against Liberal Democracy*. New York: Penguin Random House, 2018.

Eberle, Henrik, ed. *Letters to Hitler*. Translated by Steven Rendall. Cambridge, UK: Polity Press, 2012.

Ebner, Michael R. *Ordinary Violence in Mussolini's Italy*. Cambridge, UK: Cambridge University Press, 2010.

El-Kikhia, Mansour O. *Libya's Qaddafi. The Politics of Contradiction*. Gainesville: University Press of Florida, 1997.

Ellul, Jacques. *Propaganda. The Formation of Men's Attitudes*. New York: Vintage Books, 1973.

Enciclopedia Treccani. Edited by Giovanni Treccani. Milan: Istituto Trecccani, 1932.

Enrich, David. *Dark Towers: Deutsche Bank, Donald Trump, and an Epic Trail of Destruction*. New York: Custom House, 2020.

Ensalaco, Mark. *Chile under Pinochet: Recovering the Truth*. Philadelphia: University of Pennsylvania Press, 1999.

Errázuriz, Luis Hernán, and Gonzalo Leiva Quijada. *El Golpe Estético. Dictadura Militar en Chile 1973–1989*. Santiago: Ocholibros, 2012.

Esposito, Roberto. *Bios: Biopolitcs and Philosophy*. Translated by Timothy Campbell. Minneapolis: University of Minnesota Press, 2008.

Etlin, Richard, ed. *Art, Culture, and Media under the Third Reich*. Chicago: University of Chicago Press, 2002.

Evans, Richard. *The Coming of the Third Reich*. New York: Penguin, 2003.

Falasca-Zamponi, Simonetta. *Fascist Spectacle*. Berkeley: University of California Press, 1997.

Fallaci, Oriana. *Interview with History*. Translated by John Shepley. Boston: Houghton Mifflin, 1976.

Farcau, Bruce W. *The Coup. Tactics in the Seizure of Power*. Westport, CT: Praeger, 1994.

Farfán, Claudia, and Fernando Vega. *La familia. Historia Privada de los Pinochet*. Santiago: Random House Mondadori, 2009.

Fellini, Federico. *Fellini on Fellini*. Translated by Isabel Quigley. New York: Delacorte Press, 1976.

Fermi, Laura. *Mussolini*. Chicago: University of Chicago Press, 1961.

Ferrario, Rachele. *Margherita Sarfatti: La regina dell'arte nell'Italia fascista*. Milan: Mondadori, 2015.

Fest, Joachim. *Hitler*. New York: Mariner Books, 2002.

Fest, Joachim. *Plotting Hitler's Death. The Story of German Resistance*. New York: Metropolitan Books, 1996.

Finchelstein, Federico. *A Brief History of Fascist Lies*. Berkeley: University of California Press, 2020.

Finchelstein, Federico. *From Fascism to Populism in History*. Berkeley: University of California Press, 2017.

Fisher, Dana. *American Resistance: From the Women's March to the Blue Wave.* New York: Columbia University Press, 2019.

Franco, Francisco. *Discursos y mensajes del Jefe del Estado 1955–1959.* Madrid: Dirección General de Información Publicaciones Españolas, 1960.

Frantz, Erica. *Authoritarianism: What Everyone Needs to Know.* New York: Oxford University Press, 2018.

Frantz, Erica, and Natasha Ezrow. *The Politics of Dictatorship. Institutions and Outcomes in Authoritarian Regimes.* Boulder, CO: Lynne Rienner, 2011.

Franzinelli, Mimmo. *Il Duce e le donne. Avventure e passioni extraconiugali di Mussolini.* Milan: Mondadori, 2013.

Franzinelli, Mimmo. *Squadristi. Protagonisti e techniche della violenza fascista, 1919–1922.* Milan: Mondadori, 2003.

Franzinelli, Mimmo. *Il tribunale del Duce. La giustizia fascista e le sue vittime (1927–1943).* Milan: Le Scie, 2017.

Friedman, Alan. *My Way. Berlusconi in His Own Words.* London: Biteback Publishing, 2015.

Fry, Michael. *Hitler's Wonderland.* London: John Murray, 1934.

Fuller, Mia. *Moderns Abroad. Architecture, Cities, and Italian Imperialism.* New York: Routledge, 2006.

Gabowitsch, Mischa. *Protest in Putin's Russia.* Cambridge, UK: Polity Press, 2017.

Gaddafi, Muammar. *Escape to Hell and Other Stories.* Toronto: Hushion House, 1998.

Gaddafi, Muammar. *My Vision. Conversations and Frank Exchanges of Views with Edmond Jouve.* Translated by Angela Parfitt. London: John Blake, 2005.

Galeotti, Mark. *We Need to Talk about Putin: How the West Gets Him Wrong.* London: Ebury Press, 2019.

Gandhi, Jennifer. *Political Institutions under Dictatorship.* Cambridge, UK: Cambridge University Press, 2008.

Geddes, Barbara. *How Dictatorships Work. Power, Personalization, and Collapse.* Cambridge, UK: Cambridge University Press, 2018.

Gellately, Robert, and Nathan Stoltzfus, eds. *Social Outsiders in Nazi Germany.* Princeton, NJ: Princeton University Press, 2018.

Gessen, Masha. *The Future Is History: How Totalitarianism Reclaimed Russia.* New York: Riverhead Books, 2017.

Gessen, Masha. *The Man without a Face: The Unlikely Rise of Vladimir Putin.* New York: Riverhead Books, 2012.

Geyer, Michael, and John W. Boyer, eds. *Resistance against the Third Reich: 1933–1990.* Chicago: University of Chicago Press, 1994.

Geyer, Michael, and Sheila Fitzpatrick, eds. *Beyond Totalitarianism: Stalinism and Nazism Compared.* Cambrdige, UK: Cambridge University Press, 2009.

Ginsborg, Paul. *Silvio Berlusconi. Television, Power, and Patrimony.* New York: Verso, 2004.

Ginsborg, Paul, and Enrica Asquer, eds. *Berlusconismo. Analisi di un fenomeno.* Rome: Laterza, 2011.

Giovannini, Paolo, and Marco Palla. *Il fascismo dalle mani sporche. Dittatura, corruzione, affarismo.* Rome: Laterza, 2019.

Gobetti, Ada. *Diario partigiano.* Turin: Einaudi, 1972.

Gobetti, Piero. *La rivoluzione liberale. Saggio sulla politica della lotta in Italia.* Fano, Italy: Aras Edizioni, 2016.

Goebbels, Joseph. *Die Tagebücher von Joseph Goebbels.* Vol. 1. *Sämtliche Fragmente: Aufzeichnungen 1923–1941.* Edited by Elke Fröhlich. Munich: K.G. Saur Verlag, 1998–2006.

Goeschels, Christian. *Mussolini and Hitler: The Forging of the Fascist Alliance*. New Haven: Yale University Press, 2018.

Goeschels, Christian. *Suicide in Nazi Germany*. New York: Oxford University Press, 2009.

González, Mónica. *La Conjura. Los mil y un dias del golpe*. Santiago: Ediciones B Chile, 2000.

González-Ruibal, Alfredo. *An Archeology of the Contemporary Era*. New York: Routledge, 2019.

Goretti, Gianfranco, and Tommaso Giartosio. *La Città e l'Isola: Omosessuali al confino nell'Italia fascista*. Rome: Donzelli, 2006.

Görtemaker, Heike B. *Eva Braun. Life with Hitler*. New York: Knopf, 2011.

Goscilo, Helena, ed. *Putin as Celebrity and Cultural Icon*. New York: Routledge, 2013.

Goscilo, Helena, and Vlad Strukov, eds. *Celebrity and Glamour in Contemporary Russia: Shocking Chic*. New York: Routledge, 2011.

Graham, Helen. *The Spanish Civil War. A Very Short Introduction*. New York: Oxford University Press, 2005.

Green, Jeffrey Edward. *Eyes of the People. Democracy in an Age of Spectatorship*. New York: Oxford University Press, 2010.

Gross, Jan. *Neighbors. The Destruction of the Jewish Community in Jedwabne, Poland*. Princeton, NJ: Princeton University Press, 2001.

Guaaybess, Tourya, ed. *National Broadcasting and State Policy in Arab Countries*. New York: Palgrave Macmillan, 2013.

Guardiola-Rivera, Oscar. *Story of a Death Foretold. The Coup against Salvador Allende, September 11, 1973*. London: Bloomsbury, 2013.

Guenther, Irene, *Nazi Chic*. New York: Berg, 2004.

Guerriero, Leila, ed. *Los Malos*. Santiago: Ediciones Diego Portales, 2015.

Gundle, Stephen, Christopher Duggan, and Giuliana Pieri, eds. *The Cult of the Duce: Mussolini and the Italians*. Manchester, UK: Manchester University Press, 2015.

Guzzanti, Paolo. *Mignottocrazia. La sera andavamo a ministre*. Rome: Aliberti, 2010.

Hall, Todd H. *Emotional Diplomacy*. Ithaca, NY: Cornell University Press, 2015.

Han, Clara. *Life in Debt. Times of Care and Violence in Neoliberal Chile*. Berkeley: University of California Press, 2012.

Haycock, Dean. *Tyrannical Minds. Psychological Profiling, Narcissism, and Dictatorship*. New York: Pegasus Books, 2019.

Herz, Gabriele. *The Women's Camp in Moringen. A Memoir of Imprisonment in Nazi Germany 1936–1937*. Edited by Jane Caplan. New York: Berghahn, 2006.

Hetherington, Marc J., and Jonathan D. Weiler. *Authoritarianism and Polarization in American Politics*. Cambridge, UK: Cambridge University Press, 2009.

Hett, Benjamin Carter. *Burning the Reichstag*. New York: Oxford University Press, 2014.

Heywood, Paul, ed. *The Routledge Handbook of Political Corruption*. New York: Routledge, 2015.

Higginbotham, Virginia. *Spanish Film under Franco*. Austin: University of Texas Press, 1988.

Hill, Fiona, and Clifford Gaddy. *Mr. Putin. Operative in the Kremlin*. Washington, DC: Brookings Institution Press, 2013.

Hitler, Adolf. *Mein Kampf*. Translated by Ralph Manheim. Boston: Houghton Mifflin, 1999.

Hochschild, Adam. *King Leopold's Ghost: A Story of Greed, Terror, and Heroism in Colonial Africa*. New York: Houghton Mifflin, 1999.

Hochschild, Arlie Russel. *Strangers in Their Own Land: Anger and Mourning on the American Right*. New York: The New Press, 2016.

Hockenos, Paul. *Free to Hate. The Rise of the Right in Post-Communist Europe*. New York: Routledge, 1993.

Holmboe, Knud. *Desert Encounter. An Adventurous Journey through Italian Africa.* Translated by Helga Holbek. London: George G. Harrap, 1936.

Hom, Stephanie Malia. *Empire's Mobius Strip. Historical Echoes in Italy's Crisis of Migration and Detention.* Ithaca, NY: Cornell University Press, 2019.

Hughes, H. Stuart. *The United States and Italy.* Cambridge, MA.: Harvard University Press, 1953.

Hull, Isabel. *Absolute Destruction: Military Culture and the Practices of War in Imperial Germany.* Ithaca, NY: Cornell University Press, 2006.

Huneeus, Carlos. *The Pinochet Regime.* Translated by Lake Sagaris. Boulder: Lynne Rienner, 2007.

Ibrahim, Vivian, and Margit Wunsch. *Political Leadership, Nations and Charisma.* New York: Routledge, 2012.

Ignazi, Piero. *Postfascisti? Dal Movimento sociale italiano ad Alleanza Nazionale.* Bologna: Il Mulino, 1994.

Isikoff, Michael, and David Corn. *Russian Roulette: The Inside Story of Putin's War on America and the Election of Donald Trump.* New York: Twelve, 2018.

Jansen, Jan C., and Jürgen Osterhammel. *Decolonization: A Short History.* Translated by Jeremiah Riemer. Princeton, NJ: Princeton University Press, 2017.

Jensen, Geoffrey. *Franco: Soldier, Commander, Dictator.* Dulles, VA: Potomac Books, 2005.

Joachimsthaler, Anton. *Hitlers Ende: Legenden und Dokumente.* Munich: Verlag Harbig, 2003.

Jones, Raymond. *Adwa: African Victory in an Age of Empire.* Cambridge, MA: Harvard University Press, 2011.

Joubert, Alain. *Le moustache d'Adolf Hitler, et autres essais.* Paris: Gallimard, 2016.

Joyce, Kathyrn. *The Child Catchers: Rescue, Trafficking, and the New Gospel of Adoption.* New York: Public Affairs, 2013.

Jump, Jim, ed. *Looking Back at the Spanish Civil War.* London: Lawrence and Wishart, 2010.

Kakutani, Michiko. *The Death of Truth. Notes on Falsehood in the Age of Trump.* New York: Penguin, 2018.

Kalder, Daniel. *The Infernal Library: On Dictators, the Books They Wrote, and Other Catastrophes of Literacy.* New York: Henry Holt, 2018.

Kallis, Aristotle. *Fascist Ideology: Territory and Expansionism in Italy and Germany, 1922–1945.* New York: Routledge, 2000.

Kaplan, Temma. *Taking Back the Streets. Women, Youth, and Direct Democracy.* Berkeley: University of California Press, 2004.

Karklins, Rasma. *The System Made Me Do It. Corruption in Post-Communist Societies.* New York: Routledge, 2005.

Karl-i-Bond, Jean Nguza. *Mobutu, ou l'incarnation du Mal Zaïrois.* London: Rex Collings, 1982.

Kawczynski, Daniel. *Seeking Gaddafi: Libya, the West and the Arab Spring.* London: Biteback Publishing, 2011.

Kelly, Sean. *America's Tyrant. The CIA and Mobutu of Zaire.* Washington, DC: American University Press, 1993.

Kendzior, Sarah. *Hiding in Plain Sight. The Invention of Donald Trump.* New York: Flatiron Books, 2020.

Kersevan, Alessandra. *I lager italiani. Pulizia etnica e campi di concentramento fascisti per civili jugoslavi 1941–1943.* Rome: Nutrimenti, 2008.

Kershaw, Ian. *The "Hitler Myth": Image and Reality in the Third Reich.* Oxford: Oxford University Press, 1987.

Kertzer, David. *The Pope and Mussolini: The Secret History of Pius XI and the Rise of Fascism in Europe*. New York: Random House, 2014.

Kissinger, Henry. *White House Years*. Boston: Little, Brown, 1979.

Kissinger, Henry. *Years of Upheaval*. Boston: Little, Brown, 1982.

Kitchen, Martin. *A World in Flames*. New York: Routledge, 1990.

Kitchen, Martin. *Albert Speer, Hitler's Architect*. New Haven: Yale University Press, 2017.

Klaas, Brian. *The Despot's Accomplice. How the West Is Aiding and Abetting the Decline of Democracy*. New York: Oxford University Press, 2016.

Klemperer, Viktor. *I Will Bear Witness. A Diary of the Nazi Years 1933–1941*. Translated by Martin Chalmers. New York: Knopf, 1999.

Knight, Amy. *Orders to Kill. The Putin Regime and Political Murder*. New York: Thomas Dunne, 2017.

Knipp, Kersten. *Die Kommune der Faschisten Gabriele D'Annunzio, die Republik von Fiume und die Extreme des 20. Jahrhundert*. Stuttgart: WBG Theiss, 2019.

Knopp, Guido. *Hitler's Women*. New York: Routledge, 2003.

Koonz, Claudia. *The Nazi Conscience*. Cambridge, MA: Belknap Press, 2003.

Korherr, Riccardo. *Regresso delle nascite: Morte dei popoli*. Rome: Unione Editoriale d'Italia, 1928.

Kornbluh, Peter. *The Pinochet File: A Declassified Dossier on Atrocity and Accountability*. New York: The New Press, 2003.

Köttig, Michaela, Renate Bitzan, and Andrea Petö, eds. *Gender and Far Right Politics in Europe*. New York: Palgrave Macmillan, 2017.

Kretsedemas, Philip, Jorge Capetillo-Ponce, and Glenn Jacobs, eds. *Migrants and Marginality*. London: Routledge, 2014.

Kubizek, August. *The Young Hitler I Knew*. Translated by E. V. Anderson. Boston: Houghton Mifflin, 1955.

Lanzmann, Claude. *Shoah. The Complete Text of the Acclaimed Holocaust Film*. New York: Da Capo Press, 1995.

Lattuada, Alberto. *Alberto Lattuada fotografo*. Edited by Piero Berengo Gardin. Florence: Alinari, 1982.

Leeson, Robert, ed. *Hayek: A Collaborative Biography: Part XIII: "Fascism" and Liberalism in the (Austrian) Classical Tradition*. Basingstoke, UK: Palgrave Macmillan, 2018.

Lendval, Paul. *Orbán: Hungary's Strongman*. New York: Oxford University Press, 2018.

Levi, Primo. *Survival in Auschwitz*. New York: Touchstone Books, 1996.

Levitsky, Steven, and Daniel Ziblatt. *How Democracies Die*. New York: Crown Books, 2018.

Linz, Juan J. *Totalitarian and Authoritarian Regimes*. Boulder: Lynne Rienner, 2000.

Livingston, Michael. *The Fascists and the Jews of Italy: Mussolini's Race Laws, 1938–1945*. Cambridge, UK: Cambridge University Press, 2014.

Longerich, Peter. *Goebbels: A Biography*. New York: Random House, 2015.

Lower, Wendy. *Hitler's Furies: German Women in the Nazi Killing Fields*. New York: Houghton Mifflin, 2013.

Ludwig, Emil. *Talks with Mussolini*. Translated by Eden and Cedar Paul. Boston: Little, Brown, 1933.

Lupo, Salvatore. *Il fascismo. La politica in un regime totalitario*. Rome: Donzelli, 2000.

Lusane, Clarence. *Hitler's Black Victims. The Historical Experiences of Afro-Germans, European Blacks, Africans, and African-Americans in the Nazi Era*. New York: Routledge, 2002.

Luzzato, Sergio. *Il corpo del Duce: Un cadavere tra immaginazione, storia e memoria*. Turin: Einaudi, 1998.

Machtan, Lothar. *The Hidden Hitler*. Translated by John Brownjohn. New York: Basic Books, 2001.

Mack Smith, Denis. *Mussolini*. New York: Alfred A. Knopf, 1982.

Magyar, Bálint. *The Post-Communist Mafia State*. Budapest: Central European University Press, 2015.

Malaparte, Curzio. *Mussolini. Il grande imbecille*. Milan: Luni Editrice, 1999.

Malaparte, Curzio. *Tecnica del colpo di Stato*. Florence: Vallecchi, 1994.

Mangan, James Anthony, ed. *Shaping the Superman. The Fascist Body as Political Icon*. London: Frank Cass, 1999.

Mann, Thomas. *Diaries 1918–1939*. New York: Harry N. Abrams, 1982.

Manne, Kate. *Down Girl: The Logic of Misogyny*. New York: Oxford University Press, 2018.

Márquez, Gabriel García. *Clandestine in Chile. The Adventures of Miguel Littín*. Translated by Asa Zatz. New York: Henry Holt, 1986.

Maschmann, Melita. *Account Rendered. A Dossier on My Former Self*. Translated by Geoffrey Strachan. New York: Abelard-Shuman, 1965.

Matar, Hisham. *The Return: Fathers, Sons and the Land in Between.* New York: Random House, 2016.

Matard-Bonnard, Marie-Anne. *L'Italia fascista e la persecuzione degli ebrei*. Bologna: Mulino, 2007.

Mattioli, Aram. *Experimentierfeld der Gewalt: der Abessinienkrieg und seine international Bedeutung, 1935–1941*. Zürich: Orell Füssli, 2005.

Mattioli, Aram. *"Viva Mussolini!" Die Aufwertung des Faschismus im Italien Berlusconis*. Paderborn, Germany: Ferdinand Schöningh, 2010.

Matus, Alejandra. *Doña Lucia. La biografía no autorizada*. Santiago: Ediciones B, 2013.

Mayorga, Patricia. *Il condor nero. L'internazionale fascista e i rapporti segreti con il regime di Pinochet*. Milan: Sperling and Kupfer, 2003.

Mazower, Mark. *Dark Continent: Europe's Twentieth Century*. New York: Vintage, 2009.

McLean, Nancy. *Democracy in Chains: The Deep History of the Radical Right's Stealth Plan for America*. New York: Viking, 2017.

McSherry, Patrice. *Predatory States: Operation Condor and Covert War in Latin America*. Lanham, MD: Rowman and Littlefield, 2005.

Megargee, Geoffrey, and Martin Dean, eds. *Encyclopedia of Camps and Ghettos, 1933–1945*. Washington, DC: United States Holocaust Memorial Museum, 2009.

Meyer, David S., and Sidney Tarrow, eds. *The Resistance. The Dawn of the Anti-Trump Opposition Movement*. New York: Oxford University Press, 2018.

Meyer, Thomas. *Media Democracy. How the Media Colonize Politics*. Cambridge, UK: Polity Press, 2002.

Migone, Gian Giacomo. *The United States and Italy. The Rise of American Finance in Europe*. Cambridge, UK: Cambridge University Press, 2015.

Millett, Kate. *The Politics of Cruelty. An Essay on the Literature of Political Imprisonment*. New York: W. W. Norton, 1994.

Moghaddam, Fathali M. *The Psychology of Dictatorship*. Washington, DC: American Psychological Association, 2013.

Moghaddam, Fathali M. *Threat to Democracy: The Appeal of Authoritarianism in an Age of Uncertainty*. Washington, DC: American Psychological Association, 2019.

Moorhead, Caroline. *A Bold and Dangerous Family: The Remarkable Story of an Italian Mother, Her Two Sons, and Their Fight against Fascism*. New York: HarperCollins, 2017.

Moorhouse, Roger. *Killing Hitler: The Plots, the Assassins, and the Dictator Who Cheated Death*. New York: Bantam Books, 2006.

Moradiellos, Enrique. *Franco: Anatomy of a Dictator.* London: I.B. Tauris, 2018.

Mosco, Maria Laura, and Pietro Pirani. *The Concept of Resistance in Italy.* Lanham, MD: Rowman and Littlefield, 2017.

Mosse, George. *Nazi Culture. A Documentary History.* New York: Schocken Books, 1966.

Mudde, Cas. *The Far Right Today.* Oxford: Polity Press, 2019.

Mudde, Cas. *Populism: A Very Short Introduction.* New York: Oxford University Press, 2017.

Müller, Jan-Werner. *What Is Populism?* Philadelphia: University of Pennsylvania Press, 2016.

Munizaga, Giselle, and Carlos Ochsenius. *El discurso publico de Pinochet.* Buenos Aires: Consejo Latinoamericano de Ciencias Sociales, 1983.

Munn, Michael. *Hitler and the Nazi Cult of Film and Fame.* New York: Skyhorse, 2013.

Muñoz, Heraldo. *The Dictator's Shadow: Life under Augusto Pinochet.* New York: Basic Books, 2008.

Mussolini, Benito. *Corrispondenza inedita.* Edited by Duilio Susmel. Milan: Edizioni del Borghese, 1972.

Mussolini, Benito. *My Autobiography.* New York: Charles Scribner's Sons, 1928.

Mussolini, Benito. *Opera Omnia.* Edited by Edoardo and Duilio Susmel. 44 vols. Florence: La Fenice, 1951–1980.

Mussolini, Benito. *Scritti e Discorsi.* Vol. VI. Milan: Ulrico Hoepli Editore, 1934.

Mussolini, Benito. *Storia di un anno. Il tempo del bastone e della carota.* Milan: Mondadori, 1945.

Mussolini, Romano. *Il Duce Mio Padre.* Milan: Rizzoli 2004.

Nazaryan, Alexander. *The Best People: Trump's Cabinet and the Siege on Washington.* New York: Hachette, 2019.

Neustadt, Robert. *Cada Día: La Creación de un arte social.* Santigao: Editorial Cuarto Propio, 2001.

Niewert, David. *Alt-America: The Rise of the Radical Right in the Age of Trump.* New York: Verso, 2017.

Nordlinger, Jay. *Children of Monsters: An Inquiry into the Sons and Daughters of Dictators.* New York: Encounter Books, 2017.

Norris, Pippa. *Cultural Backlash: Trump, Brexit, and Authoritarian Populism.* Cambridge, UK: Cambridge University Press, 2019.

Nussbaum, Martha. *Political Emotions. Why Love Matters for Justice.* Cambridge, MA: Harvard University Press, 2013.

O'Connor, Garry. *The Butcher of Poland: Hitler's Lawyer Hans Frank.* Stroud, UK: The History Press, 2013.

O'Shaughnessy, Nicholas. *Marketing the Third Reich: Persuasion, Packaging and Propaganda.* New York: Routledge, 2018.

O'Shaughnessy, Nicholas. *Selling Hitler. Propaganda and the Nazi Brand.* London: Hurst, 2016.

Oates, Sarah. *Revolution Stalled: The Political Limits of the Internet in the Post-Soviet Sphere.* New York: Oxford University Press, 2013.

Olla, Roberto. *Il Duce and His Women: Mussolini's Rise to Power.* Richmond: Alma Books, 2011.

Optiz, May, Katharina Oguntoye, and Dagmar Schulaz. *Showing Our Colors. Afro-German Women Speak Out.* Amherst: University of Massachusetts Press, 1992.

Orsina, Giovanni. *Berlusconism and Italy: A Historical Interpretation.* New York: Palgrave Macmillan, 2014.

Ortega y Gasset, José. *Man and People.* Translated by Willard R. Trask. New York: W. W. Norton, 1957.

Orwell, George. *Homage to Catalonia.* New York: Harcourt Brace and World, 1952.

Ottaviano, Giancarlo, ed. *Le veline di Mussolini.* Viterbo, Italy: Stampa Alternativa, 2008.

Palmer, Mark. *Breaking the Real Axis of Evil: How to Oust the World's Last Dictators by 2025.* Lanham, MD: Rowman and Littlefield, 2005.

Pargeter, Alison. *Libya: The Rise and Fall of Gaddafi.* New Haven: Yale University Press, 2012.

Pavan, Ilaria. *Tra indifferenza e odio. Le conseguenze economiche delle leggi razziali in italia, 1938–1970.* Milan: Mondadori, 2019.

Pavone, Claudio. *A Civil War: A History of the Italian Resistance.* New York: Verso, 2013.

Paxton, Robert. *The Anatomy of Fascism.* New York: Vintage, 2005.

Payne, Stanley G., and Jesus Palacios. *Franco: A Personal and Political Biography.* Madison: University of Wisconsin Press, 2018.

Pedersen, Susan. *The Guardians. World War One and the Crisis of Empire.* New York: Oxford University Press, 2017.

Peet, Basharat. *A Question of Order. India, Turkey, and the Return of Strongmen.* New York: Columbia Global Reports, 2017.

Pellizzetti, Pierfranco. *Fenomenologia di Berlusconi.* Rome: Manifestolibri, 2009.

Peña, Juan Cristóbal. *La secreta vida literaria de Augusto Pinochet.* Santiago: Random House Mondadori, 2013.

Perry, John. *Torture: Religious Ethics and National Security.* Princeton, NJ: Princeton University Press, 2005.

Petacci, Clara. *Mussolini Segreto. Diari, 1932–1938.* Edited by Mauro Sutturo. Milan: RCS Libri, 2009.

Pini, Giorgio. *Filo diretto con Palazzo Venezia.* Bologna: Cappelli, 1950.

Pinochet, Augusto. *Camino Recorrido. Memorias de un Soldado.* Vols. 2 and 3. Santiago: Istituto Geografico Militar de Chile, 1991–1994.

Pinochet, Augusto. *El Dia Decisivo: 11 de Septiembre de 1973.* Santiago: Andres Bello, 1979.

Pinto, António Costa, ed. *Rethinking the Nature of Fascism: Comparative Perspectives.* New York: Palgrave Macmillan, 2010.

Pitzer, Andrea. *One Dark Night: A Global History of Concentration Camps.* Boston: Little, Brown, 2017.

Plamper, Jan. *The Stalin Cult: A Study in the Alchemy of Power.* New Haven: Yale University Press, 2012.

Policzer, Pablo. *The Rise and Fall of Repression in Chile.* Notre Dame: University of Notre Dame Press, 2009.

Pomerantsev, Peter. *Nothing Is True and Everything Is Possible: The Surreal Heart of the New Russia.* New York: Public Affairs, 2015.

Porch, Douglas. *Counterinsurgency: Exposing the Myths of the New Way of War.* Cambridge, UK: Cambridge University Press, 2013.

Post, Jerrold M. *Leaders and Their Followers in a Dangerous World: The Psychology of Political Behavior.* Ithaca, NY: Cornell University Press, 2004.

Prats, Carlos González. *Una vida por la legalidad.* Mexico City, México: Fondo de Cultura Económica, 1975.

Preston, Paul. *Franco: A Biography.* New York: Basic Books, 1994.

Pugliese, Stanislao. *Carlo Rosselli. Socialist Heretic and Antifascist Exile.* Cambridge: MA: Harvard University Press, 1999.

Pugliese, Stanislao, ed. *Fascism and Anti-Fascism.* Manchester, UK: Manchester University Press, 2001.

Putin, Vladimir. *First Person: An Astonishingly Frank Self-Portrait by Russia's President Vladimir Putin.* With Nataliya Gevorkyan, Natalya Timakova, and Andrei Kolesnikov. Translated by Catherine A. Fitzpatrick. New York: Public Affairs, 2000.

Rachetto, Piero. *Poesie della Resistenza.* Turin: Voci Nuove, 1973.

Ranald, Josef. *How to Know People by Their Hands*. New York: Modern Age Books, 1938.

Rees, Laurence. *Hitler's Charisma*. New York: Pantheon Press, 2012.

Reich, Jacqueline. *The Maciste Films of Italian Silent Cinema*. Bloomington: Indiana University Press, 2015.

Reichardt, Sven. *Faschistische Kampfbünde: Gewalt und Gemeinschaft im italienischen Squadrismus und in der deutschen SA*. Vienna and Cologne: Böhlau-Verlag Gmbh, 2009.

Rejali, Darius. *Torture and Democracy*. Princeton, NJ: Princeton University Press, 2009.

Renga, Dana, Elizabeth Leake, and Piero Garofalo. *Internal Exile in Fascist Italy*. Bloomington: Indiana University Press, 2019.

Rice, Condoleezza. *No Higher Honor. A Memoir of My Years in Washington*. New York: Crown Publishing, 2011.

Richet, Isabelle. *Women, Anti-Fascism, and Mussolini's Italy. The Life of Marion Cave Rosselli*. London: I.B. Tauris, 2018.

Roberts, David D. *Fascist Interactions. Proposals for a New Approach to Fascism and Its Era*. New York: Berghahn, 2016.

Rochat, Giorgio. *Guerre italiane in Libia e in Etiopia: Studi militari 1921–1939*. Treviso, Italy: Pagus, 1991.

Roseman, Mark. *Lives Reclaimed: A Story of Rescue and Resistance in Nazi Germany*. New York: Metropolitan Books, 2019.

Rosenberg, Bernard, and David Manning White, eds. *Mass Culture. The Popular Arts in America*. New York: The Free Press, 1957.

Rosendorf, Neal M. *Franco Sells Spain to America. Hollywood Tourism and PR as Postwar Spanish Soft Power*. New York: Palgrave Macmillan, 2014.

Rosenfeld, Gavriel. *Hi Hitler! How The Nazi Past Is Being Normalized in Contemporary Culture*. Cambridge, UK: Cambridge University Press, 2015.

Rosenfeld, Sophia. *Democracy and Truth. A Short History*. Philadelphia: University of Pennsylvania Press, 2018.

Rosenwald, Brian. *Talk Radio's America. How An Industry Took Over a Political Party That Took Over the United States*. Cambridge, MA: Harvard University Press, 2019.

Ross, Steven J. *Hitler in Los Angeles. How Jews Foiled Nazi Plots against Hollywood and America*. New York: Bloomsbury, 2017.

Rosselli, Carolo. *Oggi in Spagna, domani in italia*. Turin: Einaudi, 1967.

Rossi, Ernesto, ed. *No al fascismo*. Turin: Einaudi, 1963.

Rubin, Barry. *Modern Dictators. Third World Coup Makers, Strongmen, and Populist Tyrants*. New York: McGraw-Hill, 1987.

Rucker, Philip, and Carol Leonnig. *A Very Stable Genius: Donald J. Trump's Testing of America*. New York: Penguin, 2020.

Ruggeri, Giovanni, and Mario Guarino. *Berlusconi. Inchiesta sul signor TV*. Milan: Kaos, 1994.

Runciman, David. *How Democracy Ends*. London: Profile Books, 2018.

Sadiqi, Fatima, ed. *Women's Movements in Post–"Arab Spring" North Africa*. New York: Palgrave Macmillan, 2016.

Saini, Angela. *Superior: The Return of Race Science*. Boston: Beacon, 2019.

St. John, Ronald Bruce. *Libya: From Colony to Revolution*. London: Oneworld Publications, 2017.

Salvemini, Gaetano. *Mussolini diplomatico*. Bari, Italy: Laterza, 1952.

Sánchez, Antonio Cazorla. *Fear and Progress. Ordinary Lives in Franco's Spain, 1939–1975*. Oxford, UK: Blackwell, 2010.

Sarfatti, Margherita. *Dux*. Milan: Mondadori, 1926.

Sarfatti, Michele. *The Jews in Mussolini's Italy: From Equality to Persecution*. Madison: University of Wisconsin Press, 2006.

Satter, David. *Darkness at Dawn: The Rise of the Russian Criminal State*. New Haven: Yale University Press, 2004.

Schieder, Wolfgang. *Adolf Hitler. Politischer Zauberlehrling Mussolinis*. Berlin: De Gruyter Oldenbourg, 2017.

Schivelbusch, Wolfgang. *The Culture of Defeat: On National Trauma, Mourning, and Recovery*. New York: Picador, 2001.

Schmölders, Claudia. *Hitler's Face. The Biography of an Image*. Philadelphia: University of Pennsylvania Press, 2006.

Schoenberg, Arnold. *Letters*. Edited by Erwin Stein. Berkeley: University of California Press, 1987.

Schwartz, Margaret. *Dead Matter. The Meaning of Iconic Corpses*. Minneapolis: University of Minnesota Press, 2015.

Sciascia, Leonardo. *Le parrocchie del Regelpetra*. Milan: Adelphi, 1991.

Seara, Luis González. *La España de los años 70*. Madrid: Editorial Moneda y Crédito, 1972.

Seldes, George. *Sawdust Caesar. The Untold History of Mussolini and Fascism*. New York: Harper and Brothers, 1935.

Sharman, J. C. *The Despot's Guide of Wealth Management*. Ithaca, NY: Cornell University Press, 2017.

Shepard, Todd. *Voices of Decolonization: A Brief History with Documents*. New York: Bedford/St. Martins, 2014.

Siemens, Daniel. *Stormtroopers. A New History of Hitler's Brownshirts*. New Haven: Yale University Press, 2017.

Sims, Cliff. *Team of Vipers: My 500 Extraordinary Days in the Trump White House*. New York: Thomas Dunne, 2019.

Singh, Naumihal. *Seizing Power. The Strategic Logic of Military Coups*. Baltimore: Johns Hopkins University Press, 2014.

Snyder, Timothy. *Black Earth. The Holocaust as History and Warning*. New York: Tim Duggan Books, 2015.

Snyder, Timothy. *Bloodlands: Europe between Hitler and Stalin*. New York: Basic Books, 2012.

Sofsky, Wolfgang. *The Order of Terror. The Concentration Camp*. Translated by William Templer. Princeton, NJ: Princeton University Press, 1997.

Sperling, Valerie. *Sex, Politics, and Putin: Political Legitimacy in Russia*. New York: Oxford University Press, 2014.

Spooner, Mary Helen. *Soldiers in a Narrow World. The Pinochet Regime in Chile*. Berkeley: University of California Press, 1999.

Stanley, Jason. *How Fascism Works. The Politics of Us and Them*. New York: Random House, 2018.

Steigmann-Gall, Richard. *The Holy Reich. Nazi Conceptions of Christianity, 1919–1945*. Cambridge, UK: Cambridge University Press, 2003.

Steinbach, Gerald. *Nazis on the Run. How Hitler's Henchmen Fled Europe*. New York: Oxford University Press, 2011.

Stella, Gian Antonio, and Sergio Rizzo. *Cosi parlò il cavaliere*. Milan: Rizzoli 2011.

Stenner, Karen. *The Authoritarian Dynamic*. Cambridge, UK: Cambridge University Press, 2005.

Stent, Angela. *Putin's World: Russia against the West and with the Rest*. New York: Twelve, 2019.

Stephan, Maria, and Erica Chenoweth. *Why Civil Resistance Works.* New York: Columbia University Press, 2012.

Stern, Steve J. *Battling for Hearts and Minds. Memory Struggles in Pinochet's Chile, 1973–1988.* Durham: Duke University Press, 2006.

Stille, Alexander. *The Sack of Rome: How a Beautiful European Country with a Fabled History and a Storied Culture Was Taken Over by a Man Named Silvio Berlusconi.* New York: Penguin, 2006.

Strang, Bruce, ed. *Collision of Empires: Italy's Invasion of Ethiopia and Its International Impact.* New York: Routledge, 2013.

Stuckler, David, and Sanjay Basu. *The Body Economic: Why Austerity Kills.* New York: Basic Books, 2013.

Stutje, Jan Willem, ed. *Charismatic Leadership and Social Movements: The Revolutionary Power of Ordinary Men and Women.* New York: Berghahn, 2012.

Sullam, Simon Levis. *The Italian Executioners. The Genocide of the Jews of Italy.* Princeton, NJ: Princeton University Press, 2018.

Svolik, Milan. *The Politics of Authoritarian Rule.* Cambridge, UK: Cambridge University Press, 2012.

Taylor, Brian D. *The Code of Putinism.* New York: Oxford University Press, 2018.

Theweleit, Klaus. *Male Fantasies.* Vol. 1. *Women, Floods, Bodies, Histories.* Minneapolis: University of Minnesota Press, 1987.

Thomas, Julia Adeney, and Geoff Eley, eds. *Visualizing Fascism: The Twentieth-Century Rise of the Global Right.* Durham: Duke University Press, 2020.

Thyssen, Fritz. *I Paid Hitler.* New York: Farrar and Rhinehart, 1941.

Traverso, Enzo. *Fire and Blood. The European Civil War 1914–1945.* Translated by David Fernbach. New York: Verso, 2016.

Traverso, Enzo. *The Origins of Nazi Violence.* Translated by Janet Lloyd. New York: The New Press, 2003.

Tubach, Friedrich C. *German Voices: Memories of Life during Hitler's Third Reich.* Berkeley: University of California Press, 2011.

Tufekci, Zeynep. *Twitter and Teargas: The Power and Fragility of Networked Protest.* New Haven: Yale University Press, 2017.

Tumarkin, Nina. *Lenin Lives! The Lenin Cult in Soviet Russia.* Cambridge, MA: Harvard University Press, 1997.

Turner, Thomas, and Crawford Young. *The Rise and Decline of the Zairian State.* Madison: University of Wisconsin Press, 1985.

Tworek, Heidi. *News from Germany. The Competition to Control Wireless Communications, 1900–1945.* Cambridge, MA: Harvard University Press, 2019.

Ulrich, Volker. *Hitler: Ascent 1889–1939.* New York: Knopf, 2016.

Unger, Craig. *House of Trump, House of Putin.* New York: Dutton, 2019.

Uzal, Maria José Henríquez. *Viva la verdadera Amistad! Franco y Allende, 1970–1973.* Santiago: Editorial Unversitaria, 2014.

Vandewalle, Dirk. *A History of Modern Libya.* Cambridge, UK: Cambridge University Press, 2012.

van Genugten, Saskia. *Libya in Western Foreign Policies, 1911–2011.* New York: Palgrave Macmillan, 2016.

Varvelli, Arturo. *L'Italia e l'ascesa di Gheddafi. La cacciata degli italiani, le armi e il petrolio (1969–1974).* Milan: Baldini Castoldi Dalai, 2009.

von Hildebrand, Dietrich, and John Henry Crosby. *My Battle against Hitler: Defiance in the Shadow of the Third Reich.* New York: Image Books, 2016.

von Moltke, Freya, and Helmuth James von Moltke. *Last Letters: The Prison Correspondence, 1944–1945*. Edited by Dorothea von Moltke and Johannes von Moltke. New York: New York Review of Books, 2019.

von Plehwe, Friedrich-Karl. *The End of an Alliance. Rome's Defection from the Axis in 1943*. New York: Oxford University Press, 1971.

Wachsmann, Nicholas. *KL. A History of the Nazi Concentration Camps*. New York: Farrar, Straus and Giroux, 2016.

Ward, Vicky. *Kushner, Inc. Greed. Ambition, Corruption*. New York: St. Martin's Press, 2019.

Weber, Max. *Economy and Society: An Outline of Interpretive Sociology*. Vol. 1. Edited by Guenther Roth and Claus Wittich. Berkeley: University of California Press, 1978.

Wegren, Stephen K., ed. *Putin's Russia: Past Imperfect, Future Uncertain*. Lanham, MD: Rowman and Littlefield, 2015.

Welch, David. *The Third Reich: Politics and Propaganda*. New York: Routledge, 1993.

Whitehead, Andrew, and Samuel Perry. *Taking America Back for God: Christian Nationalism in the United States*. New York: Oxford University Press, 2020.

Wolff, Michael. *Fire and Fury. Inside the Trump White House*. New York: Henry Holt, 2018.

Wood, Randall, and Carmine DeLuca. *Dictator's Handbook: A Practical Manual for the Aspiring Tyrant*. Newfoundland: Gull Pond Books, 2012.

Woodward, Bob. *Fear: Trump in the White House*. New York: Simon and Schuster, 2018.

Worth, Owen. *Morbid Symptoms: The Global Rise of the Far-Right*. London: Zed Books, 2019.

Wright, Thomas, and Rody Oñate, *Flight from Chile. Voices from Exile*. Albuquerque: University of New Mexico Press, 1998.

Wrong, Michela. *In the Footsteps of Mr. Kurtz. Living on the Brink of Disaster in the Congo*. London: Fourth Estate, 2000.

Yavuz, M. Hakan, and Bayram Balci, eds. *Turkey's July 15th Coup: What Happened and Why*. Salt Lake City: University of Utah Press, 2018.

Yglesias, José. *Chile's Days of Terror: Eyewitness Accounts of the Military Coup*. Edited by Judy White. New York: Pathfinder, 1974.

Zakaria, Fareed. *The Future of Freedom: Illiberal Democracy at Home and Abroad*. New York: W. W. Norton, 2003.

Zayani, Mohamed, and Suzi Mirgani, eds. *Bullets and Bulletins. Media and Politics in the Wake of the Arab Uprisings*. New York: Oxford University Press, 2016.

Zucman, Gabriel. *The Hidden Wealth of Nations. The Scourge of Tax Havens*. Translated by Teresa Laven-der Fagan. Chicago: University of Chicago Press, 2015.

Zygar, Mikhail. *All the Kremlin's Men. Inside the Court of Vladimir Putin*. New York: Public Affairs, 2016.

INDEX

Page numbers after 272 refer to notes.
Page numbers in *italics* indicate photographs.